Springer Series in Design and Innovation

Volume 50

AF783552

Editor-in-Chief

Francesca Tosi, University of Florence, Florence, Italy

Series Editors

Claudio Germak, Politecnico di Torino, Turin, Italy

Francesco Zurlo, Politecnico di Milano, Milan, Italy

Zhi Jinyi, Southwest Jiaotong University, Chengdu, China

Marilaine Pozzatti Amadori, Universidade Federal de Santa Maria, Santa Maria, Rio Grande do Sul, Brazil

Maurizio Caon, University of Applied Sciences and Arts, Fribourg, Switzerland

Springer Series in Design and Innovation (SSDI) publishes books on innovation and the latest developments in the fields of Product Design, Interior Design and Communication Design, with particular emphasis on technological and formal innovation, and on the application of digital technologies and new materials. The series explores all aspects of design, e.g. Human-Centered Design/User Experience, Service Design, and Design Thinking, which provide transversal and innovative approaches oriented on the involvement of people throughout the design development process. In addition, it covers emerging areas of research that may represent essential opportunities for economic and social development.

In fields ranging from the humanities to engineering and architecture, design is increasingly being recognized as a key means of bringing ideas to the market by transforming them into user-friendly and appealing products or services. Moreover, it provides a variety of methodologies, tools and techniques that can be used at different stages of the innovation process to enhance the value of new products and services.

The series' scope includes monographs, professional books, advanced textbooks, selected contributions from specialized conferences and workshops, and outstanding Ph.D. theses.

The volumes of the series are single-blind peer-reviewed.

Keywords: Product and System Innovation; Product design; Interior design; Communication Design; Human-Centered Design/User Experience; Service Design; Design Thinking; Digital Innovation; Innovation of Materials.

How to submit proposals

Proposals must include: title, keywords, presentation (max 10,000 characters), table of contents, chapter abstracts, editors'/authors' CV.

In case of proceedings, chairmen/editors are requested to submit the link to conference website (incl. relevant information such as committee members, topics, key dates, keynote speakers, information about the reviewing process, etc.), and approx. number of papers.

Proposals must be sent to: series editor Prof. Francesca Tosi (francesca.tosi@unifi.it) and/or publishing editor Mr. Pierpaolo Riva (pierpaolo.riva@springer.com).

Daniel Brandão · Nuno Martins · Emilia Duarte
Editors

Perspectives on Design and Digital Communication V

Research, Innovations and Best Practices

Springer

Editors
Daniel Brandão
Communication and Society Research Centre
Institute of Social Sciences
University of Minho
Bargo, Portugal

Nuno Martins
Research Institute for Design
Media and Culture, School of Design
Polytechnic Institute of Cávado and Ave
Barcelos
Barcelos, Portugal

Emilia Duarte
UNIDCOM/IADE
IADE - Universidade Europeia
Lisboa, Portugal

ISSN 2661-8184 ISSN 2661-8192 (electronic)
Springer Series in Design and Innovation
ISBN 978-3-031-76158-4 ISBN 978-3-031-76156-0 (eBook)
https://doi.org/10.1007/978-3-031-76156-0

© The Editor(s) (if applicable) and The Author(s), under exclusive license to Springer Nature Switzerland AG 2025, corrected publication 2025

This work is subject to copyright. All rights are solely and exclusively licensed by the Publisher, whether the whole or part of the material is concerned, specifically the rights of translation, reprinting, reuse of illustrations, recitation, broadcasting, reproduction on microfilms or in any other physical way, and transmission or information storage and retrieval, electronic adaptation, computer software, or by similar or dissimilar methodology now known or hereafter developed.
The use of general descriptive names, registered names, trademarks, service marks, etc. in this publication does not imply, even in the absence of a specific statement, that such names are exempt from the relevant protective laws and regulations and therefore free for general use.
The publisher, the authors and the editors are safe to assume that the advice and information in this book are believed to be true and accurate at the date of publication. Neither the publisher nor the authors or the editors give a warranty, expressed or implied, with respect to the material contained herein or for any errors or omissions that may have been made. The publisher remains neutral with regard to jurisdictional claims in published maps and institutional affiliations.

This Springer imprint is published by the registered company Springer Nature Switzerland AG
The registered company address is: Gewerbestrasse 11, 6330 Cham, Switzerland

If disposing of this product, please recycle the paper.

Scientific Committee

Ana Catarina Silva, Escola Superior de Design IPCA, Portugal
Ana Clara Roberti, CITCEM, Portugal
Andreia Pinto de Sousa, Universidade Lusófona do Porto, Portugal
António Maneira, UNIDCOM—IADE Universidade Europeia, Portugal
Camila Soares, FBAUP, Portugal
Catarina Lelis, Universidade de Aveiro, Portugal
Cláudia Lima, Universidade Lusófona do Porto, Portugal
Daniel Raposo, Politécnico Castelo Branco, Portugal
Demétrio Matos, Escola Superior de Design IPCA, Portugal
Dina Riccò, Politecnico di Milano, Italy
Elga Ferreira, Politécnico de Leiria, Portugal
Eliana Penedos, Universidade do Porto, Portugal
Elisabete Rolo, Faculdade de Arquitectura—Universidade de Lisboa, Portugal
Filipa Martins de Abreu, University of Saint Joseph, Macao
Heitor Alvelos, Universidade do Porto, Portugal
João Alves de Sousa, Universidade Lusófona do Porto, Portugal
João Tiago Santos, Escola Superior de Artes e Design, Portugal
José Raimundo, Escola Superior de Design IPCA, Portugal
Karel van der Waarde, Swinburne University of Technology, Melbourne, Australia
Luís Leite, ESMAD-IPP, Portugal
Nuno Coelho, Universidade de Coimbra, Portugal
Pedro Amado, Universidade do Porto, Portugal
Pedro Cardoso, Universidade de Aveiro, Portugal
Pedro Portela, Universidade do Minho, Portugal
Priscila Farias, Universidade de São Paulo, Brazil
Rita Coelho, ESMAD, IPP, Portugal
Rita Espanha, ISCTE, Portugal
Sara Santos, Universidade de Aveiro, Portugal
Vanda Sousa, Politécnico de Lisboa, Portugal
Vítor Quelhas, ESMAD-IPP, Portugal

Preface

The world is saturated with artefacts that we have designed, impacting and transforming our lives in myriad ways. This impact is not confined to the individual level but extends to groups and society at large, with effects that are felt not only immediately but can also persist long-term. Driven by the pursuit of progress and guided by consumer-driven logic and metrics, we have embraced innovation uncritically and accepted technological determinism without hesitation [1]. We have channelled our talents and knowledge towards the creation of more things—more appealing and engaging—that keep us connected and dependent, victims of a kind of happiness dictatorship.

On the other hand, the excesses of a deregulated liberal capitalist system, operating on the principle of perpetual growth to which Design has been subjugated, have resulted in the transgression of many planetary boundaries. We now desperately attempt to mitigate these through sustainability strategies that will inevitably prove to be of limited success. Meanwhile, technological blindness and the overestimation of science and technology's capacity to resolve the problems they have created have led to the proliferation of potentially disruptive technologies with significant societal concerns and ecological footprints. Their impacts are not yet fully understood, but their effects are already becoming apparent.

The planetary challenges humanity faces make the designer's role more crucial than ever, rallying an increasing number of voices calling for a paradigm shift and the creation of a new Design. This Design should be guided by a critical spirit that does not ignore the mediating effect of artefacts or consider technology as neutral. It should be adept at understanding the systemic nature of problems, capable of distinguishing between a problem and its symptom, and discerning a good solution from a solution for good [2, 3]. This Design, alert to warnings, should position itself as a guardian of the built world, aware that design ultimately means colonising the future, adopting a very long-term vision grounded in ethical principles and values. More than specialising in studying interactions and experiences, Design should now focus on the interconnections between all living and non-living beings, adopting an ecocentric stance over an anthropocentric one—a more-than-human design approach.

Aware that paradigm change can happen and that it is desirable for it to occur through Design rather than through catastrophe, more than saying yes to new challenges, this new Design should be capable of saying no, thus contributing to paradigm shifts and advocating for the planetary regeneration and the flourishing of humanity.

The various contributions in this book reflect the great diversity of thoughts and positions characterising the expansive territory of contemporary Design. Our intention is to promote free and critical debate of existing visions and contributions, enabling us to reimagine the Design of the 21st century.

The 20 chapters of this book collectively explore the multifaceted nature of design, encompassing sustainability, well-being, cultural identity, innovation, and research methodologies. The journey begins with a focus on sustainable design principles aimed at reducing energy consumption and supporting well-being, exemplified through digital environments, smart devices for aging individuals, and inclusive digital participation of youth. It progresses to an examination of visual and cultural identity, unraveling the intricate patterns of cities like Macau and the digital transformation of typographic collections, while also decoding the behavioral dynamics in font design through eye-tracking. Innovations in design methodologies are highlighted through participatory design projects, advancements in AI for logo design, and non-linear narrative augmented reality experiences. The exploration extends to the auditory realm, where sound systems are integrated into design. The final section delves into design research and its practical applications, from developing didactical strategies using podcasts to understanding customer loyalty in online retail, overcoming challenges in computer gaming, enhancing metaphorical design, and creating phygital cookbooks. Together, these chapters illustrate the broad impact of design on various aspects of life, showcasing its potential to drive sustainable, inclusive, and innovative solutions across different contexts.

All chapters are original contributions by reputable authors selected from the best papers presented at the 7th International Conference on Digital Design and Communication (Digicom 2023), which took place in Barcelos, Portugal, November 9–11, 2023, along with several invited top researchers worldwide. All chapters submitted to this book have been subject to a double-blind peer review process by members of our scientific committee. The feedback provided by experts on the different topics covered in each chapter made it possible to strengthen the work presented by all authors.

The findings presented in this book have the capacity to motivate and offer significant support to those working in the fields of design and digital communication. Both scholars and practitioners will find value in the content, which provides insights that might help them in their respective endeavours.

Bargo, Portugal — Daniel Brandão
Barcelos, Portugal — Nuno Martins
Lisboa, Portugal — Emilia Duarte

References

1. Brandão D, Martins N, Cooper R (2023) Design and communication: Digital challenges and dilemmas. Comunicação E Sociedade 43:e023009. https://doi.org/10.17231/comsoc.43(2023).4830
2. Martins N, Brandão D, Guimarães L, Penedos-Santiago E, Brandão E (2023) The importance of communication design in the process of disseminating community practices in social neighbourhoods: The Balteiro. Comunicação E Sociedade 43:e023010. https://doi.org/10.17231/comsoc.43(2023).4455
3. Roberti AC, Martins N, Brandão D (2024) Decoding the communal self: Ethnographic documentary and design as methodologies for understanding a social phenomenon. Design Principles Pract: Int J—Ann Rev 18(1):1–22. https://doi.org/10.18848/1833-1874/CGP/v18i01/1-22

Contents

Sustainable Design and Well-Being

Seeding a Sustainable Mindset to Reduce Energy Consumption and Carbon Footprint Through Sustainable Digital Design Principles

Sónia Rafael and Seyed Mohsen Mirmotahari

Abstract To contribute to the reduction of energy consumption, carbon footprint, and the promotion of sustainable digital design principles, this article explores several key steps: education and awareness; integration of sustainability principles into the design process; utilization of sustainable technologies; collaborative work among designers, engineers, and environmentalists; assessment of the environmental impact of digital products and services; and advocacy for policies and regulations promoting sustainable digital design practices. Given the complexity of the process, our small contribution will focus on the first two topics. This study conducted a literature review and analysis of two paradigmatic case studies: the Sustainability Action Cards for digital designers, developed by the Design Group Italia, and the report from Atos, conducted by Greenspector, which measures digital energy consumption. Following this analysis, a survey was conducted with university students and junior digital designers to determine their knowledge and concern regarding digital sustainability, with the aim of seeding a sustainable mindset. However, it is important to note that this was a preliminary study.

Keywords Sustainable digital design · Carbon footprint · Energy consumption

1 Introduction

Digital consumption has been increasing exponentially in recent decades, driven by technological advancement, the proliferation of internet-connected devices, and the growing digitization of services and systems.

S. Rafael (✉) · S. M. Mirmotahari
Faculdade de Belas-Artes, ITI—Interactive Technologies Institute / LARSyS, Universidade de Lisboa, Largo da Academia Nacional de Belas Artes, 1249-058 Lisboa, Portugal
e-mail: srafael@edu.ulisboa.pt

S. M. Mirmotahari
e-mail: mirmotahari@edu.ulisboa.pt

© The Author(s), under exclusive license to Springer Nature Switzerland AG 2025

D. Brandão et al. (eds.), *Perspectives on Design and Digital Communication V*, Springer Series in Design and Innovation 50, https://doi.org/10.1007/978-3-031-76156-0_1

Internet access has expanded significantly worldwide, with billions of people connected online. Benjamin Bratton describes the world as a system of "planetary-scale computing", composed of layers of juxtaposed interfaces designed to be extensions of everyday motor and sensory experiences [1]. This has led to increased use of digital services such as social media, e-commerce, video and music streaming, and others.

The proliferation of network-connected devices such as smartphones, tablets, laptops, and Internet of Things (IoT) devices has contributed to increased digital consumption [2, 3]. Indeed, people are increasingly dependent on these devices for communication, work, entertainment, and other daily activities.

In background of digitalization, cloud storage and data centers play a fundamental role in digital infrastructure, enabling the storage and processing of large amounts of data [4, 5]. However, they also consume enormous amounts of energy, contributing to the environmental impact of digital consumption.

This growth in digital consumption has led to growing concerns, as has the disposal of obsolete electronic devices and the production of electronic waste. These topics are also discussed in the context of sustainability and digital consumption [6].

Finding strategies to reduce energy consumption and carbon footprint is essential. The research of Everts [3, 7], conducted on the topic of global data consumption, reveals the relevance and urgency of raising awareness about this issue.

We can find in design a powerful tool. Not to reverse the process, but to help reduce the impact of the digital footprint. As a discipline, design increasingly integrates ethical, humanitarian, and environmental concerns.

Aligned with design responsibility, Victor Papanek was the first designer to introduce a critique of the design and marketing practices of some multinational corporations. He also advocated for the responsibility of designers to create social and ecological methodologies, processes, and projects for mass production [8, 9].

In contemporary times, sustainable digital design focuses on reducing environmental and ecological impact through sustainable design processes and by applying ethical development practices. It delivers digital products, systems, and services that respect the principles of the Sustainable Web Manifesto: clean, efficient, open, honest, regenerative, and resilient [10].

The aim of this article is to contribute to raising awareness among young designers—both as young people and as designers—of the need to reduce energy consumption and carbon footprint through the principles of sustainable digital design. These principles can easily be adopted by designers in the digital design process.

We believe that the successful implementation of these principles depends on educating future designers during their university education. Subsequently, upon entering the profession as junior designers, it is necessary to reinforce these principles and assess whether they are being properly applied.

Of course, the implementation of environmental protection and digital sustainability measures does not depend solely on the education of designers, nor on the education of environmentally responsible citizens [11], but rather on a variety of actors, including governments, private organizations, academic institutions, and individuals.

To better understand the context of our target group, we conducted a survey to assess the mindset of digital design students and junior digital designers regarding the application of digital sustainability principles in their daily practices and design processes.

To develop this questionnaire, we conducted a literature review and analyzed two paradigmatic case studies. The first case study involved the action cards of the Sustainability Kit for Digital Designers, developed by Design Group Italia [12]. The second case study entailed analyzing a report conducted by Greenspector—an independent company specializing in measuring digital energy consumption—on the Atos brand [13]. We identified the 14 principles of digital sustainability, and some of these principles were selected to be a part of the survey.

Based on this questionnaire, we began to instill a Sustainable Mindset in students and junior digital designers, aiming to promote environmental sustainability by reducing energy consumption and carbon footprint.

2 Digital Consumption

The International Energy Agency's (IEA) annual report on the electricity sector dedicated a special section to examining data centers and their impact on energy consumption. A comprehensive analysis was conducted of the factors driving electricity consumption in data centers, revealing that such consumption could double by 2026.

In data centers, energy is predominantly consumed by two main processes: data processing itself, which accounts for about 40% of total consumption; and the cooling system for the rooms, also responsible for approximately 40%. The remaining 20% is used by associated information technology equipment [14]. There is an investment in trends that can significantly increase the carbon footprint, such as Artificial Intelligence (AI), IoT, and blockchain [15] (Fig. 1).

Based on IEA estimates, data centers, cryptocurrencies, and AI consumed about 460 terawatt-hours (TWh) of electricity worldwide in 2022, accounting for nearly 2% of total global electricity demand (Fig. 2). Data centers, along with the electricity

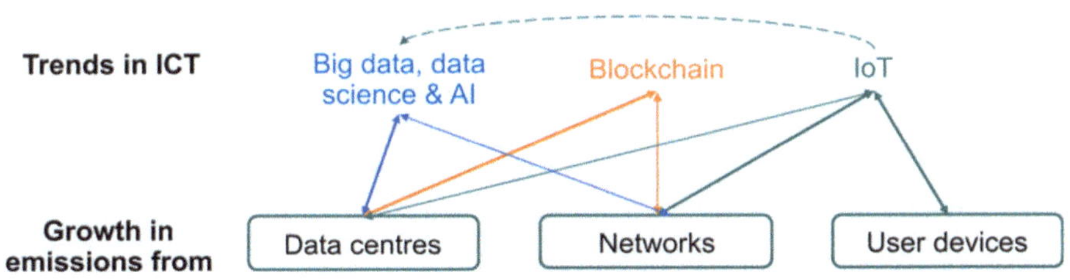

Fig. 1 The impacts that trends in ICT have on growth in emissions from data centers, networks, and devices [15]

infrastructure that powers them, are a critical component of the infrastructure that supports digitalization [14].

To meet climate change mitigation targets, the Information and Communication Technology (ICT) sector also needs to drastically reduce its own emissions.

Despite some variability in estimates, ICT is responsible for 1.5–4% of global greenhouse gas emissions (GHG), and its footprint has grown significantly [15]. The world needs to reduce its greenhouse gas emissions to stay within the 1.5 °C warming limit.

From the beginning of 2019 to the end of 2022, the global energy system was responsible for more than 140 gigatons of carbon dioxide emissions (Gt CO_2). Energy-related CO_2 emissions increased by 1% in 2022 and are expected to increase by a similar amount in 2023 (Fig. 3). These additional emissions are amplifying the occurrence of frequent heat waves, droughts, and other extreme weather events, further increasing stress on vulnerable populations and energy systems [16].

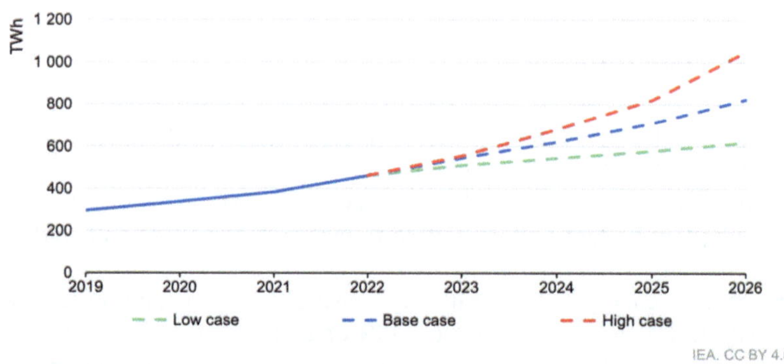

Fig. 2 Global electricity demand from data centers, AI, and cryptocurrencies, 2019–2026 [14]

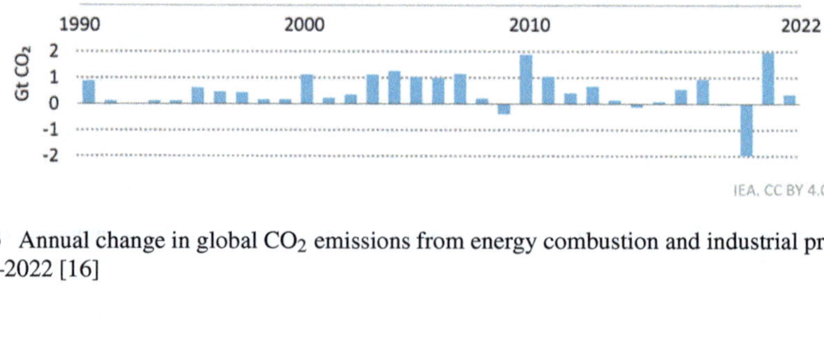

Fig. 3 Annual change in global CO_2 emissions from energy combustion and industrial processes, 1990–2022 [16]

By 2040, ICT could represent a significant contribution (over 14%) to greenhouse gas emissions on a planetary and individual scale, a percentage corresponding to more than half of the current carbon footprint of the transportation sector [17].

Energy consumption is contributing to the depletion of non-renewable natural resources, which can lead to several global problems, such as poverty, war, extremism, violence, crime, among others [18]. In fact, the survival of humanity depends on a balance between the size of the population and the productive potential of the ecosystem [19].

Energy consumption, carbon footprint, and the threat of climate change have been drawing the attention of the scientific communities, warning that our status quo must change and that we must move towards a more sustainable future [20]. The human influence on global warming mentioned by the Intergovernmental Panel on Climate Change (IPCC) highlights the urgency to drastically reduce CO_2 and other greenhouse gas emissions [21].

The tendencies of the technology industry—its tendency to follow trends, its focus on consumption, its high demand for electrical power and rare natural resources, and its rapid cycle of innovation that leads to obsolescence—may not only fall short of promoting sustainability but could potentially hasten a collapse [22].

3 Key Steps for Reducing Energy Consumption and Carbon Footprint

Considering the framework presented above, we realize that the implementation of environmental protection and digital sustainability measures goes beyond educating designers or environmentally responsible citizens [23]. It depends on a variety of other actors, such as governments, private organizations, academic institutions, and individuals. A concerted effort by all these stakeholders is needed.

Based on a literature review, we will investigate and propose a concerted strategy consisting of a 7-step process that can lead to more sustainable practices through design and the integration of digital sustainability principles (Fig. 4). Sustainable digital design focuses on reducing environmental and ecological risks through cleaner product design processes and by applying ethical development practices. The key steps for sustainable design with digital sustainability principles to reduce energy consumption and carbon footprint are:

(1) **Education and Awareness**: It is crucial to promote education and training on the importance of digital sustainability, both for designers and other stakeholders. Everyone needs to be aware of the impact that digital consumption has on energy consumption and carbon footprint. Digital citizenship, as defined by Anne Collier, involves critical thinking and ethical decision-making regarding the content we consume and produce online, and the impact that this content has on ourselves, others, and the community [24]. In the educational context, digital citizenship also refers to norms of appropriate and responsible behavior

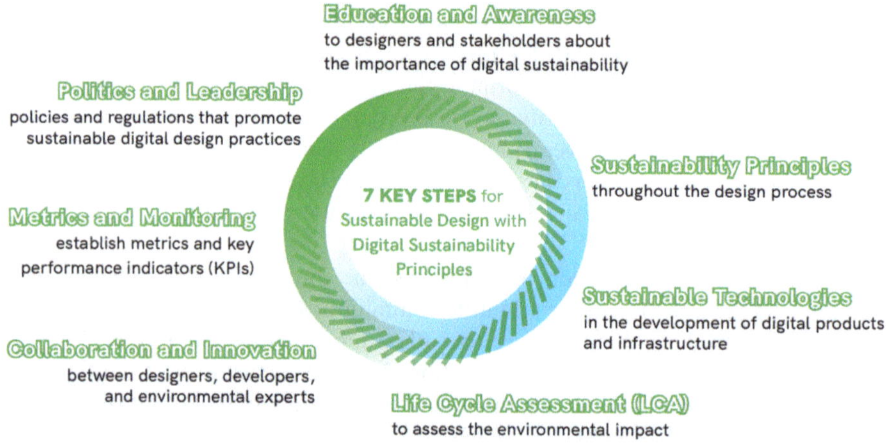

Fig. 4 Key steps for reducing energy consumption and carbon footprint

in the use of technology [25]. Just as environmental education is important for shaping conscientious citizens, it is crucial that digital literacy be used to raise awareness among students about the carbon footprint of digital consumption. This awareness should be integrated into learning environments [26, 27].

(2) **Sustainability Principles**: Sustainability principles must be integrated throughout the design process. This includes considering energy efficiency, resource conservation, and waste reduction at every stage of the design process. Since the 1960s, sustainability has been a topic of discussion in different areas of society. There is a growing trend towards the creation of new directions for design [28], new products, services, or systems that integrate the correct message and sustainable concerns throughout their process and implementation. Designers can and should contribute to developing a sustainable society. In this context, Nathan Stegall argues that the goal is not simply to create sustainable products, but rather to envision products, processes, and services that encourage widespread sustainable behavior [29]. The aim is to transform design practices to promote more sustainable outcomes. Although guided by principles such as usability, ergonomics, efficiency, and functionality, design has not always been deeply influenced by ethics, despite their inherent interconnectedness [30]. Additionally, considering sustainability in design can help designers address the political and ethical responsibility associated with persuading consumers to change their behavior [31]. Tony Fry highlights how design, even with good intentions, can have unintended side effects that can lead to undesirable changes in our collective futures [32]. The role of the designer in promoting a sustainable society goes beyond simply creating sustainable products. Rather, it involves envisioning products, processes, and services that actively promote sustainable behavior on a large scale [29]. Designers should incorporate the intention to

"encourage positive constructive ways of life" as an integral aspect of designing the artificial world [29, 33].

(3) **Sustainable Technologies**: The use of sustainable technologies is critical in the development of digital products and infrastructure. This includes incorporating renewable energy sources, energy-efficient hardware, and environmentally friendly materials. Green technology refers to technologies considered eco-friendly due to their manufacturing processes or supply chains. Green technology aims to protect the environment and, in some cases, mitigate past environmental damage [34]. The use of green technology involves renewable energy, hardware, and systems that contribute to environmental protection, minimizing the destructive effects of human activity. Given the increasing availability of studies on the negative environmental implications of ICT [35], there has been a growing adoption of Green IT (Green Information Technology) practices, particularly at the organizational level. Green IT encompasses the study and practice of designing, manufacturing, using, and disposing of computers, servers, and associated subsystems—such as monitors, printers, storage devices, and networking and communication systems—efficiently and effectively with minimal or no environmental impact [36].

(4) **Life Cycle Assessment (LCA)**: Perform life cycle assessments to evaluate the environmental impact of products, services, and digital systems from production to disposal. And identify areas for improvement and implement strategies to minimize energy consumption and carbon emissions. The ISO 14040:2006 standard establishes the principles and framework for conducting Life Cycle Analysis (LCA) [37] of products, services, or systems. This standard can assist companies and organizations in identifying opportunities for environmental improvement, making more sustainable decisions, and ensuring that results are accurate and reliable.

(5) **Collaboration and Innovation**: Foster collaboration among designers, developers, and environmental experts to innovate and develop new solutions for sustainable digital design. Encourage the sharing of best practices and the adoption of new technologies that prioritize environmental sustainability. The perspective of design integrated with principles of sustainability does not correspond to the classical traditional approaches of design or engineering. Instead, it involves viewing design as a reflective social practice, ideal for open and complex problems at the intersection with other professional domains. Integrating design with this characteristic is not a simple task but requires more fundamental changes, particularly in the training and education of these professionals [38]. There have been, for example, many discussions about the relevance, role, and integration of sustainability in the engineering curriculum [38, 39]. There is also a reflective design perspective that emphasizes a more interactive relationship between the designer, the design object, the context, and the other participants in this process. At IDEO, they call it design thinking, which they describe as a human-centered approach that goes beyond conventional problem-solving and products for new experiences [40]. With this reflective understanding of design, it is openly recognized that design does not progress

along a linear line from analysis to synthesis or from problem to solution. Instead, it moves back and forth between different domains as the design problem and solution co-evolve and are continuously subject to review [41]. The practice of reflective design could be part of a strategy to begin preparing engineers for these types of complex challenges unfolding in unfamiliar territory for engineering disciplines. It is fundamental that the approach to sustainability be an integrated strategy among various stakeholders, namely designers, engineers, and environmental experts.

(6) **Metrics and Monitoring**: Establishing metrics and key performance indicators (KPIs) to track energy consumption, carbon footprint, and other sustainability measures is crucial. Regularly monitoring and evaluating progress towards sustainability goals and adjusting based on results are essential for success. The success of sustainability initiatives relies on creating a strong system for measurement and evaluation. This means setting up metrics and KPIs to monitor progress towards sustainable goals. According to the Global Reporting Initiative (GRI) [42], these metrics should cover various environmental aspects, such as: (a) tracking energy consumption, including renewable and non-renewable sources, (b) measuring total greenhouse gas emissions, including Scopes 1, 2, and 3 as per the Greenhouse Gas Protocol [43], (c) monitoring total water usage across all activities to identify conservation opportunities [44], (d) tracking waste management efforts, including percentages recycled, reused, or sent to landfills [44]. Additionally, factors like biodiversity impact and material efficiency may also be considered, depending on the sector and specific goals [42, 44]. Regular monitoring and evaluation are crucial for ensuring progress towards sustainability goals. By collecting and analyzing data at defined intervals and comparing performance against established targets and industry standards, organizations can effectively assess the impact of their sustainability efforts.

(7) **Policy and Leadership**: Advocating for policies and regulations that promote sustainable digital design practices. Setting an example in the industry, companies, and organizations by demonstrating a commitment to sustainability and encouraging others to follow suit. Digital design has a significant environmental impact, from the energy used to power data centers to the materials used to manufacture electronic devices. Sustainable digital design practices aim to minimize this impact by using resources efficiently and responsibly. The digital ecological footprint is an indicator resulting from multiple factors and decisions made by governments, companies, organizations, and even consumers. At the industry level, companies such as GAFA (Google, Amazon, Facebook, and Apple) are the main entities targeted in managing internet infrastructures. While digital product and service design are geared towards user engagement strategies to retain users for as long as possible, there is an emerging need for environmental preservation. The commitment to using 100% renewable energy expressed by the big four reveals recognition of their negative influence regarding intensive resource exploitation, energy consumption, greenhouse gas emissions, and

their focus on reducing their negative impacts on a global scale and contemporary societies [45]. Some examples of policies and regulations may include defining energy efficiency standards by establishing minimum energy efficiency standards for electronic devices; recycling requirements by requiring electronic device manufacturers to offer recycling programs for their products; carbon taxes by imposing taxes on carbon emissions from the digital industry [46].

By incorporating these principles into digital design processes and promoting a culture of sustainability within organizations, it is possible to reduce energy consumption and carbon footprint, while simultaneously fostering environmental responsibility in the digital domain.

4 Methodology

This article seeks to contribute to the advancement of knowledge within the scope of the 1st and 2nd key steps outlined in point 3 of this article.

In the topic of education and awareness about digital sustainability, to better understand the context of our target group, we conducted a questionnaire to gauge the mindset of digital design students and junior digital designers regarding the application of digital sustainability principles in their daily practices and design process. In the topic of integrating sustainability principles into the design process, we used the analysis of two paradigmatic case studies.

The first case study is the action cards of the Sustainability Kit for digital designers, developed by Design Group Italia [12]. The second case study involves the analysis and a report on digital energy consumption conducted by Greenspector, regarding the Atos brand [13]. The action cards of the Sustainability Kit offer a broader perspective on digital sustainability principles, encompassing various guidelines to be followed by digital designers. The report on the Atos brand resides in a detailed study aligned with the purpose of providing decarbonized digital design. The chosen design elements were selected to be more sustainable, adopting methods and visual elements that minimize carbon impact [13].

We believe that by considering these two cases, we can develop a framework with topics that are easy to implement by digital designers, without significant impact for companies or organizations and without affecting the digital well-being of users.

One definition of digital well-being corresponds to a state where subjective well-being is maintained in an environment characterized by digital communication overabundance. Within a condition of digital well-being, individuals can channel digital media usage towards a sense of comfort, safety, satisfaction, and fulfilment [47].

The 14 principles of digital sustainability have been identified through the analysis of the action cards of the Sustainability Kit and Atos (Table 1). These principles are:

1. **Color selection/Screen brightness**: Using sustainable colors and reduced screen brightness consumes less energy, both on the user's device and on the servers that deliver the content.

Table 1 Comparative analysis between the two case studies (action cards and Atos)

	Sustainability principals	Kit cards	Atos
1	Color selection/screen brightness	✓	✓
2	Variable fonts/system fonts	✓	✓
3	Reduce the number of images or videos	✓	✓
4	Dark mode possibility	✓	✓
5	Ethical approach	✓	X
6	Illustrations/light icons	X	✓
7	Reduce files size	✓	✓
8	Battery/energy consumption	✓	✓
9	Accessibility/inclusion	✓	✓
10	Filter usage in images or videos	X	✓
11	Clean coding/green web host	✓	X
12	Avoid needless content	✓	X
13	Unnecessary data collection	✓	X
14	Optimize server space/cloud storage	✓	✓

2. **Variable fonts/System fonts**: Variable fonts allow a single font file to cover a wide range of styles (bold, italic, etc.), reducing the overall file size and data consumption. Using system fonts also reduces the need to download additional fonts.
3. **Quantity of images or videos**: Limiting the use of heavy visual elements, such as images and videos, can decrease file size and reduce server load, resulting in faster loading times and lower energy consumption.
4. **Dark mode possibility**: Dark mode uses dark background colors, which reduces energy consumption on devices with OLED screens.
5. **Ethical Approach**: Integrating ethical considerations at all stages of digital design, such as respecting user privacy, avoiding deceptive practices, and promoting transparency in data collection and usage. Considering the full life-cycle of the digital product, from the origin of the materials used in the device to final disposal, contributes to more sustainable practices.
6. **Illustrations/Light icons**: Opting for simple and lightweight illustrations and icons can decrease the size of image files, resulting in lighter and faster web pages, reducing data consumption.
7. **File size**: Optimizing the size of images, videos, code, and other resources reduces the amount of energy required for transmission and storage.
8. **Battery/Energy consumption**: Designing interfaces that consume less energy can extend the battery life of mobile devices and reduce the environmental impact associated with frequent battery charging.
9. **Accessibility/Inclusion**: Accessible design allows a broader audience to use the digital interface, avoiding the need to create alternative versions that would require additional resources.

10. **Filters in images or videos**: When the use of images or videos is unavoidable, applying filters to reduce excessive brightness or contrast can help reduce energy consumption when displaying these elements.
11. **Clean code/Green hosting**: Writing clean and efficient code avoids unnecessary processing, saving energy on both the device and server. Opting for green hosting services that use renewable energy sources reduces the carbon footprint.
12. **Content selection**: Redundant or unnecessary content on websites and applications increases page size and loading time, consuming more energy.
13. **Data collection**: Collecting less user data reduces the need for storage and processing, lowering energy consumption.
14. **Server space/Cloud storage**: Organizing data storage and eliminating obsolete files frees up space on servers and cloud storage services, reducing energy consumption.

With the aim of this article being to raise awareness among young designers about the need for implementing sustainable digital design principles into their design process, we conducted a questionnaire with 77 undergraduate and graduate students in digital design, as well as junior designers.

Given that this is a preliminary study, we decided to restrict the scope of the questions to the first eight principles identified. Another factor influencing this decision is that the survey sample consists of young designers, whose experience in the field of design may be limited.

The results, as presented in the following graph (see Fig. 4), indicate that out of the 77 respondents, 77.9% are between 18 and 24 years old ($N = 60$). This finding provides insight into the age distribution of our audience, aiding in understanding their perspectives on sustainability (Table 2).

Following our aim for this investigation—to identify junior digital designers, it becomes essential to determine their level of work experience. In fact, if we define "junior" as individuals with between 1 and 5 years of experience, our investigation reveals that 63.6% (50.6% + 13%) ($N = 49$) of respondents fall within this category, indicating a significant representation of junior designers in our survey (Table 3).

One of the sustainability principles outlined by the Atos brand—the implementation of a dark mode—can lead to significant energy savings, especially on OLED screens. This principle is also mentioned in the action cards of the Sustainability Kit.

Table 2 Age group

Age group	Frequency (f)	%
18–24	60	77.9%
25–34	13	16.9%
35–44	4	5.2%
Total	77	100%
Mean		23.40
Variance		24.24
St deviation		4.92

Table 3 Level of work experience

Experience (year)	Frequency (f)	%
0	21	27.3%
1–2	39	50.6%
3–5	10	13%
6–10	4	5.2%
11 or more	3	3.9%
Total	77	100%
Mean		2.12
Variance		6.75
St deviation		2.60

Table 4 Implementing the dark mode

Choices	Responses	%
Never	7	9.1%
Whenever I need to conserve battery	16	20.8%
Automatically enabled	24	31.2%
Always	30	39%
Total	77	100%
St deviation		9.98

With this concern in mind, we inquired about our users' usage of this method on their devices.

The following table (Table 4) depicts their responses, revealing that 39% of them consistently use this method, while 31.2% have it set as default on their devices, 20.8% use it whenever they need to save battery, and 9.1% never choose this method. Overall, this indicates a substantial adoption of dark mode among our junior digital designers.

It was crucial for us to understand the perspectives of junior digital designers regarding digital sustainability. This insight would help us ascertain their level of awareness and understanding. If they were aware, we needed to explore why sustainability practices were not yet widespread. Conversely, if they lacked awareness, it would signify the necessity to educate them on the subject. The results revealed that 92% of our audience possesses an understanding of digital sustainability overall, while 8% were unaware of it (Table 5).

Aligned with the principles of Atos and the action cards of the Sustainability Kit, we queried our audience on how they integrate digital sustainability principles into their projects (allowing them to select one or more options). The results showed that 35.71% are mindful of the need to optimize images/videos, 32.65% choose color selection, and 6.12% consider font selection aligned with sustainability principles. However, it was unexpected that 25.51% acknowledged not taking any actions aligned with digital sustainability (Table 6).

Table 5 Principles of digital sustainability

Choices	Actions	%
I've just heard about it and need to learn more	10	8%
Designing while considering energy consumption	32	25.6%
Designing while considering the social and ethical implications	35	28.0%
Designing with minimal environmental impact	48	38.4%
Total	125	100%
St deviation		15.78

Table 6 Sustainable digital design principles

Choices	Actions	%
Font selection (I am aware of sustainable font types)	6	6.12%
Not taking any specific action	25	25.51%
Color selection (I am aware of choosing colors that consume less energy on screens)	32	32.65%
Image/video selection (I am aware of considering size, color, and quality choices)	35	35.71%
Total	98	100%
St deviation		13.03

This discrepancy might be addressed by exploring the responses to the following question.

While we asked digital designers about the challenges, they face in promoting sustainability in their projects, 37.7% cited client demands as a significant obstacle. Additionally, 31.15% mentioned user preferences as another challenge, while 30.33% stated that digital sustainability imposes limitations in design and 0.82% lacked enough knowledge about it (Table 7).

Table 7 Challenges in promoting sustainability in the design projects

Choices	Actions	%
Don't have enough knowledge	1	0.82%
Design limitations imposed by sustainability efforts	37	30.33%
User preferences	38	31.15%
Client demands	46	37.70%
Total	122	100%
St deviation		20.07

Table 8 Perception of success of digital sustainability

From 1 to 5	Responses	%
1—Wick	8	10.4%
2—Below average	21	27.3%
3—Average	37	48.1%
4—Good	11	14.3%
5—excellent	0	0%
Total	77	100%
Mean		2.66
St deviation		14.22

While we asked them about their perception of the current success of digital sustainability, the majority response, at 48.1%, indicated that it is "average". Additionally, 14.3% rated it as "excellent", another 27.3% mentioned it as "below average", and 10.4% said it's "weak".

Interestingly, 0% stated that digital sustainability is fully successful at its aims (Table 8). These responses suggest that they recognize there is significant progress to be made in achieving success in digital sustainability.

5 Conclusions and Future Work

Sustainable digital design aims to minimize environmental impacts by adopting cleaner methods for designing digital products, services, or systems.

Following sustainability concerns, our main objective of this article is to raise awareness among young designers about thc importance of reducing energy consumption and carbon footprint through the adoption of sustainable digital design principles. We believe it is crucial to educate future designers about these principles during their university education. Additionally, as they enter the profession as junior designers, it is essential to reinforce these principles and ensure they are being applied properly.

For this purpose, a comparative analysis was conducted between two existing frameworks, which allowed us to identify some principles that have been selected to be a part of the survey conducted.

In conclusion, the survey conducted with university students and junior digital designers regarding digital sustainability revealed relevant information. Most of our audience demonstrates awareness of digital sustainability principles, highlighting a promising foundation for future initiatives in promoting sustainable practices within the field. However, our study also identified significant challenges, including accommodating client demands, addressing user preferences, and navigating the limitations imposed by digital sustainability in design processes. Despite these challenges, there is a shared recognition among the participants that digital sustainability has not yet reached its full potential, with many recognizing its state as average or below average.

The next steps of our research involve conducting a comprehensive survey on sustainable digital design principles—examining the practices, advantages, and disadvantages from the perspectives of consumers/users, companies/organizations, and digital designers, aiming to reduce energy consumption and carbon footprint. Subsequently, we plan to design a workshop to disseminate these practices to as many stakeholders as possible in the process of conceiving, developing, and implementing digital products, systems, or services.

Acknowledgements This research was funded by ITI/LARSyS: https://doi.org/10.54499/LA/P/0083/2020; https://doi.org/10.54499/UIDP/50009/2020 and https://doi.org/10.54499/UIDB/50009/2020.

References

1. Bratton, B. H.: The Black Stack. e-flux Journal, 53 (March 2014), https://editor.e-flux-systems.com/files/59883_e-flux-journal-the-black-stack.pdf, last accessed 2024/3/14.
2. Monserrate, S. G.: The Cloud Is Material: On the Environmental Impacts of Computation and Data Storage. MIT Case Studies in Social and Ethical Responsibilities of Computing, Winter (January 2022), https://doi.org/10.21428/2c646de5.031d4553.
3. Everts, T.: Ten years of page bloat: What have we learned? SpeedCurve (March 2022), https://www.speedcurve.com/blog/ten-years-page-bloat, last accessed 2024/3/10.
4. Parikka, J.: Working for systems that do not do the work: Joana Moll's the hidden life of an Amazon user. Interface Critique, 3, 81–85 (2021), https://doi.org/10.11588/ic.2021.3.81325.
5. Bridle, J.: New Dark Age: Technology and the End of the Future. Verso, UK (2018).
6. Narang, R., Tiwari, S.: Antecedents and Consequences of the Growing Popularity of Digital Consumption. In M. Khosrow-Pour D.B.A. (Ed.), Encyclopedia of Information Science and Technology, 5th Edition, pp. 1066–1084, IGI Global. https://doi.org/10.4018/978-1-7998-3479-3.ch073
7. Everts, T.: What is page bloat? And how is it hurting your business, your search rank, and your users?, SpeedCurve (July 2023), https://www.speedcurve.com/blog/page-bloat-web-performance, last accessed 2024/3/10.
8. Papanek, V.: Design for the Real World, 3rd Edition, Thames & Hudson Ltd, London (2019).
9. Ceschin, F., Gaziulusoy, L.: Evolution of design for sustainability: From product design to design for system innovations and transitions. Design Studies, 47, 118–163 (2016), https://doi.org/10.1016/j.destud.2016.09.002.
10. Sustainable Web Manifesto, https://www.sustainablewebmanifesto.com, last accessed 2024/02/21.
11. Daly, H. E.: Toward some operational principles of sustainable development. Ecological economics, 2(1), 1–6 (1990).
12. Design Group Italia.: Sustainable Digital Design. Small actions to design in a conscious way (2022), https://www.figma.com/proto/1ifbAAqhIHOVuBwwflG2kH/Sustainability-Kit-for-digital-designers-(Community)?type=design&node-id=11-3573&scaling=contain&page-id=11%3A3508&starting-point-node-id=11%3A3573, last accessed 2024/2/15.
13. Atos Group.: Ato's ecobranding principles (2021), https://atos.net/wp-content/uploads/2021/07/atos-ecobranding-report.pdf, last accessed 2024/2/14.
14. IEA. Electricity 2024, IEA, Paris. License: CC BY 4.0 (2024), https://www.iea.org/reports/electricity-2024, last accessed 2024/3/29.

15. Freitag, C., Berners-Lee, M., Widdicks, K., Knowles, B., Blair, G. S., Friday, A.: The real climate and transformative impact of ICT: A critique of estimates, trends, and regulations, Patterns, 3(8), 100576 (2022), https://doi.org/10.1016/j.patter.2021.100340.
16. IEA. World Energy Outlook 2023, IEA, Paris, License: CC BY 4.0 (report); CC BY NC SA 4.0 (Annex A) (2023). https://www.iea.org/reports/world-energy-outlook-2023.
17. Preist, C., Schien, D. Blevis, E.: Understanding and Mitigating the Effects of Device and Cloud Service Design Decisions on the Environmental Footprint of Digital Infrastructure. In Proceedings of the 34th Annual ACM Conference on Human Factors in Computing Systems, CHI, pp. 1324–1337. Association for Computing Machinery (ACM), NY (May 2016), https://doi.org/10.1145/2858036.2858378.
18. Fuchs, C.: Critical social theory and sustainable development: the role of class, capitalism and domination in a dialectical analysis of Un/sustainability, Sustainable Development, 25(5), 443–458 (2017), https://doi.org/10.1002/sd.1673.
19. Kotlarsky, J., Oshri, I., Sekulic, N.: Digital Sustainability in Information Systems Research: Conceptual Foundations and Future Directions. In Journal of the Association for Information Systems, 24(4), pp. 936–952. Association for Information Systems (2023), https://doi.org/10.17705/1jais.00825.
20. Remy, C., Bates, O., Dix, A., Thomas, V., Hazas, M., Friday, A., Huang, E. M.: Evaluation Beyond Usability: Validating Sustainable HCI Research. In Proceedings of the 2018 CHI Conference on Human Factors in Computing Systems (CHI'18), vol. 216, pp. 1–14. Association for Computing Machinery, https://doi.org/10.1145/3173574.3173790.
21. Intergovernmental Panel on Climate Change (IPCC). Climate Change 2021—The Physical Science Basis: Working Group I Contribution to the Sixth Assessment Report of the Intergovernmental Panel on Climate Change. Cambridge University Press, Cambridge (2023), https://doi.org/10.1017/9781009157896.
22. Toyama, K.: Preliminary thoughts on a taxonomy of value for sustainable computing. First Monday, 20(8) (2015), https://doi.org/10.5210/fm.v20i8.6132.
23. Herman E. D.: Toward some operational principles of sustainable development, Ecological Economics, 2(1), 1–6 (1990), https://doi.org/10.1016/0921-8009(90)90010-R.
24. Collier, A.: A definition of digital literacy & citizenship. NetFamilyNews (September 2009), https://www.netfamilynews.org/?p=28594, last accessed 2024/3/29.
25. Ribble, M., Bailey, G.: Digital Citizenship in Schools. ISTE, Washington DC (2007).
26. Elgaaïed-Gambier, L., Bertrandias, L., Bernard, Y.: Cutting the Internet's Environmental Footprint: An Analysis of Consumers' Self-Attribution of Responsibility. Journal of Interactive Marketing, 50(1), 120–135, https://doi.org/10.1016/j.intmar.2020.02.001.
27. Gnanasekaran, V., Fridtun, H., Hatlen, H., Langøy, M., Syrstad, A., Subramanian, S., De Moor, K.: Digital carbon footprint awareness among digital natives: an exploratory study, 1. NIKT: Norsk IKT-konferanse for forskning og utdanning (2021).
28. Holt, D., Cameron, D.: Cultural strategy: using innovative ideologies to build breakthrough brands. Oxford University Press, UK (2010).
29. Stegall, N.: Designing for Sustainability: A Philosophy for Ecologically Intentional Design. Design Issues, 22(2), 56–63. The MIT Press, Massachusetts (2006).
30. Verbeek, P-P.: Morality in Design: Design Ethics and the Morality of Technological Artifacts. In Kroes, P., Vermaas, P. E., Light, A. and Moore, S. A. (Eds.), Philosophy and Design: From Engineering to Architecture. Springer, Dordrecht (2008).
31. Davis, J.: Towards Participatory Design of Ambient Persuasive Technology. Presented at Persuasive Pervasive Technology and Environmental Sustainability Workshop at Pervasive (2008).
32. Fry, T.: The Voice of Sustainment: Design Ethics as Futuring, Design Philosophy Papers, 2(2), 145–156 (2005), https://doi.org/10.2752/144871304X13966215068038.
33. Blevis, E.: Sustainable interaction design: invention & disposal, renewal & reuse. In Proceedings of the SIGCHI Conference on Human Factors in Computing Systems (CHI'07), pp. 503–512. Association for Computing Machinery, NY, https://doi.org/10.1145/1240624.1240705.

34. Venkadeshwaran, K.: Green Technology and Its Effect on the Modern World. Jetir, 6(3), (2019), https://www.jetir.org/papers/JETIREW06032.pdf.
35. Røpke, I., Christensen, T.H.: Energy impacts of ICT and Insights from an everyday life perspective. Telematics and Informatics 29(4), 348–361 (2012).
36. Murugesan, S., Gangadharan, G.: Harnessing Green IT: Principles and Practices. Chichester: John Wiley and Sons (2012).
37. ISO 14040:2006. Environmental management. Life cycle assessment. Principles and framework (2006), https://www.iso.org/standard/37456.html, last accessed 2024/2/29.
38. Mulder, K.F., Segalas, J., Ferrer-Balas, D.: How to educate engineers for/in sustainable development: Ten years of discussion, remaining challenges. International Journal of Sustainability in Higher Education, 13, 211–218 (2012).
39. Boyle, C.: Considerations on education engineers in sustainability. International Journal of Sustainability in Higher Education, 5(2), 147–155 (2004), https://doi.org/10.1108/146763704 10526233.
40. Brown, T., Wyatt, J.: Design thinking for social innovation. Stanford Social Innovation Review, 8, 30–35, Winter (2010).
41. Downey, G.: Are Engineers Losing Control of Technology? Chemical Engineering Research and Design, 83, 583–595 (2005).
42. Global Reporting Initiative (2016), https://www.globalreporting.org, last accessed 2024/1/23.
43. Greenhouse Gas Protocol, https://ghgprotocol.org, last accessed 2024/1/25.
44. Lawless, J.: Sustainability KPIs—An In-Depth Guide, Purple Griffon (February 2024). https://purplegriffon.com/blog/sustainability-kpis, last accessed 2024/1/24.
45. Chugh, R., Wibowo, S., Grandhi, S.: Environmentally sustainable Information and Communication Technology usage: awareness and practices of Indian Information and Communication Technology professionals, Journal of Cleaner Production, 131, 435–446 (2016), https://doi.org/10.1016/j.jclepro.2016.05.004.
46. The Shift Project, https://theshiftproject.org/en/home, last accessed 2024/1/23.
47. Gui, M., Fasoli, M., Carradore, R.: Digital Well-Being. Developing a New Theoretical Tool for Media Literacy Research. Italian Journal of Sociology of Education (2017).
48. Hanks, K., Odom, W., Roedl, D., Blevis, E.: Sustainable millennials: attitudes towards sustainability and the material effects of interactive technologies. In Proceedings of the SIGCHI Conference on Human Factors in Computing Systems (CHI '08), pp. 333–342. Association for Computing Machinery, NY, https://doi.org/10.1145/1357054.1357111.

Digital Environment to Support Well-Being, Empowerment and Experience of Care

Piera Losciale, Alessandra Scarcelli, and Annalisa Di Roma

Abstract Starting from the definition of the theoretical paradigm of reference of the city as care and the role of digital environment systems to support holistic well-being, the case of citizen wellbeing in relation to the territorial and social context is addressed here. The transdisciplinary research approach identifies and puts into practice methods and solutions that can improve the quality of life of citizens through the use of technological facilitators and the delocalisation of services. This paper, within the service design framework for social innovation, provides the state of the art, through case studies, to support the development of a digital platform. The research method involves the definition of criteria (sustainability, inclusion, memory) used as foundations for the mapping of places, services, projects and needs, the subject of the case studies analysed. In particular, the research focuses on the case of the Apulian territory.

Keywords Digital environment · Citizens' well-being · Platform society

1 Introduction

The present research is part of the ongoing project NXT Digital Platform[1] and in particular reports the desk phase aimed at defining the theoretical reference model for the emergence of the needs and constraints to be placed at the basis of the analysis and data collection phases for the future design of a digital platform for the Italian city of Bari.

---

[1] Research Project NXT Digital Platform—Contract for research activities between NTT DATA ITALIA S.p.A. and Politecnico di Bari. Coordinator Prof. A. Di Roma, OR1: Analysis of technologies and methodologies enabling the NXT Digital Platform (Research Team: Di Roma, A., Scarcelli, A., Neglia, A. L., Losciale, P., Ricci, M., Lafortuna, L., Simone, R.).

P. Losciale (✉) · A. Scarcelli · A. Di Roma
Department of Architecture, Construction and Design, Polytechnic University of Bari, Bari, Italy
e-mail: p.losciale1@phd.poliba.it

© The Author(s), under exclusive license to Springer Nature Switzerland AG 2025

D. Brandão et al. (eds.), *Perspectives on Design and Digital Communication V*, Springer Series in Design and Innovation 50, https://doi.org/10.1007/978-3-031-76156-0_2

The multidisciplinary approach of the research, identifies and implements methods and solutions that can improve the quality of life of citizens through the use of technological enablers and the delocalisation of services.

The general objective is the development of a model that defines the 'city as care' starting from the construction of the state of the art through a transdisciplinary approach, the identification and analysis of case studies, the definition of criteria to be applied to the mapping of these selected cases.

Specifically, the study of methodologies, theoretical and/or applied, aimed at improving the quality of life of citizens, is combined with the research activity of the existing macro-project related to services for citizens (i.e. 'city of 15 min', urban planning), in order to improve their experience in the city through the use of technology. Particular attention is given to understanding the specific context, the diversity of society and the capacity of citizenship, permanent or temporary, to absorb the impact of the solutions in the cases described.

Following the introductory section, the paper provides for the restitution of the theoretical-critical paradigm, the methodology used with the analysis criteria, the selected case studies, the role of the digital environment and in particular of digital platforms in supporting citizen well-being, and the conclusions with the respective future research perspectives.

2 The Theoretical-Critical Paradigm

In contemporary society, characterised by urbanisation, the city is understood as its essence and symbol, where evolution is not only guaranteed, but also particularly dynamic [1]. The city, born out of millennia of progressive domestication of ecosystems and landscapes, is considered the primary care for human needs, as it is simultaneously the object of nature and the subject of culture, the individual and the group [2]: the city plays a crucial role as it is the primary place of encounter, coexistence and social interaction [3].

As a consequence of its evolution, the city has introduced harmful elements into itself [1] and from being a care for human needs it has become an organism in need of care. In fact, following industrialisation, the city emerged as the main context for capitalist exchange, competitiveness and individual consumption. These new dynamics have profoundly transformed the very nature of urban places, redefining their main function in economic and productive terms. However, despite the fact that cities have become engines of cultural and economic development, they have often struggled to adapt to social needs and the impacts of environmental and landscape transformations [4]: fragmented and incoherent cities, lacking organic planning, complex and inequitable.

2.1 *Quality of Life, Well-Being, Health and Care*

The focus of theoretical studies on life in urban contexts developed from the need for their reconstruction following the two World Wars. The concept of 'quality of life', understood as well-being closely linked to a habitat [5, 6], is introduced by the reasoning of some European scholars of urban geography in the 1970s. In these same years it is the idea of well-being that undergoes a change. From being strictly connected to economic possibilities, thus brought back to the standard of living and to the ability of individuals to place themselves with their own resources at the top of the hierarchical pyramid [7], the concept of quality of life begins to consider social and psycho-sociological components that were previously completely ignored.

While in the past the level of well-being was mainly assessed by traditional indicators such as GDP, per capita income and life expectancy, in the 1980s, indicators related to natural wealth, climate and associated life began to be considered as well. This idea collaborated in the formation of the idea of sustainable development, which was first reported in 1987 by the Brundtland Report [8].

The concept of 'health', the primary essence of wellbeing, is broadened and deepened at the same time as the idea of quality of life and wellbeing. From being considered exclusively as the mere absence of disease or limited to the bio-physiological condition, the notion of health begins to be interpreted as a more complex concept involving different dimensions of human experience. Although the definition of health by the World Health Organisation in 1948 already refers to health as a state of 'physical, mental and social well-being', it was in the 1970s that it began to be considered as a harmonious condition between the physical, mental and social dimensions and as a virtuous relationship between man and the environment: a determining factor for the promotion of health and collective well-being [9].

Nowadays, it is a common understanding that health, and thus quality of life, is influenced by circumstances, opportunities and the capacity for dynamic integration with the surrounding environment, including urban, natural and social spheres.

2.2 *The City as a Cure*

Therefore, the interrelationship between cities, well-being, and health has transformed into a bond of mutual interconnectedness and interdependence. The perspective of 'city as care' and 'city care' is considered not as two alternative options, but rather as two equally necessary and sufficient conditions. On the one hand, health should be regarded as a resource for everyday life, not as the ultimate goal of life [10]; on the other hand, a good city is first and foremost a city in which people live well, a city that is healthy and promotes healthy lifestyles that enable as many individuals as possible to realise their full biological potential and lead a satisfying and fulfilling existence [7].

The research tends towards the model of the city of proximity [11], a model also known as the 'city of 15 min' in which proximity is not only understood in terms of the reduction of distances, but also in terms of relationships. The need to overcome the idea of the city as a set of services of which citizens are customers or users is compelling.

2.3 The Systemic Model of Study and Observation of the City

Building upon these general reflections, the research establishes a complex and multifaceted mode of observation, study, and analysis of the urban context. To study the city, both as a subject of care and an object of care, it is necessary to hybridize methods and observation techniques originating simultaneously from technical disciplines such as architecture and design, as well as from humanities disciplines such as urban and media sociology, cultural studies, and language theory. Therefore, the research proposes a multidisciplinary approach.

As emphasized by the semiotician Gianfranco Marrone [12]:

"È convinzione ormai diffusa fra gli studiosi di spazi urbani che la città non si esaurisce nella differenziazione dei suoi spazi (strade, piazze, giardini, fiumi e spiagge, terreni vaghi...) e nell'articolazione delle cose che li riempiono (edifici, chiese e monumenti, segnaletica, affissioni, luci, servizi vari). Si insiste sul fatto che a costituire una città – di qualsiasi dimensione e complessità, densità o rarefazione – sono soprattutto i cittadini, siano essi stanziali o meno, residenti o passanti, pendolari o turisti, che vivono i luoghi urbani, li attraversano secondo percorsi variamente stabilizzati, valorizzandoli, disvalorizzandoli e rivalorizzandoli di continuo. Da una parte ci starebbe allora lo spazio, naturale e costruito, condizione di possibilità dell'ambiente urbano in quanto forma ideale astratta; dall'altra si collocherebbero invece le persone, soggetti individuali e collettivi che in quello spazio si trovano in vario modo situati, costituendone la sostanza sociale. Il tutto all'interno di una storia e di una memoria che mitiga le forze entropiche del tempo consolidando uomini e cose, costruendo e mantenendo scampoli di identità".[2]

[2] Trad. "It is now widely believed among scholars of urban spaces that the city does not exhaust itself in the differentiation of its spaces (streets, squares, gardens, rivers and beaches, vacant lands…) and in the articulation of the things that fill them (buildings, churches and monuments, signage, advertisements, lights, various services). It is emphasized that what constitutes a city – of any size and complexity, density or rarity – are primarily the citizens, whether they are stationary or not, residents or passers-by, commuters or tourists, who experience urban places, traverse them along variously stabilized paths, continuously valuing, devaluing, and revaluing them. On one hand, there would be space, natural and built, as the condition of possibility of the urban environment as an abstract ideal form; on the other hand, there would be people, individual and collective subjects who are in various ways situated in that space, constituting the social substance. All within a history and memory that mitigates the entropic forces of time by consolidating people and things, constructing and maintaining fragments of identity".

The study of care dynamics within the city thus occurs from a systemic and relational perspective: when actions are taken for the care of the city, this automatically implies caring for the people, and vice versa.

Users or Consumers? Ideal Type, Proto-Personas, Personas

The definition of city users involves considering a broad group of consumers, including both resident and non-resident citizens, each bringing specific instances of care and well-being. Therefore, in the desk phase, the research initially relies on the sociological category of the Weberian ideal type, which will later evolve into proto-personas and personas in the field phase.

The term "ideal type" refers to an abstract but plausible model useful for understanding the world: a conceptual framework that is not reality but is expressed in a schema assumed as an example. This concept is closely related to the concept of personas adopted for user research in a Human-Centered approach within the field of interaction design. The concept of personas was first introduced in 1999 by Alan Cooper in the book "The Inmates Are Running the Asylum," following the need to introduce imaginary characters to represent different types of users during the design of user experience. Therefore, this concept is an evolution of the ideal type concept coined by Max Weber in the early twentieth century and subsequently used in numerous sociological and political research studies.

From ideal types, which can be defined as generative theoretical tools that identify critical hypotheses of users whose needs, behaviors, and practices can be imagined, proto-personas are constructed. These proto-personas, through the definition of more specific data, can evolve into personas.

Through the identification of different types of users, the research attempts to observe the city as an adaptive system that responds differently to various needs and instances. What is of interest to investigate is the reciprocal influence exerted by the city and its users to identify forms of virtuous coexistence functional to health and well-being.

3 Research Methodology

The present study specifically concerns the city of Bari, but initially broadens its analytical scope to the entire Apulian regional territory. Its primary aim is to investigate to what extent the typical city of the analyzed context cares for its inhabitants and to what extent it simultaneously requires care to ensure a higher quality of life.

Given the complexity of the analysis to be conducted, the research initially conducted an exploratory theoretical analysis, followed by an examination of places, services, projects, and needs. This process defined a method of analysis that identifies indicators for systematic and comparative observation. In this regard, three macro-indicators (inclusion, memory, sustainability) were identified, further subdivided into more specific sub-indicators, with the aim of identifying all those factors that effectively act as elements of care and well-being for individuals and the entire community. Subsequently, the research conducted a specific analysis of some appropriately selected case studies.

Following the described phases, a review of the theoretical literature regarding the role of the digital environment, particularly digital platforms, was conducted, and an emblematic case study was reported. All these steps facilitated the development of a model of the "city as care."

3.1 Indicators

Inclusion

The first macro-indicator is that of "inclusion." Inclusion is conceptualized here by adopting the perspective of Ronald Mace's universal design. It is defined as the ability to conceive all products, environments, and processes in a way that makes them accessible to all individuals, regardless of the presence or absence of physical disabilities, age, abilities, and social conditions. Such an idea of inclusion certainly relates to accessibility, a concept understood here as encompassed within that of inclusion, but also to the integration of all types of disadvantage or cultural, economic, linguistic, or cognitive diversity. True inclusion, therefore, is realized in equitable use and in the full participation of all individuals in social life.

In the case at hand, more specific indicators include all strategies for reducing environmental barriers, policies aimed at social and gender inclusion, and actions directed towards linguistic and cultural integration implemented at the regional and city levels.

Sustainability

The second macro-indicator is that of "sustainability." Sustainable development is understood as the capacity to meet the needs of the present without compromising the ability of future generations to meet their own needs. The concept of sustainability, as understood here, in line with its evolution over time, not only considers purely ecological aspects but also economic and social components. Sustainable progress implies overall well-being, whether it be environmental, social, or economic.

In the case at hand, more specific indicators include all strategies implemented for the preservation of the environment and energy resources, as well as actions aimed at technological integration at the regional and city levels.

Memory

The third macro-indicator is that of "memory." Memory refers not only to the capacity to safeguard and preserve but also to critically renegotiate identity and cultural elements, traditional and ritualistic components, and historical awareness. This concept of memory encompasses all forms of "unconscious modernity." The indicator of memory becomes crucial in the analysis of a city understood as an articulated adaptive system and as a complex human-environmental relationship. Keeping in mind the history, culture, and traditions of a place allows for the assessment of the relevance of any intervention aimed at care and well-being and evaluating its effectiveness in context.

In the case at hand, more specific indicators include all strategies implemented for the protection of cultural heritage, policies aimed at enhancing local traditions, and the social impact of all cultural initiatives undertaken at the regional and city levels.

3.2 Case Studies

The case studies under examination concern the territorial scale of the Apulia region and consider two specific dimensions of analysis (see Fig. 1).

- The first social dimension (in red) concerns activities promoted, coordinated, and organized by associations in private spaces within the territory.
- The second social dimension (in blue) refers to the physical spaces of the city, focusing on care and well-being promoted through the strategic enhancement of public spaces present in the territory.

The case studies have been selected based on their relevance to the previously identified indicators. The adopted analysis method involved the design and compilation of technical sheets for the selected case studies. These sheets contain descriptive metadata of the case under examination (name, year, entity, location, sources to consult), the critical assignment of values to the indicators of inclusion, sustainability, and

Fig. 1 Case studies on the territory of Apulia (first and second dimensions)

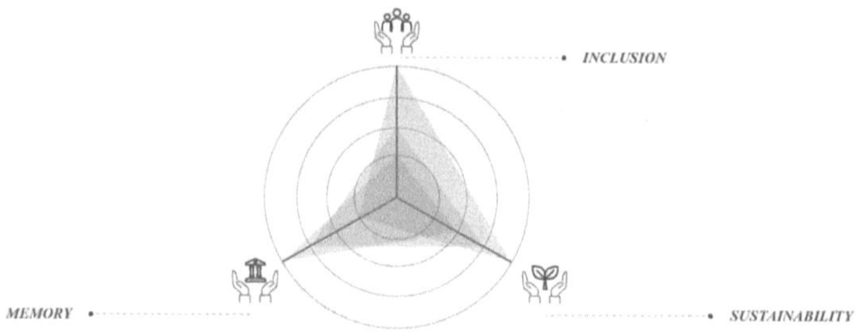

Fig. 2 Kiviat diagram with selected variables

memory (graphical representation and textual description), and photographic documentation. In this context, only some of the case studies analyzed by the research are reported, in a layout different from the original indexing but containing the same information for optimal graphical representation.

For assigning values to the indicators, the Kiviat diagram is used, an effective graphical representation for visualizing data on multiple variables. This type of graph consists of a series of rays extending from a central point and forming equal angles with each other; each ray represents one of the considered variables, specifically inclusion, sustainability, and memory (see Fig. 2). The distance from the center of the graph of the point positioned on the ray is proportional to the value of the variable compared to the maximum achievable value. The points on the rays are then connected by segments, allowing for an immediate comparison between the values of the different variables.

4 Case Study Analysis

The analysis of the case studies reported below is divided by belonging dimension (first or second). Furthermore, for each selected case, a general description is provided, along with the corresponding Kiviat diagram, photographic documentation, and a systematic analysis of the indicators.

4.1 First Dimension: Activities, Initiatives

The case studies reported for the first dimension include the initiative "Don't BeeScared" [13], promoted by the cultural association Facelia composed of young beekeepers engaged in urban educational beekeeping in the territory of Bari; the urban workshop "Ortodomingo" [14], supported by the Social Promotion Association Parco Domingo, which aims to socially include those experiencing mental or physical difficulties through a new formula of social aggregation based on empathy,

Fig. 3 Don't BeeScared—Bari (BA)

environmental sustainability, and sharing; the project "Terrazza Tutti al mare" [15], born from an idea of the founder of the association 2HE-Center For Human Health and Environment, and the "IO POSSO" project, aimed at promoting initiatives to improve the quality of life of people with disabilities.

Don't BeeScared

It is the first urban apiary in Bari, born in 2019 from the idea of young beekeepers, where activities of information and awareness about the world of bees are promoted (see Fig. 3).

- Inclusion: Their commitment to inclusion is reflected in the creation of educational programs such as "OlimpiAPI," targeted workshops for children, schools, and families that involve everyone in the discovery of the wonderful world of bees. They aim to break down barriers of knowledge by offering as wide an audience as possible the opportunity to actively participate in role-playing games that promote environmental awareness and respect for bees. Inclusion is their foundational value, as they believe that everyone should have access to information and activities that contribute to environmental conservation.
- Sustainability. Sustainability is at the core of their mission to care for bees in the territory of Bari. Through initiatives such as "Le Cronache un'Arnia," they offer stories tailored for an adult audience, promoting awareness of the need to preserve bees and the ecosystem in which they live. Additionally, the visit to the hives allows them to demonstrate concretely how they contribute to sustainability, illustrating the structure of the hives, their inhabitants, and production materials such as pollen, wax, propolis, royal jelly, and bee venom. They support the health of bees and the environment, thus contributing to a more sustainable future for all.
- Memory. Memory is essential for preserving the history of bees and their connection with them. Through activities such as honey tasting, they celebrate the tradition and history of these industrious creatures. Each taste of honey is a sensory journey that connects them to bees and their essential role in the ecosystem. They preserve the memory of bees not only through stories and hive visits but

Fig. 4 Ortodomingo—Bari (BA)

also through sensory experiences, keeping alive awareness of their importance in history and the present.

Ortodomingo

The project, started in 2015, involves the creation of an urban workshop initiated by a social promotion association, where individuals can socialize or engage in cognitive stimulation activities for those experiencing mental or physical challenges (see Fig. 4).

- Inclusion. In the specific context of the first "smart" urban workshop in Bari, active efforts are underway to promote inclusion through the implementation of new models of social aggregation. The approach is based on the valorization of empathy as a fundamental element, aiming to create an exemplary Community of Civilization. In this perspective, the establishment of a community website dedicated to the development of circular economy processes is promoted. The goal is to encourage the sharing of best practices and innovative solutions in the Smart City context, promoting the active participation of all community members.
- Sustainability. The urban workshop sets the ambitious goal of implementing environmental sustainability in every aspect of community life. An essential pillar of this project is the creation of a Solidarity Purchasing Group, which encourages the purchase of locally sourced products with the "Made in Sud" formula. In this way, it aims to stimulate collective awareness towards responsible and sustainable choices, reducing the environmental impact associated with consumption. In parallel, the group works together to achieve significant savings on individual energy and waste management costs, promoting an eco-friendly lifestyle.
- Memory. The urban workshop does not limit itself to practical and tangible aspects but also aspires to preserve the memory and history of the community. Another objective is to promote the inclusion of specialized operators from other associations in the territory. These professionals, with a solid skills base, provide assistance to individuals facing physical or mental difficulties. This inclusion of specialized operators not only contributes to individual well-being but also constitutes an important piece in the construction of collective memory.

Fig. 5 Terrazza Tutti al mare—Area of Salento (LE)

Terrazza Tutti al Mare

The project was born in 2015 from an idea by Gaetano Fuso, founder of the association 2HE and promoter of the "IO POSSO" project, aimed at promoting initiatives to improve the quality of life of those affected by disabilities (see Fig. 5).

- Inclusion. IO POSSO has quickly involved a significant number of volunteers, whose contingent continues to grow both in Italy and abroad. The active participation of the community is evident in the three locations where the terrace has been implemented: San Foca, Gallipoli, and Porto Cesareo. This involvement reflects a widespread commitment to supporting accessibility to the sea and promoting an inclusive environment for all.
- Sustainability. The project's objectives, resulting in continuous growth, include providing access to the sea with adequate and free services for both guests and their caregivers. The construction of nursing stations and the employment of specialized personnel in assistance contribute to ensuring a safe and welcoming bathing experience. Additionally, the commitment to breaking down existing barriers reflects the willingness to make the entire bathing experience accessible to all people, regardless of their physical abilities.
- Memory. Finally, the project represents a significant step forward in providing the first equipped access to the sea for individuals with SLA, neuromuscular diseases, and other severe motor disabilities. The memory of these achievements will endure over time, as IO POSSO continues to stand as a beacon of inclusivity and accessibility, inspiring future efforts and projects aimed at improving the quality of life for all people, regardless of the challenges they face.

4.2 Second Dimension: Public Physical Spaces of the City

The case studies reported for the second dimension concern the "Percorso vita" [16] at the Pane e Pomodoro beach in Bari; the "Bimbiland" playground [17] at the Nassiriya public area in Triggiano; the "Parco Giochi Diffuso" [18] in the city of Manduria.

Fig. 6 Percorso vita—Bari (BA)

Percorso Vita

In 2023, the Municipality of Bari, in collaboration with Pfizer s.r.l., promoted an awareness campaign on metastatic breast cancer in women. The campaign involved the installation of fitness equipment at the Pane e Pomodoro beach, aiming to encourage outdoor physical activity (see Fig. 6).

- Inclusion. The installation is intended to benefit women affected by breast cancer, as physical activity is considered an important means to increase strength and physical endurance, facilitate completion of daily activities, help manage fatigue, and boost self-esteem. Simultaneously, the initiative aims to promote physical activity among all citizens by extending the use of the equipment to everyone. This contributes to raising awareness within the community about the importance of well-being and health in general, spreading information about breast cancer, and socially including women affected by this condition.
- Sustainability. The initiative adds value to the sports offerings of the city beach by integrating with the existing calisthenics path. Sustainable redevelopment interventions in the city's natural areas contribute to the goal of making the city greener. In this context, the creation of an "outdoor gym" fits perfectly into intervention strategies, leading to an increase in the number of people practicing sports, particularly in outdoor areas, with significant health benefits for citizens of all ages.
- Memory. The selection of the location for the installation is not random: the Municipality aims to promote holistic health by positively intervening in iconic places of the city, such as the symbolic beach "Pane e Pomodoro". The fitness area in this location, one of the most beloved by the residents of Bari and frequented by tourists, helps preserve and pass on the identity of the place, making it accessible and lived by the city community.

Parco Giochi Bimbiland

In 2017, the Municipality of Triggiano, in collaboration with a group of volunteers, created an inclusive playground designed to accommodate all children, both typically developing and differently-abled, with particular attention to motor and sensory disabilities (see Fig. 7).

Fig. 7 Parco giochi Bimbiland—Triggiano (BA)

- Inclusion. The park is designed without architectural barriers, ensuring accessibility for all and guaranteeing the right to have a green area where children can play freely. It promotes interaction and integration among children with different physical abilities, fostering social inclusion and education on diversity. The park is not just a recreational space but also a place where children learn to respect differences and collaborate with each other, contributing to creating a more supportive and inclusive community. The playground equipment features various functions and structures, from swings accessible even with wheelchairs to sensory games designed for children with cognitive differences. The park can accommodate up to 30 children aged between 2 and 12 years old simultaneously, offering them the opportunity to play and have fun together in an inclusive and safe environment.
- Sustainability. Environmental sustainability aspects are minimally present in this case, except for the redevelopment of a disused public area in the city.
- Memory. The preservation of memory is minimally present in this case (Fig. 8)

Parco Giochi Diffuso

In 2023, the Municipality of Manduria realized a project of playful installations, distributed in various locations throughout the city, inspired by traditional street games, ensuring families the right to play while fully complying with safety regulations (see Fig. 9).

Fig. 8 Parco Giochi Diffuso—Manduria (TA)

Fig. 9 WeMi digital wealth platform [https://wemi.comune.milano.it/]

- Inclusion. Viewing families as integral parts of the community, the project encourages the sharing of values such as cooperation, inclusion, civic sense communication, environmental respect, and mutual respect among the city's younger citizens. Moreover, the activities enhance and stimulate children's creativity, providing them with spaces and opportunities to express themselves freely through play and imagination. This not only contributes to their personal development but also to the construction of a more cohesive, supportive, and inclusive community.
- Sustainability. The installations are designed to harmoniously integrate with the urban environment, avoiding the introduction of bulky elements and instead featuring colorful lines that blend with the street pavement. However, the project does not specifically focus on the implementation of green public areas in the city.

Memory. The playful installations seamlessly blend into the history and culture of Manduria's territory. By promoting, integrating, and valorizing local traditions among the younger generation, the project, through fun and recreation, strengthens the tangible bond between children and their community, enriching the city's social and cultural fabric.

The Platform Society

The construction of community is the starting point for the realization of a proximity city, aimed at care, well-being, and health. Proximity is understood here as the condition of being physically close in space, but also in the feeling derived from the awareness of sharing something with someone. The proximity city thus sees an ecosystem of people, organizations, places, products, and services that collectively demonstrate a mutual capacity for care and well-being. The proximity city becomes a social and material resource for all its citizens who contribute to its production and must bear its burden.

Therefore, to thoroughly investigate the influence mutually exerted by cities and city users in order to identify virtuous coexistence forms functional to health and well-being, it is necessary to focus attention on the modalities through which real and virtual communities are created in the context. It is necessary to study how, why, and especially through which physical and virtual spaces, and through which communication channels, modern communities are created.

Sociology, particularly media sociology, sociosemiotics, and cultural studies, have long been concerned with concepts such as urban communities and subcultures, but alongside these theoretical definitions, the concept of the Platform Society is becoming increasingly influential. Western societies, in fact, are increasingly dependent on the infrastructural services of the so-called Big Tech companies (Google, Amazon, Facebook, Microsoft, Apple). They are "platformized" societies, which build, live, and modify themselves predominantly through virtual spaces. This means that the study of the platform society is a necessary prerequisite for understanding the mechanisms of constitution and functioning of both digital and real society, i.e., the so-called "communities of sense", whether it be a street, a neighborhood, or even an entire city.

In a fragmented social context, the development of aggregation and social network reconfiguration services is crucial to respond to the pluralization and changing needs, and digital services are capable of defining new services, inducing, or facilitating proximity interactions.

Even the more complex and holistic conception of well-being and health that is prevalent today cannot ignore the evolution of technologies and their transformative impact on society, which has promoted the shift from a model where people felt and acted as passive consumers to a reality that promotes collaboration, the production of common goods, and mutual support among individuals and towards the planet. In this perspective, digital services become collaborative sociotechnical systems that define community networks and relationships, facilitating resource sharing, cooperation, and mutual care.

In particular, welfare platforms are based on the principle of multiple people providing collaborative responses to needs, actively involving social actors, and creating interactions, thereby strengthening community resources. The platform, in this context, serves as the main infrastructure that connects the demand and supply of goods and services through their reorganization. Consequently, digital platforms contribute to promoting greater economic and social sustainability by reorganizing collective services.

4.3 Welfare Platforms: The Case of WeMi

Digital platforms can thus be used as tools to support and facilitate a hybrid mode of service delivery, having the ability, through their digital dimension, to connect not only those who are physically distant but also those who live in a condition of physical proximity. They become tools to stimulate and enable encounters in the digital space that lead to encounters in the physical one: tools for a new hybrid proximity.

In support of this, an example in the welfare sector is represented by the WeMi program promoted by the Municipality of Milan in 2015. This initiative is characterized by the integration of the digital dimension with the physical one in providing services to the community. The digital platform is a key element of the program, offering a range of services accessible online. However, these services have been designed to be rooted in the physical context of the city through a network of local services known as "WeMi Spaces." These spaces have been strategically placed in bars and other places frequented by residents of various neighborhoods, thus ensuring tangible and immediate accessibility to the services offered by the WeMi program. The WeMi platform proposes five categories of services (offered by the Municipality and entities affiliated with it): personal well-being, family support, household management, socialization and sharing, and financial education. The services provided are diverse and range from home meal delivery to support for the transportation of differently abled individuals, babysitting, pet care, home maintenance, and the purchase and delivery of medications at home. Furthermore, being an open system where everyone can express and pose their questions, the platform acts as a facilitator, capable of capturing needs that services organized in traditional delivery could not bring out.

On the other hand, the WeMi spaces (16 mapped in 2021) (see Figs. 10 and 11) serve as the physical interface of the platform: managed by cooperatives and associations in agreement with the Municipality of Milan and located in existing places, they have become centers for neighborhood meetings and initiatives. In these spaces, citizens find operators who advise them on how to find solutions more suitable to their needs, but also help them to build a network of relationships, to get in touch with each other, and to plan initiatives. The hybrid nature of this project, enabled by the use of the digital platform, allows the construction of communities that are hybrid yet deeply rooted in the city.

Fig. 10 WeMi Voltri (*source* https://spazioapertoservizi.org/servizi/wemi-voltri/)

Fig. 11 Rab-WeMI San Gottardo (*souce* http://consalezrossi.com/projects/rab-wemi.html)

5 Conclusions and Research Perspectives

The research phase reported represents a fundamental part of the entire project, as it lays the scientific and methodological foundations to support the design of the system to be implemented, requiring an in-depth understanding of multiple aspects. In this contribution, the desk phase of the research was described, which made it possible to define the theoretical reference model for the emergence of the needs and constraints underlying the analysis and data collection phases. This model has been outlined starting from the construction of the state of the art, in particular through the study of cases, considered relevant in the metropolitan/regional context in various fields, and analysed according to an interdisciplinary approach determined by the involvement of expertise belonging to different areas of knowledge, from service design to socio-semiotics, from landscape design to interaction design.

To achieve the objective, it was necessary to understand the context, the diversity of society and the capacity of the citizenry, permanent or temporary, to absorb the impact of the solutions in the use cases described.

This approach will evolve, in the second field phase, with a human-centric and inclusive focus, aimed at building a cyber-responsible society.

References

1. Indovina, F.: La città sostenibile: sosteniamo la città. Archivi di studi urbani e regionali. 77, (2003).
2. Strauss, C.L.: Tristi tropici. il Saggiatore (1960).
3. Bookchin, M.: Dall'urbanizzazione alle città. Elèuthera, Milano (2023).
4. Wu, J.: Urban ecology and sustainability: The state-of-the-science and future direction. Landsc Urban Plan. 125, 209–221 (2014).
5. Northan, R.M.: Urban Geography. Wiley, Hoboken (1975).
6. Johnston, R.J.: City and society. An outline for Urban Geography. Penguin Books, London (1980).
7. Toppetti, F., Ferretti, L.V.: La cura della città. Politiche e Progetti. Quodlibet, Macerata (2022).
8. World Commission on Environment and Development: Our Common Future. Oslo (1987).
9. Cardinali, L., Guidetti, L.: Benessere. In: Criconia, A., Cortesi, I., and Giovannelli, A. (eds.) 40 parole per la cura della città. Lessico dei paesaggi della salute. p. 70. Quodlibet, Macerata (2021).
10. The Ottawa Charter for Health Promotion: La carta di Ottawa. Ottawa (1986).
11. Manzini, E.: Abitare la prossimità: Idee per la città dei 15 minuti. EGEA S.p.A. (2021).
12. Marrone, G.: Figure di città. Spazi urbani e discorsi sociali. Mimesis, Milano (2013).
13. Don't BeeScared, https://www.dontbeescared.it/, last accessed 2024/03/19.
14. Parco Domingo, https://www.associazioneparcodomingo.org/, last accessed 2024/03/19.
15. IO POSSO. Terazza Tutti al mare, https://www.ioposso.eu/tag/terrazza/, last accessed 2024/03/19.
16. Quotidiano di Puglia, https://www.quotidianodipuglia.it/bari/bari_palestra_mare_pane_e_pomodoro_cantiere_lavori_progetto_come_sara-7314133.html, last accessed 2024/03/19.
17. Parchi per tutti, http://www.parchipertutti.com/bimbiland/, last accessed 2024/03/19.
18. Reti dei comuni sostenibili, https://www.comunisostenibili.eu/2023/09/14/arriva-a-manduria-il-parco-giochi-diffuso/, last accessed 2024/03/19.
19. Weber, M.: L'oggettività conoscitiva della scienza sociale e politica (1904).
20. Alan, C.: The Inmates Are Running the Asylum. Sams (1999).
21. Cassano, F.: Il pensiero meridiano. Editori Laterza, Bari (1966).
22. Pais, I.: Futuro prossimo. Città delle prossimità e piattaforme digitali. In: Manzini, E. (ed.) Abitare la prossimità: Idee per la città dei 15 minuti. EGEA S.p.A. (2021).
23. van Dick, J., Poell, T., de Waal, M.: Platform society. Valori pubblici e società connessa. Guerini, Milano (2019).
24. Kazepov, Y., Cefalo, R.: La dimensione territoriale delle politiche sociali. Parolechiave. 28, (2009).
25. Kazepov, Y., Barberis, E.: Il welfare frammentato. Le articolazioni regionali delle politiche sociali italiane. Carocci (2013).
26. Arcidiacono, D., Pais, I., Zandonai, F.: Plat-firming welfare: trasformazione digitale nei servizi di cura locali (2021).
27. Fosti, G.: Sharing Welfare? In: Polizzi, M. and Bassoli, M. (eds.) Le politiche della condivisione. La sharing economy incontra il pubblico. Giuffrè (2016).
28. Fosti, G.: Rilanciare il welfare locale: ipotesi e strumenti: una prospettiva di management delle reti. Egea S.p.A. (2013).
29. Gillespie, T.: The politics of "platforms." New Media Soc. 12, 347–364 (2010).
30. WeMi. La città per il welfare, https://wemi.comune.milano.it/, last accessed 2024/03/19.

Developing a Smart Pill Dispenser to Support Aging Individuals

Óscar T. Viana, Octávio Lima, Miguel Terroso, and João L. Vilaça

Abstract As a person ages, there is a tendency for the progressive degeneration of the body, which usually manifests as a loss of motor, cognitive and sensory abilities. This introduces new challenges to the independent accomplishment of previously routine tasks. Through the analysis of this issue, the authors identify that the adherence to complex medication regimes might pose a particularly difficult challenge for elderly patients, whose limitations can introduce the risk of ineffective treatments and health hazards by the wrongful taking of medicine. The solution proposed is the development of an automatic pill dispenser, designed to counteract the adverse effects of aging and enable the elderly to retain a degree of autonomy in their daily care, or support family and professional caretakers. This chapter will follow the projects' development through the identification and analysis of the challenges faced by elderly individuals; a comparative study of the options currently available to support them in the identified issue; the proposal of a solution; and concluding with the construction of a preliminary prototype.

Keywords Smart pill dispenser · Design for aging · Prototype development

Ó. T. Viana (✉) · O. Lima · J. L. Vilaça
2Ai – School of Technology, IPCA, Barcelos, Portugal
e-mail: osviana@ipca.pt

O. Lima
e-mail: olima@ipca.pt

J. L. Vilaça
e-mail: jvilaca@ipca.pt

M. Terroso
ID+ - Research Institute in Design, Media and Culture, School of Design, IPCA, Barcelos, Portugal
e-mail: mterroso@ipca.pt

© The Author(s), under exclusive license to Springer Nature Switzerland AG 2025
D. Brandão et al. (eds.), *Perspectives on Design and Digital Communication V*, Springer Series in Design and Innovation 50, https://doi.org/10.1007/978-3-031-76156-0_3

1 Introduction

Declining birth rates and increased life expectancy have resulted in a progressively more elderly population, usually defined as people over the age of sixty-five (Orimo et al., 2006; Gonçalves & Carrilho, 2006). Individuals belonging to this group are usually faced with a natural accumulation of cellular damage that brings about a progressive degradation of the body (World Health Organization, 2015a). This results in arising chronic illness, generalized decline of motor, sensory and cognitive faculties; impacting the ability to autonomously maintain a routine (Abdi et al., 2019; Górska et al., 2013; Martin et al., 2012; Nicholson et al., 2012; Nyman et al., 2017). Consequently, this health degradation introduces new responsibilities in the form of progressively stronger and more complex medication treatments, the adherence to which is challenged by the same issues it is meant to counteract. It is estimated that 45% of elderly patients faced difficulties when managing their daily medication routine (Advinha, 2017), skipping or repeating doses, leading to ineffective treatments. Further exacerbating the situation is the lack of supervision of these individuals, with social isolation being identified in 7–24% of individuals above the age of 60 (Iliffe et al., 2005). Considering these combined factors, the authors identify, as an opportunity to enable individuals to retain a degree of autonomy, the development of an automatic pill dispenser. Targeting elderly patients, in personal residences or assisted living care facilities, the device would be capable of recurring to audible, visible and tactile alerts to aid with following complex medication regimes. Family members and healthcare professionals would be enabled to keep surveillance of the patient through the device's smart features, such as the capability for direct communication, in the form of video and audio calls, and the recording of behaviors concerning the adherence to treatments.

1.1 Development Method

Through this chapter, the device development is presented sequentially, divided into three stages that encompass different aspects of the design process and culminate in a complete product proposal. As is shown in Fig. 1, the process is initiated with defining the problem to be tackled. This is done by first identifying the characteristics of the target userbase, categorizing them into specified needs and from them create a list of requirements that the product must fulfil to adequately respond to the problem. The next stage regards the proposal of a theoretical solution, that is reached through the analysis of currently available products that target the same problem, investigating the state of the art for ambient assisted living and how a product might fit into that structure. Considering the collected data, a Business Model and User Experience are proposed. The final stage presented consists in the concrete development of a product following the guidelines identified throughout the earlier stages. Beginning with defining the technical architecture of hardware components, through

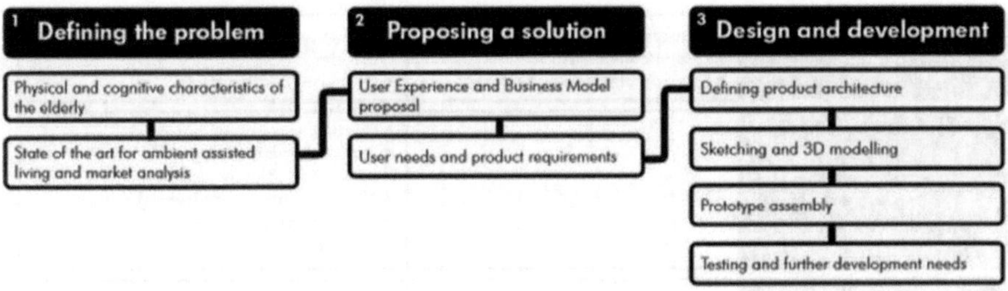

Fig. 1 Organizational chart with summary of the main design and development phases

form explorations and reaching the development of an early prototype, recurring to 3D printing techniques, that is then tested and evaluated, to identify areas for future improvement.

2 Defining the Problem

2.1 Physical and Cognitive Characteristics of the Elderly

The aging process may manifest as a degradation of physical and cognitive faculties, introducing new challenges that might impact one's self-sufficiency.

Consequently, these developments can also impact the individual's ability to interact with a product, requiring careful analysis before a product can be developed to adequately respond to those characteristics. From the literature analysis, Fig. 2 was constructed, summarizing the developments that can occur with age and the adverse effects they have on the abilities of the user.

Studies regarding the target population reveal that these changes produce an impact on a physical, cognitive and social level, often overlapping and causing distress.

Physically, aging people are faced with phenomena such as sarcopenia, the loss of skeletal muscle mass and strength brought about by old age (Walston, 2012). This accounts for an increased effort threshold to perform previously natural movements and routine tasks. When associated with sedentary living and excessive caloric intake this condition can evolve to become sarcopenic obesity, leading to additional movement restriction (Donini et al., 2022).

Along with these conditions, during the aging process a person's height might be reduced by 2–4 cm, being brought about by spine deformations caused by the effects of sarcopenia but also arthritis, spine inflammation and herniated discs, among others (Fernihough & McGovern, 2015; Huang et al., 2013).

Physical		• Reduction of muscle mass. • Loss of bone density. • Spine deformation and arthritis.	• Restriction of movement speed and breadth. • Difficulties bearing loads.
Cognitive		• Memory degradation.	• Difficulty recalling routine actions. • Reduced understanding and acquisition of knowledge. • Slower information processing. • Issues remembering events, conversations and instructions.
Sensorial	Sight	• Development of sight related illnesses (Cataracts; Glaucoma; Age-related Macular Degeneration)	• Reduction of central and peripheral vision. • Lack of focus and definition. • Difficulty adapting to darker environments.
Sensorial	Hearing	• Gradual loss of hearing from cumulative damage.	• Issues communicating. • Reduction of spacial awareness. • Not recognizing alerts and alarms.
Sensorial	Haptics	• Loss of tactile sensibility.	• Difficulty recognizing textures. • Insensitivity to vibrations. • Reduction of thermal sensitivity.
Sensorial	Proprioception	• Reduced speed of sensorial stimuli. • Reduction of limb sensibility.	• Reduction of fine motor skills. • Difficulty keeping balance while standing and walking without support. • Movements become slower and less precise.
Sensorial	Taste and Smell	• Reduced sensitivity to taste and smell.	• Difficulty identifying and distinguishing tastes and smells. • Loss of appetite.

Fig. 2 Summary of common physical and cognitive effects of the aging process

In terms of cognitive impact, with the appearance of illnesses such as Alzheimer's, aging has the greatest effect on memory, degrading various recollection mechanisms and, consequently, cognitive processing. Memory is divided into functional categories, and those most impacted by the aging process are the sectors of:

- Prospective memory, referring to the retention of actions to be performed at a future time, such as remembering to take medication at a specific time (Grady, 2000; Nilsson, 2003; Tulving, 1985; Zimmermann & Meier, 2006).
- Working memory, that encapsulates small bits of information required for routine cognitive processes, completing sentences, tasks and following lines of reasoning (Cowan, 2014).
- Episodic memory, responsible for the recollection of life events. Identified as a sector facing a severe decline after the age of 60 (Mitchell et al., 1990; Nyberg et al., 2003, 2012; Verhaeghen & Salthouse, 1997).

The manifestation of the physical and cognitive degradation mentioned above induces a consequent reduction in sensorial capabilities, such as sight, haptics, proprioception, taste and smell.

According to a study by the WHO (World Health Organization, 2015b), the main pathologies causing reduced eyesight and blindness are cataracts, glaucoma and age-related macular degeneration. The latter, referred to as AMD, is the leading cause of vision loss for aging individuals, resulting in a blurring of the central vision reducing the ability to see and recognize faces, read or perform other close-up tasks. Other conditions that arise from gradual tissue degeneration can also cause difficulty in focusing, reduce the field of view or damage the eye's capacity to adapt to different lighting environments (*Age-Related Macular Degeneration (AMD) | National Eye Institute*, n.d.; Czaja et al., 2019; Owsley, 2011; Resnikoff et al., 2004; World Health Organization, 2019).

Hearing loss occurs gradually as the sensitive inner ear receptors are worn by life-long exposure to various degrees of noise, resulting in a progressive and continuous reduction of their sensitivity. Plainly, old age represents longer exposure to these damaging factors and therefore more degradation of the hearing ability (Cruickshanks et al., 1998; Gopinath et al., 2009; Lin et al., 2011). Studies have found that as many as 60% of adults over the age of 70 are faced with hearing problems (Lin et al., 2011).

Loss of haptic sensitivity translates as a reduced ability to identify textures, temperatures and vibrations (Czaja et al., 2019). In a study conducted by Norman et al. (2016), when prompted to recognize various objects through texture alone, individuals over the age of 70 fared worse than younger test subjects. This reduced sensitivity increases the risk of burns and other incidents and also damages the recognition of buttons and switches on devices.

Proprioception refers to the self-perception of the body, the ability to control posture, retain balance and adjust movement. Peripheral nerve damage causes a reduced awareness of the body, leading to the loss of balance, imprecise movements and slower reaction to sensorial stimuli. In an attempt to rectify these limitations, the afflicted might consciously reduce the frequency and speed of their movements (Czaja et al., 2019; Lord & Ward, 1994; Walker et al., 1997).

Apart from the risks brough about by the inability to distinguish tastes and smells, degradation of this sense can also lead to an unbalanced diet, be it through reduced appetite and consequent weight loss, or overdependence on flavors enhancers such as sugar and salt, leading to the development of pathologies such as diabetes or high blood pressure (Boyce & Shone, 2006; Doty et al., 1984; Neumann et al., 2016; Paula et al., 2008; Schiffman & Zervakis, 2002).

2.2 State of the Art of Ambient Assisted Living and Support Devices

A desire present in many aging individuals is the continued residence in a familiar domestic environment in favor of institutionalized care facilities. The past years, motivated by the growing elderly population, have seen advancements in research

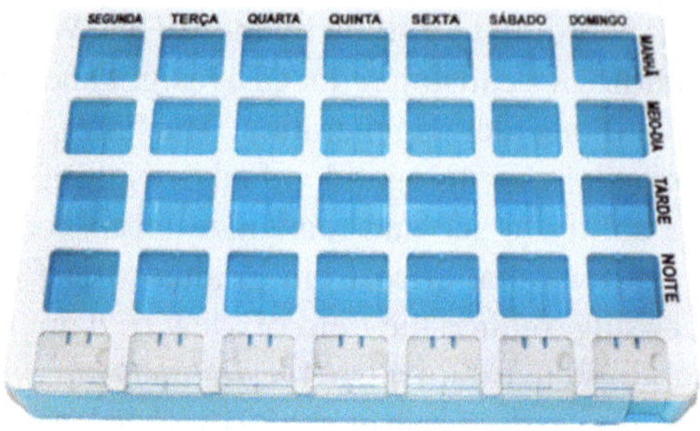

Fig. 3 Example of a conventional weekly pill organizer. *Source* afarmaciaonline.pt

for aging in place, technologies and systems that create an environment that promotes more comfortable and autonomous experience for the elderly in dealing with their daily tasks (Vasunilashorn et al., 2012). This is the idea behind Ambient Assisted Living, that information and communication technologies can produce a space that aids its inhabitants in retaining independence as they age (Do et al., 2018; Vimarlund et al., 2021).

Transposing this philosophy to the proposed issue, adherence to daily medication regimes, a number of solutions have already been developed. These appear in the form of medication dispensers, enabling users to organize and keep track of their prescribed doses. Conventionally, these consist of containers with divisions for separating medication into individual doses, commonly extending for a day or a full week. These products require routine manual refilling of small compartments, during which, lack of finesse can cause the user to place medicine in the incorrect compartment. Furthermore, as analog products, the patient is responsible for keeping track of dose times (Fig. 3).

However, with technological developments, these shortcomings have begun being addressed by electronic pill dispensers imbued with the smart technologies referenced in *Ambient Assisted Living* environments. For example, the GMS (*GMS Automatic Pill Dispenser: Review*, 2020), Medacube (*MedaCube Medication Dispenser: Review*, 2020), MedMinder (*MedMinder, Maya: Review*, 2020), HeroHealth (*Hero Medication Dispenser: Review*, 2020) and Pria (*Black & Decker, Pria: Review*, 2020) are devices that take advantage of computing power to introduce features such as alerts, accompanied medicine taking and device refilling procedures, remote adherence management and communication with family and caretakers.

When analyzing and comparing the devices mentioned, it was identified that Pria and HeroHealth have the most prominent **designs** in the list. While both feature a system in which medicine is dispensed into a cup, they differ in terms of interface. The Pria is fitted with a touchscreen, while the Hero includes physical buttons. However, its screen has reduced dimensions that could make it difficult for users with impaired vision to understand instructions.

Medacube and HeroHealth have the most efficient **refilling** process, as they automatically select and dispense medication according to predefined plans. For the Medacube the plan is programmed directly on the device's screen while the Hero can connect to a mobile app where the plan can be introduced, managed, and changed remotely. At the programmed times, the device will select and dispense the required pills.

The main hindrance while using these devices is the refilling process, which is why some include **service** networks. The MedMinder is supported with a weekly medicine tray that is mailed from pharmacies, requiring only the replacement of the spent tray. As for the Hero, the device keeps track of stock and refills are ordered for depleted medication, not resolving, however, the issue with the refilling process, that needs to be done manually.

When it comes to **alerts**, Pria and Hero are the most effective, using both visual and auditory alerts. Pria features a feminine voice that alerts the user while Hero's alert is a common doorbell style sound. At the scheduled times, both illuminate the base of the medicine cup and ask for confirmation that the dispensed medication is correct, with the Hero alerting the user to return the cup after use. Other devices, MedMinder and Medacube enable the user to personalize these alerts with the voice of family or caretakers, which could have a powerful impact in helping the user feel comfortable with the device.

Pria is the standout in terms of **supervision**. The device's main goal is reducing the gap between users and caretakers and for this it can connect to a mobile app that enables accompaniment of regime adherence, alerting for failed doses, refilling needs and the capacity for communication through messages and video calls.

To ensure **safety**, Medacube and Hero block the medicine compartments requiring a key for access, while also keeping parts of the interface secured with pin codes, preventing unauthorized individuals from adjusting the medication program. Furthermore, the Medacube stands out by including a battery that sustains the device for up to 24 h in case of energy failures. An interesting safety feature, present only in the Pria, is device unlocking via facial recognition, ensuring medication is taken only by the correct user.

The characteristics analyzed in this short comparison of the devices were classified, evaluated, and then displayed as the radial graph in Fig. 4. In this way facilitating the identification of where some devices excel or falter, enabling the process of extracting desirable features to be incorporated in a more balanced and effective product proposal, that is outlined in the following segments of this document.

3 Proposing a Solution

3.1 User Experience and Business Model Proposal

Proceeding with development, context-based user experiences were outlined, for domestic, hospital and continued care facility usage. These were narrated referencing Benyon's (2005) sequence model and graphically represented (Figs. 5, 6 and 7).

In domestic use, at the scheduled time for taking medication, the device alerts the patient through vibration, auditory and visual stimuli. Simultaneously, the connected

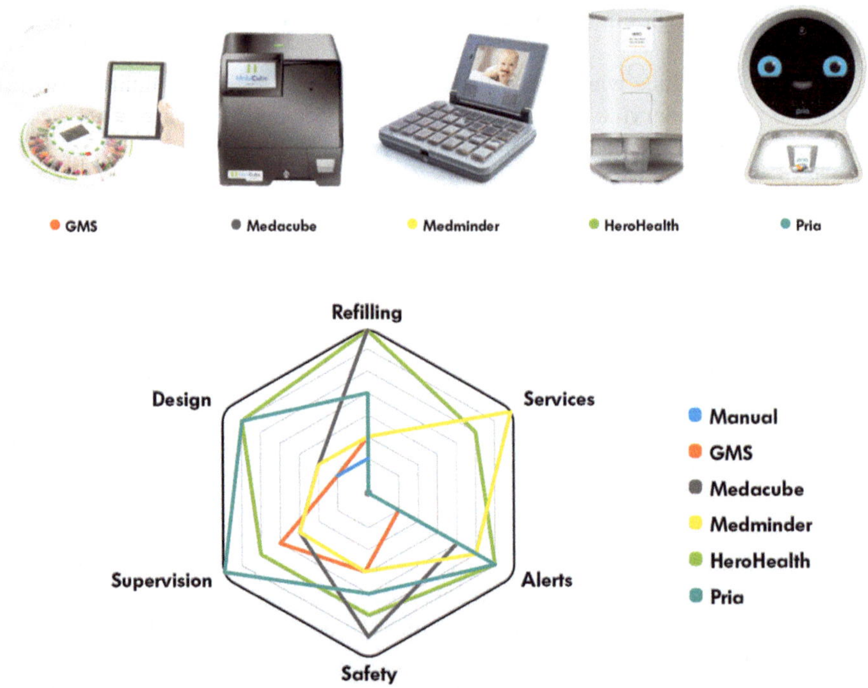

Fig. 4 Comparing already available electronic pill dispensers

smartphone app receives a notification. The user approaches the device, and, after facial recognition validation, the medication is dispensed into a cup. The user is prompted to verify if the dosage is correct (displaying correct dose information onscreen) and if so, consume the medication.

When a cartridge needs refilling, a technician collects the depleted cartridge and performs any necessary maintenance on the device. Collected cartridges are sterilized and directed to pharmaceutical facilities when they are refilled according to patient files and sent back. [Did you check if pharmacists or wholesalers would be able to do this?]

The product and services are accessible through bundles, A and B, offering different experiences. The sale of which, is handled by a team including an administrator (1), who interviews the user, creating a budget, and the family doctor, for an accurate medication regimen. Data is collected in the company servers and used by administrator (2) when managing orders for pharmaceutical labs and redirecting them to the refill site.

In a hospital context the experience would begin with the device alerting a healthcare technician, dispensing the pills into a disposable cup and requesting correct dose validation (displaying correct dose information onscreen). Simultaneously, the nurse responsible for the patient is notified for medication pickup at the pharmaceutical

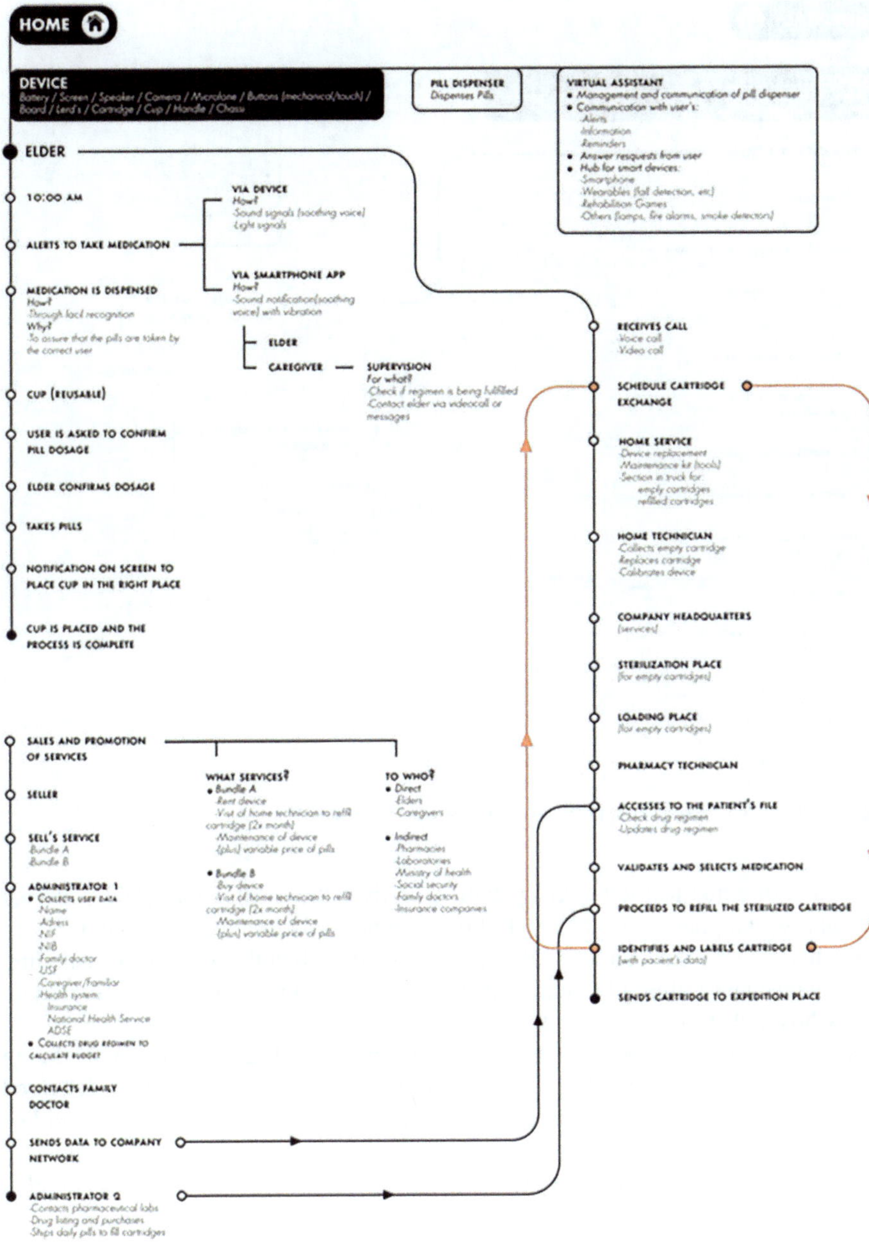

Fig. 5 Sequence diagram of the home environment experience

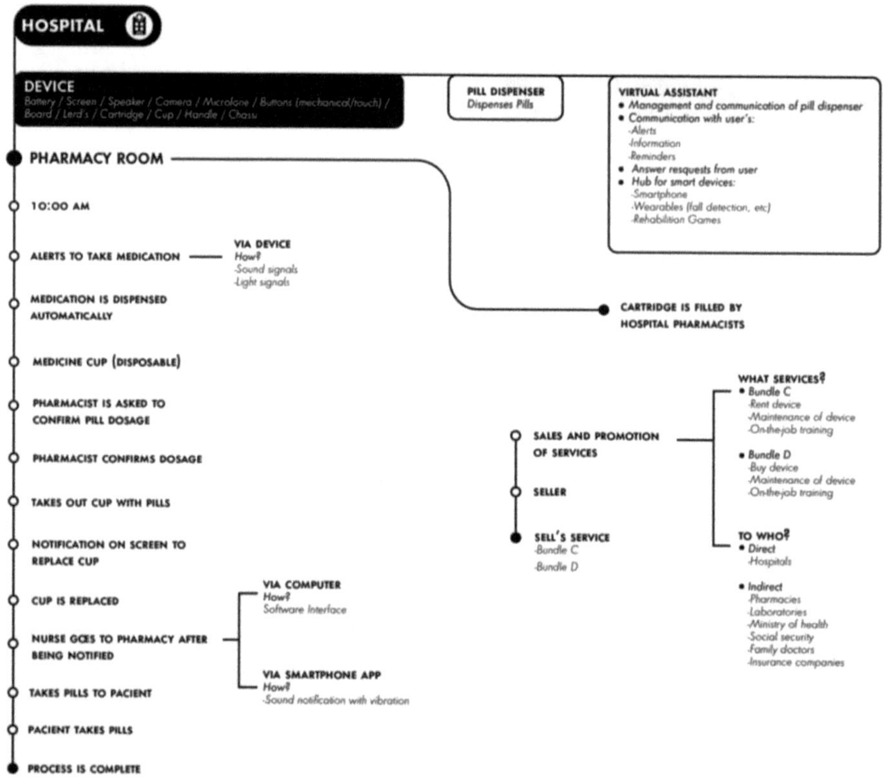

Fig. 6 Sequence diagram of experience in a hospital environment

office and directed to the correct patient to deliver the medication. [Did you visit several hospital pharmacies to check if this manner of working is possible?]

In this context the commercial department offers bundles C and D, including maintenance and training but not cartridge refilling, as this would be performed on site by hospital staff.

Similarly, in continued care facilities, the experience begins with a nurse being alerted by the device, the medication being dispensed and validated and then delivered to the patient. Commercial service bundles are the same as for hospitals (C and D).

Sourcing data from these experiences, the business model was defined, following the canvas structured by Osterwalder and Pigneur (2010). This structure is divided into nine essential business elements:

- The *Key Partners*, in this case, the labs and pharmacies responsible for supplying the medication, the institutions where the service would be implemented (hospitals, nursing facilities) and those responsible for service adoption (insurance providers, solidarity institutions, private care administrators and national health services).

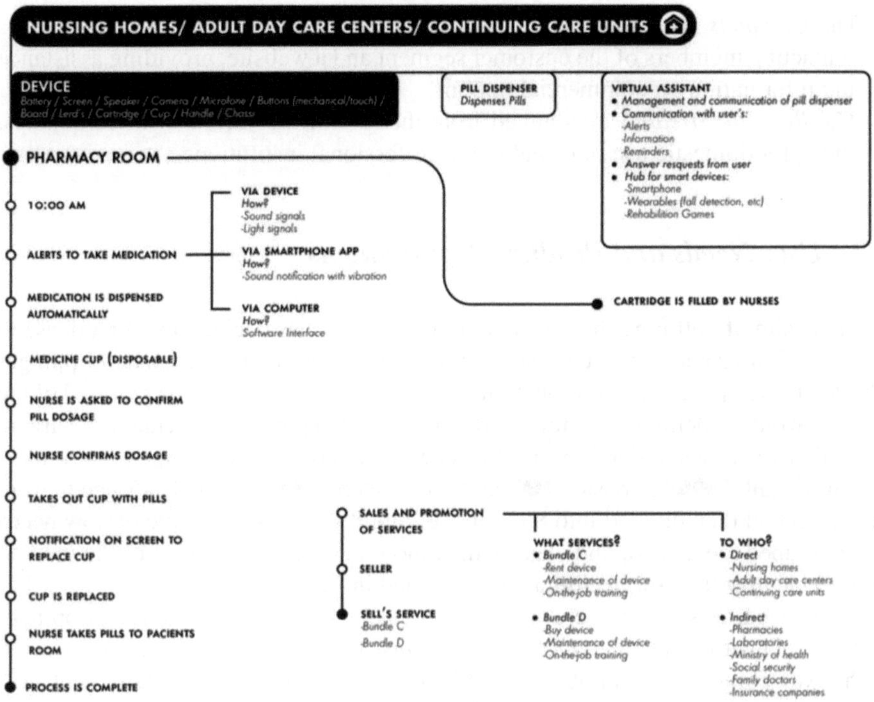

Fig. 7 Sequence diagram of experience in nursing homes, day centers and long-term care

- The *Key Activities*, the main services provided. Those being the sale and distribution of medication management devices, technical, maintenance and refilling services as well as training for implementation of the device ecosystem.
- The *Key Resources* includes technical resources (devices, vehicles, real estate, computer systems and networks), human resources (technicians, administrators, sales representatives, pharmacists) and intellectual property (patents, client and business partner information) as the main assets of the company.
- The *Customer Segments* the targets for product distribution, the direct (hospitals, nursing facilities, healthcare providers and the elderly) and indirect consumers (pharmacies, insurance providers, ministry of health).
- The *Cost Structure* includes routine operation expenses and costs for research, certification, production, and distribution.
- The Customer Relationships. The main contact with costumers occurs when providing personal assistance for service needs.
- The *Value Proposition*, what value is offered to the customer segment. In this case being the reduced risk for inadequate medication taking, reducing possible harm, and enabling a more independent daily routine to elders while also facilitating better supervision by healthcare professionals.

- The *Channels*. The company's services are distributed by sales representatives contacting members of the customer segment and a website, providing assistance and information on commercial options.
- The *Revenue Streams* are sourced from the sale of the various service bundles, and B for domestic use or C and D for professional institutions.

3.2 User Needs and Product Requirements

With the aim of outlining the system requirements, it was decided in a first phase to identify the user needs, through the methodology described by Ulrich and Eppinger (2015). This requires the identification of the functions that would be required of the device, avoiding definite solutions or descriptions, keeping the statements abstract.

In this way, needs identified in the state of the art will be grouped and ranked as "important ●●●", "basic ●●" and "low interest ●". In total, 45 needs were identified and then divided into 8 groups. Figure 8 shows an example of how needs were grouped, described, and classified. A more detailed description of the method used to identify the user needs can be consulted in Lima (2022).

To proceed, these needs were analyzed and, again through the Ulrich and Eppinger method, converted into *Product Requirements*. For this, a table was constructed with seven columns: (1) numbers to facilitate the identification of requirements; (2) description of the requirement; (3) effects exerting influence over the requirement (dimensions, required connections, materials, form, etc.); (4) define specifications based on those factors; (5) the potential cost to fulfil the requirement, classified as "high", "medium" or "low"; (6) classification of requirements by importance, as previously, with "important •••", "basic ••" and "low interest •"; (7) the identifying number of the user needs this requirement would fulfill.

	The device meets the physical and cognitive needs of the elderly.	
01	The device uncomplicates the pill-taking process, promoting better adherence.	●●●
02	The device enables caregivers/family members to supervise and help the elderly more efficiently.	●●●
	The device alerts the users efficiently without provoking anxiety on elders.	
03	The device alerts the users to take the pill dosage with a feminine soothing voice.	●●●
04	The device allows to personalize the voice comands with the voice of family members.	●●

Fig. 8 Sample extracted from the needs table. The statements are numbered and divided into groups by the black bars, that also identify those groups

FUNCTIONAL

N°	REQUIREMENT	INFLUENCE FACTORS Factors that influence the requirements	SPECIFICATION	COST-BENEFIT	REQUIREMENT IMPORTANCE	NEEDS
01	The device must include a touch screen.	• **Dimensions:** - Between 8 and 10.1 inches • **Resolution:** - Between 1024x600 and 1280x800px • **Tactile feedback** • **Connection to PCB board** • **Connection to chassis**	• **Quantity:** - 1 unit • **Dimensions:** - 10.1 inches • **Resolution:** - 1280×800px	€€€	●●●	05 25 06
02	The device must include a microphone.	• **Quantity:** - Between 2 and 6 microphones • **Type of microphone:** - Long reach • **Connection to PCB board** • **Connection to chassis**	• **Quantity:** - 6 units • **Type of microphone:** - Long reach	€€	●●	29 40 41 42 43

Fig. 9 Two examples of requirements from functional category

Furthermore, the requirements were organized according to categories: (1) Functional, those relating to the essential hardware for device function; (2) Usability, the ones presenting functions promoting ease of use, from ergonomic concerns to the design of the digital user interface; (3) Aesthetics, collecting requirements advising the form, materials, textures and colors of the device; and finally (4) Security, encompassing safety measures to ensure adequate access to the pill storage and device settings.

Figure 9 shows a sample of functional requirements and how they all are numbered, described, rated according to cost–benefit and importance, as well as reference the relevant needs, from the previous list.

The requirements established for the device can be consulted in full, for all stipulated categories and in greater detail, in the following publications (Lima et al., 2022; Lima, 2022).

4 Design and Development

4.1 Defining Product Architecture

The requirements allowed to move forward with the definition of the product architecture, defining all the essential elements for the device, namely external and internal components. Proceeding to the development of the device, and according to the previously listed requirements, the first step was the definition of the product's electronic components, required hardware whose volumes would influence the device's form.

The essential hardware elements selected to ensure device basic functionality are as follows: a 10.1-inch touchscreen, a 12 V 3 A power source, a 12.6 V 6000 mAh battery pack, a BMS (Battery Management System), a 5 V buck converter, a Raspberry Pi microcomputer, a 20 W sound amplifier and two speakers, a wide view camera, a long-range microphone board (Fig. 10).

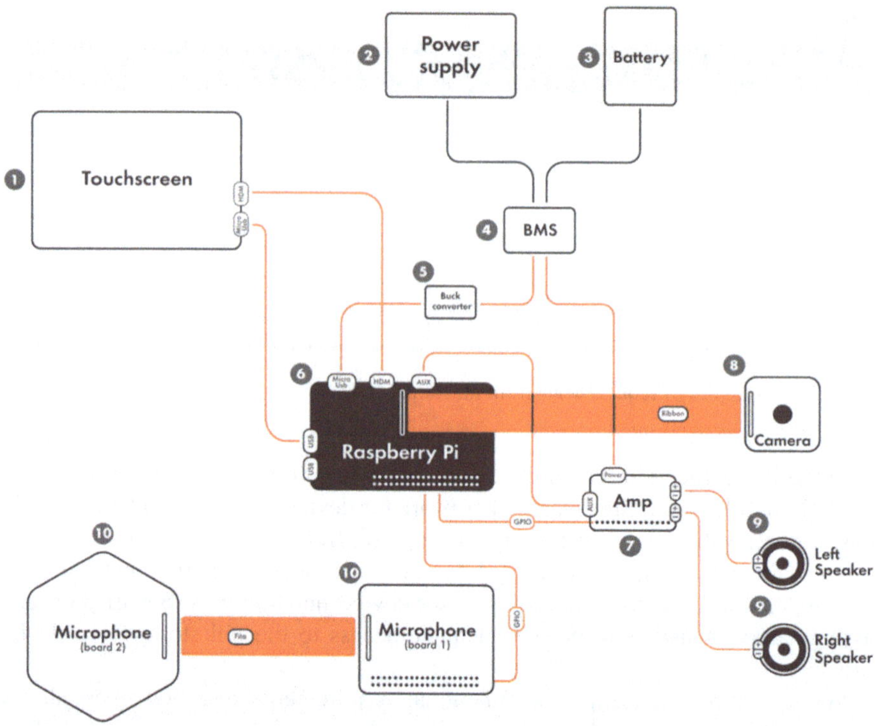

Fig. 10 System electronics diagram

Based on data sourced in the commercial platforms where these components were available, a cardboard model, representing the basic volume, was built of each component. These were then arranged in different configurations to visualize possible geometries of the device.

For the device's architecture the exterior the device features a handle, to facilitate displacement and support during operation, such as opening the device for refilling the cartridge. Below this handle is placed the touchscreen, through which interactions with the digital interface are mediated and a camera, implemented to enable video calls but also functions such as facial recognition, to increase security of the device and ensure the correct user is taking the medication. The buttons presented on the central area of the device were intended to facilitate interaction by users unfamiliar with touchscreens, however, after further exploration of the form and hardware space availability these were deemed redundant and excluded from following iterations. At the lower front are located the cup, to which medication is dispensed, the LEDs to provide alerts and the Speakers. Below the device a rotating mechanism was implemented to facilitate reorientation without requiring the device to be lifted. At the back is the access point for the cartridge containing medicine.

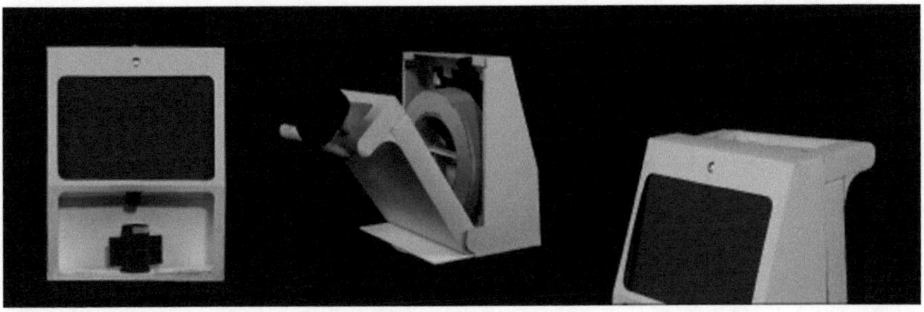

Fig. 11 Views of the device full-size paper model

4.2 Sketching and 3D Modeling

The process continued with sketching until a shape was reached that would be capable of housing the hardware components while taking into account the previously defined requirements, needs and architecture. Until this stage, the pill dispensing mechanism was not yet defined, but through exploration of possible geometries a favorable and space-efficient solution was identified in the form of a rotating segmented circular cartridge. Each segment in the cartridge would correspond to a dose of medication, and these would be released at the programmed times by dispensing the contents of the correct segment through a canal, connecting the cartridge to a vessel from which the user would then take the dose. A full-size paper model was constructed to address dimensioning and ergonomic concerns, such as handle placement and touchscreen inclination (Fig. 11).

After approval by the team, the next stage was creating a digital model based on this experiment, on the 3D modelling software Solidworks, an industry standard platform for production-oriented modelling. From inception, 3D printing was decided as the production method for the product, ensuring that from the early stages of design considerations such as print orientation, support requirements, print plate dimensions, material selection and assembly were considered. The model was created in full detail, including all hardware elements and electrical connections so it could be used as a guide in the subsequent prototype assembly (Fig. 12).

4.3 Prototype Assembly

When preparing the digital model for 3D printing, one of the challenges faced was the limited printing space available. Therefore, to accommodate the reduced dimensions of the available printers, parts of the model were subdivided, to be reassembled after separate printing. To facilitate this task, additional fitting geometry was added to the model, to ensure solid and accurate reassembly (Fig. 13). The parts were then exported in STL format to the Prusa Slicer software that generates a version of the

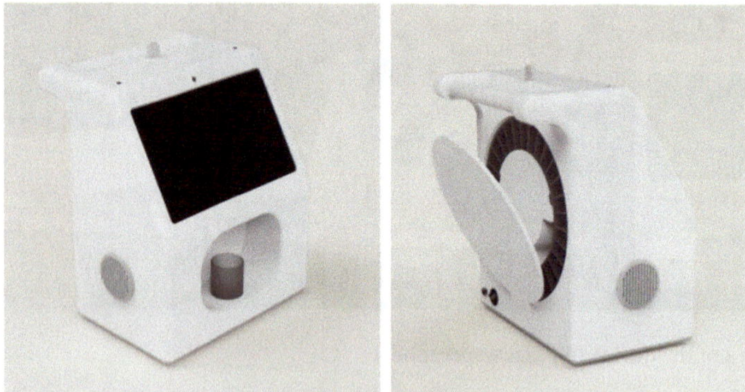

Fig. 12 Render of the device with front and back views

model sliced into layers that are recreated by the 3D printer. During this stage the print speed and infill preferences are adjusted and is added the support material, that serves as scaffolding to accurately maintain the model's geometry during the printing process. Printing of all parts lasted approximately 153 h. Nevertheless, 3D printing proved an accessible and cost-efficient solution for fast prototyping (Gibson et al., 2015).

After printing, parts were sanded, assembled, and, in some points of additional stress, supplementary fixing elements were added. The assembled shell was then painted and, finally, the hardware and electronic elements were installed.

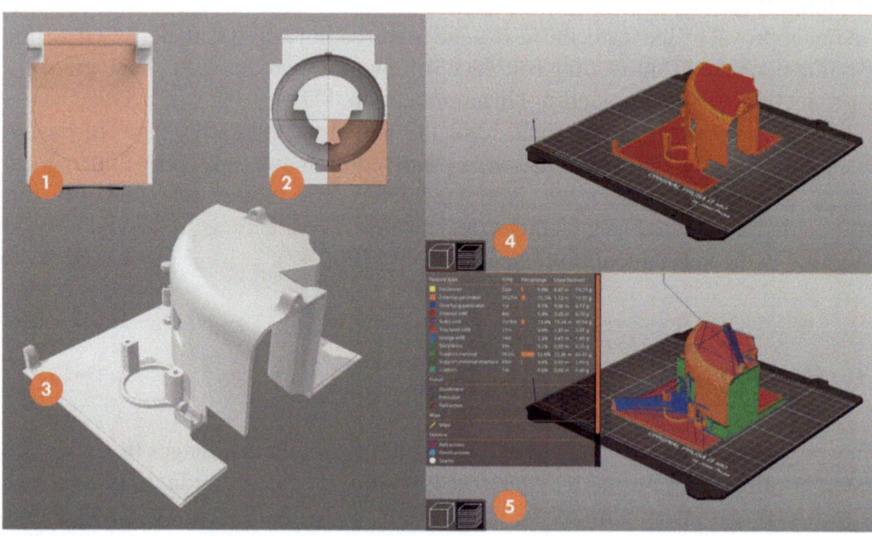

Fig. 13 Software processing for 3D printing

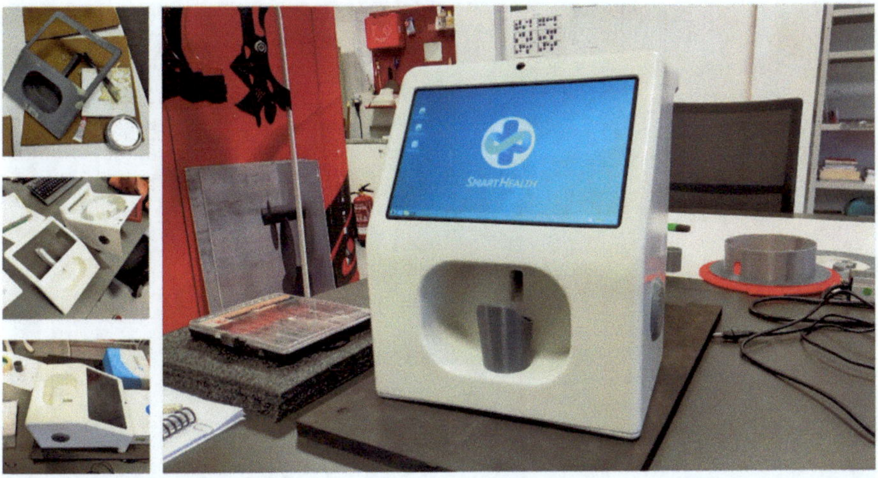

Fig. 14 Final prototype assembly

Preliminary mockups were created of what might become the graphical user interface, the development of which accounted for observations made in the research stage. To accommodate the target userbase, the interface would be constructed with large, distinguished interactive elements, readable typefaces, common icons accompanied by text, calming colors and simple, thoughtfully limited interactions (Figs. 14 and 15).

4.4 Testing and Further Development Needs

Having all parts in place the next step was testing the components: the touchscreen, camera, microphone, speakers, and dispensing mechanism. Powering up the Raspberry Pi connected to the touchscreen correctly displayed the desktop environment and touch inputs were recognized, validating that both components and the connections were correctly functioning. To test the voice and sound components, the software Audacity was installed on the Raspberry Pi and used to record a short sound clip, later reproduced by the speakers. Some electrical interference was heard; however, this issue could be resolved by installing a filter in future versions and both components were validated as functioning.

To test the dispensing mechanism, an online guide was followed to correctly connect the Raspberry Pi to the step motor driver, and, after calculating the necessary steps to rotate the cartridge for one pill-containing segment, a basic program was written to execute this function. When activated, the motor would engage the mechanical parts and the task would be completed, with the pills being delivered to the cup through the dispensing canal. It was detected, however, that on occasion, the

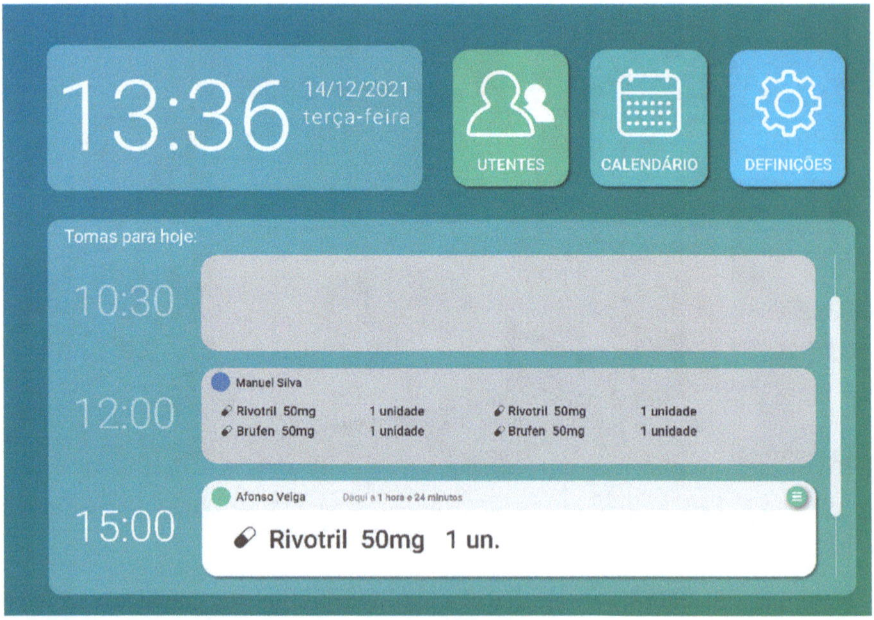

Fig. 15 Preliminary interface mockup

motor would not engage the printed gears correctly, leading to failure in rotating the cartridge, an error that might be fixed by revising geometry and positioning of these parts (Weaver, 2018).

During this test it was identified that the cup's geometry would not always correctly capture the dispensed pills. To improve on this, the cup was elongated in parts, creating a tapered brim on one side. Additionally, magnets were inserted at the bottom of the cup to force correct placement and orientation which, in further tests, proved efficient in increasing the cup's ability to properly collect the pills.

Additional issues were categorized and collected in Table 1, to be tackled in future prototyping efforts. Electrical refers to changes to be made in the circuit, Structural when concerning the assembly's integrity and Functional, for problems disrupting basic functions of the device.

Future steps in this project would address these issues by finding and implementing solutions to create an enhanced prototype, that would be subjected to more testing, with the goal of iterating in the device to the point it became acceptable for contextual trials.

Table 1 Issues identified and suggested corrections

Electrical	Structural	Functional
Diode to avoid backflow	Add fixation point in base	Round edges of cartridge lid to prevent blocking
Bypass RaspberryPi for powering the screen	Thicken fitting lops	Adjust gear placement to avoid skipped steps
Filter to reduce noise from speakers	Add more stable supports for the screen	Create adequate cavities for magnets in the cup and cartridge lid
	Add supportive roller bearings below the cartridge for smoother rotation	Replace current camera incompatible with RaspberryPi model

5 Conclusion

Presented throughout this document was the development of a device for use in nursing homes, clinics and the domestic environment, capable of storing and dispensing medication according to patients' needs. The developed device fulfills these tasks and aims to integrate a virtual assistant, connecting patients, caregivers, and healthcare professionals. Research was carried out on the characteristics of the elderly and problems resulting from aging, which allowed us to understand the complete spectrum of the physical and cognitive body of the elderly. An analysis was also carried out on support technologies for the elderly, in which several products on the market were analyzed, such as medication dispensers and virtual assistants.

These themes were essential for the follow-up and implementation of the next phases of the project. All user experiences were defined in this way, which made it possible to define the business model. Following this research, the user needs and device requirements were defined as 46 clear statements, which were then referenced during development of the product, by first defining the hardware to be included in the device and creating a basic 2D representation of where to allocate each component.

The 3D modeling of the device was challenging, as it had a large engineering component, as it was necessary to understand all the electronic and mechanical components, as well as the electrical connections between them. The electronic component ended up imposing some restrictions on the design of the device, however the result of the prototype was well achieved.

Acknowledgements This work was funded by the project "NORTE-01–0145-FEDER-000045", supported by Northern Portugal Regional Operational Programme (Norte2020), under the Portugal 2020 Partnership Agreement, through the European Regional Development Fund (FEDER).

References

Abdi, S., Spann, A., Borilovic, J., de Witte, L., & Hawley, M. (2019). Understanding the care and support needs of older people: a scoping review and categorisation using the WHO international classification of functioning, disability and health framework (ICF). *BMC Geriatrics, 19*(1), 195. https://doi.org/10.1186/s12877-019-1189-9

Advinha, A. M. M. (2017). *Avaliação da Capacidade Funcional da População Idosa na Gestão da Sua Medicação.*

Age-Related Macular Degeneration (AMD) | National Eye Institute. (n.d.). Retrieved February 8, 2024, from https://www.nei.nih.gov/learn-about-eye-health/eye-conditions-and-diseases/age-related-macular-degeneration

Benyon, D., Turner, P., & Turner, S. (2005). *Designing Interactive Systems.* Addison Wesley.

Black & Decker, Pria: Review. (2020, January 25). Tech-Enhanced Life. https://www.techenhancedlife.com/reviews/black-decker-pria

Boyce, J. M., & Shone, G. R. (2006). Effects of ageing on smell and taste. *Postgraduate Medical Journal, 82*(966), 239–241. https://doi.org/10.1136/pgmj.2005.039453

Cowan, N. (2014). Working Memory Underpins Cognitive Development, Learning, and Education. *Educational Psychology Review, 26*(2), 197–223. https://doi.org/10.1007/s10648-013-9246-y

Cruickshanks, K. J., Wiley, T. L., Tweed, T. S., Klein, B. E. K., Klein, R., Mares-Perlman, J. A., & Nondahl, D. M. (1998). Prevalence of Hearing Loss in Older Adults in Beaver Dam, Wisconsin: The Epidemiology of Hearing Loss Study. *American Journal of Epidemiology, 148*(9), 879–886. https://doi.org/10.1093/oxfordjournals.aje.a009713

Czaja, S. J., Boot, W. R., Charness, N., & Rogers, W. A. (2019). *Designing for Older Adults.* CRC Press. https://doi.org/10.1201/b22189

Do, H. M., Pham, M., Sheng, W., Yang, D., & Liu, M. (2018). RiSH: A robot-integrated smart home for elderly care. *Robotics and Autonomous Systems, 101*, 74–92. https://doi.org/10.1016/j.robot.2017.12.008

Donini, L. M., Busetto, L., Bischoff, S. C., Cederholm, T., Ballesteros-Pomar, M. D., Batsis, J. A., Bauer, J. M., Boirie, Y., Cruz-Jentoft, A. J., Dicker, D., Frara, S., Frühbeck, G., Genton, L., Gepner, Y., Giustina, A., Gonzalez, M. C., Han, H.-S., Heymsfield, S. B., Higashiguchi, T., … Barazzoni, R. (2022). *Consensus Statement Definition and Diagnostic Criteria for Sarcopenic Obesity: ESPEN and EASO Consensus Statement.* https://doi.org/10.1159/000521241

Doty, R. L., Shaman, P., Applebaum, S. L., Giberson, R., Siksorski, L., & Rosenberg, L. (1984). Smell Identification Ability: Changes with Age. *Science, 226*(4681), 1441–1443. https://doi.org/10.1126/science.6505700

Fernihough, A., & McGovern, M. E. (2015). Physical stature decline and the health status of the elderly population in England. *Economics & Human Biology, 16*, 30–44. https://doi.org/10.1016/J.EHB.2013.12.010

Gibson, I., Rosen, D., & Stucker, B. (2015). *Additive Manufacturing Technologies* (2nd ed.). Springer. https://eprints.ukh.ac.id/id/eprint/183/1/2015_Book_AdditiveManufacturingTechnolog.pdf

GMS Automatic Pill Dispenser: Review. (2020, January 25). Tech-Enhanced Life. https://www.techenhancedlife.com/reviews/gms-automatic-pill-dispenser

Gonçalves, C., & Carrilho, M. L. (2006). Ageing—An increasing phenomenon with geographical differences. *Revista de Estudos Demográficos, 40*, 21–37.

Gopinath, B., Rochtchina, E., Wang, J. J., Schneider, J., Leeder, S. R., & Mitchell, P. (2009). Prevalence of Age-Related Hearing Loss in Older Adults: Blue Mountains Study. *Archives of Internal Medicine, 169*(4), 415. https://doi.org/10.1001/archinternmed.2008.597

Górska, S., Forsyth, K., Irvine, L., Maciver, D., Prior, S., Whitehead, J., Flockhart, J., Fairnie, J., & Reid, J. (2013). Service-related needs of older people with dementia: perspectives of service users and their unpaid carers. *International Psychogeriatrics, 25*(7), 1107–1114. https://doi.org/10.1017/S1041610213000343

Grady, C. (2000). Changes in memory processing with age. *Current Opinion in Neurobiology, 10*(2), 224–231. https://doi.org/10.1016/S0959-4388(00)00073-8

Hero Medication Dispenser: Review. (2020, January 16). Tech-Enhanced Life. https://www.techenhancedlife.com/reviews/hero-medication-dispenser

Huang, W., Lei, X., Ridder, G., Strauss, J., & Zhao, Y. (2013). Health, Height, Height Shrinkage, and SES at Older Ages: Evidence from China. *American Economic Journal: Applied Economics, 5*(2), 86–121. https://doi.org/10.1257/APP.5.2.86

Iliffe, S., Kharicha, K., Harari, D., Swift, C., & Stuck, A. E. (2005). Health risk appraisal for older people in general practice using an expert system: a pilot study. *Health & Social Care in the Community, 13*(1), 21–29. https://doi.org/10.1111/j.1365-2524.2005.00525.x

Karl T. Ulrich, & Steven D. Eppinger. (2015). *Product Design and Development* (6th ed.). McGraw-Hill Education.

Lin, F. R., Thorpe, R., Gordon-Salant, S., & Ferrucci, L. (2011). Hearing Loss Prevalence and Risk Factors Among Older Adults in the United States. *The Journals of Gerontology Series A: Biological Sciences and Medical Sciences, 66A*(5), 582–590. https://doi.org/10.1093/gerona/glr002

Lima, O. (2022). Smarthealth-desenvolvimento de um dispensador de comprimidos com assistente virtual para idosos.

Lima, O., Terroso, M., Dias, Nuno., Vilaça, J., Matos, D., (2022). Development of a pill dispenser: system requirements and product architecture. https://doi.org/10.1007/978-3-031-20364-0_29

Lord, S. R., & Ward, J. A. (1994). Age-associated Differences in Sensori-motor Function and Balance in Community Dwelling Women. *Age and Ageing, 23*(6), 452–460. https://doi.org/10.1093/ageing/23.6.452

Martin, F., Turner, A., Wallace, L. M., Choudhry, K., & Bradbury, N. (2012). Perceived barriers to self-management for people with dementia in the early stages. *12*(4), 481–493. https://doi.org/10.1177/1471301211434677

MedaCube Medication Dispenser: Review. (2020, January 14). Tech-Enhanced Life. https://www.techenhancedlife.com/reviews/medacube-medication-dispenser

MedMinder, Maya: Review. (2020, January 14). Tech-Enhanced Life. https://www.techenhancedlife.com/reviews/medminder-maya

Mitchell, D. B., Brown, A. S., & Murphy, D. R. (1990). Dissociations between procedural and episodic memory: Effects of time and aging. *Psychology and Aging, 5*(2), 264–276. https://doi.org/10.1037/0882-7974.5.2.264

Neumann, L., Schauren, B. C., & Adami, F. S. (2016). Sensibilidade gustativa de adultos e idosos. *Revista Brasileira de Geriatria e Gerontologia, 19*(5), 797–808. https://doi.org/10.1590/1809-98232016019.150218

Nicholson, C., Meyer, J., Flatley, M., Holman, C., & Lowton, K. (2012). Living on the margin: Understanding the experience of living and dying with frailty in old age. *Social Science & Medicine, 75*(8), 1426–1432. https://doi.org/10.1016/J.SOCSCIMED.2012.06.011

Nilsson, L. G. (2003). Memory function in normal aging. *Acta Neurologica Scandinavica, 107*(179), 7–13. https://doi.org/10.1034/J.1600-0404.107.S179.5.X

Norman, J. F., Adkins, O. C., Hoyng, S. C., Dowell, C. J., Pedersen, L. E., & Gilliam, A. N. (2016). Aging and the Haptic Perception of Material Properties. *Perception, 45*(12), 1387–1398. https://doi.org/10.1177/0301006616659073

Nyberg, L., Lövdén, M., Riklund, K., Lindenberger, U., & Bäckman, L. (2012). Memory aging and brain maintenance. *Trends in Cognitive Sciences, 16*(5), 292–305. https://doi.org/10.1016/j.tics.2012.04.005

Nyberg, L., Maitland, S. B., Rönnlund, M., Bäckman, L., Dixon, R. A., Wahlin, Å., & Nilsson, L.-G. (2003). Selective adult age differences in an age-invariant multifactor model of declarative memory. *Psychology and Aging, 18*(1), 149–160. https://doi.org/10.1037/0882-7974.18.1.149

Nyman, S. R., Innes, A., & Heward, M. (2017). Social care and support needs of community-dwelling people with dementia and concurrent visual impairment. *Aging & Mental Health, 21*(9), 961–967. https://doi.org/10.1080/13607863.2016.1186151

Orimo, H., Ito, H., Suzuki, T., Araki, A., Hosoi, T., & Sawabe, M. (2006). Reviewing the definition of "elderly." *Geriatrics and Gerontology International*, *6*(3), 149–158. https://doi.org/10.1111/j.1447-0594.2006.00341.x

Osterwalder, A., & Pigneur, Y. (2010). *Business Model Generation*. John Wiley & Sons.

Owsley, C. (2011). Aging and vision. *Vision Research*, *51*(13), 1610–1622. https://doi.org/10.1016/j.visres.2010.10.020

Paula, R. da S., Colares, F. C. de J., Toledo, J. O. de, & Nóbrega, O. de T. (2008). Alterações gustativas no envelhecimento. *Rev. Kairós*, 217–235. http://revistas.pucsp.br/index.php/kairos/article/viewFile/2518/1603

Resnikoff, S., Pascolini, D., Etya'ale, D., Kocur, I., Pararajasegaram, R., Pokharel, G. P., & Mariotti, S. P. (2004). Global data on visual impairment in the year 2002. *Bulletin of the World Health Organization*, *82*(11), 844–851.

Schiffman, S. S., & Zervakis, J. (2002). *Taste and smell perception in the elderly: Effect of medications and disease* (pp. 247–346). https://doi.org/10.1016/S1043-4526(02)44006-5

Tulving, E. (1985). How many memory systems are there? *American Psychologist*, *40*(4), 385–398. https://doi.org/10.1037/0003-066X.40.4.385

Vasunilashorn, S., Steinman, B. A., Liebig, P. S., & Pynoos, J. (2012). Aging in Place: Evolution of a Research Topic Whose Time Has Come. *Journal of Aging Research*, *2012*, 1–6. https://doi.org/10.1155/2012/120952

Verhaeghen, P., & Salthouse, T. A. (1997). Meta-analyses of age–cognition relations in adulthood: Estimates of linear and nonlinear age effects and structural models. *Psychological Bulletin*, *122*(3), 231–249. https://doi.org/10.1037/0033-2909.122.3.231

Vimarlund, V., Borycki, E. M., Kushniruk, A. W., & Avenberg, K. (2021). *Ambient Assisted Living: Identifying New Challenges and Needs for Digital Technologies and Service Innovation*. https://doi.org/10.1055/s-0041-1726492

Walker, N., Philbin, D. A., & Fisk, A. D. (1997). Age-Related Differences in Movement Control: Adjusting Submovement Structure To Optimize Performance. *The Journals of Gerontology Series B: Psychological Sciences and Social Sciences*, *52B*(1), P40–P53. https://doi.org/10.1093/geronb/52B.1.P40

Walston, J. D. (2012). *Sarcopenia in older adults*. https://doi.org/10.1097/BOR.0b013e328358d59b

Weaver, K. (2018, May 28). *Controlling Stepper Motors using Python with a Raspberry Pi*. Medium. https://keithweaverca.medium.com/controlling-stepper-motors-using-python-with-a-raspberry-pi-b3fbd482f886

World Health Organization. (2015a). *World report And Ageing on Health*.

World Health Organization. (2015b). *World Report on Ageing and Health*. www.who.int

World Health Organization. (2019). *World Report on Vision*.

Zimmermann, T. D., & Meier, B. (2006). The Rise and Decline of Prospective Memory Performance across the Lifespan. *Quarterly Journal of Experimental Psychology*, *59*(12), 2040–2046. https://doi.org/10.1080/17470210600917835

Children and Youth Participation in Digital Environment: A Systematic Literature Review

Conceição Costa, Sara Pereira, Daniel Brandão, Diana Pinto, and Carolina Jardim

Abstract In both online and offline environments, children and youth have the right to freedom of expression and participation. Research on children's participation and voice in the media is expanding, although the objectives and the actual actions of their participation are less studied. In this study, using conceptualisations of children and youth media participation as social interaction, political and civic participation (Giddens, 2006; Carpentier, 2011, 2015; Dahlgren, 2013), a literature review (2017–2022), on children's participation in media and in society through media was conducted in the field of Communication Sciences. The "Communication Abstracts" database and the Prisma 2020 methodology were used to answer the following research questions: (a) What is the object of analysis and methodological approach in sources? (b) What are the goals of children mediated participation reported by studies? (c) What types of *action* are conducted by children in the media and in society through media? After the application of the eligibility criteria, 78 studies were included in the review. Overwall, the results suggest that social interaction followed by political participation were the main goals of children (mediated) participation in those studies. Belonging to a community seems to be the main motivation for children's content creation and sharing, followed by activism and social change. Identity building, prestige and recognition are more connected with children content creation, while political engagement actions rely more on sharing content. Only four sources mention participation in media organisations. Children use social media, particularly YouTube, and game platforms to participate with diverse levels

C. Costa
Lusófona University - CICANT, Lisbon, Portugal
e-mail: conceicao.costa@ulusofona.pt

S. Pereira (✉) · D. Brandão
University of Minho, Communication and Society Research Centre, Braga, Portugal
e-mail: sarapereira@ics.uminho.pt

D. Pinto
ICNOVA – NOVA Institute of Communication, Lisbon, Portugal
e-mail: dianapinto@fcsh.unl.pt

C. Jardim
Research Centre on Education, University of Minho, Braga, Portugal

© The Author(s), under exclusive license to Springer Nature Switzerland AG 2025

D. Brandão et al. (eds.), *Perspectives on Design and Digital Communication V*, Springer Series in Design and Innovation 50, https://doi.org/10.1007/978-3-031-76156-0_4

of intensity. Formal education, and particularly civic and media education, have a relevant role in youth participatory actions in media.

Keywords Children and media · Participation · Media production · Literature review

1 Introduction

The daily life of young people is marked by a digital and convergent media culture (Mihailidis & Viotty, 2017; Poyntz & Hoechsmann, 2011) which has led to a growing attention of researchers on children's interaction with media (Kalmus & O'Neill, 2021; Pereira et al., 2020; Staksrud & Milosevic, 2017). Smart technology and the multiplication of screens, devices and mobile platforms in constant evolution are ubiquitous and offer young people countless opportunities for media consumption and production (Vandenplas & Picone, 2021; Carrera et al., 2020; Vieira, 2018).[1]

Some research claim that children are active in several forms of media production and participation (Kaskazi & Kitzie, 2021; James & Cotnam-Kappel, 2020; Caron et al., 2019) and they also disseminate content through digital media (De Paula, 2021; Scolari et al., 2018; Campos & Simões, 2014). Specific forms of production include creation and publishing of photographs, videos, and texts on social media as well as the production of videogames, films, multimodal texts, digital stories, and poetry (De la Fuente Prieto et al., 2019; Drotner, 2020; Kovalik & Curwood, 2019; Wargo & Claytron, 2018). Moreover, several studies claim that young people use digital media to engage in several practices of political, civic participation and expression (Kaskazi & Kitzie, 2021; Kligler-Vilenchik & Literat, 2018; Mihailidis, 2020; Raby et al., 2018). They can engage in political action in social media, through discussions, comments, videos (Ekström & Shehata, 2018; Kaskazi & Kitzie, 2021) and through experiences of social and political activism (e.g., Cortés-Ramos et al., 2021). Some research (e.g., Pereira, 2021; Pereira et al., 2018) pointed out that youth media production is often unprepared, poorly structured and with content addressed essentially towards friends and family. Furthermore, in the digital environment, children have the right to freedom of expression as well as to participate: "to engage in play and to peaceful assembly and association, including through online communication, gaming, networking, and entertainment" (Council of Europe, 2018, p. 15).

Participation is a dynamic and fluid concept (Carpentier, 2011, 2015) and claims about the educational and symbolic value of youth digital participation need to be critically examined (Literat et al., 2018). In the political approach, participation is a process linked to power with several participatory intensities (Carpentier, 2016; Pateman, 1970). For instance, in Pateman (1970) conceptualisation of full participation all actors involved in the decision-making have equal power. Although this ideal

[1] Children and youth in this study mean ages until 18 years old.

of equal power can be helpful for theoretical purposes, this is controversial since *total equalisation* is utopic even in democratic societies or relationships (Carpentier, 2011, 2015).

In the sociological approach, concepts such as engagement to participate (Dahlgren, 2013) and interaction, as any form of socio-communicative relationships between individuals (Giddens, 2006), could be considered participation. In this perspective, people's interaction with media objects (technology) and other people in a digital environment is a form of participation, which is a broad use of participation and not without critique. Carpentier (2015) states that participation differs from (media) interaction since the power positions of elite actors (big technological companies such as YouTube) tend to be protected.

Socio-cultural views on media participation among children are discussed using several concepts, such as participatory media, youth media, youth media production, community-based media production, and creative media engagement (e.g. Charmaraman, 2013; Hopkins, 2010). In terms of audience activity Carpentier (2011) distinguishes between participation in media and participation in society through media. Participation in media relates to the production of media content and engagement with the decision-making of media organisations, while participation in society through media refers to mediated participation in several public spaces.

The present study considers children's media participation as social interaction (for self-expression, pleasure, fun, identity (ies) building and sense of belonging), political participation (to advance children and human rights, activism, and social change) and civic participation (any form of engagement or action in supporting and developing their communities) building on conceptualisations of Giddens (2006), Carpentier (2011, 2015) and Dahlgren (2013). To advance the state of the art in children media participation in the field of Communication Sciences and Media Studies a systematic literature review (SLR) was conducted. The database Communication Abstracts was chosen since it brings together the main scientific production and the main journals in the field of Communication Sciences. This SLR was guided by the following research questions:

a. What is the object of analysis and methodological approach in those studies?
b. What are the goals of children mediated participation reported by studies?
c. What types of *action* are conducted by children in the media and in society through media?

2 Method

To conduct the SLR, the Preferred Reporting Items for Systematic Reviews and Meta-Analyses (PRISMA 2020) statement checklist was followed (Page et al., 2021).

Eligibility Criteria

In the identification phase only peer-reviewed academic articles published in journals and published between March 2017 and February 2022 were selected. Records where children under 18 are not present were excluded, as well as studies whose object of analysis is not children participation and representation in media. Records that did not check the language eligibility criteria (not available in English, Portuguese, French or Spanish) were excluded, as well the ones which full text were not available for retrieval. Other reasons for exclusion during the process are presented in the next section.

Information Sources and Search Strategy

For the review, the leading database in the communication and media studies area—'Communication Abstracts'—was selected. Since this database includes the main journals in this area, a vast and representative range of scientific production in the field can be found in a single database. The search was performed in February 2022 and the following combination of keywords was applied: *(child* OR young* OR youth OR teen* OR adolesc*) AND (media OR Internet OR online OR social networks OR television OR TV OR radio OR magazines OR news* OR book* OR game*) AND (participation OR creation OR expression* OR production OR voice*)".*

Selection and Data Collection Process

In the identification phase 2984 results were found. To narrow the search according to the SLR goals filters were applied: only peer-reviewed studies, published between March 2017 and February 2022 and written in English, Portuguese, French or Spanish. This resulted in the exclusion of 2339 excluded records. For the screening phase 645 records were included. In Table 1 the criteria to include/exclude sources are presented.

In the first step of the screening phase the records' individual abstracts, titles and keywords were reviewed by two researchers, using Microsoft Excel spreadsheet. This process resulted in 460 records excluded, resulting in a total of 185 records eligible for the second screening phase: full-text reading. Similarly, Microsoft Excel was used to perform this task, which allowed to exclude the records with no full text available (EXC7; $n = 7$), duplicate records (EXC8; $n = 1$), opinion papers or commentary opinion articles that did not meet the eligibility criteria for a Scientific study (EXC1; $n = 3$), an article that was not peer-reviewed (EXC2; $n = 1$), studies with unrelated themes to the scope of this study (EXC5; $n = 41$) and studies that did not focus on children or adolescents, with participants predominantly with more than 18 years old (EXC6; $n = 54$). This analysis resulted in a total of 78 records included in the review (see Fig. 1).

Data Coding and Analysis

To systematically review the literature, a thematic analysis was performed by 2 researchers with NVivo 12 Plus. A coding guide was created from scratch by researchers (Table 2).

In terms of 'Goals for Youth Participation' the main categories in coding guide are: (a) social interaction as 'engagement to participate' (Dahlgren, 2013) and 'interaction' as any form of socio-communicative relationships between individuals (Giddens, 2006); (b) political participation as a process linked to power with several

Table 1 Reasons for inclusion and exclusion

	Inclusion criteria (INC)	Exclusion criteria (EXC)
Type of document	INC1 Journal article—Scientific study	EXC1 Conference papers, Proceedings, books or book chapters, reports, essays, opinion articles, biographies, book reviews
Revision by peers	INC2 The study is peer-reviewed	EXC2 The study is not peer-reviewed
Publication date	INC3 Published from March 2017 to February 2022	EXC3 Papers published before March 2017 or after February 2022
Language	INC4 Papers written in English, Portuguese, French or Spanish	EXC4 Articles not available in English, Portuguese, French or Spanish
Scope/theme	INC5 Papers about the study's theme scope: children (ages from 12–18 years old) participation and expression (s) in and through the media	EXC5 Papers were unrelated to the study's theme scope: children (ages from 12–18 years old) participation and expression (s) in and through the media
Target age	INC6 Studies considering children and adolescents (until 18 years old)	EXC6 Studies focusing on ages above 18 years old and/or not mentioning participants' age
Availability of full text	INC7 The full text of the paper is available	EXC7 Full text not available
Document duplication	INC8 Non-duplicated record	EXC8 Duplicate record

participatory intensities (Carpentier, 2016; Pateman, 1970); (c) civic participation as youth involvement (action) in community life and in the construction of shared experiences (e.g. Head, 2011; Percy-Smith, 2010; Bloustien, 2007); (d) youth voice meaning youth as "participants in the larger social fabric" (Qvortrup et al., 2009, p. 5); and (e) (media) education as the development of personal and social skills related to media, such as action to promote media literacy competencies in and out of school context.

Risk of Bias

Inter Coder Reliability (ICR) was computed as a preliminary phase of the thematic analysis. Cohen's Kappa was adopted as the ICR indicator. Multiple coding was applied to 11.54% of the coded material (9 papers and 2 coders), which is above the minimum recommended (O'Connor & Joffe, 2020). Cohen's Kappa, agreement rate, and disagreement rate for each node were computed in NVivo 12 Plus and averages and standard deviations for the full sample were calculated on MS Excel. An average Kappa of 0.89 ($SD = 0.31$) for the full coding was obtained which represents "substantial" correspondence (Landis & Koch, 1977). With an average agreement of 99.66% ($SD = 2.10$) and an average disagreement of 0.34% ($SD = 2.10$). The obtained scores are acceptable and represent "substantial" correspondence, mainly for an exploratory approach (O'Connor & Joffe, 2020).

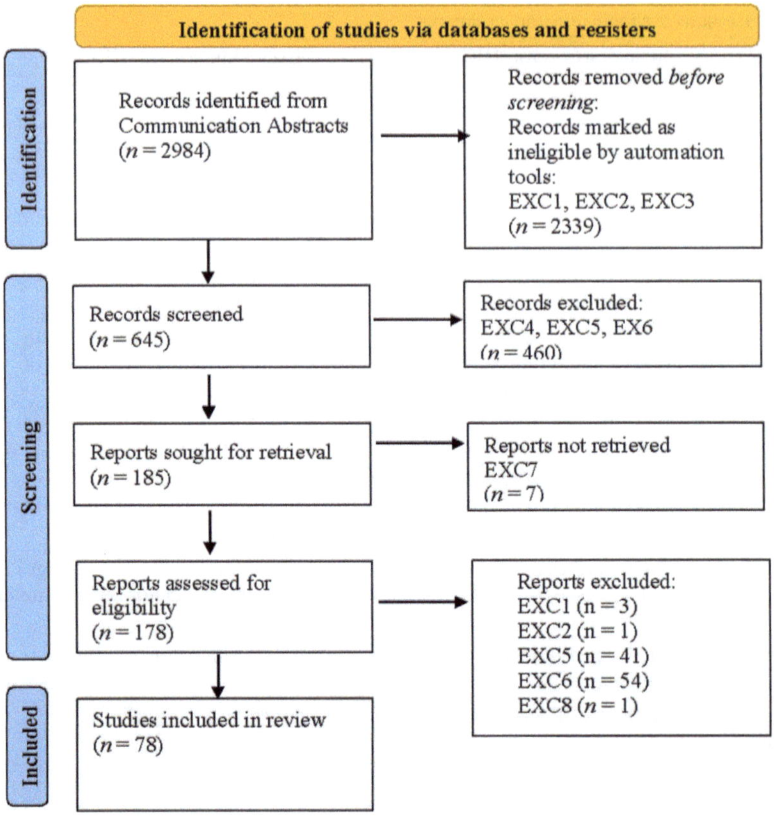

Fig. 1 PRISMA 2020 flow diagram

3 Results

The word cloud of one hundred frequent exact words in code "Participation and Media", show that *young/youth, political, social media online and hashtags*, are central to the articles included in the review, followed by *participation* and *civic issues* (Fig. 2).

Codification of Sources in NVivo 12 Plus

The coding guide, created by four researchers is presented in Table 2 and results from two approaches: a top-down approach based on theoretical foundations and research questions, and a bottom-up approach that emerged from the data.

Publication Year

Regarding the pattern of the publishing evolution of children and youth media participation, the results show a linear process from 2017 to 2020, which presents a growing

Table 2 Coding guide and sources codification

Name	Files	References
Publication year	78	114
Type of article	78	810
Participation and media	77	1149
Goals for participation	77	654
Social interaction	52	172
Belonging to communities	37	69
Self-expression	21	29
Building identity	19	35
Pleasure and fun	11	21
Prestige and recognition	11	16
Political participation	38	159
Activism and social change	16	55
Political engagement	15	23
Children rights	5	15
Civic participation	29	149
Climate change	13	36
Gender issues	10	44
Help others-social support	6	34
Civic engagement	5	10
Children voices	28	94
Education	16	43
Development of personal and social skills	5	21
Critical thinking	4	5
Digital media-arts practices	3	3
Promote or improve wellbeing	3	4
Multimodal learning	2	3
Type of action in and through media	59	320
Participation in society trough media	47	160
Participation in media	4	15
Children youth age	61	91

interest in the subject. In 2021, there was a breakdown of publications on children and youth participation, which could reflect the delays in scientific research during the pandemic and/or that children and youth participation in media was not a trendy theme in communication and media research. In 2022 there was no publishing activity, as expected since in this SLR the search was performed in February 2022.

Fig. 2 The most 100 frequent exact words in participation and media code

Publications

In the present SLR sample ($n = 78$) sources were published in 30 peer-reviewed journals being 'Learning, Media and Technology' ($n = 20$) where more publications were found. The journal 'Information, Communication & Society' is the second in ranking ($n = 6$), followed by 'New Media & Society' ($n = 5$) and 'Comunicar'. 'Journal of Communication' and 'Convergence: The International Journal of Research into New Media Technologies' had four publications ($n = 4$). Moreover, five journals had three publications each ($n = 3$), 'Discourse: Studies in the Cultural Politics of Education', 'Journal of Children and Media', 'Media Practice and Education', 'Media, Culture and Society' and 'Written Communication'. There are 3 journals with two publications each ($n = 2$), namely, 'Journalism and Mass Communication Quarterly', 'Political Communication' and 'Revista Latina de Comunicación Social'. The remaining journals have one publication only.

Sample, Object of Analysis and Method in Sources

A total of 96% of the studies in the sample are empirical ($n = 75$) with 4% ($n = 3$) being conceptual papers (Table 3). Children and youth samples vary from 1 to 3665 subjects. In terms of media artefacts, the sample range is 1–14,202. Several sources ($n = 21$) do not indicate sample size.

The majority of empirical studies have children and young people ($n = 43$) as objects of analysis. A significant number of articles ($n = 18$) focus their analysis on participants and on the digital artefacts produced by them, such as videos, films, games, digital stories, photos, illustrations, posts published in social media or in online communities and memes. Fourteen ($n = 14$) studies focused exclusively on analysis of media artefacts produced by children and youth.

The qualitative approach ($n = 50$) is the most frequent in sources when compared to quantitative ($n = 17$) or mixed methods ($n = 8$). Moreover, case studies ($n =$

Table 3 Studies' sample, object of analysis and methodological approach

Study	Citation	*N*	Studied sample	Object of analysis	Methodological approach
1	Andrade-Vargas et al. (2021)	2115	Young people (12–18 years old)	Socio economic profile of young people concerning the consumption and creation of content, and their virtual world related to social inequalities	Questionnaire
2	Aparici et al. (2019)	NA	Young people (12–15 years old)	Critical analysis of the commodification of the creative work produced by young people on the web	Conceptual paper
3	Bhatia and Pathak-Shelat (2020)	49	Children and Young people (9–12 years old)	The communal divide in interfaith societies	Ethnography (field notes, photo stories submitted by participants; semi structured interviews)
4	Blum-Ross (2017)	NA	Young people (12–21 years old); adults	How 'empowerment' in youth produced films moves from abstract discourse to on-the-ground practice	Case study (Semi-structured interviews, participant-observation and analysis of textual documents)
5	Bowden (2019)	2	Young people (10 years old)	Multimodal cultural production in children's interaction with Scratch	Video ethnographic study (Video recordings of the boys working on their Scratch game)
6	Bowden and Aarsand (2020)	NA	Young people (10 years old)	Practices of game design critique in a 4th grade classroom	Ethnomethodology and conversation analysis
7	Caron (2017)	55	Vlogs posted on YouTube	Vlogging and the ways civic discussions can foster discursive forms of engagement and activism	Multimodal content analysis of vlogs

(continued)

Table 3 (continued)

Study	Citation	*N*	Studied sample	Object of analysis	Methodological approach
8	Caron et al. (2019)	2 videos	Videos addressing gender inequality	Youth information and communication technology–enabled politics in vlogs	Case study (Multimodal analysis of videos)
9	Catalina-García et al. (2018)	NA	The age of the youth is not specified	Social media and the political-civic participation of young people	Qualitative analysis (literature review)
10	Chu (2020)	NA	The age of the youth is not specified	The meaning of youth participation in several contexts	10 Focus group
11	Dahya (2017)	3 girls' (students)	Young people (10–13 years old)	Voice and representation in youth digital media production in educational settings	Feminist Ethnography (interviews, students' audio–video productions, video-recordings, fieldnotes)
12	Dahya and King (2020)	48 participant mobile videos; 12 pitches; 125 videos of participants at work; 145 clips of raw footage; 2 final films	14 young people (13–18 years old)	Race, racial difference, and representation in feminist youth media production	Participatory visual research (analysis of visual artefacts, participant videos, fieldnotes and reflections)
13	De la Fuente Prieto et al. (2019)	47	Children and young people (8–14 years old)	The processes of media literacy of young people: the practices and audiovisual discourses that adolescents developed through new media	Action research, virtual ethnography, and visual methods (audiovisual recordings of workshops and audiovisual creations made by participants)
14	de Paula (2021)	NA	Young people (13–18 years old)	Reflexivity in research on digital media production	Conceptual paper

(continued)

Table 3 (continued)

Study	Citation	*N*	Studied sample	Object of analysis	Methodological approach
15	Dejmanee (2018)	15	Fashion blogs authored by girls between the ages of 11–16,	The popular feminism expressed through teen girl fashion blogs	Critical cultural analysis of blogs
16	Drotner (2020)	171	Young people (6–16 years old)	Children's digital content creation as creative processes of production	Case study (observation and interview)
17	Dussel and Dahya (2017)	NA	The age of the youth is not specified	Voice and representation in youth digital media production in educational settings	Conceptual paper
18	Edgerly et al. (2018)	1505 parent–child dyads	Young people (12–17 years old) and one associated parent	The relationship between news youth exposure and participation	Online survey
19	Ekström and Shehata (2018)	Cohort 1: 904; 883; 843; 723; 695 Cohort 2: 892; 807; 740; 467	Young people (cohort 1—13–14 years old; cohort 2—16–17 years old)	The role of social media on youth political engagement	Five-wave panel study
20	Fisher and Jenson (2017)	39	Young people (11–16 years old)	Girls and gaming	Qualitative ethnographic methods (a short survey, semi-structured interviews, observations, audio and video recordings, and textual analysis of student-produced media)
21	Friesem (2020)	4 students	Children (8–9 years old)	How the pedagogy of media production can improve self-reflection and self-efficacy of students	Case study (Participant observation, interviews, and analysis of artefacts)

(continued)

Table 3 (continued)

Study	Citation	*N*	Studied sample	Object of analysis	Methodological approach
22	Gleason (2018)	3	Young people (16, 17 years old)	Teenagers' new literacies practices on twitter	Case-study (virtual research methods; interviews)
23	González (2018)	NA	Young people (15–20 years-old)	The use of YouTube in the cultural practices of young electro dancers	Ethnographic approach (participant and non-participant observation; analysis of videos)
24	Guerrero-Pico et al. (2019)	216 young people (167 produce videos, 117 take photos, 38 draw and design, and 38 write stories)	Young people (12–19 years old)	Types of knowledge put into practice by teenagers in the creation of their media content	Short-term ethnography (survey; creative participatory workshops to collect teenagers' media production, in-depth interviews and media diaries, and online observation)
25	Hauge (2020)	1	Children (7 years old)	Bana Alabed digital engagement and democratic practice	Case study (analysis of twitter posts)
26	Heiss and Matthes (2017)	294	Young people (15–20 years-old)	Adolescents' political Social Network Sites use	Survey
27	Heiss et al. (2020)	294	Young people (15–20 years old)	Use of Social Network Sites (SNS) and political engagement among adolescents	Survey
28	Hickey (2020)	NA	Children and young people (8–10 years old)	The intergenerational media practice pedagogy at work in the Generation Animation project	Participatory Action Research methodology
29	Hilte et al. (2020)	434,537 social media posts written by 1384 teenagers	Young people (13–20 years old)	The impact of the sociodemographic profile on lexical patterns in adolescents' online writing	Quantitative text analysis of social media posts

(continued)

Table 3 (continued)

Study	Citation	*N*	Studied sample	Object of analysis	Methodological approach
30	Hollett (2019)	150	Young people (16–17 years old)	The symbiotic learning partnerships formed between teen skateboarders and teen videographers	Short ethnographic Study (observations, conversations, and semi-structured interviews)
31	James and Cotnam-Kappel (2020)	38	Young people and adults (15–25 years old)	How youth define and carry out political dialogue on social media platforms	Qualitative exploratory study (in-depth interviews and artefact analysis)
32	Jimenez et al. (2021)	34	Young people (11–14 years old) and adults	How do youth exercise empowerment in youth/adult settings of youth media co-production	Observation, fieldnotes, semi-structured Interviews
33	Kahne and Bowyer (2018)	1033	Young people (15–27 years old)	The influence of friendship-driven and interest-driven online activity on forms of political action	Survey
34	Kang (2017)	NA	Young people and children under 19	Youth internet activism and street politics	Critical discourse analysis of the online discourses and street performances through postings in an online community
35	Khalil (2017)	NA	Young people (15–25 years old) and adults	The reconstruction of Lebanese youth and the exercise of children's participation rights through the #YouStink movement	Analysis of fieldwork interviews and social media online discourses
36	Kim et al. (2017)	Cohort 1: 864; 717 Cohort 2: 532; 575	Young people (cohort 1–16 years old; cohort 2–22 years old)	The role played by the Internet in young people's political lives	Two-wave panel study

(continued)

Table 3 (continued)

Study	Citation	*N*	Studied sample	Object of analysis	Methodological approach
37	Kligler-Vilenchik and Literat (2018)	1,116 creative artefacts and 14,202 responses posted in online communities	Young people (12–30 years old)	Election-related content uploaded to online sites	Case studies (qualitative content analysis of artefacts and responses, which included textual comments and multimodal responses, such as reaction videos or remixes)
38	Leurs (2017)	16	Young people and adults (15–34 years old)	The usage of social media among young refugees, human rights' discourse, and technology	Participatory action research (in-depth interviews; participant observation and follow-up conversations)
39	Li et al. (2020)	36 students; 9 teachers	Young people (14–16 years old) and teachers	Students' engagement with a video-sharing app to realise their dreams of socio-economic mobility	Observations, interviews, and analysis of artefacts created by participants
40	Lim and Toh (2020)	Videos produced by 3 children (number not specified)	Children (8–10 years old)	Children's out-of-school digital multimodal composing practices on learning and teaching in the formal educational context	Qualitative case study approach method (content analysis of the videos produced)
41	Lindell and Sartoretto (2018)	NA	Young people (15–20 years-old)	The relation between social classes and young people's news practices and news preferences	Focus group; interviews
42	Literat and Kligler-Vilenchik (2018)	1116 media artefacts and 14,202 comments posted on them in 3 non-political online spaces	Young people (13–18 years old)	The significance of youth political expression in non-political online spaces, and its implications for civic education	In-depth qualitative content analysis of artefacts (games, animations, stories, illustrations)
43	Literat and Kligler-Vilenchik (2019)	1651	Youth-created videos on social media	Young people's political expression on tik tok	Quantitative and qualitative content analyses of videos

(continued)

Table 3 (continued)

Study	Citation	*N*	Studied sample	Object of analysis	Methodological approach
44	Literat et al. (2018)	13	Young people (15–22 years old)	Assessment of youth digital participation forms and outcomes	Case studies (qualitative content analysis of depth interviews)
45	Literat et al. (2020)	Two games produced by 6 young people	Young people (10–14 years old)	Encourage and capture youth reflection, discussion, and participation around news literacy topics	Video and audio recordings of participatory game design workshops; content analysis of the artefacts of the game design process; surveys and fieldnotes
46	Mandau (2021)	157 posts written by 104 girls	Young people (11–20 years old)	Image-based sexual abuse (IBSA) with the use of digital technologies	Qualitative thematic analysis of posts
47	Marchi (2017)	NA	Young people (15–20 years old)	The use of Internet for newsgathering among low-income immigrant youth	Interviews
48	Marchi and Clark (2021)	14	Young people (15–17 years old)	The contribution of social media to youth voice, collective identity, and political engagement	Ethnographic research (interviews)
49	McInroy (2020)	3665	Young people and adults (14–29 years old)	Online fandom communities as a source of social support and resilience for sexual and gender minority youth	Mixed methods (online survey; qualitative content analysis)
50	Mihailidis (2020)	93	Young people (13–16 years old)	Young people attitude towards memes and hashtags for civic purposes	Survey (Exploratory design)
51	Moeller et al. (2018)	904; 883; 843;723;695;668	Young people (13–14 years old)	Mechanisms and processes stimulating the long-term development of political interest during adolescence	Longitudinal panel survey (six annual waves)

(continued)

Table 3 (continued)

Study	Citation	*N*	Studied sample	Object of analysis	Methodological approach
52	Moon and Bai (2020)	2584	Young people (13–17 years old)	Digital literacy as a predictor of civic engagement	Survey
53	Moreno-Almeida and Banaji (2019)	NA	Young people (17–30 years old)	Youth attitudes toward the usage of digital media in political, civic, cultural and artistic networks	Case studies (qualitative interviews, focus group, participant observation, and field notes)
54	Morris (2019)	8	Young people (16–18 years old)	Multimodal media production within the juvenile justice system and restorative justice	Exploratory qualitative research design (interviews; analysis of digital stories)
55	Notley and Dezuanni (2019)	1000	Young people (8–16 years old)	Young people's news practices and experiences	Survey
56	Olaortua et al. (2018)	2426	Young people (12–16 years old)	Online audio-visual content consumption, creation, and dissemination among adolescents	Survey
57	Pandya and Low (2020)	180	Children and young people (8–10 years old)	Children's perceptions of the audiences of digital videos they made	Design based research (interviews and video analysis)
58	Parry et al. (2020)	NA	Young people (14–25 years old)	Young people's media production project run in libraries	Mix-method research (survey, interviews, workshops)
59	Pereira and Moura (2019)	679	Young people (17–18 years old)	Evaluation of media literacy competencies in Portuguese youth	Survey
60	Pereira et al. (2018)	281	Young people (12–19 years old)	Media uses and production practices of teens from Portugal, Spain and Italy	Short-term ethnography with a mostly qualitative approach (observation, survey, interviews, workshops, media diaries)

(continued)

Table 3 (continued)

Study	Citation	*N*	Studied sample	Object of analysis	Methodological approach
61	Pienimäki (2019)	NA	Young people (15–22 years old)	The potential of including media participation to support at risk youth, to become active agents in their lives	Mixed-method research (observation diaries, interviews, media content produced by participants, surveys)
62	Pyles (2017)	14	Young people (14–20 years old)	Youth created films about their lives and communities	Cases studies (semiotic analysis of youth-produced films; Interviews; observation and fieldnotes; audio–video taping)
63	Reichert and Print (2017)	3513	Young people (15–16 years old)	How the use of traditional and online media affect youth's participation in politics	Survey
64	Richardson (2017)	NA	Young people (16–17 years old)	The construction of gender and identity in youth media production	Mix-methods (survey, focus group, in depth interviews, analysis of videos)
65	Shule et al. (2019)	NA	Young people (11–19 years old)	Enabling children to engage in radio production, addressing children's rights	Interviews, focus group discussions and live broadcasts and recordings
66	Smirnov and Lam (2019)	2 clips from a youth-produced news show	Young people (12–18 years old)	Youth media production to represent, legitimate, and reimagine experiences of hyper criminalization	Social semiotics and critical discourse analysis of 2 videos
67	Starkey et al. (2019)	68	Children and young people (9–11 years old)	How preadolescent children, from 14 different communities, participate in the digital world	Mixed-method research (survey and semi-structured group interviews)

(continued)

Table 3 (continued)

Study	Citation	*N*	Studied sample	Object of analysis	Methodological approach
68	Stornaiuolo and Thomas (2018)	2 young people; one short documentary film	Young people (18 years old)	The practices of youth digital media producers to navigate experiences of social injustice	Longitudinal ethnographic inquiry (analysis of the documentary film produced by young people, artefacts related to the film and 6 semi-structured interviews)
69	Sugihartati (2020)	NA	The age of the youth is not specified	Youth fans of 'the Mortal Instruments' in Indonesia and the "free digital labourer"	Textual analysis and discourse analysis of In-depth interview and focus group discussion
70	Taddeo and Tirocchi (2021)	263	Young people (11–19 years old)	The consuming and producing digital media practices of teenagers	Multiple methodologies (survey, in-depth interviews, workshops and media diaries)
71	Theo (2019)	NA	The age of the youth is not specified	Social change and awareness of critical human rights in youth, through making films	Semiotic analysis of films produced by young people
72	Thorson et al. (2018)	1505 parent–child dyads	Young people (12–17 years old) and 1 parent	The impact of parent socioeconomic status, the amount of political communication in the home and the development of youth political interest	Two-wave national online survey
73	Tuzel and Hobbs (2017)	84	Young people (12–14 years old)	The use of social media among young people to promote cultural understanding	Case study (interviews, documents, observations, video recordings)
74	Valdivia (2017)	15 young people; two adults	Young people (12–14 years old) and adults	Analysis of digital creations as a strategy for the self-expression of children and adolescents	Survey; ethnographic observations of multimedia workshops; audio recorded data; interviews; a field diary; digital stories and photos produced by young people

(continued)

Table 3 (continued)

Study	Citation	*N*	Studied sample	Object of analysis	Methodological approach
75	Vizcaíno-Verdú et al. (2021)	603	Young people (16–35 years-old)	The self-perception of young youtubers in intertextual and transmedia competencies	Survey
76	Vozmediano et al. (2018)	400 videos	The age of the youth is not specified	Contexts in teen video making and sharing in YouTube	Content analysis of videos
77	Wargo and Clayton (2018)	23	Young people (15–19 years old)	Young people's multimodal composition, and video production as a nexus of 'participatory politics'	Mediated discourse analysis (observations, fieldnotes, informal conversations, interviews, multimodal artefacts, group videos)
78	Winocur (2019)	NA	Young people (17 years old)	Memes as symbolic resources to youth social inclusion–exclusion	Online ethnography (online observation; face-to-face interviews)

13) and ethnographies ($n = 9$) are frequent methodological approaches. The data in sources was preferentially collected through interviews ($n = 34$), and through the analysis of youth media artefacts ($n = 34$), such as videos, photographs, audio-visual creations, digital stories, photo stories and social media posts. Surveys were also a frequent research technique.

3.1 Children and Media Participation in Literature

Goals of Media Participation

In terms of goals for children's participation, 'social interaction' ($n = 52$) is the most frequent in the analysed sources, followed by political participation ($n = 38$), civic participation ($n = 29$) and youth voice ($n = 28$). In social interaction participants are main actors in their identity (ies) construction and socio-communicative actions.

In political participation, youth activism and social change ($n = 16$) and political engagement ($n = 15$) (as motivation to participate or minor acts of participation) are the most frequent goals of participation action, initiated by children and youth. In civic participation, climate change ($n = 13$) and gender issues—mainly related to women and LGBT rights—are the most frequent themes in sources ($n = 10$).

Under the category Education, the action is initiated by adults in formal and informal learning spaces with the goal of citizenship development, social inclusion, youth knowledge on their own and *otherness* rights and development of media literacy competencies.

Type of Action in Media and in Society Through the Media

Two main categories emerged from data: 'Creating and Sharing'. While these online activities are not exclusive, creating audio-visual content is the most frequent action by participants and include video production and animation mainly to be shared on YouTube platform. 'Creating' ($n = 50$) is the most referred action in sources, particularly audio-visual content ($n = 22$) and games ($n = 10$), followed by news ($n = 9$). When the type of content created by youth is crossed with goals of participation 'Audiovisual content', 'Games' and 'Digital Storytelling" are the most frequent. 'Games' are the most frequent content created in the context of Education activities. Since in sources children/youth ages are between 8 and 18 years old, it is outside school context that children/youth create news, memes and written comments to express themselves and conduct political and civic action. The creation of audiovisual content and games, as well as digital storytelling, means that children and youth invest some time to express themselves in the media (Fig. 3).

In 'Sharing' ($n = 31$), posting and reposting ($n = 19$) and audio-visual content ($n = 11$) are the most frequent actions referred in sources (Fig. 5). When the category 'Sharing' is crossed with the goals of participation 'personal views on social media', online 'collective action' is more frequent than 'likes' (Fig. 4), meaning they commit to their actions, for instance they choose their audiences (using hashtags).

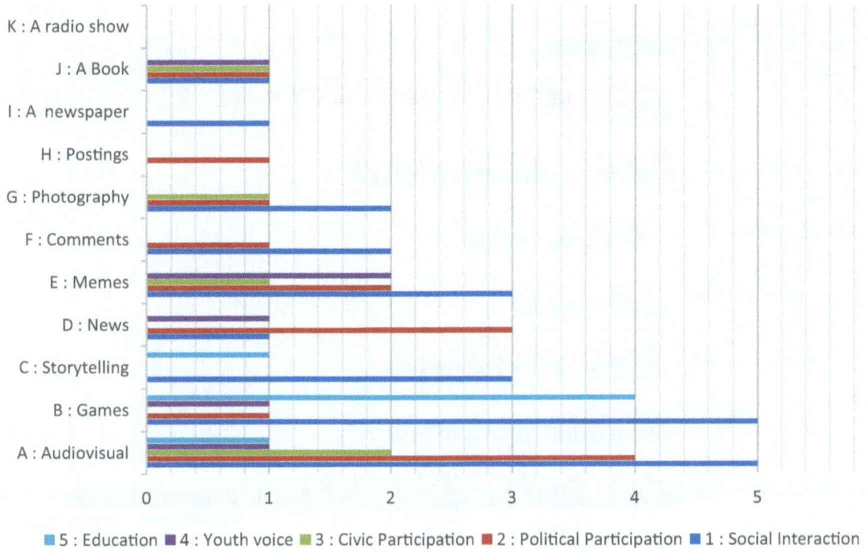

Fig. 3 Matrix coding query: type of content created by youth versus goals for participation

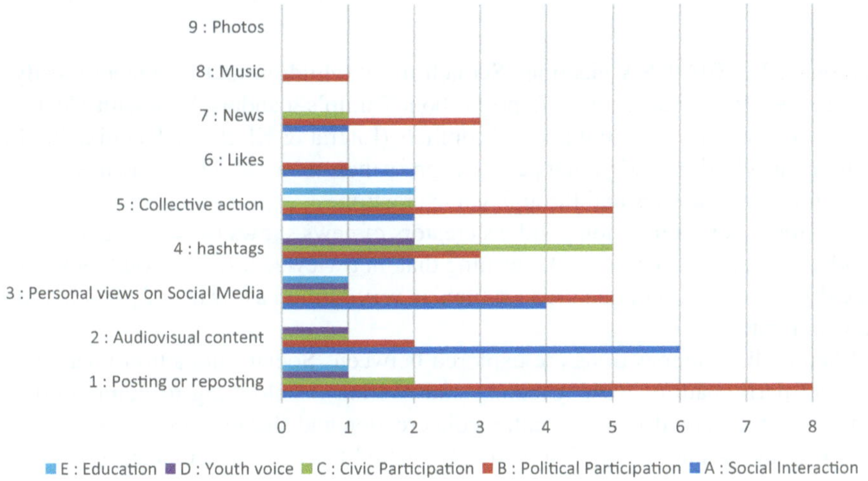

Fig. 4 Matrix coding query: type of content shared by youth versus goals for participation

Children and Youth Mediated Participation

In our sample, children and youth participation is mainly mediated social participation ($n = 47$) and participation in society through social media ($n = 33$). YouTube is the most referred social media in sources ($n = 12$) used for participation among youth. In 'Game Creation' ($n = 10$) the online game engine Scratch is the most

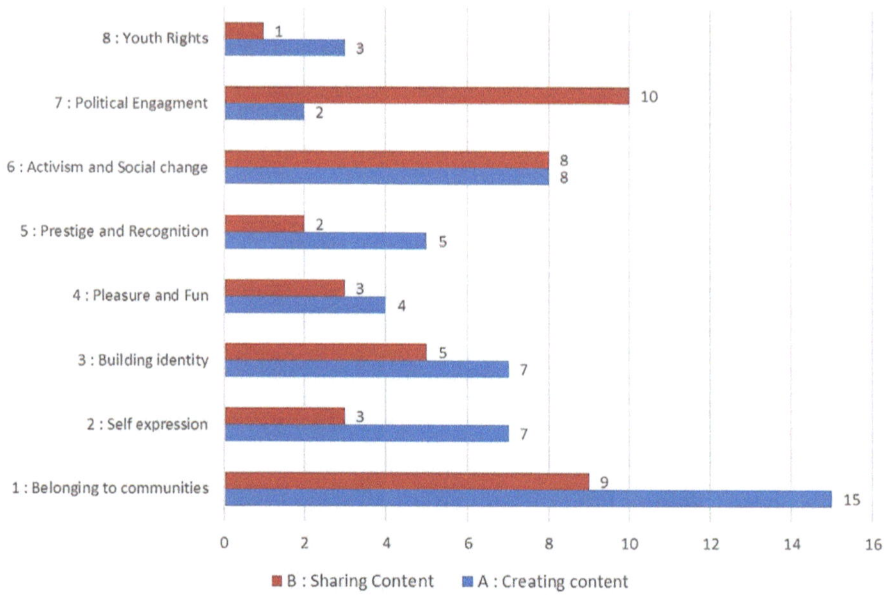

Fig. 5 'Creating' and 'sharing' in social interaction goals and political participation

mentioned. In 2016 USA elections Scratch users (children and teenagers mostly) have created 598 artefacts and 9775 posts about Trump's scandals; Wall with Mexico; Nuclear warfare and potential nuclear conflicts (Literat & Kligler-Vilenchik, 2018), meaning that children and young people express themselves about political issues in non-political online sites and through game creation.

Only four sources mention youth as creators of news shows ($n = 3$), a book ($n = 1$) and a youth magazine ($n = 1$), meaning that, in reviewed articles, youth power to make decisions within media organisations is very limited as forms of participation and youth voice.

When coding intersections are explored between 'Social interaction goals' and 'Political participation' with 'Creating and sharing', 'belonging to communities' seems to be the main driver of youth media creation and sharing in sources (Fig. 5). "Activism and Social Change" are equally related to creating and sharing actions, while 'Political Engagement' among participants seems to be more connected with shared content. 'Building Identity' and 'Prestige and Recognition' are more connected with creating content by participants.

4 Discussion and Conclusion

The present study reviews recent research on children and young people's media participation, production, and voice in the field of communication and media studies.

Regarding the analysed data, the journal ‘Learning, Media and Technology’ has a significant number of publications in this area, followed by ‘Information, Communication and Society’ and ‘New Media and Society’.

Most of the papers in the sample are empirical studies and the qualitative approach is the most frequent in the analysed sources. The data was preferentially collected through interviews, media production analysis, and surveys in and out-of-school contexts.

The results demonstrate that researchers who study children and/or young people’s participation and production in media and in society through media, focus on young people as an object of analysis, as well as on their produced artefacts.

When addressing youth participation goals and actions in media and in society through the media, social interaction is the most frequent in sources and belonging to communities the most prominent in data. Such results are consistent with engagement to participate and interaction conceptualisations as forms of participation (Dahlgren, 2013; Giddens, 2006). Social Interaction is followed by political participation, civic participation, and youth voice, consistent with the literature (Caron et al., 2019; James & Cotnam-Kappel, 2020; Kaskazi & Kitzie, 2021).

For ‘Type of action in media and in society through the media’, the categories creating and sharing content emerged from the data. Both have important contributions to ‘activism and social change’ and ‘sharing content’, more than ‘creating’ is related to political engagement. In the analysed studies, social media is the most referred digital environment used by participants to content creation and sharing, especially YouTube, followed by Facebook and game creation platforms. Indeed, these findings align with the perspective that young people use social networks to produce and share creative content, such as texts, photos, and videos (e.g., Choi & Behm-Morawitz, 2020; De la Fuente Prieto et al., 2019; Kovalik & Curwood, 2019).

Children and youth participation in media organisations is residual, which is expected facing the imbalance of power within media organisations. It is worth noting that in this SLR analysis, several civic and political actions are decided by adults in formal and informal learning environments. However, many sources (47 in 78) document participation in society initiated by youth, which is aligned with Peter Dalghren’s (2013) concept of online civic cultures and the democratic potential of the internet and social media.

Children and young people express themselves and participate in society through social media mainly, most of the time to communicate with their peers but as they approach adult age, they use memes and other formats to political activism.

One important finding from this literature review is that some children and young people are committed to their participation in society through social media and other online platforms, investing time in creating complex media formats, such as games and in targeting audiences for their content. This goes against the idea that young people do not participate or only do so via *sharing* and *likes*. Another important finding is that ‘Political Engagement’ among children/youth seems to be more connected with shared content, and it open up an important question for future research: do they read and reflect on the content they are sharing?

As a limitation, this SLR was carried out using only the database 'Abstracts Communication'. It would be of interest, in future work, to cross-reference the analysis with publications from other areas, particularly in the field of education, since as found in sources there are participatory actions that are initiated from formal and informal learning spaces. To do this, it would be relevant to use other databases, thus broadening the scope of the study.

Acknowledgements This study is financed by national funds through FCT—Fundação para a Ciência e a Tecnologia, I.P., under the project entitled "bYou—Study on children and young people's experiences and expressions of the media" [PTDC/COM-OUT/3004/2020]—https://doi.org/10.54499/PTDC/COM-OUT/3004/2020.

Disclosure Statement No potential competing interest was reported by the authors.

References

Andrade-Vargas, L., Iriarte-Solano, M., Rivera-Rogel, D., & Yunga-Godoy, D. (2021). Young people and social networks: Between the democratization of knowledge and digital inequality. *Comunicar, 69*(29), 85–95. https://doi.org/10.3916/C69-2021-07

Aparici, R., García-Marín, D., & Díaz-Delgado, N. (2019). Vampires on the Web. The exploitation of youth culture. *Revista Latina de Comunicación Social, 74*, 197–213. https://doi.org/10.4185/RLCS-2019-1327

Bhatia, K.V., & Pathak-Shelat, M. (2020). Reimagining religiously segregated spaces: building interfaith sites through participatory photography. *Journal of Communication Inquiry, 44*(4), 321–353. https://doi.org/10.1177/0196859920918543

Bloustien, G. (2007). 'Wigging people out': youth music practice and mediated communities. *Journal of Community & Applied Social Psychology, 17*(6), 446–462. https://doi.org/10.1002/casp.938

Blum-Ross, A. (2017). Voice, empowerment and youth-produced films about 'gangs'. *Learning, Media and Technology, 42*(1), 54–73. https://doi.org/10.1080/17439884.2016.1111240

Bowden, H.M. (2019). Problem-solving in collaborative game design practices: epistemic stance, affect, and engagement. *Learning, Media and Technology, 44*(2), 124–143. https://doi.org/10.1080/17439884.2018.1563106

Bowden, H.M., & Aarsand, P. (2020). Designing and assessing digital games in a classroom: an emerging culture of critique. *Learning, Media and Technology, 45*(4), 376–394. https://doi.org/10.1080/17439884.2020.1727500

Campos, R., & Simões, J.A. (2014). Digital participation at the margins: Online circuits of rap music by Portuguese afro-descendant youth. *Young, 22*(1), 87–106. https://doi.org/10.1177/1103308813512931

Caron, C. (2017). Speaking up about bullying on YouTube: teenagers' vlogs as civic engagement. *Canadian Journal of Communication, 42*, 645–668. https://doi.org/10.22230/cjc.2017v42n4a3156

Caron, C., Raby, R., Mitchell, C., Théwissen-LeBlanc, S., & Prioletta, J. (2019). How are civic cultures achieved through youth social-change-oriented vlogging? A multimodal case study. *Convergence: The International Journal of Research into New Media Technologies, 25*(4), 694–713. https://doi.org/10.1177/1354856518795094

Carpentier, N. (2011). The concept of participation. If they have access and interact, do they really participate?. *CM Communication Management Quarterly, 6*(21), 13–36. https://doi.org/10.4013/fem.2012.142.10

Carpentier, N. (2015). Differentiating between access, interaction and participation. *Conjunctions: Transdisciplinary Journal of Cultural Participation, 2*(2), 7–28. http://dx.doi. org/https://doi.org/10.7146/tjcp.v2i2.22844

Carpentier, N. (2016). Beyond the ladder of participation: An analytical toolkit for the critical analysis of participatory media processes. *Javnost - The Public, 23*(1), 70–88. https://doi.org/10.1080/13183222.2016.1149760

Carrera, P., Blanco-Ruiz, M., & Andújar, C.S. (2020). Media consumption among Teenagers. New media and Old Stories in Transmedia context. *Historia y Comunicacion Social, 25*(2), 563–574. https://doi.org/10.5209/hics.72285

Catalina-García, B., López, M. C. L. A., & Nieto, M.R. (2018). Social media and the political-civic participation of young people. A review of the digital citizenship debate. *Doxa Comunicación, 27*, 81–97. https://doi.org/10.31921/doxacom.n27a4

Charmaraman, L. (2013). Congregating to create for social change: urban youth media production and sense of community. *Learning, Media and Technology, 38*(1), 102–115. https://doi.org/10.1080/17439884.2011.621956

Choi, G. Y., & Behm-Morawitz, E. (2020). Discovering hidden digital producers: Understanding motivation and creativity in social media production. *Psychology of Popular Media, 9*(3), 318–327. https://doi.org/10.1037/ppm0000240

Chu, D. (2020). Civic intentionality in youth media participation: the case of Hong Kong. *Learning, Media and Technology, 45(*4), 363–375. https://doi.org/10.1080/17439884.2020.1809450

Cortés-Ramos, A., García, J. A. T., Landa-Blanco, M., Gutiérrez, F. J. P., and Mesa, M. T. C. (2021). Activism and social media: Youth participation and communication. *Sustainability, 13*(18), 1–13. https://doi.org/10.3390/su131810485

Council of Europe (2018). Recommendation CM/Rec (2018)7 of the Committee of Ministers. Strasbourg, France.

Dahlgren, P. (2013). Tracking the civic subject in the media landscape: Versions of the democratic ideal. *Television and New Media, 14*(1), 71–88. https://doi.org/10.1177/1527476412458809.

Dahya, N. (2017). Critical perspectives on youth digital media production: 'voice' and representation in educational contexts. *Learning, Media and Technology, 42*(1), 100–111. https://doi.org/10.1080/17439884.2016.1141785

Dahya, N., & King, W. E. (2020). Politics of race, gender, and visual representation in feminist media education. *Discourse: Studies in the Cultural Politics of Education, 41*(5), 673–690. https://doi.org/10.1080/01596306.2020.1769934

Dejmanee, T. (2018). Popular feminism and teen girl fashion blogs. *Continuum, 32*(3), 345–354. https://doi.org/10.1080/10304312.2018.1430744

De La Fuente Prieto, J., Díaz, P. L., & Martínez-Borda, R. (2019). Adolescents, social networks and transmedia universes: Media literacy in participatory contexts. *Revista Latina de Comunicacion Social, 74*, 172–196. https://doi.org/10.4185/RLCS-2019-1326

de Paula, B. (2021). Reflexivity, methodology and contexts in participatory digital media research: making games with Latin American youth in London. *Learning, Media and Technology, 46*(4): 435–450. https://doi.org/10.1080/17439884.2021.1901114

Drotner, K. (2020). Children's digital content creation: Towards a processual understanding of media production among Danish children. *Journal of Children and Media, 14*(2), 221–236. https://doi.org/10.1080/17482798.2019.1701056

Dussel, I., & Dahya, N. (2017). Introduction: problematizing voice and representation in youth media production. *Learning, Media and Technology, 42*(1), 1–7. https://doi.org/10.1080/17439884.2016.1205602

Ekström, M., & Shehata, A. (2018). Social media, porous boundaries, and the development of online political engagement among young citizens. *New Media and Society*, *20*(2), 740–759. https://doi.org/10.1177/1461444816670325

Edgerly, S., Vraga, E.K., Bode, L., Thorson, K., & Thorson, E. (2018). New Media, new relationship to participation? A closer look at youth news repertoires and political participation. *Journalism & Mass Communication Quarterly, 95*(1), 192–212. https://doi.org/10.1177/1077699017706928

Fisher, S., & Jenson, J. (2017). Producing alternative gender orders: a critical look at girls and gaming. *Learning, Media and Technology, 42*(1), 87–99. https://doi.org/10.1080/17439884.2016.1132729

Friesem, Y. (2020). It's all about control: how giving kids control over access, content, and format of their media production advances social and emotional learning. *Media Practice and Education, 21*(4), 261–274. https://doi.org/10.1080/25741136.2020.1832828

González, A.C. (2018). Why do electro dancers also dance on YouTube? The media logic of the cultural practices in the electro dance youth style. *The Communication Review, 21*(4), 277–295. https://doi.org/10.1080/10714421.2018.1535727

Guerrero-Pico, M., Masanet, M., & Scolari, C. A. (2019). Toward a typology of young produsers: Teenagers' transmedia skills, media production, and narrative and aesthetic appreciation. *New Media & Society, 21*(2), 336–353. https://doi.org/10.1177/1461444818796470

Giddens A. (2006). *Sociology (5th Edition).* Polity Press.

Gleason, B. (2018). Thinking in hashtags: exploring teenagers' new literacies practices on twitter. *Learning, Media and Technology, 43*(2), 165–180. https://doi.org/10.1080/17439884.2018.1462207

Hauge, C. (2020). Girl with a voice: Bana Alabed's digital engagement and democratic practice. *Discourse: Studies in the Cultural Politics of Education, 41*(5), 691–707. https://doi.org/10.1080/01596306.2020.1769935

Head, B.W. (2011). Australian experience: Civic engagement as symbol and substance. *Public Admin. Dev., 31*, 102–112. https://doi.org/10.1002/pad.599

Hopkins, L. (2010). YouthWorx Increasing youth participation through media production. *The Australian Sociological Association, 47*(2), 181–197. https://doi.org/10.1177/1440783310386827

Heiss, R., & Matthes, J. (2017). Who 'likes' populists? Characteristics of adolescents following right-wing populist actors on Facebook. *Information, Communication & Society, 20*(9), 1408–1424. https://doi.org/10.1080/1369118X.2017.1328524

Heiss, R., Knoll, J., & Matthes, J. (2020). Pathways to political (dis-)engagement: motivations behind social media use and the role of incidental and intentional exposure modes in adolescents' political engagement. *Communications, 45*(s1), 671–693. https://doi.org/10.1515/commun-2019-2054

Hickey, A. (2020). Generation animation: participatory action research and intergenerational pedagogy. *Media Practice and Education, 21*(2), 109–120. https://doi.org/10.1080/25741136.2020.1769952

Hilte, L., Daelemans, W., & Vandekerckhove, R. (2020). Lexical Patterns in Adolescents' Online Writing: The Impact of Age, Gender, and Education. *Written Communication, 37*(3), 365–400. https://doi.org/10.1177/0741088320917921

Hollett, T. (2019). Symbiotic learning partnerships in youth action sports: Vibing, rhythm, and analytic cycles. *Convergence: The International Journal of Research into New Media Technologies, 25*(4), 753–766. https://doi.org/10.1177/1354856517735840

James, C., & Cotnam-Kappel, M. (2020). "Doubtful dialogue": how youth navigate the draw (and drawbacks) of online political dialogue. *Learning, Media and Technology, 45*(2), 129–150. https://doi.org/10.1080/17439884.2020.1686013

Jimenez, C., Clark, S. L., Kennedy, H., Nisle, S., Engle, Matyasic, C. S., & Anyon, Y. (2021). The art of youthful restraint: negotiating youth-adult relations in digital media literacy. *Learning, Media and Technology, 46*(2), 190–203. https://doi.org/10.1080/17439884.2021.1888118

Kahne, J., & Bowyer, B. (2018). The Political Significance of Social Media Activity and Social Networks. *Political Communication, 35*(3), 470–493. https://doi.org/10.1080/10584609.2018.1426662

Kalmus, V., & O'Neill, B. (2021). Through mature and yet fresh eyes: Researching emerging issues in the field of children and media. *Communications, 46*(3), 327–331. https://doi.org/10.1515/commun-2021-2050

Kang, J. (2017). Internet activism transforming street politics: South Korea's 2008 'Mad Cow' protests and new democratic sensibilities. *Media, Culture & Society 39*(5), 750–761. https://doi.org/10.1177/0163443717709444

Kaskazi, A., & Kitzie, V. (2021). Engagement at the margins: Investigating how marginalized teens use digital media for political participation. *New Media and Society, 25*(1), 72–94. https://doi.org/10.1177/14614448211009460

Khalil, J.F. (2017). Lebanon's waste crisis: An exercise of participation rights. *New Media & Society, 19*(5), 701–712. https://doi.org/10.1177/1461444816686321

Kligler-Vilenchik, N., & Literat, I. (2018). Distributed creativity as political expression: Youth responses to the 2016 U.S. presidential election in online affinity networks. *Journal of Communication, 68*(1), 75–97. https://doi.org/10.1093/joc/jqx005

Kim, Y., Russo, S., & Amnå, E. (2017). The longitudinal relation between online and offline political participation among youth at two different developmental stages. *New Media & Society, 19*(6), 899–917. https://doi.org/10.1177/1461444815624181

Kovalik, K., & Curwood, J. S. (2019). #poetryisnotdead: understanding Instagram poetry within a transliteracies framework. *Literacy, 53*(4), 185–195. https://doi.org/10.1111/lit.12186.

Landis, J.R., & Koch, G.G. (1977). The measurement of observer agreement for categorical data. *Biometrics, 33*, 159–174. https://doi.org/10.2307/2529310

Leurs, K. (2017). Communication rights from the margins: politicising young refugees' smartphone pocket archives. *The International Communication Gazette, 79*(6–7), 674–698. https://doi.org/10.1177/1748048517727182

Li, M., Tan, C. K. K., & Yang, Y. (2020). ShehuiRen: cultural production and rural youths' use of the Kuaishou video-sharing app in Eastern China. *Information, Communication & Society, 23*(10), 1499–1514. https://doi.org/10.1080/1369118X.2019.1585469

Lim, F.V., & Toh, W. (2020). Children's digital multimodal composing: implications for learning and teaching. *Learning, Media and Technology, 45*(4), 422–432. https://doi.org/10.1080/17439884.2020.1823410

Lindell, J., & Sartoretto, P. (2018). Young People, class and the news. *Journalism Studies, 19*(14), 2042–2061. https://doi.org/10.1080/1461670X.2017.1310628

Literat, I., & Kligler-Vilenchik, N. (2018). Youth online political expression in non-political spaces: implications for civic education. *Learning, Media and Technology*, *43*(4), 400–417. https://doi.org/10.1080/17439884.2018.1504789

Literat, I., Kligler-Vilenchik, N., Brough, M., & Blum-Ross, A. (2018). Analyzing youth digital participation: Aims, actors, contexts and intensities. *The Information Society, 34*(4), 261–273. https://doi.org/10.1080/01972243.2018.1463333

Literat, I., & Kligler-Vilenchik, N. (2019). Youth collective political expression on social media: The role of affordances and memetic dimensions for voicing political views. *New Media and Society, 21*(9), 1988–2009. https://doi.org/10.1177/1461444819837571

Literat, I., Chang, Y.K., & Hsu, S. (2020). Gamifying fake news: Engaging youth in the participatory design of news literacy games. *Convergence: The International Journal of Research into New Media Technologies, 26*(3), 503–516. https://doi.org/10.1177/1354856520925732

Mandau, M. B. H. (2021). "Snaps", "screenshots", and self-blame: A qualitative study of image-based sexual abuse victimization among adolescent Danish girls. *Journal of Children and Media, 15*(3), 431–447. https://doi.org/10.1080/17482798.2020.1848892

Marchi, R., & Clark, L.S. (2021). Social media and connective journalism: The formation of counterpublics and youth civic participation. *Journalism 22*(2), 285–302. https://doi.org/10.1177/1464884918807811

Marchi, R. (2017). News Translators: Latino Immigrant Youth, Social Media, and Citizenship Training. *Journalism & Mass Communication Quarterly, 94*(1), 189–212. https://doi.org/10.1177/1077699016637119

McInroy, L.B. (2020). Building connections and slaying basilisks: fostering support, resilience, and positive adjustment for sexual and gender minority youth in online fandom communities. *Communication & Society, 23*(13), 1874–1891. https://doi.org/10.1080/1369118X.2019.1623902

Mihailidis, P., & Viotty, S. (2017). Spreadable Spectacle in Digital Culture: Civic Expression, Fake News, and the Role of Media Literacies in "Post-Fact" Society. *American Behavioral Scientist, 61*(4), 441–454. https://doi.org/10.1177/0002764217701217

Mihailidis, P. (2020). The civic potential of memes and hashtags in the lives of young people. *Discourse, 41*(5), 762–781. https://doi.org/10.1080/01596306.2020.1769938

Moeller, J., Shehata, A., & Kruikemeier, S. (2018). Internet use and political interest: Growth curves, reinforcing spirals, and causal effects during adolescence. *Journal of Communication, 68*(6), 1052–1078. https://doi.org/10.1093/joc/jqy062.

Moon, S.J., & Bai, S.Y. (2020). Components of digital literacy as predictors of youth civic engagement and the role of social media news attention: the case of Korea. *Journal of Children and Media, 14*(4), 458–474. https://doi.org/10.1080/17482798.2020.1728700

Moreno-Almeida, C., & Banaji, S. (2019). Digital use and mistrust in the aftermath of the Arab Spring: beyond narratives of liberation and disillusionment. *Media, Culture & Society, 41*(8),1125–1141. https://doi.org/10.1177/0163443718823143

Morris, J. (2019). Exploring the affordances of digital storytelling in a media-arts restorative justice program. *Visual Communication, 18*(2), 205–230. https://doi.org/10.1177/1470357217752749

Notley, T., & Dezuanni, M. (2019). Advancing children's news media literacy: learning from the practices and experiences of young Australians. *Media, Culture & Society, 41*(5), 689–707. https://doi.org/10.1177/0163443718813470

O'Connor, C., & Joffe, H. (2020). Intercoder reliability in qualitative research: Debates and Practical Guidelines. *International Journal of Qualitative Methods, 19*, 1–13. https://doi.org/10.1177/1609406919899220

Olaortua, A.F.A., Arrillaga, I.L., & Sesumaga, L.E. (2018). Digital natives: Online audiovisual content consumption, creation and dissemination. *Comunicar, 57*(26), 61–69. https://doi.org/10.3916/C57-2018-06

Page, M., McKenzie, J.E., Bossuyt, P.M., Boutron, I., Hoffmann, T.C., Mulrow, C.D., Shamseer, L., Tetzlaff, J,M., Akl, E.A., Brennan, S.E., Chou, R., Glanville, J., Grimshaw, J.M., Hróbjartsson, A., Lalu, M., Li, T., Loder, E.W., Mayo-Wilson, E., McDonald, S.…Moher, D. (2021). The PRISMA 2020 statement: an updated guideline for reporting systematic reviews. *BMJ, 71*, 1–9. https://doi.org/10.1136/bmj.n71

Pandya, J.Z., & Low, D.E. (2020). Theorizing the Addressive Audience in Children's Digital Video Production. *Written Communication, 37*(1), 41–68. https://doi.org/10.1177/0741088319880509

Parry, R., Howard, F., & Penfold, L. (2020). Negotiated, contested and political: the disruptive Third Spaces of youth media production. *Learning, Media and Technology, 45*(4), 409–421. https://doi.org/10.1080/17439884.2020.1754238

Pateman, C. (1970) *Participation and democratic theory*. Cambridge University Press.

Percy-Smith, B. (2010). Councils, consultations and community: rethinking the spaces for children and young people's participation. *Children's Geographies, 8*(2), 107–122. https://doi.org/10.1080/14733281003691368

Pereira, S. (2021). *Crianças, Jovens e Media na Era Digital: Consumidores e Produtores?* UMinho Editora.

Pereira, S., & Moura, P. (2019). Assessing media literacy competences: A study with Portuguese young people." *European Journal of Communication* 34 (1): 20–37. https://doi.org/10.1177/0267323118784821.

Pereira, S., Moura, P., MaSanet, M. J., Taddeo, G. & Tirocchi, S. (2018). Media uses and production practices: Case study with teens from Portugal, Spain and Italy. *Comunicacion y Sociedad*, 33: 89–114. https://doi.org/10.32870/cys.v0i33.7091.

Pereira, S., Ponte, C. & Elias, N. (2020). Children, youth and media: current perspectives. *Comunicação e Sociedade* 37: 9–18. https://doi.org/10.17231/comsoc.37(2020).2687.

Pienimäki, M. (2019). Improving the wellbeing of at-risk youth through media Participation. *Media Practice and Education, 20*(4), 364–377. https://doi.org/10.1080/25741136.2018.1541371

Poyntz, S. R., & Hoechsmann, M. (2011). Children's media culture in a digital age. *Sociology Compass, 5*(7), 488–498. https://doi.org/10.1111/J.1751-9020.2011.00393.X

Pyles, D.G. (2017). A social semiotic mapping of voice in youth media: the pitch in youth video production. *Learning, Media and Technology, 42*(1), 8–27. https://doi.org/10.1080/17439884.2016.1095209

Qvortrup, J., Corsaro, W.A. & Honig, M-S. (2009). Why social studies of childhood? An introduction to the handbook. In Qvortrup, J., Corsaro, W.A. & Honing, M-S. (Eds.) *The Palgrave Handbook of Childhood Studies* (pp. 1–18). Palgrave Macmillan.

Raby, R., Caron, C., Théwissen-LeBlanc, S., Prioletta, J., & Mitchell, C. (2018). Vlogging on YouTube: the online, political engagement of young Canadians advocating for social change. *Journal of Youth Studies, 21*(4), 495–512. https://doi.org/10.1080/13676261.2017.1394995

Reichert, F., & Print, M. (2017). Mediated and moderated effects of political communication on civic participation. *Information, Communication & Society, 20*(8), 1162–1184. https://doi.org/10.1080/1369118X.2016.1218524

Richardson, J.M. (2017). The promposal: youth expressions of identity and 'love' in the digital age. *Learning, Media and Technology, 42*(1), 74–86. https://doi.org/10.1080/17439884.2016.1130055.

Scolari, C. A., Masanet, M. J., Guerrero-Pico, M., & Establés, M. J. (2018). Transmedia literacy in the new media ecology: Teens' transmedia skills and informal learning strategies. *Profesional de La Informacion, 27*(4), 801–812. https://doi.org/10.3145/epi.2018.jul.09

Shule, V., Boothby, H., Ahmed, S. & Hansen, A.H. (2019). Radio waves, children's rights and community communication: A radio for children's rights project in Africa. *Journal of African Media Studies, 11*(1), 3–19. https://doi.org/10.1386/jams.11.1.3_1

Smirnov, N., & Lam, W.S.E. (2019). "Presenting our perspective": Recontextualizing youths' experiences of hypercriminalization through media production. *Written Communication, 36*(2), 296–344. https://doi.org/10.1177/0741088319827594

Starkey, L., Eppel, E.A., & Sylvester, A. (2019). How do 10-year-old New Zealanders participate in a digital world? *Information, Communication & Society, 22*(13), 1929–1944. https://doi.org/10.1080/1369118X.2018.1472795

Stornaiuolo, A., & Thomas, E.E. (2018). Restorying as political action: authoring resistance through youth media arts. *Learning, Media and Technology, 43*(4), 345–358. https://doi.org/10.1080/17439884.2018.1498354

Staksrud, E., & Milosevic,T. (2017). Adolescents and children in global media landscape: from risks to rights. *Annals of the International Communication Association, 41*(3–4), 235–241. https://doi.org/10.1080/23808985.2017.1387503

Sugihartati, R. (2020). Youth fans of global popular culture: Between prosumer and free digital labourer. *Journal of Consumer Culture, 20*(3), 305–323. https://doi.org/10.1177/1469540517736522

Taddeo, G., & Tirocchi, S. (2021). Transmedia teens: the creative transmedia skills of Italian students. *Information, Communication & Society, 24*(2), 241–257. https://doi.org/10.1080/1369118X.2019.1645193

Theo, L. J. (2019). LGBTQ "selves" in films from the Reel-Lives project as signifiers of political and social change, and of personal value. *Social Semiotics, 29*(4), 476–491. https://doi.org/10.1080/10350330.2018.1459422

Thorson, K., Xu, Y. & Edgerly, S. (2018). Political inequalities start at home: Parents, children, and the socialization of civic infrastructure Online. *Political Communication, 35*(2), 178–195. https://doi.org/10.1080/10584609.2017.1333550

Tuzel, S., & Hobbs, R. (2017). The use of social media and popular culture to advance cross-Cultural understanding. *Comunicar, 51*(25), 63–72. https://doi.org/10.3916/C51-2017-06

Valdivia, A. (2017). What was out of the frame? A dialogic look at youth media production in a cultural diversity and educational context in Chile. *Learning, Media and Technology, 42*(1), 112–125. https://doi.org/10.1080/17439884.2016.1160926

Vandenplas, R., & Picone, I. (2021). Media as the great emancipators? Exploring relations between media repertoires and cultural participation in Flanders. *Convergence: The International Journal of Research into New Media Technologies, 27*(5), 1439–1461. https://doi.org/10.1177/1354856521990246

Vieira, J. (2018). Media and generations in Portugal. *Societies, 8*(3), 61. https://doi.org/10.3390/soc8030061

Vizcaíno-Verdú, A., Contreras-Pulido, P., & Guzmán-Franco, M. (2021). Youtube musicians and self-perceived multimedia, hypermedia, intertextual and transmedia competencies. *Learning, Media and Technology, 46*(4), 515–530. https://doi.org/10.1080/17439884.2021.1941099

Vozmediano, M.M., Jiménez, A.G. & Sendra, J.M. (2018). Teen videos on YouTube: Features and digital vulnerabilities. *Comunicar, 54*(26), 61–69. https://doi.org/10.3916/C54-2018-06

Wargo, J. M., & Clayton, K. (2018). From PSAs to reel communities: exploring the sounds and silences of urban youth mobilizing digital media production. *Learning, Media and Technology, 43*(4), 469–484. https://doi.org/10.1080/17439884.2018.1534859

Winocur, R. (2019). The tribe of memes. A virtual territory of inclusion-exclusion among adolescents. *Comunicación y Sociedad,* 1–22. https://doi.org/10.32870/cys.v2019i0.7327

Exploring the Factors Affecting the Wayfinding Experience of Elderly Users in General Hospitals: A Multi-Criteria Decision-Making Perspective

Jieqiong Fan and Albert Young Choi

Abstract This study focuses on the wayfinding experiences of general elderly users in Tianjin Medical University General Hospital, aiming to identify and optimize the main factors affecting their wayfinding experiences. Initially, hypotheses were proposed and the importance of various factors influencing the elderly users' wayfinding experiences was quantitatively evaluated by applying Multi-Criteria Decision-Making (MCDM) methods, particularly the Analytic Hierarchy Process (AHP). Subsequently, qualitative research methods, including field surveys, wayfinding tests, and interviews, were employed to collect data and verify the applicability and accuracy of the AHP theoretical assumptions in practical wayfinding experiences. The results revealed key factors affecting the wayfinding experiences of elderly users, such as the complexity of the building structure, the ease of use and comprehensibility of the signage system, and the environmental friendliness. Finally, based on these key factors, targeted improvement suggestions and design guidelines for the wayfinding system in Tianjin Medical University General Hospital were proposed.

Keywords Wayfinding experience · Factors · Wayfinding system · Multi-criteria decision making · General elderly users · Analytic hierarchy process

---

J. Fan
Graduate School, College of Design, Hanyang University ERICA, Ansan, South Korea
e-mail: fanjieqiong351@gmail.com

A. Y. Choi (✉)
Faculty of Graduate School, Communication Design, College of Design, Hanyang University ERICA, Ansan, South Korea

© The Author(s), under exclusive license to Springer Nature Switzerland AG 2025
D. Brandão et al. (eds.), *Perspectives on Design and Digital Communication V*, Springer Series in Design and Innovation 50, https://doi.org/10.1007/978-3-031-76156-0_5

1 Introduction

Research background: in modern society, general hospitals, as a core component of the healthcare system, play an important role in providing comprehensive healthcare services to the community and promoting medical research and medical education. However, the complex architectural structures and bustling environment often pose challenges for visitors and patients in wayfinding these facilities. Factors like unclear signage, insufficient navigational information, high foot traffic, and temporary changes and construction exacerbate the difficulty, making wayfinding a critical aspect of healthcare facility design that directly impacts the spatial quality of the facility's quality [1]. General hospitals cater to diverse populations with varying needs and preferences. With changes in demographics [2], addressing the specific needs of elderly users and enhancing their quality of life has become a crucial societal task. As people age, elderly users face issues such as slower cognitive processing speed, reduced attention and memory, and decreased information processing ability. For elderly users who are visiting the hospital for the first time or infrequently use wayfinding systems, these issues can increase their stress and anxiety [3]. Although studies indicate that individuals with visual or cognitive impairments face numerous challenges in wayfinding within hospitals, this research primarily focuses on the wayfinding experiences of general elderly users. This focus is justified by the rapidly growing elderly population worldwide, who frequently use medical facilities and commonly experience declines in cognitive and physiological functions. Therefore, studying the wayfinding experiences of general elderly users holds significant practical importance.

In general hospitals, wayfinding systems typically rely on static wayfinding information systems such as signage, maps, colors, numeric codes, and environmental cues [4]. However, these may not offer sufficiently simple cues for elderly individuals with declining cognitive and physiological functions, making wayfinding tasks more challenging for them. To reduce anxiety among elderly users during hospital visits, general hospitals need to allocate resources to optimize and simplify wayfinding systems, thus improving the wayfinding experience for this demographic.

A well-designed wayfinding system is the foundation of a good wayfinding experience, according to Karimi (2015), there is a sufficient body of research that proves that there are several aspects associated to the wayfinding experience and the physical elements of the buildings that affect the wayfinding process and consequently result in navigation errors [5]. Karimi (2015) present seven aspects that can increase the errors made throughout a wayfinding experience, such as the visual access to destinations, the individual spatial capabilities, the existing navigational clues, the cognitive map created, the spatial learning capabilities, the wayfinding strategies adopted, and the characteristics of the physical environment and buildings' structure [6]. Even in terms of management, issues such as the maintenance of wayfinding systems and inadequate personnel guidance may affect the wayfinding experience of elderly users (see Table 2).

Research aims and methods: this study aims to identify and optimize the main factors affecting the wayfinding experience of elderly users in general hospitals. Initially, a literature review is conducted to identify the main factors affecting user wayfinding. Subsequently, based on opinions from researchers and experts, a Multi-Criteria Decision-Making (MCDM) approach—specifically, the Multi-Attribute Decision Making (MADM)—Analytic Hierarchy Process (AHP), is utilized to hypothesize evaluation criteria. This is followed by a quantitative analysis to assess and rank the importance of various factors affecting the wayfinding experience of elderly users. Furthermore, qualitative research methods, such as on-site surveys, wayfinding tests, and interviews, are employed to collect data directly from the real-life experiences of elderly users, thereby validating the practical applicability of the AHP theoretical assumptions. Finally, based on the findings, specific measures, and design guidelines to improve the wayfinding experience of elderly users are proposed. The methodological framework of this study ensures the scientific accuracy and practicality of the research results, providing evidence-based recommendations for improvements in general hospitals.

Hospital selection: Tianjin Medical University General Hospital was chosen as the research site for three main reasons. Firstly, established in 1954, the Department of Geriatrics at Tianjin Medical University General Hospital is one of the earliest geriatric departments in China. It serves as a comprehensive geriatric medical center, integrating medical treatment, teaching, scientific research, and healthcare. With extensive experience in elderly care, it provides valuable insights for the research topic. Secondly, having access rights to get the participation of hospital administrators and geriatric patients is more operational and practical for the research. Thirdly, the hospital boasts complex architectural structures and wayfinding systems, highlighting the intricacies of wayfinding experience research.

2 Theoretical Background

2.1 Multiple Criteria Decision Making (MCDM)

Multiple criteria decision making (MCDM) is also known as multi-criteria decision analysis (MCDA), is a systematic decision analysis method used to handle complex relationships among multiple decision criteria or objectives. Multi-criteria decision making is divided into two categories: multiple-attribute decision making (MADM) and multi-objective decision making (MODM) [7]. MCDM solutions help the decision makers to examine the various scenarios and practical utility of the proposed solutions in a quite flexible manner. It is characterized by a finite number of criteria and feasible alternatives [7], the process of MCDM analysis is governed by three steps: (1) determine relevant criteria and alternative solutions, (2) assign numerical values to criteria, (3) utilize formal mathematical procedures for analysis.

This study chooses to utilize the MCDM model, which comprises various elements depending on the nature of the decision problem, common elements include decision, preference, outcome, criteria, alternatives, and decision variables [7]. In the context of navigating through a general hospital, elderly users may feel unfamiliar with their surroundings, prompting them to seek information from the external environment and utilize sensory cues to guide them to their destination. Acting as decision-makers during the wayfinding process, elderly users need to plan and execute decisions at each decision point to determine their course of action [8]. Factors such as building structure, environmental characteristics, and visual elements are considered crucial factors influencing these decisions. Each criterion may impact the wayfinding experience of elderly users differently, leading to the selection of various alternative routes based on individual preferences. The flexibility and systematic approach of MCDM enable decision-makers to gain a comprehensive understanding of the actual effects of various solutions, thereby optimizing the wayfinding system in general hospitals to meet the special needs of elderly users and enhance their wayfinding experience.

2.2 *Application of Multi-Criteria Decision-Making in Wayfinding Problems*

The aforementioned principles/guidelines and models for wayfinding design have provided objective guidance, aiding in addressing wayfinding issues and understanding the design of wayfinding systems. However, designers still lack a detailed guidance. Existing design principles and models are primarily based on planning and internal architectural structures (such as density, visibility, depth, integration, and connectivity), largely dependent on the interaction between individuals, spaces, and environmental factors. They overlook individual psychology, behavior, and preferences, thus having certain limitations in predicting wayfinding experiences.

The classification of multi-criteria decision making has been mentioned above, and in this study, the applied hierarchical analysis in multi-attribute decision making (MADM) was chosen, MADM refers to making preference decisions by evaluating and prioritizing a limited set of alternatives based on multiple conflict attributes [9]. The Analytic Hierarchy Process (AHP) hierarchically decomposes decision problems, aiming to determine the relative importance of each element in the decision by comparing each pair of alternative solutions at each level. It begins with the construction of a decision matrix, representing the relative importance of various attributes relative to each other [7]. For example, from the perspective of elderly patients, in the design of wayfinding systems in general hospitals, what is the importance of comprehensibility relative to ease of use (e.g., operational simplicity), accessibility (e.g., convenience), user-friendliness (e.g., user experience), and safety (e.g., accident prevention)? Decision-makers are required to assess the importance of comprehensibility based on "importance intensity" (such as "very important," "more important," etc.), as shown in Table 1.

Table 1 The Saaty rating scale

Intensity of importance	Definition	Explanation
01	Equal importance	Two factors contribute equally to the objective
03	Somewhat more important	Experience and judgement slightly favor one over the other
05	Much more important	Experience and judgement strongly favor one over the other
07	Very much more important	Experience and judgement very strongly favor one over the other Its importance is demonstrated in practice
09	Absolutely more important	The evidence favoring one over the other is of the highest possible validity
02, 04, 06, 08	Intermediate values	When compromise is needed

A simple undervaluation is used for rating attributes. For example, if comprehensibility A is considered "very important" compared to safety B, then according to Table 2, its rating is 7, and the importance rating of B to A is 1/7. Finally, in AHP analysis, consistency ratio (CR) is highly significant. Consistency ratio is employed to assess the consistency level of expert judgments. Experts are required to compare each pair of factors, determine the weights of each level, and ultimately synthesize the optimal solution.

3 Research Method

3.1 Elements for Comparison

Based on comprehensive research findings, we found that the evaluation criteria for wayfinding systems involve multiple integrated factors. We horizontally divided them according to different domains or types, including architectural structure, environmental features, and wayfinding systems. Additionally, we vertically classified the evaluation criteria based on various aspects or levels, including usability, understandability, accessibility, user-friendliness, and safety. Comparison elements, based on these two main classification dimensions, facilitate a comprehensive capture of the multifaceted factors affecting the wayfinding experience of elderly users, allowing for more accurate identification of key areas for optimization efforts.

Table 2 Researchers' related research on elderly users' wayfinding

Researchers	Research content
Passini (1984), Arthur and Passini (1992), Carpman and Grant (2001), Huelat (2007) and Rooke et al. (2010b), Haq and Zimring (2003)	The importance of legible physical settings (e.g. architectural clues and other forms of visual and tactile cues) is emphasised. Arthur and Passini, for example, point out that wayfinding in buildings and groups of buildings is most affected by the logic of the architectural arrangement and design. Haq and Zimring, Huelat highlight specific characteristics of the spatial layout of the environment that affect the paths people take. Haq and Zimring (2003) pay attention to the overall structure of the system of rooms and corridors stating that the naming, numbering, and general organization of the parts of a building is a critical organizational aspect of a wayfinding plan
Werner and Schindler (2004) Ruddle and Peruch (2004)	Highlight properties of building layout that facilitate or impede movement. For example, give better wayfinding performance than those with angled intersections. Ruddle and Peruch assert that well-designed signs are likely to be quite ineffective in a building that is highly complicated and does not provide simple cues that enable natural movement
Weisman (1981), Hölscher et al. (2013), Slone et al. (2015)	There are four important characteristics of a building's architectural configuration that influence the wayfinding experience. The greatest impact is the morphological complexity of the layout, also known as layout configuration, which in order of impact is architectural differentiation; visual access; and lighting
Huelat (2007:11)	Asserts that signage should support 'the good bones' of the physical environment. She calls for a clear organized set of sign elements which should provide four types of information: informational, directional, identifying, and regulatory. These, she adds should be integrated into design in a logical, consistent, and user-friendly way

(continued)

Table 2 (continued)

Researchers	Research content
Carpman and Grant (1993)	Point out that any good wayfinding system should go beyond mere signage and the use of colour codes to differentiate various areas. They call for an integration of coordinated elements, such as visible and easy-to-understand signs and numbers; graphic symbols; clear and consistent verbal directions; consistent and clear paper, mail-out, and electronic information
Rodrigues (2019)	Wayfinding is more than signs as it encompasses the overall configuration, layout or physical arrangement, space differentiation, landmarks, and other architectural group of aids that should work together to help guide the users. The signage system and its graphical characteristics can help the effectiveness of the wayfinding system
Karimi (2015)	Karimi (2015) present seven aspects that can increase the errors made throughout a wayfinding experience, such as the visual access to destinations, the individual spatial capabilities, the existing navigational clues, the cognitive map created, the spatial learning capabilities, the wayfinding strategies adopted, and the characteristics of the physical environment and buildings' structure

3.2 Establishing a Hierarchy

This study aims to optimize the wayfinding experience of elderly users in a general hospital using the analytic hierarchy process (AHP) method. We establish a hierarchical structure composed of decision objectives, evaluation criteria, and improvement measures for analysis, as shown in Fig. 1. The core decision objective is to "optimize the wayfinding experience of elderly users in a general hospital." All subsequent analyses and decisions will revolve around how to achieve this goal. Based on literature review and preliminary research hypotheses, we identified five initial evaluation criteria as key factors in measuring the success of optimizing the wayfinding experience. These evaluation criteria include complexity of the architectural structure, usability of the wayfinding system, understandability, environmental friendliness, and accessibility of information. For each evaluation criterion, we will explore possible improvement measures to optimize the wayfinding experience of elderly users. Specific improvement measures will be formulated based on subsequent data analysis.

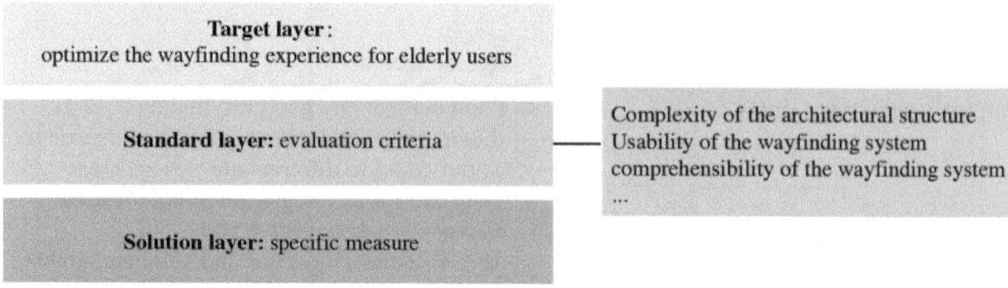

Fig. 1 Hierarchy diagram

3.3 Construct a Judgment Matrix and Determine Relative Weights

This process is accomplished by comparing the relative importance of the evaluation criteria with respect to the decision objective, aiming to quantify their roles and significance in achieving the goal.

Constructing of the Judgment Matrix. For the previously proposed five hypothetical evaluation criteria (Architectural Complexity, Usability of the Wayfinding System, Understandability of the Wayfinding System, Environmental Friendliness, and Accessibility of Information), we need to assess their relative importance to the decision-making goal and construct a judgment matrix accordingly. Based on the experience of experts and practitioners in the field and their understanding of the wayfinding experience of the elderly (see Table 2), an assessment of each pair of evaluation criteria was carried out, employing the 1–9 scale by Saaty mentioned earlier (see Table 1). It is assumed that their importance decreases in the order of Architectural Complexity, Usability of the Wayfinding System, Understandability of the Wayfinding System, Environmental Friendliness, and Accessibility of Information. Architectural Complexity is the most crucial, therefore it is assigned a value of 1 when compared with itself. The Usability of the Wayfinding System, being the second most important, is assigned a value of 1/3 when compared to Architectural Complexity (since it is less important). The Understandability of the Wayfinding System, being the third most important, is given a value of 1/5. Environmental Friendliness is fourth in importance, meriting a value of 1/7. Lastly, the Accessibility of Information is deemed the least important, warranting a value of 1/9. Consequently, the judgment matrix is presented as Table 3.

Normalized Judgment Matrix and Weights. To determine the relative importance values, first, each cell value in Table 3 is divided by the total of its column to normalize the values (for example, 1/7.87 = 0.559, 1/3/1.787 = 0.187, 3/4.676 = 0.642). Next, sum the numbers in each column of the normalized judgment matrix. The purpose of the normalized judgment matrix is to ensure that the sum of the elements in each column equals 1. Lastly, sum each row in the normalized matrix and then divide each row sum by the number of evaluation criteria, which is 5, to obtain the weight for each

Table 3 Judgment matrix for wayfinding evaluation criteria

Criteria	Architectur complexity	Wayfinding system usability	Understandability	Environmental friendliness	Information accessibility
Architectural complexity	1	3	5	7	9
Wayfinding system usability	1/3	1	3	5	7
Wayfinding system understandability	1/5	1/3	1	3	5
Environmental friendliness	1/7	1/5	1/3	1	3
Information accessibility	1/9	1/7	1/5	1/3	1
Sum of column	1.787	4.676	9.533	16.33	25

evaluation criterion, thus completing the normalized judgment matrix (see Table 4). According to Table 4, it can be concluded that Architectural Complexity has the most substantial influence, with a weight of 0.5028. The remaining factors are ranked in descending order of their weights as follows: Usability of the Wayfinding System at 0.2604, Understandability of the Wayfinding System at 0.1344, Environmental Friendliness at 0.0678, and Accessibility of Information at 0.0346.

Consistency Test. After completing the normalized judgment matrix, to ensure the rationality and logical coherence of our judgments, we perform a consistency test on the judgment matrix. First, we calculate the Consistency Vector (CV) by multiplying each column's values in Table 3 by the corresponding weights (from the 'Weight' column in Table 4), generating vertical vectors in columns 1–5 in Table 5. For example, the 'Architectural Complexity' column vector (1, 1/3, 1/5, 1/7, 1/9) from Table 3 by the 'Architectural Complexity' weight (0.5028) from Table 4 will generate a vertical vector in column 1 from Table 5.

Next, sum the values from the first to the fifth column for each row in Table 5 to create a 'Row Sum'. Divide the 'Row Sum' by the corresponding weight to create the Consistency Vector (CV), as in Table 5.

Lastly, calculate the Consistency Index (CI) and the Consistency Ratio (CR). CI = (λmax − n) / (n − 1), where λmax is the maximum eigenvalue of the judgment matrix (λmax is the total of the Consistency Vector column divided by the number of evaluation criteria), and n is the number of evaluation criteria (which is 5). CR = CI / RI, where RI is the Random Consistency Index, a predetermined value associated with the number of evaluation criteria (see Table 6), and because the matrix order is 5, RI is 1.12. If CR is less than 0.1, the consistency of the judgment matrix is considered acceptable.

$\lambda max = (5.45 + 5.42 + 5.19 + 5.02 + 5.13) / 5 = 5.242.$

$CI = (\lambda max - n) / (n - 1) = 5.242 - 5/5 - 1 = 0.0605.$

Table 4 Normalized judgment matrix

Criteria	Architectural complexity	Wayfinding system usability	Understandability	Environmental friendliness	Information accessibility	Weight
Architectural complexity	0.559	0.642	0.524	0.429	0.36	**0.5028**
Wayfinding system usability	0.187	0.214	0.315	0.306	0.28	**0.2604**
Wayfinding system understandability	0.112	0.071	0.105	0.184	0.20	**0.1344**
Environmental friendliness	0.080	0.043	0.035	0.061	0.12	**0.0678**
Information accessibility	0.062	0.030	0.021	0.020	0.04	**0.0346**
Sum of column	1	1	1	1	1	1

Table 5 Consistency vector

Criteria	Architectural complexity	Wayfinding system usability	Understandability	Environmental friendliness	Information accessibility	Sum of row	Weight	Consistency vector (CV)
Architectural complexity	0.5028	0.7812	0.6720	0.4746	0.3114	**2.742**	**0.5028**	**5.45**
Wayfinding system usability	0.1659	0.2604	0.4032	0.3390	0.2422	**1.4107**	**0.2604**	**5.42**
Wayfinding system understandability	0.0106	0.0868	0.1344	0.2034	0.1730	**0.6981**	**0.1344**	**5.19**
Environmental friendliness	0.0718	0.0521	0.0448	0.0678	0.1038	**0.3403**	**0.0678**	**5.02**
Information accessibility	0.0553	0.0372	0.0269	0.0226	0.0346	**0.1776**	**0.0346**	**5.13**

Table 6 Average random consistency index RI standard

Matrix order	1	2	3	4	5	6	7	8	9	10
RI	0	0	0.58	0.90	1.12	1.24	1.32	1.41	1.45	1.49

$CR = CI / RI = 0.0605/1.12 = 0.054 < 0.1.$

In this thesis, the Analytic Hierarchy Process (AHP) is applied based on a comprehensive review of literature or expert opinions to hypothesize the necessary evaluation criteria and their levels of importance. Through the construction of a judgment matrix, normalization of the judgment matrix, and consistency testing, the consistency and reliability of these weights are verified. The successful passage of these tests demonstrates that, although these weights are established based on hypothetical evaluation criteria, they maintain logical consistency and can serve as a foundation for decision-making, providing a quantitative analysis basis for subsequent research. Furthermore, this study will continue to collect data through qualitative methods such as field surveys, wayfinding tests, and in-depth interviews to further validate the applicability and accuracy of these theoretical assumptions in real-world wayfinding experiences.

3.4 Data Collection and Analysis

Through a variety of qualitative research methods, such as on-site surveys, wayfinding tests, and interviews, empirical data on the wayfinding experiences of elderly users in hospital environments was collected. The purpose of this phase is to verify and refine the evaluation standard weights previously derived from the Analytic Hierarchy Process (AHP), and to further explore the key factors affecting the wayfinding experience of elderly users. By combining quantitative analysis with qualitative observation, this section aims to provide a comprehensive perspective, thereby gaining a deeper understanding of the wayfinding challenges encountered by elderly users in hospital environments and laying a solid foundation for subsequent improvement recommendations and design guidelines based on empirical data.

On-site surveys. Field research was conducted at Tianjin Medical University General Hospital. Following the previously mentioned criteria, the content of the field research focused on two main classification dimensions: horizontally, it included architectural structure, environmental features, and wayfinding systems. Vertically, it was divided into the usability, understandability, accessibility, friendliness, and safety of the wayfinding system.

The analysis of building structure primarily focuses on its internal construction, layout, and spatial design, including corridors, staircases, and rooms (see Fig. 2). Environmental features mainly encompass the hygiene and lighting, facilities conditions within and around the hospital premises (see Fig. 2). The study of way-finding systems primarily revolves around signage, wayfinding signs, maps, promotional materials, and advertisements (see Fig. 2). Detailed analyses are presented in Tables 7 and 8. Based on on-site research and observation, the preliminary assessment indicates that the most significant factors affecting the wayfinding experience for elderly individuals are the complexity of the architectural structure and the usability and understandability of the wayfinding system.

Wayfinding test. To ensure the accuracy of the research results, we designed a wayfinding test. The participants consisted of three groups of elderly individuals, with two participants in each group, aged on average 63 years, 69 years, and 78 years, respectively. All these elderly participants were first-time visitors to Tianjin Medical University General Hospital. The task involved navigating from the hospital entrance (outdoors) to the Geriatrics Department (internal medicine for the elderly). Each group of participants was informed of the starting and ending points of the task before beginning and was required to find the destination independently without any assistance. Additionally, each group was accompanied by an observer responsible for documenting the participants' behaviors and reactions during the wayfinding process, particularly noting any difficulties encountered or instances of getting lost. The observer recorded the participants' walking paths, dwell times, and any signs of confusion or anxiety displayed during the wayfinding task. In this experiment, the three groups departed at 8:30 a.m. (Group 1), 11:00 a.m. (Group 2), and 2:30 p.m. (Group 3), respectively. For Group 1, the two participants set off five minutes apart, while the participants in the other two groups departed simultaneously. The experimental data and observation results are presented in Table 9.

Analysis of wayfinding test results. In the wayfinding experiment conducted with three groups of elderly users, distinct behavior patterns and wayfinding abilities were observed. During the experiment at 8:30 a.m., participants A and B from Group 1 demonstrated high wayfinding efficiency in a relatively quiet hospital environment. Participant A completed the task smoothly, without getting lost or pausing, showcasing excellent spatial orientation skills; Participant B hesitated slightly and got a

Fig. 2 Hospital internal architectural structure, environment and wayfinding system

Table 7 Analysis of integrated factors affecting wayfinding experience (horizontally)

Domains or types	Content of analysis		Impact on the wayfinding experience
Architectural structure	Layout configuration	Tianjin Medical University General Hospital is divided into five independent buildings based on functionality: outpatient building, emergency building, and first, second, and third inpatient buildings. The complex architectural structure features asymmetrical spatial shapes, a high number of rooms, and corridors of various shapes, including straight, L-shaped, T-shaped, and circular	Orientation challenge, cognitive memory load, confusion in pathways, mobility obstacles, decision-making fatigue, longer wayfinding times. Significantly
Environmental features	Lighting	The indoor space is vast, making it difficult to utilize natural light for illuminating functional areas. The main source of illumination is provided by overhead fluorescent lamps, supplemented by the internal lighting of signage. The light intensity is relatively weak, leading to insufficient illumination	Decreased sense of direction perception, decreased sense of direction perception, difficulty and slowness in decision-making process
	Hygienic	The internal cleanliness is good, with moderate hygiene overall. However, the indoor air circulation is weak, and the facilities are old, with building materials showing slight signs of aging	The impact is weak

(continued)

Table 7 (continued)

Domains or types	Content of analysis			Impact on the wayfinding experience
	Facilities		Medical, hygiene, safety, and convenient service facilities are complete and well-maintained, relatively clean, but the surfaces of the facilities appear slightly outdated, and although functional, they lack human-centered design	Hardly affects their wayfinding abilities
Wayfinding systems	Static wayfinding information	Signage	The signage system has undergone noticeable modifications and patches over time. While the hierarchy of signs is clear, the styles are varied and inconsistent. The color contrast is strong, but there is inconsistency in text styles, and an excess of professional terminology	Cognitive memory load, decisions are prone to confusion, increasing the complexity and uncertainty of wayfinding, thereby reducing wayfinding efficiency. The impact is strong
		Maps	The map is based on a structural diagram of the building, complete and clear lines, but for the function of wayfinding, the information is incomplete, the functionality is very weak, the map for the main entrances, exits, key facilities, navigation routes are not labeled	

(continued)

Table 7 (continued)

Domains or types	Content of analysis			Impact on the wayfinding experience
		Promotional materials	In the corridors, there are often promotional materials disseminating medical knowledge. However, the design styles of these materials are inconsistent, and their sizes and installation positions vary, leading to visual and spatial clutter	
	Digital wayfinding information	Mobile app	Users can scan a QR code to access navigation services without needing to download a separate app, making it quick and convenient. Once opened, the app can activate GPS and indoor positioning systems, offering digital maps and route planning with real-time updates and navigation instructions. The app is fully functional and user-friendly but lacks a version specifically designed for the elderly	The usage of digital wayfinding systems among elderly individuals varydepending on individual differences

bit lost when faced with unclear destination information but quickly took proactive steps by asking the staff for assistance and successfully found the way. This reflects the importance of confidence and actively seeking help in enhancing wayfinding efficiency.

Participants C and D from Group 2 faced more challenges during the wayfinding test at 11 a.m. Both experienced intermittent pauses and instances of getting lost. This time is typically busier in hospitals, with increased foot traffic, including visitors, medical staff, and other patients. This surge in people not only causes congestion in corridors and common areas but may also raise noise levels, adding external distractions that can hinder elderly users' spatial wayfinding. Participant D showed significant anxiety and hesitation when looking for signs and landmarks, suggesting that the added visual and auditory distractions in a complex environment could exacerbate wayfinding difficulties, especially among older adults whose cognitive functions may have begun to decline. This observation suggests that as age increases, elderly users may become more dependent on environmental cues, highlighting the importance of providing clear and easily recognizable wayfinding information for elderly users.

Table 8 Analysis of integrated factors affecting wayfinding experience (vertically)

Various aspects	Content of analysis		Impact on the wayfinding experience
Usability	The layout of signage	Indoor signage: clear layout, easy understanding. Outdoor signage: aging appearance, visible damage, hollow-style text, difficult identification. Weaker usability compared to indoor signage	This may increase the cognitive load on older users during wayfinding and decision making
	Interactivity	Visual interaction, perceptual interaction, operational interaction	
	Feedback mechanism	Confirmation feedback: confirming whether the information provided on the wayfinding sign matches their expected or needed information	
Comprehensibility	Navigation information	The map information is not clear and the use of excessive terminology and lack of use of graphics in the wayfinding information detracts from understanding	Prone to making poor wayfinding decisions
Accessibility	Facility accessibility	There are numerous accessible facilities set up at stair corners, but there are hardly any wayfinding facilities specifically designed for elderly and disabled individuals	Difficulty in mobility and increased risk of accidents
	Route planning	The route planning fails to meet the needs of different users	

(continued)

Table 8 (continued)

Various aspects	Content of analysis		Impact on the wayfinding experience
User-friendliness	User experience	Able to accomplish basic wayfinding tasks, but there may be instances of decision hesitation or confusion during the process	Hesitation and confusion may cause anxiety in the elderly, but proactive service boosts trust. Yet, it might hinder staff efficiency
	Service attitude	The hospital staff was responding to inquiries for directions individually	
Safety	Navigation safety	The wayfinding system can guide users safely to their destinations, but there are instances of elderly users deviating from designated paths	The provision of safety features facilitates more confident and secure wayfinding decisions among elderly users
	Environmental safety	The wayfinding system provides safety cues and warnings about the surroundings. Handrails and resting seats are installed in the corridors to assist elderly users in avoiding accidents	

The performance of Participants E and F in Group 3 further reinforced this finding. Although they took the wayfinding test together at 2:30 p.m., a time when foot traffic slightly decreases compared to 11 a.m., both exhibited a marked tendency to get lost and prolonged periods of pausing. Participant E showed intense anxiety and frequently sought help from others, indicating a high level of external dependence. In contrast, Participant F relied heavily on E's wayfinding actions, showing less initiative and acting more as a follower. This phenomenon reveals the potential decline in independent wayfinding ability and the increased need for interpersonal assistance or environmental support among older elderly users.

Overall, the test results highlight the impact of ageing on the wayfinding abilities of older users and the importance of providing them with appropriate support in complex environments.

Interview. To further explore the details behind these findings and understand the real experiences and needs of elderly users, we conducted one-on-one interviews with participants of the wayfinding test. The interviews were semi-structured, lasting approximately 8–10 min, with the questions outlined in Table 10. The focus of the

Table 9 The experimental data and observational results

Groups 1	Participant A	Participant B
Age	62	64
Time spent on tasks	5 min	6 min
Difficulty or getting lost	×	×
Duration of pauses	×	25 s
Number of mistakes	0	0
Walking path	Hospital entrance. Cross the street. Second inpatient department. Second floor of the second inpatient department. Healthcare medical department	Hospital entrance. Enter the outpatient hall. Exit the outpatient hall. Cross the street. Second inpatient department. Second floor of the second inpatient department. Healthcare medical department
Behavior or reactions	Without displaying anxiety, the individual directly approached the staff for directions, received precise information, and proceeded to the destination, periodically verifying the route with the wayfinding signage encountered along the way	Mild anxiety, looks for the guide sign first, hesitates slightly when he realizes there is no destination information, and walks quickly towards the staff member to make inquiries
Groups 2	Participant C	Participant D
Age	68	70
Time spent on tasks	7 min	7 min 25 s
Difficulty or getting lost	√	√
Duration of pauses	30 s	40 s
Number of mistakes	1	0
Walking path	Hospital entrance. Enter the outpatient hall. Information desk. Exit the outpatient hall. Cross the street. Second inpatient department. Second floor of the second inpatient department. Healthcare medical department	Hospital entrance. Enter the outpatient hall. Long hallway. Information desk. Exit the outpatient hall. Cross the street. Second inpatient department. Second floor of the second inpatient department. Healthcare medical department
Behavior or reactions	Mild anxiety, repeats walking past previous routes, asks staff halfway through, misses exit	Moderate anxiety, occasionally stopping to look around for guide signs or landmarks, asking staff midway through, tone of voice anxious
Groups 3	Participant E	Participant F

(continued)

Table 9 (continued)

Groups 1	Participant A	Participant B
Age	75	81
Time spent on tasks	8 min 10 s	8 min 10s
Difficulty or getting lost	√	√
Duration of pauses	1min 20 s	1min 20 s
Number of mistakes	3	3
Walking path	E and F departed together, companions on the route. Hospital entrance. Entered the outpatient hall. Traversed two corridors. Information desk. Exited the outpatient hall. Crossed the parking lot and street second inpatient department. Second floor of the second inpatient department. Healthcare medical department	
Behavior or reactions	E exhibited severe anxiety, frequently pausing to survey the surroundings, displaying passive behavior as if awaiting assistance. E engaged often in interactions with passersby and staff, seeking help with high frequency and making errors often. F, being advanced in age, relied on E's actions, showing limited initiative, and acting more as a follower	

interviews was on their experiences during the navigation process, the obstacles encountered, and specific feedback on the environment.

Following interviews with participants, we garnered a wealth of insightful feedback, highlighting the common experiences and needs of elderly users within the hospital environment. Participants A and B specifically emphasized the crucial role of clear signage and intuitive layouts in enhancing wayfinding efficiency, agreeing on the importance of actively seeking help in uncertain situations. B also mentioned that some wayfinding signs with department names were difficult to understand, and sometimes lacked the necessary information. C and D expressed an increased reliance on the wayfinding system in scenarios of high foot traffic and noise, noting that it

Table 10 Interview questions

Q. no	Questions
Q1	In today's wayfinding test, did you find it easy to locate your destination?
Q2	During your journey through different areas of the hospital, which layout features affected your wayfinding experience?
Q3	How did you utilize the hospital's wayfinding system (signage) in today's navigation process? Please describe whether they were helpful or if there's room for improvement
Q4	Did you encounter any signage that were difficult to understand or recognize?
Q5	In what areas do you think the hospital could improve to make wayfinding easier for you and other elderly users like yourself?

was sometimes challenging to locate the next sign, and certain signs were confusingly designed, mistakenly leading them to think an emergency exit was a staircase. On the other hand, E and F pointed out that the complexity of the building layout brought challenges to their independent wayfinding. The guidance system provided limited help and was prone to confusion, especially the lack of coherence between signage. And the font size of some text information is too small, which can only be recognized at a close distance, and it is difficult to see clearly from a distance. This feedback compiles the primary challenges and suggestions for improvement faced by elderly users in the complex hospital environment, underscoring the necessity of fully considering the specific needs of elderly users when designing wayfinding systems. Providing a clear structural layout, an easy-to-understand and use wayfinding system, and considering their physiological characteristics are key to enhancing their wayfinding experience in hospitals.

4 Research Result

In Chap. 3, the importance of various factors affecting the wayfinding experience of elderly users in a comprehensive hospital was quantitatively assessed through multi-criteria decision-making methods, particularly the Analytic Hierarchy Process (AHP).

Subsequently, qualitative research methods such as on-site surveys, wayfinding tests, and interviews were used to collect data, assisting in verifying the applicability and accuracy of the theoretical hypotheses of the AHP in actual wayfinding experiences.

Field research conducted at Tianjin Medical University General Hospital revealed key factors affecting the wayfinding experience of elderly users, especially the complexity of architectural structures, the usability and understandability of the wayfinding system. The wayfinding tests further demonstrated that variations in pedestrian flow and environmental changes at different times significantly affected their wayfinding efficiency and experience. Interview results deepened the understanding of the wayfinding experience of elderly users in the hospital, highlighting their need for clear signage and intuitive layouts, as well as reflecting a tendency to seek help in complex environments.

To validate the generalizability of these findings, similar research was conducted at Peking Union Medical College Hospital and Longhua Hospital Affiliated to Shanghai University of Traditional Chinese Medicine. At Peking Union Medical College Hospital, the study found that a unified, clear wayfinding system devoid of excessive promotional information significantly reduced instances of elderly users getting lost, especially during peak times. The efficient signage system mitigated the navigation complexity brought by the building structure. During interviews, most elderly users reported being able to quickly locate their destinations through the wayfinding system, with volunteers and staff displaying a positive attitude. At Longhua Hospital

Affiliated to Shanghai University of Traditional Chinese Medicine, findings indicated that although the hospital's architectural structure was not complex, the signage system was outdated, with evident modifications and patches. The variety of signage types, unclear information hierarchy, and excessive density often caused visual confusion and comprehension difficulties, adversely affecting the wayfinding experience. Interview results indicated that elderly users were more inclined to rely on hospital staff for assistance, particularly when the wayfinding system was not intuitive.

Synthesizing data from Tianjin Medical University General Hospital, Peking Union Medical College Hospital, and Longhua Hospital Affiliated to Shanghai University of Traditional Chinese Medicine, field surveys, wayfinding tests, and interviews revealed several common issues: elderly users often face challenges with architectural structure and spatial layouts, thus relying heavily on clear and wayfinding information. Crowding and noise in the environment also posed interference to the wayfinding capabilities of elderly users. These findings validate the assumptions in the AHP analysis, indicating that the pre-set weights in the construction of the judgment matrix are largely consistent with actual experience.

Design recommendations: based on the weights of importance from the Analytic Hierarchy Process, and informed by the findings from on-site surveys, wayfinding tests, and interviews, targeted recommendations are presented for improving the wayfinding system of Tianjin Medical University General Hospital. The focus areas include the complexity of the architectural structure, the usability and understandability of the wayfinding system, environmental friendliness, and the accessibility of information. Specific design suggestions are detailed in Table 11.

5 Conclusions

This study utilized Multi-Criteria Decision-Making methods, particularly the Analytic Hierarchy Process, to explore and assess the key factors affecting the wayfinding experience of elderly users in general hospitals. The research findings indicate that multi-criteria decision models can effectively evaluate the impact of various factors on elderly users' wayfinding experiences, emphasizing that the wayfinding experience results from the interaction between elderly users and multiple factors. This highlights the potential of multi-criteria decision-making methods in addressing wayfinding issues and designing wayfinding systems.

As a systematic decision analysis method, multi-criteria decision-making can handle complex relationships between multiple decision criteria or objectives, thereby meeting the needs and preferences of different user groups. This user-centered approach is not only suitable for the elderly but also considers the special needs of individuals with disabilities, providing personalized services for various user groups.

Field research, wayfinding tests, and interviews conducted at Tianjin Medical University General Hospital, Peking Union Medical College Hospital, and Longhua

Table 11 Design suggestions

Categories	Design suggestions
Architectural structure	(1) For hospital architecture, simplifying the internal structure of an existing building presents a significant challenge. It is recommended that considerations for wayfinding be integrated at the initial design stage, avoiding convoluted corridors in favor of straightforward or standard L-shaped or T-shaped layouts, which aid elderly individuals in recognizing directions and remembering routes (2) In the existing architectural structure, conspicuous landmarks should be set up at each key turning point, such as art installations, specially designed murals, or characteristic plant displays, to help the elderly understand the different areas
Wayfinding system usability	(1) Update existing signage to ensure the consistency of indoor and outdoor signage systems (including design styles, colors, fonts, and symbols) to avoid damaged or outdated signage (2) Use a sans-serif font with thicker strokes and remove the border lines from the font style (3) Increase the use of maps, graphics and symbols. Maintain the continuity of signage information and avoid information interruption
Wayfinding system understandability	(1) Place maps at entry points, ensuring they are clear and understandable. Maps should contain necessary details, such as major entrances and exits, key facilities and their designations, pathways, and your current position (2) Offer graphic wayfinding aids, like straightforward icons and charts, to help users comprehend directions more effectively (3) Textual details in the signage system should align with the descriptions provided by the staff verbally (4) Avoid technical terminology, favoring symbols and common language instead
Environmental friendliness	(1) Foster a serene and safe setting in the hospital by introducing more seating and rest zones to alleviate crowding in the hallways and improving interior lighting to minimize visual barriers (2) Enhance cleaning standards and air circulation, and update aging infrastructure to make the environment more welcoming and agreeable (3) Unify the dimensions, mounting methods, and placement of promotional graphics in the corridors to avoid visual clutter and distraction (4) Ensure the adequacy of accessibility facilities, such as ramps, elevators, and wide doorways, to accommodate the assistive tools that elderly users may use, such as wheelchairs or canes
Information accessibility	(1) Provide multimodal navigation information, integrating visual, auditory, and tactile signals, to offer various forms of wayfinding assistance. For example, use different textures on the floor or auditory cues to offer additional guidance for elderly users with limited vision or cognitive functions

Hospital Affiliated to Shanghai University of Traditional Chinese Medicine validated the applicability and accuracy of the AHP theoretical assumptions in different environments. The research results revealed that the complexity of building structures, the usability and understandability of the wayfinding systems, are critical factors affecting the wayfinding experience of elderly users. Additionally, environmental crowding and noise were found to interfere with the wayfinding ability of elderly users. These findings provide valuable references for architects, planners, and designers.

However, this study has some limitations. Firstly, there is a lack of cross-analysis with other hospitals and facilities, meaning that the research results are mainly applicable to the specific hospitals investigated. This makes the study appear somewhat narrow and limited when aiming to develop global wayfinding design guidelines. Secondly, the number of participants in the wayfinding tests was relatively small, and the observations were primarily subjective, leading to potential inaccuracies compared to instrument-based observations. Further research is needed to corroborate these findings.

Future research can expand the scope of the study to include more types and regions of hospitals, improve user characterization methods, incorporate more architectural features, and enhance data precision. Exploring multi-modal wayfinding information systems by effectively integrating visual, auditory, and tactile sensory information is also recommended. Designing and implementing these multi-modal wayfinding systems, along with studying new technologies and methods, will further enhance the wayfinding experience and overall satisfaction of elderly users in general hospitals.

References

1. Samah, Z. A., Ibrahim, N., & Amir, J. S. (2013). Translating quality care factors to quality space: design criteria for outpatient facility. Procedia-Social and Behavioral Sciences, 105, 265–272.
2. World Health Organization. (2023). Progress report on the United Nations decade of healthy ageing, 2021–2023. In Progress report on the United Nations decade of healthy ageing, 2021–2023.
3. Fan, J., & Choi, A. Y. (2023, October). Cognitive Load Theory Analysis of Medical Signage System for Seniors Based on General Hospitals in Shanghai. In International Conference on Design and Digital Communication (pp. 542–554). Cham: Springer Nature Switzerland.
4. Morag, I., Sonmez, V., Van Puyvelde, A., & Pintelon, L. (2024). Improving wayfinding in hospitals for people with diverse needs and abilities: An exploratory approach based on multi-criteria decision making. Applied Ergonomics, 114, 104149.
5. Rodrigues, R. S. Q. (2019). Healthcare Signage Design: Guidelines to support the development of signage systems centered on the users.
6. Karimi, H. A. (Ed.). (2015). Indoor wayfinding and navigation. CRC Press.
7. Thakkar, J. J. (2021). Multi-criteria decision making (Vol. 336, pp. 1–365). Singapore: Springer.
8. Mustikawati, T., Yatmo, Y. A., & Atmodiwirjo, P. (2017). Reading the visual environment: Wayfinding in healthcare facilities. Environment-Behaviour Proceedings Journal, 2(5), 169–175.
9. Feng, J., Yan, Y., Huang, M., Du, Y., Lu, Z., & Li, B. (2022). A study on the multi-attribute decision theory and methods. Procedia Computer Science, 214, 544–551.

Visual and Cultural Identity

The Relational Infrastructures of Knowledge: Inclusiveness and Innovation for Made in Italy

Pietro Pantano, Patrizia Ranzo, Arrigo Bertacchini, and Salvatore Carleo

Abstract Made in Italy represents a branded manifestation of authenticity, encompassing key sectors such as design, fashion, agrifood products, and mechanical automation. These sectors collectively form the backbone of our nation's production and embody the diverse natural and cultural heritage of Italy. This heritage is a valuable asset that requires strategic enhancement through integrated approaches, linking research, regional development, enterprises, and human capital. This chapter aims to explore how Italy's design and creativity facilitate the translation of intangible qualities, such as cultural expressions and local specialties, into tangible products. The study underscores the role of design in offering innovative solutions by addressing emerging needs and values through collaborative methodologies. In response to contemporary challenges and geopolitical instability, there is a need for new social, production, and consumption models. European values provide a crucial framework not only for environmental and social advancement but also for establishing a secure European market aligned with common goals. The chapter adopts a literature review methodology to examine how inclusivity, collaboration, and intelligent digital infrastructures can enable companies to implement models that prioritize cohesion and access to research and innovation, rather than solely focusing on profit. Key findings reveal that embracing these values and infrastructures can significantly contribute to sustainable development and market stability. The study concludes with recommendations for leveraging Italy's design expertise to foster innovative, inclusive, and sustainable economic growth.

Keywords Made in Italy · Knowledge society · Design for inclusiveness · Digital infrastructure · Digital collaboration

P. Pantano
Dipartimento di Fisica, Università della Calabria, Rende, Italia

P. Ranzo · A. Bertacchini · S. Carleo (✉)
Dipartimento di Architettura e Disegno Industriale, Università degli Studi della Campania "Luigi Vanvitelli", Aversa, Italia
e-mail: salvatore.carleo@unicampania.it

© The Author(s), under exclusive license to Springer Nature Switzerland AG 2025

D. Brandão et al. (eds.), *Perspectives on Design and Digital Communication V*, Springer Series in Design and Innovation 50, https://doi.org/10.1007/978-3-031-76156-0_6

1 Introduction: Cohesion and Competitiveness in Made in Italy

Made in Italy, with an estimated value of over 1.9 trillion dollars, stands as a significant pillar of the global economy, renowned for its quality products derived from a unique blend of heritage, creativity, and intensive research and development (Veronesi & Schiavello, 2023). The essence of Made in Italy, as articulated by Carcano and Lojacono (2019), encompasses two complementary aspects: a cultural amalgam of legacy and tradition, and the craftsmanship combined with creativity, uniqueness, and aesthetic vocation, resulting in unparalleled quality of products and services.

Italy leads Europe in the number of design companies and ranks third in earnings, highlighting the economic importance of its design sector. The fashion industry, with its complex supply chain of highly specialized small and medium-sized businesses, exemplifies the intricate nature of Italian production (Giumelli, 2016). The TAC sector (Textile, Clothing, Footwear) does not fully capture the sophisticated nature of Italian fashion, whose greatest value lies in the intersection of culture, creativity, know-how, and local territories (Ferlito, 2024). This characteristic generates a globally recognized level of quality, defining Italy's identity through its diverse natural and cultural specificities.

This chapter aims to explore how Italy's design and creativity facilitate the translation of intangible qualities, such as cultural expressions and local specialties, into tangible products. It emphasizes the role of design in providing innovative solutions by addressing emerging needs and values through collaborative methodologies. The extended supply chain, referred to as TAC+ (including sectors such as accessories, goldsmithing, eyewear, cosmetics), presents a differentiated landscape in terms of productivity levels. Despite technological disparities among enterprises, the synergy of excellent craftsmanship, advanced companies, and micro-enterprises fuels the dynamism of the Italian fashion system.

In response to contemporary challenges and geopolitical instability, there is an urgent need for new social, production, and consumption models. European values provide a crucial framework not only for environmental and social advancement but also for consolidating a secure European market aligned with shared objectives. Italy's promising data on sustainability—leading Europe in recycled waste percentage and renewable energy consumption—illustrates its commitment to environmental stewardship. The furniture sector, for example, boasts a high content of recycled materials, and the agrifood sector ranks among the top globally for organic production.

Regarding European challenges, Made in Italy reports positive data: Italy is the European country with the highest percentage of recycled waste (79% of the total) and the first in the renewable energy sector in terms of total energy consumption (18.3%); the Italian furniture sector has been at the forefront for years due to the high content of recycled materials in its products; over 95% of waste resulting from wood processing becomes raw material for the production of semi-finished products

(Source: FederlegnoArredo Research Office on UN COMTRADE data); in the agri-food sector, Italy is among the first countries in the world for the number of organic crops with 70,000 organic agricultural producers (Source: Symbola, Coldiretti elaboration on Sinab/Eurostat/FIBL-IFOAM data); our agriculture is among the most sustainable, with just 7.2% of all national emissions (Source: Symbola, Coldiretti elaboration on Eurostat 2017 data).

In terms of the data on the food and wine sector, Made in Italy products are world leaders in quality and safety, with the lowest quantity of chemical residues beyond legal limits (Source: Symbola, Bonifiche Ferraresi, Coldiretti on EFSA data).

The Italian fashion industry has increasingly embraced sustainability, driven by trade associations such as the "Manifesto sulla Sostenibilità" by the Camera Nazionale della Moda Italiana and "Viaggio verso la sostenibilità della filiera" by Sistema Moda Italia. This reflects a broader trend towards prioritizing the quality and health of people, alongside preserving territorial differences and local cultures. Italian design research has significantly contributed to addressing environmental sustainability through a systemic vision of products, processes, and services.

Given the evolving market dynamics, only those who adapt and meet new consumer expectations will thrive. This chapter will delve into the necessary social, production, and consumption models that can leverage European values to enhance the resilience and competitiveness of Made in Italy. The concept of the cohesive company, which transcends traditional growth models based on resource exploitation and immediate profits, will be explored. This model emphasizes human capital, technology sharing, and co-production models, where consumers play a central role.

In alignment with the Next Generation EU recovery plan and the Italian National Research Program (PNR) 21–27, inclusiveness in addressing social inequalities and exclusion is a crucial and cross-cutting issue alongside digital sustainability. This is because envisioning a more sustainable world necessitates addressing the access to and dissemination of knowledge required for both sustainable and digital transitions" (Ranzo & Carleo, 2024). It promotes business models oriented towards a collaborative and digital society 5.0, innovations based on human-centered philosophy, and the valorization of intellectual capital.

This chapter aims to provide a comprehensive understanding of how these values and models can be integrated to foster innovative, inclusive, and sustainable economic growth in the context of Made in Italy. To analyze these problems within the context of Made in Italy, we employ the lens of *inclusive design*. This review synthesizes existing studies on inclusive design, summarizing the current state of the field and highlighting key insights and methodologies. By examining previous research, we aim to provide a comprehensive overview of how inclusive design principles have been applied and their impact on the Italian design and manufacturing sectors.

Inclusive design is a design methodology that aims to create products, environments, and systems that are accessible and usable by as many people as possible, regardless of their age, ability, or background. This approach goes beyond traditional design paradigms by actively considering the diverse needs of the population from the outset, ensuring that the final outcomes do not inadvertently exclude any user groups

(Design Council, 2008; Clarkson et al., 2013). Inclusive design seeks to provide solutions that accommodate a wide range of abilities and preferences, promoting equality and enhancing the user experience for everyone (Keates & Clarkson, 2003). It integrates principles from Universal Design, Design for All, and similar frameworks to foster inclusivity in both the design process and the resulting products (Mace, 1985; Steinfeld & Maisel, 2012). By emphasizing empathy, user engagement, and iterative feedback, inclusive design not only addresses the needs of marginalized groups but also benefits the broader population, creating more innovative, adaptable, and effective solutions (Hanson, 2009; Lidwell et al., 2010).

Following the introduction, the second section investigates into the value of inclusiveness in the knowledge-based society, the third section examines advances and issues in the discipline of design for inclusion, and the fourth section explores the technological infrastructures supporting knowledge sharing in design.

2 The Value of Inclusiveness in the Knowledge-Based Society

2.1 The Discipline of Design for Inclusion: Advances and Issues of Interest

Building upon the literature concerning digital infrastructures and their strategic importance for facilitating shared access to knowledge, this section critically examines the concept of inclusion within knowledge-based societies, with a special focus on the 'Made in Italy' initiative. It underscores the essential role of inclusion in scientific research, particularly in contexts characterized by rich cultural and industrial heritage. Through an in-depth review of pertinent scholarly works, this discussion identifies and elaborates on key concepts, terms, and references that significantly enhance our understanding of inclusion. Additionally, the analysis highlights the strengths and challenges associated with utilizing different databases, thereby providing a detailed evaluation of the existing research landscape in this area. Social interaction and possible convergences among multiple types of individuals from different backgrounds and with different needs stimulate the movement of streams of ideas and call for the development of a more equitable and dynamic method of analysis in response to the necessary adoption of an inclusive approach in science.

An inclusive research allows, in fact, the analysis of a plurality of experiences and points of view, going to constitute fertile ground for a broader understanding of the issues to be addressed, as well as laying the foundations of a more shared, interconnected and open access knowledge. In what Rifkin calls "the age of access" (2012), the world of Made in Italy research cannot, therefore, do without strategies that facilitate the integration of ideas and propose solutions more in line with social equality.

At present, the boundless amount of knowledge contained in the countless databases queried daily by researchers potentially extends the possibilities of research to infinity. With access to such a large amount of verified information comes the need to develop new instrumentation and appropriate methods, formulated with a view to wide-ranging selection and better metabolization of sources. The realization of a methodology of knowledge inclusion can help build a "new narrative atmosphere" for Made in Italy research, that is, to open new perspectives that reflect the complexity of contemporaneity, offering new resources useful for its understanding and progress in collective terms.

Inclusive design, as a methodology, extends beyond creating accessible products to embedding inclusiveness throughout the entire research process. This paradigm is not only concerned with the final outcomes—ensuring that they are usable by people with a wide range of abilities—but also emphasizes the incorporation of diverse perspectives during the research stages themselves.

In this context, inclusive research is defined as a methodological approach that integrates the principles of Universal Design, Inclusive Design, and Design for all into the research process (Clarkson et al., 2013). It involves engaging stakeholders from different backgrounds in all phases of research—from conception and planning to execution and dissemination (Steinfeld & Maisel, 2012). The goal is to ensure that research outcomes are not only technically sound and universally accessible but also contextually relevant and responsive to the needs of a diverse population.

Our approach ensures that the process of inquiry actively includes diverse perspectives, which is crucial for addressing the "needs of the population." This holistic approach to inclusivity allows for a broader understanding of the impacts of design and helps in developing solutions that are genuinely inclusive (Keates & Clarkson, 2003).

Thus, this research employs an inclusive methodology that is both procedural and outcome-focused, tailored to the specific demands of the Made in Italy label, reflecting the principles of inclusive design at every stage. By integrating these principles, the research aligns with a comprehensive vision of inclusivity, crucial for maintaining the high standards of craftsmanship and innovation that define Made in Italy products. This approach aims to produce results that are beneficial across various user demographics, ensuring that made in Italy goods continue to meet the diverse needs and preferences of global consumers while being practical in addressing the unique challenges faced by different groups within society. By doing so, it supports the sustainability and global competitiveness of the Made in Italy brand in an increasingly interconnected and inclusive marketplace.

Inclusive knowledge design: a review of the scientific literature. In line with the concept of social inclusion that has emerged in recent decades and specifically in Europe, the need to integrate new individuals within an already structured and established social structure is based on exogenous characteristics, such as differences related to gender, territory of birth, household of origin, economic situation or ethnicity (Governo Italiano, 2021; Unione Europea, 2020; Commissione Europea, 2024).

Based on the above formulation and in order to establish the principles of developing a methodology for inclusive knowledge sharing, research queries were defined and employed in an initial analysis of the relevant scientific literature on the topic.

These research queries should be related to the elements of design-oriented scientific knowledge and the different nuances contained in the definition of social inclusion.

Twelve queries were thought of (Fig. 1) and each was used to conduct a search in three different databases—Research Gate, Google Scholar and Academia.edu—selecting a total of 36 open source scientific articles published in the period between 2020 and 2024.

These publications were examined and the analysis perpetrated on each of them showed that most (28 to be precise) address social inclusion issues while not explicitly mentioning scientific dissemination and knowledge sharing. Of greater relevance to the thesis argued in this contribution, however, are 8 other publications, from which it was possible to identify and extrapolate concepts, keywords and references in line with the theme expressed therein.

The study of these first 8 submissions made it possible to highlight additional research queries, thanks to which it will be possible to select new, more specific data

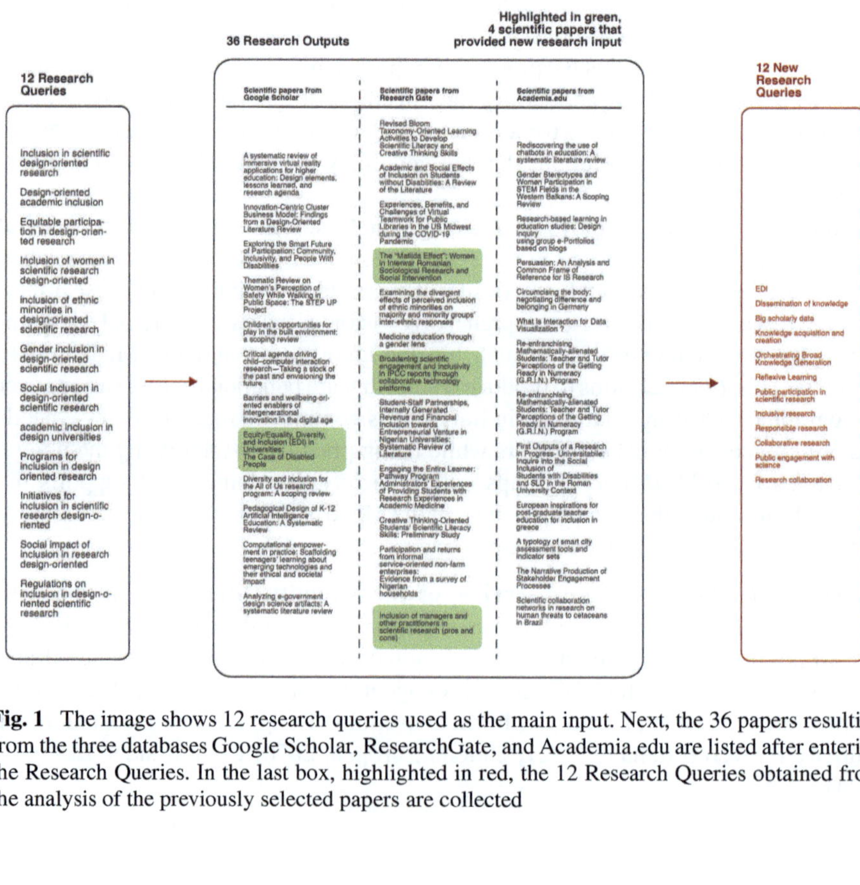

Fig. 1 The image shows 12 research queries used as the main input. Next, the 36 papers resulting from the three databases Google Scholar, ResearchGate, and Academia.edu are listed after entering the Research Queries. In the last box, highlighted in red, the 12 Research Queries obtained from the analysis of the previously selected papers are collected

relevant to the future development of research in the field of design for inclusive knowledge (Fig. 1).

Big data of scientific knowledge: quantitative analysis. The amount of academic big data (Xia et al., 2017) is growing at an ever-increasing rate, which calls for hypothesizing new approaches and processes designed specifically for analyzing such immense amounts of knowledge.

Based on the information collected, it was also possible to carry out an initial quantitative analysis of the use of the databases mentioned above. In this preliminary research phase, the positive and negative aspects derived from the use of the three selected databases were screened and, as in the table contained in Fig. 2, the comparison shows very discordant values with the same search filters entered, given the different characteristics of each bank. In fact, each makes use of its own dataset (which in turn contains a number of publications based on possible updates); each bank uses different indexing algorithms (which consequently return different outputs despite the fact that the same input is used for all databases); individual databases have their own structure and interface, thus, the possibility of using different search filters (which substantially affects the results).

The data obtained confirm the urgent need to think about new approaches to analyzing "academic big data," with a view to greater inclusion of regular and new users.

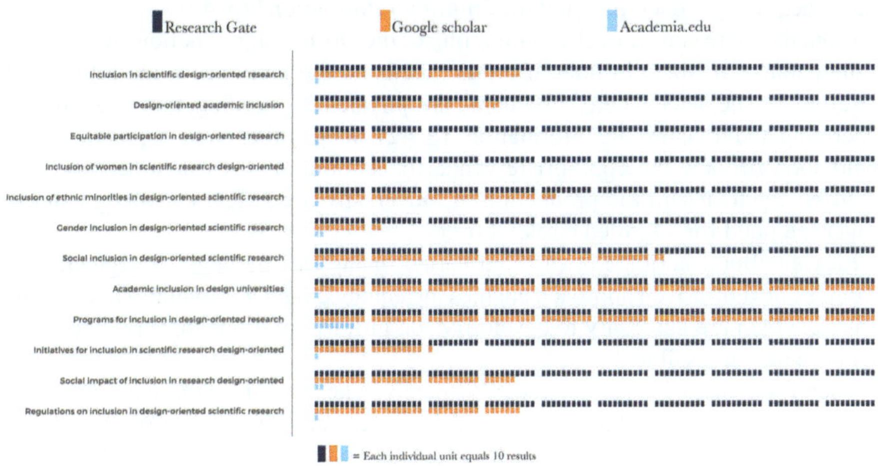

Fig. 2 In the image is a bar graph comparing the amount of results for each of the three databases: Google Scholar, ResearchGate, and Academia.edu. This comparison is made considering the same inputs entered into the respective databases

2.2 *The Value of Design for Inclusion in Contemporary Society*

In industrially advanced countries founded on the knowledge economy as Italy is for example, factors of social, gender, ethnic or economic inclusion become indispensable to the creation and sharing of knowledge: the democratization of these processes could provide an opportunity to establish an inclusive, more equitable and universally accessible knowledge society.

In contemporary society, information and knowledge take on the guise of raw material that can be manipulated and take the form of a project; however, at present the possibilities or skills in the transformation of information and knowledge are not globally widespread among individuals (Floridi, 2017, p. 96).

Vilém Flusser (1999), in his work "Shape of things: A philosophy of design" referring to the third industrial revolution, theorizes that in human history human beings also evolved through the use of different tools, and "the more complex these became, the more abstract their function became" (p. 40). Compulsory schooling, for Flusser, stems from the need to educate future workers during the 20th and 21st centuries, and the advent of AI-educated intelligent machinery suggests that the human worker will be sufficiently competent precisely as a result of such training: "this gives us a clue as to what the factories of the future will be like: school-like (p. 41). The factories of the future will be the place where "producing equal learning, that is, acquiring, generating and transmitting information" (p. 42).

From the increasingly declared mingling of the worlds of production and research in the context of Made in Italy, if on the one hand the factories of the future will, therefore, be the place where "producing is equivalent to learning, that is, acquiring, generating and transmitting information" (p. 42), on the other hand, research centers could soon become the appropriate venue for learning and research activity itself could be equated with the production of universally accessible knowledge and no longer intended for a limited circle of users.

Italy's cultural heritage is vast and varied; using this heritage strategically and through a design-driven approach enables the enhancement and evolution of creative centers, which are necessary to develop Made in Italy solutions that are innovative, inclusive and accessible.

Therefore, inclusiveness in today's society takes on an extremely significant significance in light of the processes of democratization and expanding access to knowledge itself. It is crucial to teach citizenship to take an active part in "the game of knowledge" (p. 96) so that it ceases to be merely a passive spectator.

2.3 Access to Knowledge as the Primary Value of the Knowledge Society

In recent decades, industrially advanced countries, such as Italy, have developed societies whose economy is based on the input of knowledge in all its products—material and virtual (Rifkin, 2012, p. 72).

New technologies make it possible to exponentially increase the complex knowledge generated by specialist researchers and at the same time to rework that scientific know-how into more accessible and manageable knowledge, thanks in part to the use of asynchronous and connected tools or visual outputs (De-Gol et al., 2023).

In this context, research-dependent access to knowledge is central because it facilitates the cultural advancement and mature inclusion in society of user-citizens, operationally and concretely promoting participation in public life.

Design criteria for knowledge access. The transformations of a contemporary society require a research perspective aimed at identifying solutions that can fairly establish digital and environmental transition processes. The scope of this research is inclusive and connected knowledge sharing from an Open science and Open Innovation perspective and conducted so that as many people as possible can be involved in this transition process, with the aim of reducing inequalities and promoting social inclusion.

In addition, new technologies and artificial intelligence make it possible to exponentially increase the collection and analysis of data and information as well as the production and processing of advanced forms of knowledge.

In this context, new perspectives open up for the interception of different types of target groups, which can be divided mainly into five macro-areas:

1. In-house researchers, i.e. a group of trainees, researchers and lecturers, trained on Design for Made in Italy and specialised in 5 different sub-categories inherent to the following fields: Social inclusion; Sustainable innovation of systems, products and services; Technological and digital transition; Manufacturing and new economic and Business models; Cultural heritage of Made in Italy.
2. External researchers, therefore trainees, researchers and teachers interested in sharing and expanding knowledge with the community of internal researchers, necessary to face the challenges arising from the recent change in society.
3. Companies that are part of the Made in Italy supply chain, engaged in processes of inclusion and digital and sustainable transition, and that need to be guided in the identification of emerging innovation needs or companies that need to acquire specific skills or certifications related to these areas.
4. Public administration, local authorities and institutions, which can benefit from the contents of the system so that they can then become participating actors and be able to involve a wider sphere of society in this process.
5. General users who need to have access to information regarding the content generated by the system for work or personal reasons and can also experience

learning this information through chatbots that enable them to develop conversations suited to different types of users and guide them in the use of useful information.

Research Questions for Exploring Digital Transformation in Made in Italy Industries

The following research questions have guided the investigation reported in this work:

1. **How does the integration of digital technologies enhance the competitiveness and innovation of the 'Made in Italy' sectors, particularly in design, fashion, and agrifood products?**
   - This question aims to explore the specific impacts of technologies such as Big Data, IoT, and AI on traditional Italian industries, focusing on improvements in product quality, production efficiency, and market reach.
2. **What role do collaborative and inclusive design practices play in sustaining the cultural and economic values of Made in Italy in the global market?**
   - This inquiry would assess how collaborative methodologies and inclusive design principles are being utilized to ensure that Made in Italy products continue to meet the evolving needs of global consumers while maintaining their unique cultural identity.
3. **How can digital transformation within Made in Italy sectors be managed to promote sustainable development and social inclusiveness?**
   - This question seeks to understand the strategies necessary to ensure that the adoption of digital technologies does not only drive economic growth but also contributes to a more sustainable and socially inclusive business model.
4. **What are the challenges and opportunities associated with implementing Corporate Digital Responsibility (CDR) within the Made in Italy sectors?**
   - This research would examine how Made in Italy companies address ethical concerns related to digital transformation, such as data privacy, fairness, and the avoidance of algorithmic biases, under the framework of Corporate Digital Responsibility.
5. **How does the interaction between physical and digital infrastructures enhance the educational and operational capacities of institutions involved in the Made in Italy sectors?**
   - This question investigates how the blending of physical assets and digital innovations at educational institutions and companies supports knowledge sharing, skills development, and ultimately, innovation within the Made in Italy ecosystem.

These questions aim to provide a structured approach to understanding the multifaceted impact of digital transformation on the Made in Italy sector, focusing on technological integration, cultural preservation, ethical management, and global competitiveness.

3 Technological Infrastructures for Knowledge Sharing in Design

In the dynamic realm of design, the essence of innovation, collaboration and progression is deeply intertwined with knowledge sharing and dissemination, enriched by a unique integration that is a characteristic of the Made in Italy brand. As a multifaceted discipline spanning several fields, including graphic design, industrial design and user experience design (UX), the field thrives on a continuous exchange of ideas, methodologies and creative insights. This intricate process of knowledge sharing is significantly supported by technological infrastructures, which not only act as catalysts for creative endeavours, but also as pivotal platforms for collaboration and educational growth (Kolko, 2012). In recent years, the digital revolution has profoundly transformed these infrastructures, facilitating a more continuous and extended network that allows designers to navigate and contribute to the collective intelligence of the community (Buchanan, 1992).

Added to this is the fact that the Italian approach brings with it a distinctive blend of tradition and innovation, in which the deep-rooted craftsmanship and unparalleled quality inherent in the Made in Italy brand could be perfectly integrated with modern technological advances.

Digital platforms, collaborative tools, and virtual repositories have emerged not only as essential instruments for individual designers but also as foundational elements that sustain the broader design ecosystem. These technologies enable a democratization of knowledge, making it more accessible and facilitating a culture where sharing becomes a key driver for innovation (Brown & Katz, 2009). Current platforms such as Behance and Dribble exemplify this trend by allowing designers to showcase their work and engage in feedback loops with peers, thereby fostering a community-oriented approach to design (Lockwood, 2009). Similarly, collaborative tools like Figma and Adobe XD have revolutionized the design process by enabling real-time collaboration across geographies, thereby breaking down traditional barriers to teamwork and co-creation (Friedman, 2017). The evolution of these technological infrastructures from mere tools of creation to comprehensive ecosystems for collaboration, highlights a paradigm shift towards open innovation in design (Chesbrough, 2003). Furthermore, educational platforms and open-source repositories have become invaluable resources for learning and innovation, offering access to a wide range of courses, templates, and code that support both novice and experienced designers alike (Norman & Draper, 1986). Rane (2023) explores the convergence of artificial intelligence (AI), the Internet of Things (IoT), and big data technologies within the architecture, engineering, and construction (AEC) industry.

The author emphasizes the transformative potential of integrating these leading-edge technologies to create smart and sustainable solutions across the AEC sector. However, Rane also explores the significant challenges that accompany the adoption of such advanced technologies, including issues related to data privacy, interoperability between different systems, and the need for substantial investment in infrastructure and training. The main questions that emerge are future directions for research and application that would realize the full potential of AI, IoT and big data in making industry more efficient, sustainable and responsive to societal needs. In the evolving educational landscape of the 21st century, a significant change in university infrastructure is underway, marked in particular by the transformation of universities. These institutions are no longer isolated bastions of knowledge, but are becoming shared systems where knowledge is produced, exchanged and applied beyond their physical boundaries. This transition is not just about the integration of digital platforms with traditional brick-and-mortar structures but extends to creating a symbiotic relationship between universities, the communities they serve, and the industries they connect with. The article "Redefining University Infrastructure for the 21st Century: an Interplay between Physical Assets and Digital Evolution" by BI Omodan (2024), sheds light on this reorganization. It articulates how universities are actively re-imagining their infrastructural identity to harmonize their tangible physical assets with the burgeoning realm of digital evolution. This strategic integration enhances both learning and administrative experiences, offering dynamic, flexible, and comprehensive educational encounters that transcend traditional spatial and temporal constraints. More than just facilitating a modern learning paradigm, this infrastructural metamorphosis has broader implications, notably its significant role in driving economic development. By fostering a synergistic effect between physical and digital infrastructures, universities are not only enhancing academic excellence but also positioning themselves as pivotal entities in addressing and navigating global challenges. This redefines them as resilient and forward-looking institutions, equipped to set forth an educational blueprint for the future.

The integration of physical and digital infrastructures within universities implies a transformative era. It shapes a holistic, adaptable, and enriched academic environment, poised to meet the challenges of the 21st century. This study tries to analyze the collective impact of tangible university assets and digital innovations on education and broader economic trajectories, indicating a profound shift towards shared systems of knowledge production and exchange between universities, their surrounding communities, and the interconnected web of global industries.

The comprehensive exploration of digital transformation provided by Paul et al. (2024) investigates into the profound and multi-layered impact of digital transformation across various sectors and technologies, including Internet-of-Things, social media, mobile apps, artificial intelligence including ChatGPT, augmented reality, virtual reality, and the metaverse. The study systematically examines how these digital innovations are not only reshaping consumer behavior and business models but also highlights the significant challenges and opportunities that come with their integration into everyday practices. The article stresses the importance of Corporate Digital Responsibility (CDR) in ensuring that the deployment and management of these technologies are conducted ethically, prioritizing user privacy, fairness, and the prevention of potential ethical dilemmas. It acknowledges the dynamic nature of digital transformation and its capacity to enhance operational efficiencies, customer experiences, and create new value propositions in sectors ranging from healthcare, retail, banking, and beyond. One of the key insights from this study is the evolving nature of consumer engagement facilitated by these technologies, emphasizing the shift towards more personalized, immersive, and interactive experiences. The discussion on AI and ChatGPT underscores their potential in automating and optimizing business processes, yet calls for vigilance against the risks associated with data privacy, algorithmic bias, and the ethical use of AI. The exploration of AR and VR highlights their role in creating immersive customer experiences and their potential in marketing, education, and entertainment, underscoring the need for further research on their sensory and ethical implications. Similarly, the examination of the metaverse offers a glimpse into the future of digital interactions and transactions, underlining the transformative potential of this technology in creating interconnected digital spaces.

The article champions a multidisciplinary approach to grasp the essence of digital transformation, calling for cooperation across various domains to maximize the benefits of digital technologies while minimizing their risks. The authors outline a research agenda that highlights the importance of exploring the impact of digital transformation on society, the economy, and personal well-being. They propose a strategy that seeks a balance between innovation and ethical considerations, aiming for societal benefits. Paul et al. (2024) offer a detailed overview of digital transformation's current landscape and its potential future paths. They advocate for a method that equally values technological progress, ethical integrity, responsible management, and a dedication to improving the common good. This approach aims to ensure that digital transformation acts as a force for positive change. The melding of physical and digital infrastructures in universities and other sectors marks a significant move towards more cooperative and shared systems for producing and exchanging knowledge. Such a shift not only improves academic and administrative experiences but also contributes crucially to economic growth and social advancement. In this era of digital transformation, it's essential to tackle the inherent challenges and promote a method that emphasizes both innovation and ethical, responsible management. The collective advancements in the Architecture, Engineering, and Construction (AEC) industry, educational sectors, and beyond are steering us towards a future that is both interconnected and digitally enhanced, ready to meet the needs of the 21st century. Acknowledging the Metaverse as a novel phase in the Internet revolution, powered by extended reality and artificial intelligence, the research conducted by Wang and his team in (2022) delves into its capability to enhance learning. They envision immersive, 3-D virtual worlds that merge physical and digital realities, facilitating social interactions and activities reminiscent of the real world. The research presents a theoretical framework for creating educational experiences within the Metaverse, organized around four key areas: instructional Design and Performance Technology; Knowledge; Research and Technology; Talent and Training. These sectors are aimed at improving pedagogical methods, developing content and curriculum, integrating

Metaverse technologies into education, and enhancing the skills of educators and students looking to navigate and utilize the Metaverse for educational ends.

The framework's success hinges on three critical elements, described as "wheels": infrastructure, Business Industry, and Communication; Technology Access and Equity; User Rights, Data Security, and Privacy Policy. These components are fundamental in establishing the Edu-Metaverse, ensuring equitable access to technology, and safeguarding ethical considerations and user data within the Metaverse environment.

The authors believe this detailed framework can significantly impact the ongoing research and development of Metaverse applications in education, laying the groundwork for future explorations and innovations. This effort is not just about enhancing the scholarly conversation around the Edu-Metaverse; it also aims to inspire further inquiry into the Metaverse's role in the future of education. This integration embodies a structured method for creating educational content, technologies, and skills within the Edu-Metaverse. It focuses on sparking innovation and ensuring that education through the Metaverse is equitable, secure, and accessible.

The backbone of this shared infrastructure is represented in Fig. 3.

However, navigating this evolution presents its own set of challenges, such as issues surrounding intellectual property, data privacy, and the digital divide. These

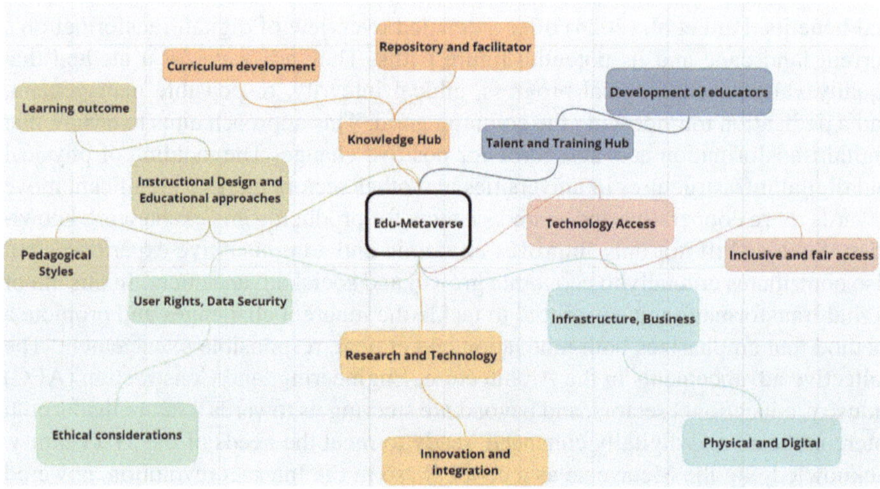

Fig. 3 This diagram visualizes a comprehensive framework for creating educational experiences in the Metaverse, organized around four main hubs: instructional design and performance technology, knowledge, research and technology, and talent and training. These hubs are supported by three essential components or "wheels": infrastructure, business industry, and communication; technology access and equity; and user rights, data security, and privacy policy. Together, they form a structured approach to developing educational content, technologies, and skills within the Edu-Metaverse, aiming to foster innovation and ensure equitable, secure access to Metaverse-based education

are hurdles that the design community and others venturing into digital transformation must address to maintain these technological infrastructures as inclusive and equitable platforms for sharing knowledge. Despite these obstacles, the potential for future advancement is considerable, especially with the integration of artificial intelligence and machine learning. These technologies promise to elevate collaborative creativity and knowledge discovery within the design realm and beyond.

4 Conclusions

In conclusion, this article has examined the critical role of inclusivity within the framework of Made in Italy, particularly in relation to the integration of digital infrastructures and their impact on knowledge-based societies. We have explored how digital advancements facilitate shared access to knowledge, promoting collaborative and inclusive growth across various sectors integral to the Made in Italy label. Our review of the relevant literature has highlighted essential concepts and challenges, emphasizing the necessity for inclusive approaches in scientific research and industry practices.

As Made in Italy continues to evolve in the face of technological advancements and global market demands, it becomes increasingly important to ensure that these innovations are implemented in ways that respect and enhance social and cultural inclusivity. The findings suggest that embracing these values not only contributes to sustainable development but also strengthens the competitive edge of Italian industries on the global stage.

Future research should continue to focus on refining digital and inclusive strategies, ensuring that the growth of the Made in Italy sectors remains aligned with both ethical considerations and the principal goal of universal accessibility. This will not only strengthen the reputation of Italian products but will also ensure that innovation and tradition blend to create a more rightful and wealthy society.

References

Brown, T., & Katz, B. (2009). *Change by design: How design thinking transforms organizations and inspires innovation.* Harper Business.

Buchanan, R. (1992). *Wicked problems in design thinking.* Design Issues, 8(2), 5–21.

Carcano, L., & Lojacono, G. (2019). *Made in Italy Industries: Managerial issues and best practices.* EGEA spa.

Chesbrough, H. (2003). *Open innovation: The new imperative for creating and profiting from technology.* Harvard Business Press.

Clarkson, J., Coleman, R., Keates, S., & Lebbon, C. (2013). *Inclusive Design: Design for the Whole Population.* Springer.

De-Gol, A. J., Le Quéré, C., Smith, A. J., & Aubin Le Quéré, M. (2023). Broadening scientific engagement and inclusivity in IPCC reports through collaborative technology platforms. *NPJ Climate Action, 2*(1), 49.

Design Council. (2008). *The principles of inclusive design (they include you).* London: Design Council.
European Commission. (2024). *Horizon Europe. 2024 General Guide.*
Ferlito, R. (2024). Industry 4.0 and sustainability: the case of the Italian textile district of Prato. *Competitiveness Review: An International Business Journal.*
Floridi, L. (2017). *La quarta rivoluzione: come l'infosfera sta trasformando il mondo.* Raffaello Cortina Editore.
Flusser, V. (1999). Shape of things: A philosophy of design. Reaktion Books.
Friedman, K. (2017). Theory construction in design research: Criteria, approaches, and methods. *Design Studies, 24*(6), 507–522.
Giumelli, E. (2016). The Meaning of the Made in Italy Changes in a Changing World. *Italian Sociological Review, 6* (2), 241–263.
Governo italiano. (2021). *Piano nazionale di ripresa e resilienza.* Ministero dell'Economia e delle Finanze.
Hanson, V. L. (2009). Age and Web access: The next generation. In Proceedings of the 2009 International Cross-Disciplinary Conference on Web Accessibility (W4A) (pp. 7–15).
Keates, S., & Clarkson, P. J. (2003). *Countering Design Exclusion: An Introduction to Inclusive Design.* Springer.
Kolko, J. (2012). *Wicked problems: Problems worth solving.* AC4D.
Lidwell, W., Holden, K., & Butler, J. (2010). *Universal Principles of Design.* Rockport Publishers.
Lockwood, T. (2009). Design Thinking: Integrating Innovation, Customer Experience, and Brand Value.
Mace, R. (1985). *Universal Design: Barrier-Free Environments for Everyone.* Designers West.
Norman, D. A., & Draper, S. W. (1986). *User centered system design: New perspectives on human-computer interaction.* Lawrence Erlbaum Associates.
Omodan, B. I. (2024). Redefining university infrastructure for the 21st century: An interplay between physical assets and digital evolution. *Journal of Infrastructure, Policy and Development, 8*(4).
Paul, J., Ueno, A., Dennis, C., Alamanos, E., Curtis, L., Foroudi, P., Kacprzak, A., Kunz, W., H., Liu, J., Marvi, R., Sreekumaran Nair, S., L., Ozdemir, O., Pantano, E., Papadopoulos, T., Petit, O., Tyagi, S., & Wirtz, J. (2024). Digital transformation: A multidisciplinary perspective and future research agenda. *International Journal of Consumer Studies, 48*(2), e13015.
Rane, N. (2023). Integrating leading-edge artificial intelligence (AI), internet of things (IOT), and big data technologies for smart and sustainable architecture, engineering, and construction (AEC) industry: Challenges and future directions. *Engineering and Construction (AEC) Industry: Challenges and Future Directions* (September 24, 2023).
Ranzo, P., & Carleo, S. (2024). Inclusiveness of Knowledge and Knowledge for Inclusiveness. Collaborative Digital Technology for Made in Italy. In: Martins, N., Brandão, D. (eds) Advances in Design and Digital Communication IV. DIGICOM 2023. Springer Series in Design and Innovation, vol. 35. Springer, Cham. https://doi.org/10.1007/978-3-031-47281-7_50
Rifkin, J. (2012). *L'era dell'accesso: "la" rivoluzione della new economy.* Arnoldo Mondadori Editore.
Steinfeld, E., & Maisel, J. (2012). *Universal Design: Creating Inclusive Environments.* Wiley.
Unione Europea. (2020). *NextGenerationEU.*
Veronesi, V., & Schiavello, M. (2023). *The Evolution of Made in Italy.* Springer Books.
Wang, M., Yu, H., Bell, Z., & Chu, X. (2022). Constructing an edu-metaverse ecosystem: A new and innovative framework. *IEEE Transactions on Learning Technologies, 15*(6), 685–696.
Xia, F., Wang, W., Bekele, T. M., & Liu, H. (2017). Big scholarly data: a survey. *IEEE Trans. Big Data 3,* 18–35.

Macau Cultural Tapestry: Unravelling a City's Visual Identity Through Its Patterns and Textures—*Digital Archive and Mapping*

Filipa Martins de Abreu, Mamadú Seck, Francisco Vizeu Pinheiro, and Gérald Estadieu

Abstract Cities present different personalities influenced by their physical and cultural characteristics, which work together to shape their identity. In this research project, we investigate a city's identity through its visual and tactile components, examining how they are indissolubly linked to the urban environment. To address the research objectives, we are mapping the city's textures and patterns, placing them within a visual terminology and identity framework, allowing us to delve into the visual character and its relationship with the urban environment, as well as how these patterns influence people's interactions and the significance of their impact. To preserve the city's visual character, we are documenting and categorising textures and patterns that are being corroded and some lost by the urban growth and development and the passage of time. To ensure that this data is accessible to all, we are developing a digital archive/repository that will include a variety of photography types, videos, vectorised images, icons, swatch libraries, texture and pattern libraries, keywords, historical information, of the various infrastructures, and a physical artefacts library for our students, professors, and the local community to use. These textures and patterns may be used to create prototypes and designs for the city's visual identity and cultural heritage. We seek to emphasise the significance of the city's visual identity in the greater cultural context while also categorising and conserving it through digital archiving and producing visual elements.

Keywords Macau · Preservation · Heritage · Patterns · Textures · Mapping · Digital archive/repository · Cultural · Interaction · Tactile · Visual and identity

F. M. de Abreu (✉) · M. Seck · F. V. Pinheiro · G. Estadieu
University of Saint Joseph, Macao, China
e-mail: filipa.martins@usj.edu.mo

M. Seck
e-mail: mamadu.seck@usj.edu.mo

F. V. Pinheiro
e-mail: francisco.pinheiro@usj.edu.mo

G. Estadieu
e-mail: gestadieu@usj.edu.mo

© The Author(s), under exclusive license to Springer Nature Switzerland AG 2025

D. Brandão et al. (eds.), *Perspectives on Design and Digital Communication V*, Springer Series in Design and Innovation 50, https://doi.org/10.1007/978-3-031-76156-0_7

1 Introduction

1.1 Background

We will begin this paper by discussing the title briefly: "*Macau Cultural Tapestry: Unravelling a City's Visual Identity through its Patterns and Textures—Digital Archive and Mapping*" mentions that the term "cultural tapestry" is used metaphorically for Macau's richness and intricate urban environment. Like a tapestry, the city is woven from many threads, while the cultural tapestry is formed from diverse traditions, religions, languages, and artistic expressions that define the city's surroundings. The concept of a cultural tapestry refers to how the city's culture is interlaced with many influences. Unravelling denotes discovering or deconstructing, for example, the city's visual identity. We're looking into the city's tapestry threads and the relation between the visual identity and its overall aesthetic character. The patterns and textures are the distinctive visual aspects that define the city's look and feel.

As a former Portuguese territory, the urban fabric of Macau breathes life into the city's identity, infusing it with a rich blend of history and a rich tapestry of diverse cultural influences. It encompasses the layout, organisation, and spatial arrangement of streets, squares, parks, and buildings, each element playing its part in shaping the city's unique character and evoking a palpable sense of place. Like an artist's canvas, the urban fabric serves as a medium for the city to express itself through a symphony of textures, patterns, colours, and visual language, creating a truly immersive experience for residents and visitors [1, 2].

The "Historical Spaces in Macao" was a foundation for the genesis of this research, the book focuses on the historical spaces that created Macau's identity, and it discusses the city's architectural past via rigorous study and clever analysis, revealing the hidden stories buried inside its ancient structures and landmarks. It provides a comprehensive explanation of Macau's rich cultural history [3], which includes great colonial architecture and religious temples. The authors describe the physical areas and investigate their social, political, and cultural significance, giving light on Macau's history and its long-lasting impact on the city's current identity.

Various identity aspects of the city of Macau focus on its visual patterns, textures, rich typography, culture, architecture, urban spaces, and the compelling interplay of East meets West. This study aims to unravel the rich tapestry embodying Macau's unique culture and colonial heritage. The fusion of Chinese, Portuguese, and European architectural styles has provided Macau with a distinctive visual identity. The intricate ornamentation of Chinese temples coexists harmoniously with the so-called colonial charm of Portuguese buildings, e.g. churches, official buildings, and heritage sites, creating a balance of Eastern and Western aesthetics. This architectural dialogue between cultures weaves the city's past and present, reinforcing Macau's identity as a cultural crossroads.

Chinese Calligraphy and Roman letters contribute to the visual language of Macau, serving as powerful tools for cultural expression, as seen in (Fig. 1). The presence of Chinese (Traditional writing) and Portuguese languages in signage, shop

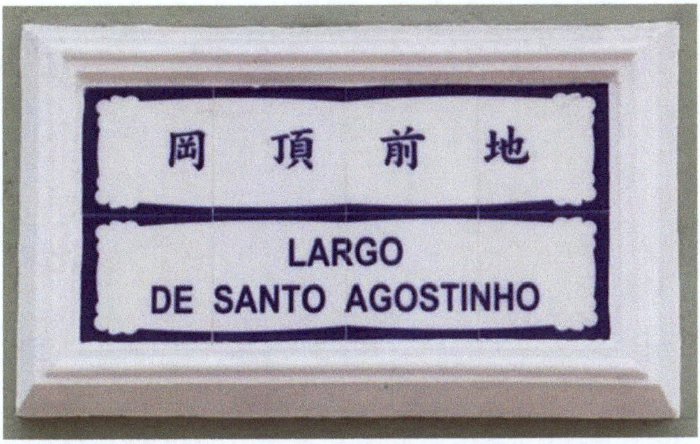

Fig. 1 Signage "Largo de Santo Agostinho", photo taken by the authors

names, and official documents reflects Macau's linguistic diversity. The contrast of these languages in typography creates a visually compelling landscape, symbolising the city's social equilibrium of two distinct cultural identities.

Macau's visual identity [4] combines Eastern and Western aspects, enticing visitors and promoting cultural exchange. The city's visual language, which combines Eastern and Western features, is a key to attracting tourists and gaining international recognition. The "East meets West' culture, or Hybrid Culture [5], is critical to defining Macau's identity. The notion of city branding and identity is crucial to Macau's positioning as a worldwide cultural hub [6].

The patterns of Chinese pottery and the vivid Portuguese tiles covering territorial structures provide a sophisticated tapestry of visual language representing the confluence of hybrid aesthetics. These patterns adorn the architectural elements and serve as tangible expressions of Macau's history and cultural identity. The patterns and textures create a captivating visual tapestry that reflects the city's Portuguese and Chinese origins. Walking through Macau's streets reveals many patterns and textures that reflect the story of the city's cultural fusion and historical past, and these patterns usually include geometric shapes and floral themes that convey elegance and nostalgia. The Portuguese tiles, Azulejos, [7] adorn the buildings, indicating the city's Portuguese influence, as seen in (Fig. 2), which create stunning mosaics to beautify the streets, evoking Macau's colonial history.

In contrast, Macau's Chinese (mostly Traditional Chinese writing) past is reflected in the bright patterns and textures of Chinese architecture and cultural items. Temples, shrines, and traditional Chinese architecture feature elaborate natural motifs such as dragons, phoenixes, and lotus blossoms. These intricate designs reflect Chinese culture's deep-rooted spiritual beliefs, folklore, and symbolism. They establish a visual language that tells the story of the city's relationship to its Chinese roots and the long-standing traditions that define its identity, and the contrast of Macau's colonial and Chinese patterns and textures produces a visual dialogue that elegantly

Fig. 2 Azulejos—"Largo da Sé" photo taken by the authors

integrates various cultural influences. Walking across the city, one can see the subtle integration of these many aesthetic languages, which reveals a distinct visual character. The patterns and textures connect Macau's ancient legacy to its modern landscape. Beyond the architectural facades, its traditional crafts and textiles reflect the patterns and textures.

The intricate embroidered fabrics, woven tapestries, and delicate porcelain are embellished with national pride and skill motifs. These ancient arts and crafts demonstrate the ability and knowledge passed down through generations, reinforcing Macau's cultural history and preserving its visual tradition.

To summarise, Macau's patterns and textures closely incorporate the city's colonial and Chinese past; these elaborate tiles and ornamental motifs of Portuguese buildings blend with the bright patterns of Chinese architecture, resulting in a visual symphony celebrating Macau's cultural fusion [8]. These patterns and textures add to the city's picturesque qualities and serve as powerful visual narrative tools, capturing the spirit of the city's abundant history, culture, and distinct, distinctive cultural identity. The eroded façades of historic buildings, the clean surfaces of modern architecture, and the rough textures of cobblestone streets all contribute depth and tactile richness to the urban experience. Patterns, ranging from elaborate ornamentation [9] on façades to recurring windows and door groups, enhance visual attractiveness while expressing cultural histories. Vibrant or subdued colours evoke emotions and reflect a city's cultural and environmental context [10].

1.2 Significance

Macau's visual identity holds great significance. Macau's visual language, patterns, and textures are indicators of its historical fusion and cultural legacy. By researching the city's unique patterns, textures, and design elements, we may appreciate the artistic expressions and artistry profoundly ingrained in its infrastructure, urban areas, and cultural artefacts. To understand a city's nature as a cultural bridge between East and West, we should examine the cultural importance and fusion of Eastern and Western characteristics represented in its roots. In addition to strengthening our understanding of Macau's history, exploring its visual identity allows us to understand better the concepts of city branding, cross-cultural engagement, and the preservation of cultural assets in a global context.

1.3 Objectives

A city's visual identity, the intricate interactions of textures, patterns, colours, and signage, reflects its historical heritage and gives it its unique character. Macau is not an exception to this phenomenon, given the diversity of its cultures. However, structures need to be preserved, and some are being demolished as regions grow. Our research project focuses on Macau's visual identity through photography, vector drawings and historical research, evaluating patterns and textures throughout the territory to understand the relevance of the infrastructure (e.g. our starting point was religious infrastructures since we wanted to start with Macau's religious influences) features allows us to examine their role in developing the city's historical and cultural legacy, as well as impacting the local community's perception of and interaction with the built environment.

A. Mapping Macau's Visual Identity: Thoroughly understand Macau's historical legacy and cultural manifestations by going into the city's visual identity by examining its textures, patterns, colours, and signage.
B. Preservation and Documentation: Our study aims to organise and maintain the textures and patterns in the visuals that are frequently ignored over time. Through data collection, analysis, classification, and storage, we aim to build an open-access file system to enable these patterns and textures across various design fields.
C. Role of Textures and Patterns in Promoting the City: It is important to understand Macau's visual marketing and cultural representation, which can be gained by looking into textures and regional patterns' role in advertising the city and its history.
D. Local Community Interaction and Perception: Understanding how pattern and texture design influences the local community and how they perceive and interact with it is essential for a user-centred design approach.

E. Identity and Visual Culture: To learn how Macau's patterns and textures contribute to its particular character and feeling of place by investigating and analysing the city's identity and visual culture.

By meeting these objectives, our study hopes to build a diverse and valuable resource that celebrates Macau's creative past while providing inspiration and information for many artistic activities, encouraging a fresh appreciation for the cultural heritage while also promoting the creation of new creative initiatives that contribute to the city's preservation and renewal by preserving and revitalising its distinct identity.

2 Theoretical Framework

2.1 Unveiling the City's Narrative—Understanding Visual Identity

The visible characteristics that shape how a city is seen and represented are called its "visual identity" and compile all aspects of a location's visual language, such as colours, textures, patterns, typography, and signs. A city's visual identity is essential in urban planning because it creates a distinct sense of place and fosters connections between the city, its residents, and visitors. These visual features are structured and built using design principles, ensuring uniformity, harmony, and meaningful representation within the urban fabric. Lynch's "The Image of the City" looks at urban vision and mental maps, arguing that people's perceptions of cities are affected by their interactions with the urban environment; his theories [11] highlight the significance of identity, coherence, and intelligibility in producing gratifying urban experiences and developing a sense of place[12], considerably influencing planning and urban design.

A city's visual identity is the sum of its perceptive characteristics that have specific elements: Colours—Palette reflecting historical influences, cultural preferences, and emotional associations; Textures—Materiality of the buildings, natural elements, and surface treatments that give tactile experiences; Patterns—Recurring architectural motifs, street layouts, or even fashion that reveal cultural narratives; Typography—Styles of typefaces used in signage that create a sense of place and historical continuity; Signage—Informational and directional elements evolving with communication needs.

2.2 *Decoding Layers—Historical Evolution and Design Principles*

The patterns, textures, and signage have evolved due to creative, technological, and cultural developments, as well as changes in materials, crafting methods, and aesthetic preferences, demonstrating a variety of artistic representations, ranging from intricate designs in traditional pottery to modern digital patterns. With communication technology, signage has drastically changed from handcrafted physical displays to digital displays. Various globalisation strategies, urbanisation changes, and cultural shifts have affected signage's visual language, resulting in a hybrid of traditional and modern design elements, and knowing the history of patterns, textures, and signs can aid in understanding the technological, social, and cultural influences that shaped them.

Historical Evolution—Creative and Technological Techniques—Materials, crafting methods, and communication technologies that influence design, e.g., handcraft signs versus. Digital signs.

Cultural Development—Aesthetics preferences and Artistic Expressions, e.g., intricate traditional tiles and pottery—modern digital patterns created by those traditional ones.

Design Principles—Lynch's "The Image of the City" highlights the importance of:
Identity—Clear and recognisable character.
Coherence—Harmony and Consistency in Visual Elements.
Intelligibility—Ease of understanding and navigating the urban environment.

2.3 *Case Study: Cultural Significance of Macau's Visual Identity and Its Unique Characteristics*

The city's infrastructure incorporates hybrid construction structures, highlighting its cultural and historical significance with vibrant patterns and tiles that encourage international discourse and community relationships. The city's visual identity also embraces current trends such as urbanisation and globalisation, as well as contemporary design aspects and technological advancements resulting from its fast expansion and global nature. Macau's visual identity reflects its complicated historical history and cultural legacy, which includes more than simply patterns, textures, and signs. It represents the diverse populations that shape the city and the constant debate between modernity and tradition (Fig. 3).

This framework strengthens the connection between visual elements, historical influences, and cultural significance, focusing on Macau as a case study.

Fig. 3 Primary areas that are being researched to understand and define the visual identity of the city of Macau and thus build the digital archive—(first square—Visual Identity of a City I second square—History and Heritage characteristics cultural and visuals from Macau City I third square—Visual Identity of the city of Macau)

3 Methodology

Our methodology focuses on the visual identity that characterises the city of Macau and consists of the following steps: State-of-the-art and conceptualisation: Conceptual study on Urban Visual Identity—historical research of what has already been produced about Macau's identity and visual characteristics. Research the visual culture that characterises the city by gathering information through photographs, videos, maps, and illustrations. Literature and historical data on the visual identity that characterises the city.

The methodology used in this study is to analyse Macau's visual identity thoroughly and define it, delving into the deep concepts, patterns, and structures that contribute to the city's distinct character that we integrate into both qualitative and quantitative methods as a multifaceted approach which focuses on a historical investigation of the urban growth and documentation of the evolution of the city's visual identity over time. Furthermore, an in-depth investigation of current literature, design studies, and city branding theories deepens the study's theoretical framework.

Our observations and documentation are used in the field to record essential visual aspects such as textures, patterns, and signage around the city. Furthermore, our research uses digital mapping (Google Maps and customised Interactive Map being created) to produce a visual database that aids the organisation and analysis of the acquired data.

This analytical framework provides a thorough understanding of Macau's visual identity while allowing for a greater appreciation of its cultural legacy and current adaptation in response to technology breakthroughs and urban transformations.

3.1 Data Collection Methods for Patterns and Textures

We are gathering information on patterns and textures essential to studying the city's design and architectural analysis since they help reveal a built environment's aesthetic qualities and cultural relevance. A city's patterns and textures have been photographed and documented using various data collection techniques. Direct observation is a frequently employed technique in examining and recording the fine details and surface characteristics of the structures, facades, and streetscapes throughout vision. This method thoroughly assists us in understanding the components, the workmanship, and the design features that make up the urban fabric. Furthermore, we are also using 360° photography, aerial high-resolution photography, with a drone (Figs. 8 and 9), where we also record complex patterns and textures on a bigger scale, which has helped us preview various patterns and textures without the need to go to a computer every time. The accurate recording is made possible by using these new techniques, which also yield helpful information for analysis, preservation, and the creation of visual identity standards for a city's planning. We also gather the historical background, cultural legacies, and aesthetic elements that influence a city's visual identity by methodically gathering this data and analysing patterns and textures.

3.2 Phases of the Research

(i) **Traditional Research**

1. Historical Analysis:
   - Examine the progression of Macau's urban landscape over time.
   - Determine the historical variables that have influenced visual identity.
2. Literature Review and Theoretical Foundation:
   - Examine relevant literature, design research, and theories of city branding.
   - Create a solid theoretical foundation for the research.
3. Research and survey of historical information of the place in terms of:
   1. the city's visual standards (Figs. 4, 5 and 6);
   2. the city's textures;
   3. the city's patterns;
   4. the city's colours;
   5. the city's signage.

Our research focuses on the visual identity that characterises Macau and consists of the following steps:

State of the Art and conceptualisation; Conceptual study on Urban Visual Identity. Historical research of what has already been produced about Macau's identity and

Fig. 4 E.g. of a pattern part of Macau's heritage; format: photographic image—"Templo Sam Po"

Fig. 5 Pattern detail; format: photographic image—"Templo Sam Po"—image not cleaned

visual characteristics. Research on the visual culture that represents the city—gathering information through photographs, videos, maps and illustrations. Literature and historical information on the visual identity that characterises the city. This research focuses on traditional methods with visual documentation to explore Macau's visual history. The study uses argumentative and conceptual writing and a collection of photographic materials to examine various aspects of its identity, such as the many textures, signs, and colours that contribute to the visual landscape of the urban environment, with an emphasis on city standards. This study aims to understand the city's identity via textual and visual representations of its historical and physical features.

(ii) **Fieldwork**—Visual Database and Mapping (Figs. 15, 16, 17, 18, 19, 20 and 21).

Fig. 6 Detail of the pattern—low resolution with low colour, with the background; format: vectorial—"Templo Sam Po"—vector not cleaned—test for basic tracing

1. Fieldwork and Data Collection:
    - Conduct fieldwork on-site to gather visual features.
    - Direct observation is used to record textures, patterns, and signage.
    - Using drone (Fig. 14) photography, standard photography, and short videos.
    - *Observations*:
        1. On-site (geographical location) (Figs. 15 and 16) and in historical context;
        2. Geographic annotations of the site;
        3. Physical notes and architectural structure;
        4. Colour annotations;
        5. Annotations of dimensions;
        6. Annotations of visual forms;
        7. Text annotations.
2. Digital Mapping and Visual Database:
    - Creation of various digital maps (Figs. 15, 16, 17, 18, 19, 20 and 21).
    - Creation of the visual database.
    - Organise and analyse the data.
    - Mapping Macau's visual identity.

Our fieldwork focuses on the need to capture and integrate data on-site into a comprehensive visual database and mapping archive of the visual elements and images; our fieldwork includes direct observation and documentation of the physical environment, as well as the gathering of visual elements such as textures, patterns, colours, and signs that contribute to the city's character. The information is then sorted and stored in a database for easy access and categorisation, and the gathered data is visually represented through photos, vectors, and physical artefacts, revealing important insights into the spatial distribution and characteristics of the city's visual identity. This visual database provides a more complete awareness of the urban landscape in one single place.

All the locations explored related to these structures or spaces follow these specific details:

Patterns

Types of Patterns: Portuguese Tile Patterns I Traditional Chinese Ornamentation I Cobblestone Street Patterns I Cultural Festival Patterns (Macau Grand Prix, Dragon Boat Festival) I Architectural Façade I Street Market Patterns I Macanese Tile Patterns I Casino and Resorts Patterns I Signage I Visual Forms.

Tiles: Portuguese Azulejos I Chinese Roof Tiles I Terracotta Tiles I Granite Tiles I Marble Tiles I Ceramic Tiles I Porcelain Tiles I Mosaic Tiles.

Signage: Street Signs I Directional Signs I Building Signs I Directional Signs I Cultural and Heritage Signs I Advertising Signs I Public Transportation Signs I Wayfinding Signs I Digital and Electronic Signs.

> **Typography**: Chinese Typography I Portuguese Typography I Macanese Typography I Modern and Contemporary Typography I Neon Signage Typography I Artistic and Decorative Typography I Multilingual Typography I Digital Typography.

Visual Forms: Geometric Patterns I Floral/Garden Patterns I Symmetrical Patterns I Grid Patterns I Textile Patterns I Grid Patterns I Ornamental Patterns I Rhythmic Patterns I Cultural/Motifs Patterns.

Textures

Types of Textures: Architectural Textures I Natural Textures I Paved Textures I Surface Textures I Textures of Public Art I Organic Textures I Infrastructure Textures I Interactive Textures.

Interactive Textures: Playgrounds I Public Art Installations I Interactive Exhibits I Sensory Gardens I Urban Installations or Events.

Textured Materials: Smooth Texture Materials (glass, polished metal, plastics) I Rough Texture Materials (brick, stone, rough concrete) I Texture Surfaced Materials (stucco, terracotta, textured paints) I Organic texture Materials (wood, natural fibres) I Tactile Texture Materials (fabric and rubbery materials).

Colours:

Terracotta I Pastel shades (e.g., pale yellows, pinks, blues) I Vibrant reds I Earth tones (e.g., browns, beiges) I White (commonly used in colonial-style buildings) I Blue (commonly used in Portuguese azulejo tiles) I Gold (often used in decorative elements) I Light Green.

Understanding these colours in Macau's visual identity and design principles can produce a more true-to-life portrayal of the city's architectural colour scheme.

Styles:

Historical Information I Categories I TypologiesI Dates I Dimensions I Urban Flooring I Overall space in which it is located I Design Structures.

(iii) **Design Research**—reproducing and analysing images and data

- Qualitative and Quantitative Analysis: Analyse the qualitative and quantitative information gathered during fieldwork.
- Identify patterns and trends in Macau's visual identity around the city landscape.
- Create digital files—visual database:
  1. The advantage of having a database centred on Macau is that everyone can consult and use the information.
- Understand and implement technical notions of Macau's design characteristics:
  1. Based on the information obtained, it is intended to understand and implement technical notions of the design characteristics of Macau.
- We are focusing on a Visual image categorisation based on the following:
  - Mapping the city through its visual characteristics—Longitudinal/ Latitude—sizes thus creates its visual identity.
  - Preservation of patterns, textures, colours and signage around the city through photographs, graphics, texts and videos—in digital format.
    1. Location Photo.
    2. Photographic image of the general patterns.
    3. Detail photographic image.
    4. Low-quality vector Image creation with or without background (similar to the photograph but in vector format).
    5. High-resolution vectorial image without a background—focus only on the module silhouette.
    6. Aerial/Drone Photography.
    7. 360° Photography.
- Creation of a vector format database based on all specific photography.
- *Digital Archive*: Creation of a digital file (e.g. visual database) with the geographical location of Macau; photographs of patterns, textures, signs and colours of the city; vectorial reproductions and illustrations of the city's textures and patterns; audiovisual documentation related to the city's textures, patterns, colour and historic signs, creation of vector files in 2D for use in 2D and 3D digital assets (Fig. 7).

4 Data Collection, Organisation and Construction of Archive

The goal is to identify, define, and map the city's visual patterns through photographs, videos, written files, and other data (Figs. 8 and 9).

There was a need to make spatial, categorical and priority divisions and subdivisions. In the first instance, the territory is divided into four main areas, Macau,

Fig. 7 Pattern/texture—city pattern location—"Sam Po Temple"

Fig. 8 Infrastructure location: e.g. Capela da Santa Cruz—Drone photography

Fig. 9 Igreja de Nª Srª das Dores (Ká Hó)[1]

Taipa, Cotai, and Coloane, with Cotai not being a priority[2] at the moment and thus, focusing more on the other three, which were also sub-divided into parishes and recently focusing more on the urban zone divisions following the mapping lines established by the local government.

Regarding categories, we divided bodies of interest for the project, such as sites and buildings. The focus, for now, is on Churches, Chapels, Temples, and buildings of Architectural Interest and Heritage. As for other sites, priority was given to squares and complexes that carry some local cultural value.

So far, we have chosen 23 buildings in the category of Churches and Chapels, 23 in the category of Temples and 23 in the Buildings of Architectural Interest, Heritage and Sites category.

Currently, the way to include two more categories is being considered: Schools and Health Centres.[3] All buildings and spaces accounted for above are duly listed in a folder under the project shared drive to facilitate remote access and collaboration by any team member and external access. Each structure has a brief historical information, description, and relevant facts in its folder, and some images obtained from official government web pages and other private pages duly referenced.

We will reference all the steps currently being taken on the following pages.

[1] We have noted that most of the religious infrastructures are deteriorated and not well preserved, even if they are part of the cultural heritage.

[2] Cotai is not a priority at this research stage, although it is an excellent source of textures and patterns; we are focusing on heritage sites or sites with Portuguese and/or Chinese influences that are not Casinos or Hotels. This could be considered in further iterations of the research.

[3] These categories are being considered because various buildings are part of cultural heritage and have social value.

4.1 Infrastructures Detail Data

Churches

E.g. *Capela da Santa Cruz (Macau).*

- Total Raw Pictures for use: more than 3800
- Total Short Videos: more than 30 (Figs. 10 and 11).

One of the goals of this research is to focus on the development of patterns and textures in vector software so that we may establish swatch libraries (Fig. 12). Our efforts have resulted in the development of a sophisticated set of patterns and swatch libraries that may significantly streamline the design process for consumers. These materials provide direct advantages to our students, educators, and the design community.

It is also important to note that the research has some shortcomings, although for example, while the patterns, textures, and swatch libraries are robust, they may not cover all possible use cases or special design needs. More complex patterns may need more work and testing to assure the greatest levels of usability and visual quality.

We are also creating 3D texture libraries for 3D software objects. Using the same patterns as textures on 3D objects enables for seamless integration of design elements across mediums (Fig. 13).

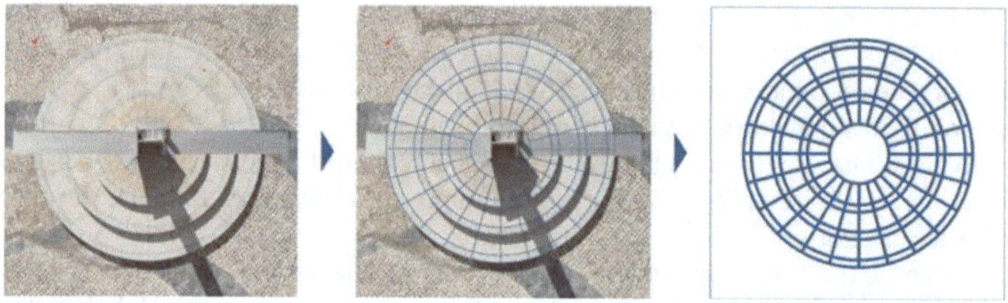

Fig. 10 E.g., Capela da Santa Cruz—a visual guideline example of vectorisationn

Fig. 11 E.g., Capela de Santa Cruz,—visual guideline example for vectorisationn

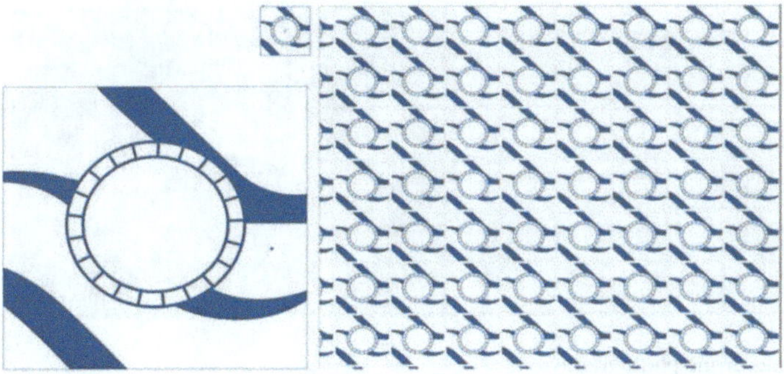

Fig. 12 Digital library assets: vectorised pattern construction using vector software

Fig. 13 E.g., of how to use the vector patterns as 3D textures

Temples

E.g. *Templo de Tin Hau (Coloane).*

- Total Raw Pictures for use: more than 3600
- Total Short Videos: more than 30.

Photos cleaned and ready for digital display: more than 500

Fig. 14 Aerial drone photography

Photos/Vectors Created—Patterns: more than 290

Photos/Vectors Created—Textures: more than 170.

Infrastructures focused on until now: 23 churches and 23 temples total (not all data isfinalisedd); however, all the Infrastructures—Churches and temples selected in Coloane Island were completed, including Taipa, except for one temple (Templo de Sam Po).

All the photos and videos of the city were captured using a DJI Mini 3 Pro, providing a unique aerial perspective and allowinfg for great visuals of the infrastructures and urban landscapes (Fig. 14).

4.2 *Mapping the City with Textures and Patterns*

The maps of the various divisions are being completed, but here are some examples in field study format and digital format already prepared to be placed on the digital archive (Fig. 22) where patterns/modules are replacing the photos.

We have been creating several maps of all the locations where we have gathered data and using these maps to assist us with the fieldwork and all the places and spaces we have been photographing and collecting information.

We have also mapped all the locations using Google Maps (Figs. 17 and 18), utilising a detailed pattern or texture image complemented with a powerful infrastructure shot. We created, processed, and presented all the data and identified the locations of the sites with textures and patterns. It is a digital archive (Fig. 23) that displays spatial data. The map is viewable on any platform and helps us observe, interpret, and interact with the images from the digital archive (Fig. 24).

4.2.1 Fieldwork Mapping

See Figs. 15 and 16.

Fig. 15 First version of the maps created in the project with the Macau Churches for fieldwork purposes

4.2.2 Digital Mapping Created for the Digital Archive (e-Library)

Our map structure created for the digital archive helps us organise the city's visual identity elements. The maps offer an interactive platform for viewers to explore the city's patterns and textures. This project output allows its users to find their desired pattern or texture, and these resources are essential for documenting and managing the asset's growing visual identity landscape and accessibility (Figs. 17, 18 and 19).

4.2.3 Localisationn—Churches and Temples

See Figs. 20 and 21.

Fig. 16 First version of the maps created in the project with the Macau Temples for fieldwork purposes

4.3 *Digital Archive (Data Repository)*

See Figs. 22 and 23 and 24.

The data repository is being developed, with metadata aiding the structure of the database. It should be noted, however, that the repository is still a work in progress, particularly categorising numerous detailed photographs and videos, because we still need to add the accompanying text created in Portuguese, English, and Chinese. These categories include location-based images that provide specific geographic context, detailed photographs capturing intricate visual elements, signage photographs documenting various signs and symbols as well as the road signage part of the East and West background, photographs highlighting diverse pavement photographs showcasing different types of walking surfaces, ceramic images capturing the unique

Fig. 17 The digital format of infrastructure mapping is already prepared to be placed in the digital e-library

ceramic artworks and installations, azulejos, patterns illustrating the vast array of visual structural and urban patterns, database structure (Fig. 25).

5 Preservation and Promotion of Macau's Visual Identity

Preserving the city's recognisable cultural legacy depends primarily on keeping and enhancing its visual identity, which includes devising strategies to retain its distinctive patterns, textures, and signage; the respective stakeholders may help preserve and restore Macau's visual character by engaging in community activities and safeguarding cultural assets. Our digital archive will also facilitate the sharing of documentation and photography of the city's visual heritage, fostering inclusion and knowledge exchange, making it possible to understand how the visual identity is viewed and experienced is critical to preserving its cultural importance and forming a meaningful relationship with the city's patterns and textures.

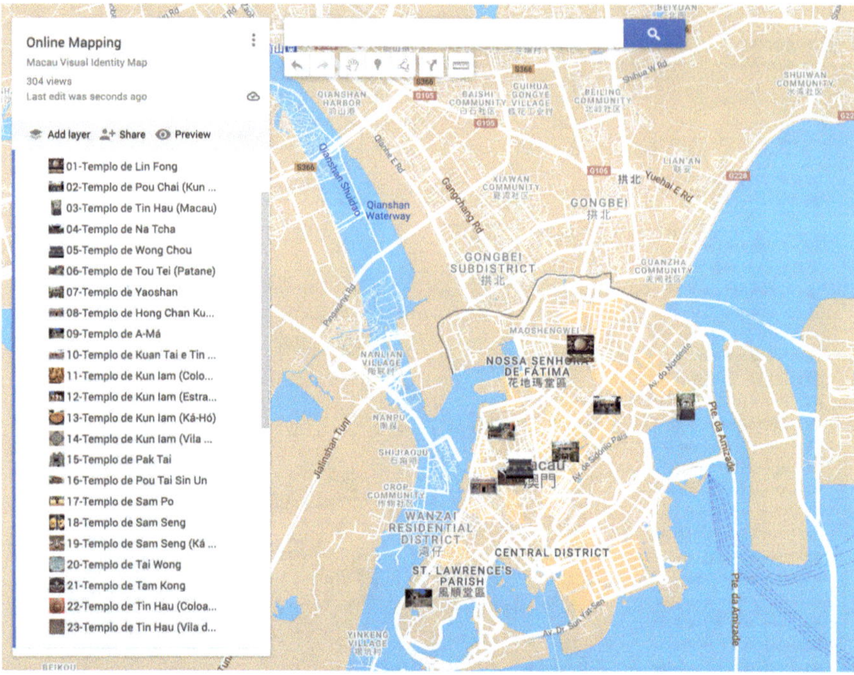

Fig. 18 Digital format of infrastructure mapping—details map

5.1 *Textures and Patterns (Vectorized Data)*

A few guidelines (Figs. 26, 27, 28, 29, 30, 31, 32, 33, 34, 35, 36 and 37) are being developed for all team members so that we can extract, understand, create, and design how to standardise all the photographs by cleaning them and focusing on the textures and patterns across the project, having various team members work on different photographs at a time.

Multiple guidelines are being created to make it easier for all team members to understand the project processes and outcomes.

We also encourage creative exploration and variation by developing extra vector variations, as seen in (Fig. 32), after generating the final vectorised images for our visual identity database. These additional vectors were inspired by the authors' inventive interpretations of the textures and patterns they saw, providing for a more diverse range of visual representations.

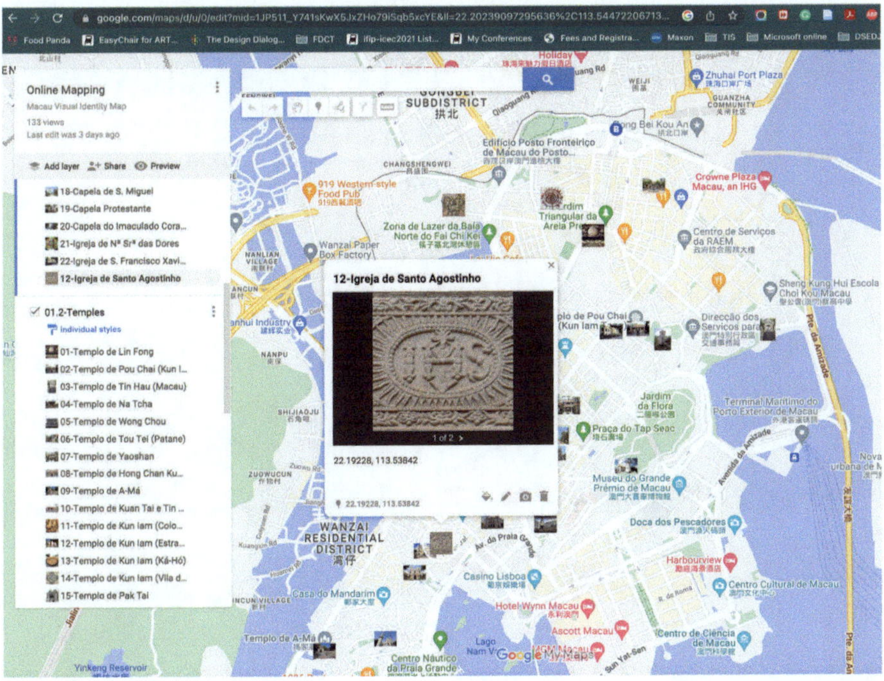

Fig. 19 Augmented texture detail of the infrastructure "Igreja de Santo Agostinho"—vector elements are being created to replace specific module photos

6 Conclusion and Future Directions for Research and Development

In conclusion, exploring Macau's visual identity via the lenses of infrastructures, visual textures, text, typography, and visual language has proven to be extremely fruitful. Every element reflects the city's eclectic blend of Eastern and Western influences. The visual language encompasses signage, typography, symbols, and branding strategies. The digital library highlights the diversity of the metropolitan region around each institution by including photos of colours and textures that not only give crucial information but also represent the city's character and goals, affecting residents' and tourists' perceptions and interactions. Fieldwork is currently being conducted to gather new photographs and first-hand information on the covered urban areas, ensuring accuracy and completeness.

Overall, the digital archive seeks to be a complete visual resource that faithfully and methodically reflects the city's visual character. One of the long-term aims of this research is to continue recording the visual identity, textures, patterns, signs, and colours throughout its documented history, resulting in visual patterns and textures that are frequently lost or damaged by municipal usage. To obtain more data, categorise it, store it, distribute it, and finally load the digital archive with

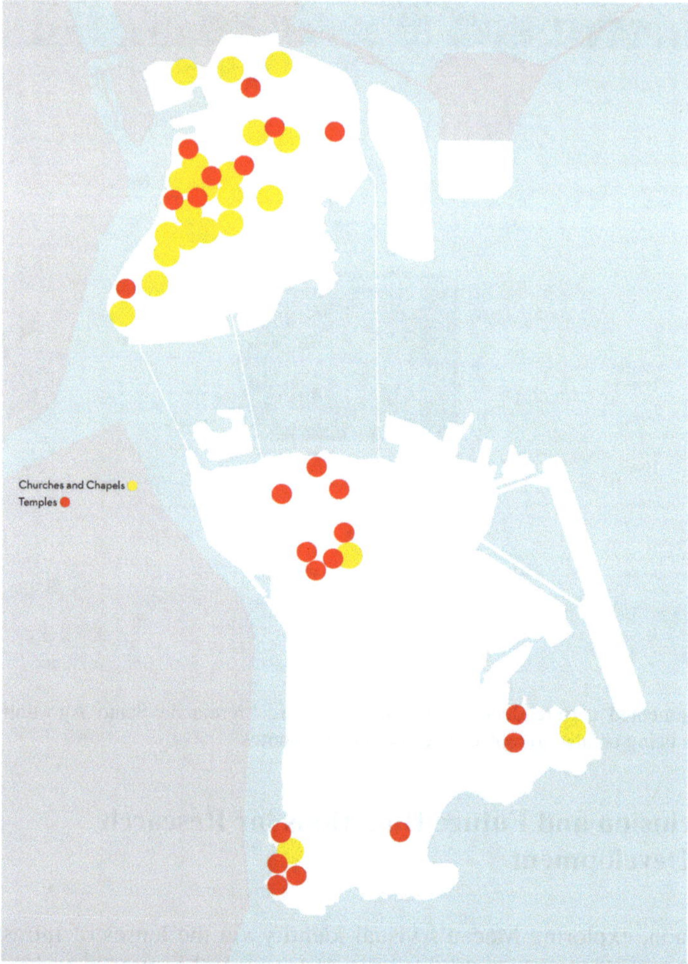

Fig. 20 Graphical map with all the churches and temples from which we have gathered data. Yellow colour represents churches, red colour represents temples

various patterns and textures collected in the latter stages of the project. We will continue to collect local textures and patterns to promote and chronicle the city's history, including building dates and styles. We will also continue creating texts and documents explaining the city's identity and visual culture throughout each city's zone.

Using new production processes, we create objects using 3D printing, laser cutting and engraving, embroidery, and screen printing, and we use sustainable and recyclable materials using new production processes. Our panel base of the Holy Cross Chapel (Figs. 38 and 39) serves as an example of how textures and patterns can

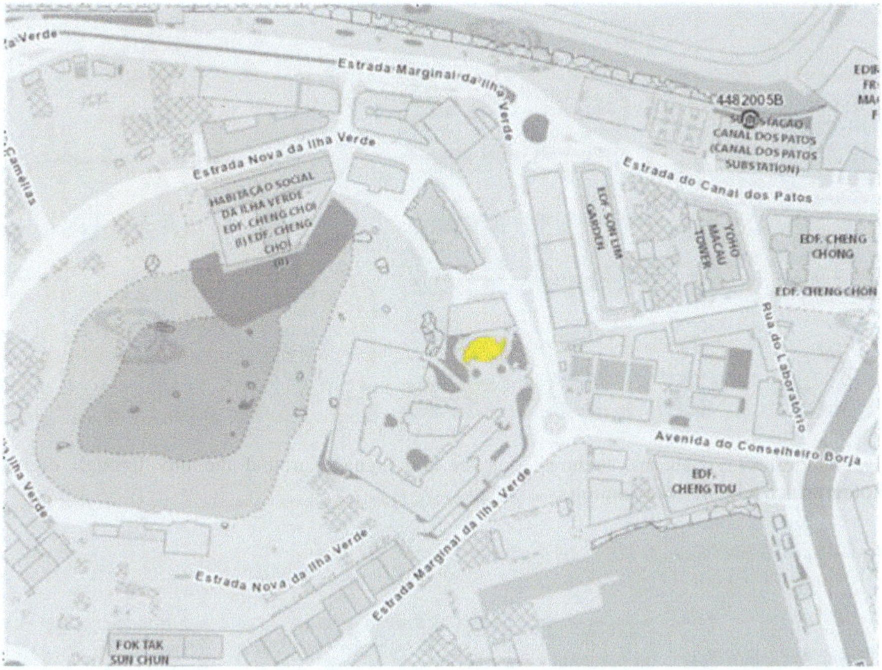

Fig. 21 E.g., a detailed map of the "Capela da Santa Cruz" infrastructure plan

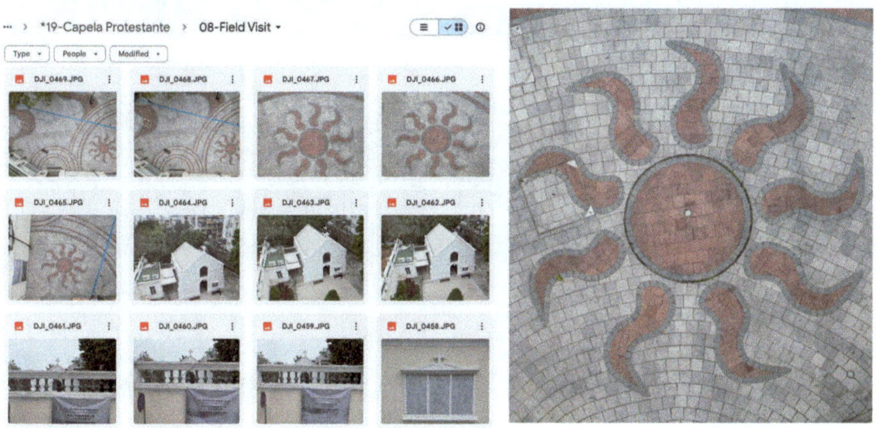

Fig. 22 Preservation of patterns, textures, colours and signage around the city through photographs—in digital format—raw images

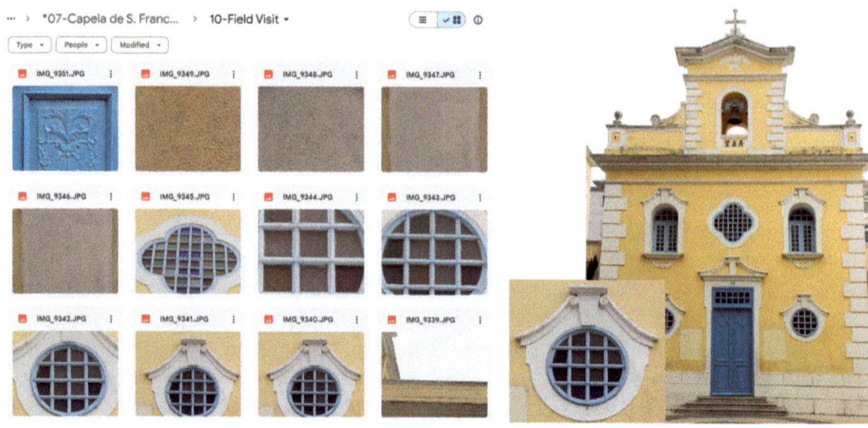

Fig. 23 Preserving patterns, textures, colours and signage around the city through digital photographs ready for vectorisation

Fig. 24 Preservation of patterns, textures, colours and signage around the city through photographs—in digital format—fieldwork details—ready for details cleaning

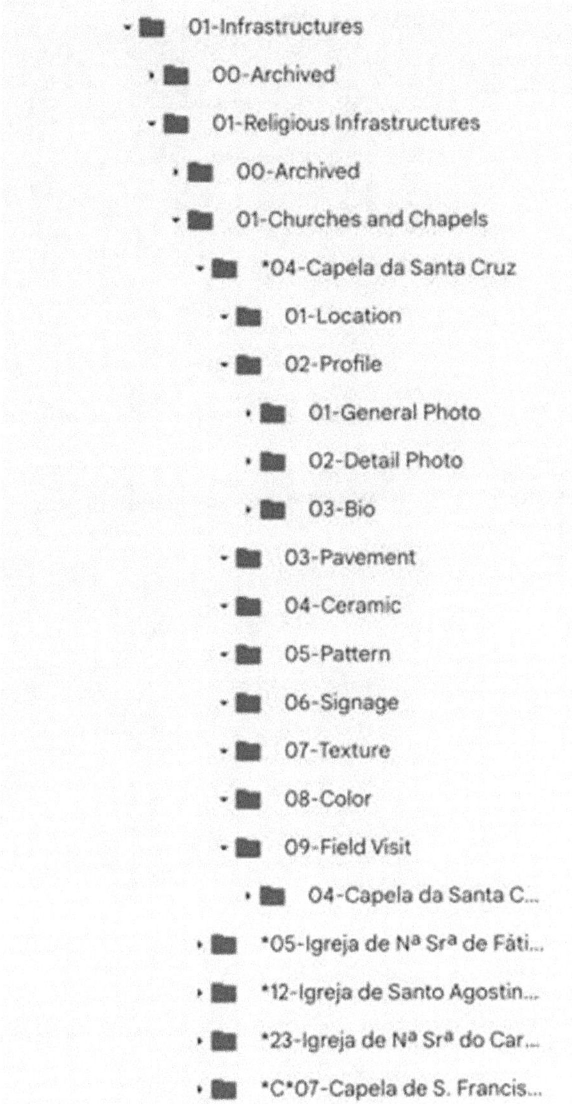

Fig. 25 Instruction—example of the database structure under the project servers—digital archive e-library

be used in various materials for prototyping, cultural preservation, and celebration of cultural artefacts, integrating traditional design with modern and diverse manufacturing techniques, demonstrating how heritage can be adapted to contemporary contexts. The blend of old and new can result in unique artefacts bridging the gap between traditional and contemporary. The goal also includes education,

Fig. 26 Instruction—Step 1—base image—focus on strategic image spots from which we can build solid and clean patterns

Fig. 27 Instruction—Step 2—define and emphasise the selected area with the help of a square for guidance (preferably)

Fig. 28 Instruction—crop the image to the boundaries of the previously created square and create a colour palette of the selected area

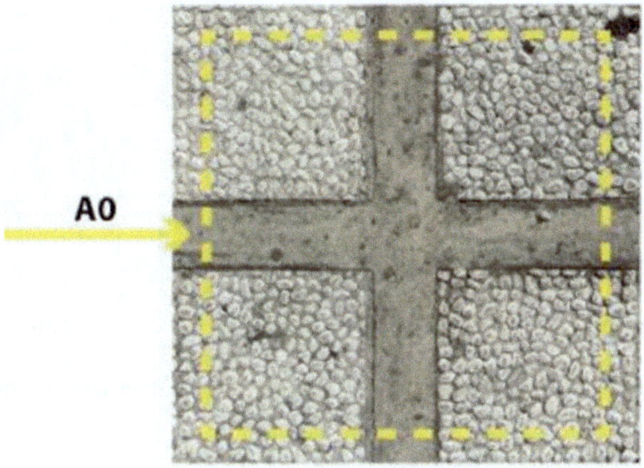

Fig. 29 Instruction—resize the image to the size of an AO, in this case, 841 × 841 mm instead of 841 × 1189 mm (regular AO) so it can be square (either by cropping or scaling)

Fig. 30 Instruction—convert the image to Black and White and clean up by eliminating small obstructions or rebuilding missing, damaged parts

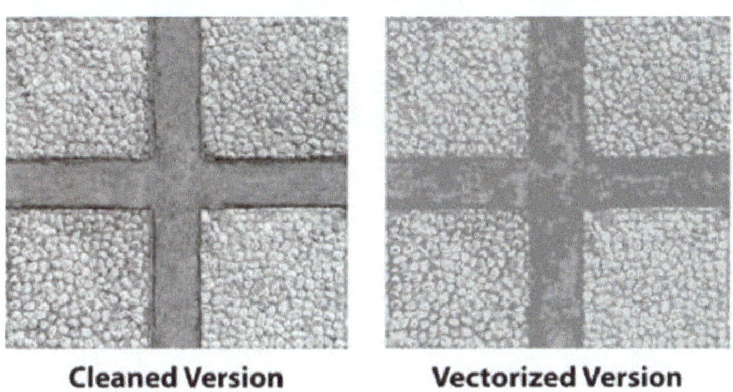

Fig. 31 Instruction vectorising the image—image trace with three colour options

Fig. 32 Instruction—expand and ungroup the image to have the three colours composed from the vectorisation

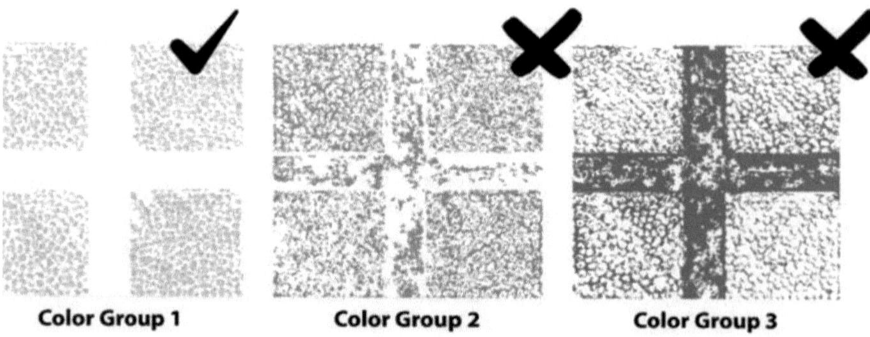

Fig. 33 Selection process—the one that seems cleaner

tourism, economic opportunities, creative discovery and expression, customisation and personalisation, sustainability, and efficiency.

Fig. 34 Instruction—recleaning process—remove unwanted vector points

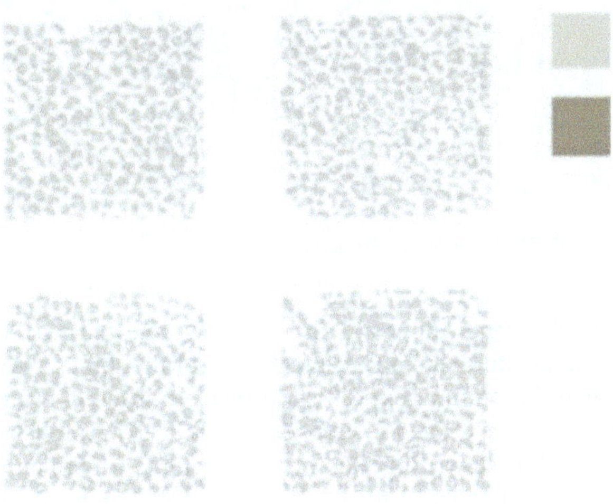

Fig. 35 Instruction—apply the colours previously created from the image palette to its elements and background

We will continue our research and increase the archive by creating digital data, physical objects, and artefacts.

The research objectives were met effectively, offering useful insights and setting a firm basis for what to do and not do in the future regarding design procedures and data criteria. The findings and amount of vectors developed for our digital library

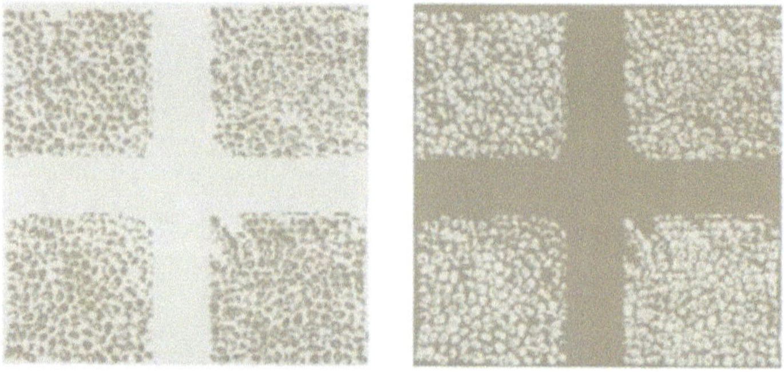

Fig. 36 Instruction—final vectorised images

Fig. 37 Instruction vectorised variation examples

are enormous, and the applications are diverse. However, it is crucial to emphasise that some areas require further improvement. One of the things we've seen is that different books in different libraries across Macau have different infrastructures, and some of the books are in restricted sections or do not exist in English or Portuguese, only in Traditional Chinese writing. So, this is something we are currently working on. As we get to the next phase of the project, more research needs to be done. The next phase will focus on overcoming some of our constraints and refining the work already completed.

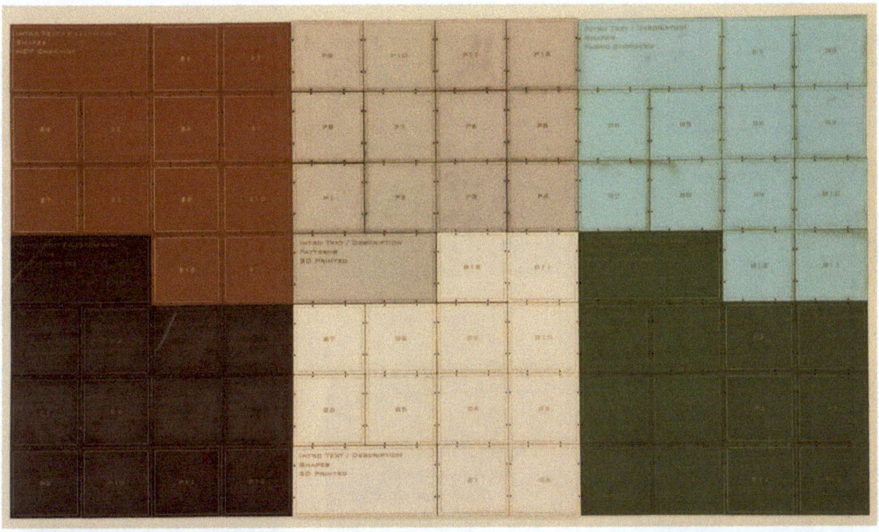

Fig. 38 Panel Base Setup for Vector Assets in various materials and using different techniques

Fig. 39 Panel of artifacts in various materials and using different techniques. Physical artifacts library of patterns and textures of the "Capela de Santa Cruz"—under development

Many textures and patterns are being created around Macau, and they can be found in various databases. Still, none have the historical background, descriptions, and vectorisation processes we use for 2D and 3D technologies, printing or laser cutting, with various materials and prototypes required in Macau's schools. Furthermore, as of today, no archive has been developed for this type of visual record and mapping

Fig. 40 Primary areas that are being researched to understand and define the visual identity of the city of Macau and thus build the digital archive—(first square—Visual Identity of a City I second square—History and Heritage characteristics cultural and visuals from Macau City I third square—Visual Identity of the city of Macau) III New Areas that are going to be researched and worked on—(first square bottom—Re-Imagening patterns and textures I second square bottom—the creation of objects and artefacts, digital and physical I third square—using diverse technologies for the creation of objects and artefacts)

(Fig. 21), which will be quite valuable for our students' projects and for the Macau community.

Signage study may give insight into Macau's history, cultural legacy, and the interplay of several visual languages, enabling the creation of practical, culturally sensitive communication approaches to accommodate the city's diverse cultures (Fig. 40).

Acknowledgements Research funded by Macau Foundation Academic Research Scheme (Fundação Macau)—https://www.fmac.org.mo—2022–2023 II 2023–2024.

References

1. Poulin, R. (2018). The language of graphic design revised and updated: An illustrated handbook for understanding fundamental design principles. Rockport Publishers.
2. Dmitrenko, A. (2019). The image of the United Kingdom in Chinese history textbooks of the 1930–1940s. Vestnik Sankt-Peterburgskogo Universiteta. Seriâ 13, Vostokovedenie, Afrikanistika, 11(2), 252–261. https://doi.org/10.21638/spbu13.2019.209

3. Pinheiro, F. V. *Espaços Históricos de Macau.* Macau, China: Instituto para os Assuntos Cívicos e Municipais, 2016.
4. Riza, M. N. Doratli, and M. Fasli, 'City Branding and Identity', Procedia - Social and Behavioral Sciences, vol. 35, pp. 293–300, 2012, https://doi.org/10.1016/j.sbspro.2012.02.091.
5. Wong, B. I. A. McKercher, and X. Li, 'East Meets West: Tourist Interest in Hybrid Culture at Postcolonial Destinations', Journal of Travel Research, vol. 55, no. 5, pp. 628–642, May 2016, https://doi.org/10.1177/0047287514563984.
6. Edmonds, R. L. 'Macau and Greater China', The China Quarterly, vol. 136, pp. 878–906, Dec. 1993, https://doi.org/10.1017/S0305741000032379.
7. Mitchell, R. 2017. Portuguese art: Portuguese azulejo. In: Donne, Elisabetta Delle, (ed.) Fine arts in Europe: the last 10 centuries. Michelangelo Project / Pixel, [online], pp. 341–360.
8. Porter, '"The Past Is Present": The Construction of Macau's Historical Legacy', History and Memory, vol. 21, no. 1, p. 63, 2009, https://doi.org/10.2979/his.2009.21.1.63.
9. Moussavi, Farshid, and Kubo M. The Function of Ornament. Actar, 2020.
10. Smith, Peter F. Syntax of Cities. 0 ed., Routledge, 2013. (Crossref), https://doi.org/10.4324/9780203717332.
11. Consulta pública sobre o Projecto do Plano Director da Região Administrativa Especial de Macau (2020–2040), Portal do Governo da RAE de Macau, April 30, 2021. https://www.gov.mo/pt/consulta-de-politicas/consulta-publica-sobre-o-projecto-do-plano- director-da-regiao-administrativa-especial-de-macau-2020–2040/ (accessed June 29, 2023).
12. Lynch, K. (1964). *The image of the city.* MIT Press.

Flexible Visual Identity Systems in Cultural Institutions

Maria Figueira, Daniel Raposo, and João Brandão

Abstract This article aims to contribute to knowledge about the characteristics of a Visual Identity System, including a design exploratory study for the Museu Marítimo de Ílhavo, Portugal. The study focuses on Flexible Visual Identity Systems in the context of cultural organisations, particularly museums. The methodology includes non-interventionist components such as a literature review, a descriptive case study, direct observation, interviews, and active research through an exploratory case in a design project. The results contribute to knowledge about the seven components of a visual identity system, the essential characteristics of a Visual Identity System, namely flexibility and coherence, as well as the design process of a flexible visual identity system for cultural organizations.

Keywords Flexible visual identity systems · Dynamic visual identity · Brand mark · Museu Marítimo de Ílhavo

1 Introduction

The concept of Visual Identity (VI) defines an integrated and coherent system of elements that materialize, represent, and graphically characterize an entity, brand, product, service or event in a given context or market, identifying and differentiating

M. Figueira · D. Raposo (✉) · J. Brandão
CIAUD, Lisbon School of Architecture, Universidade de Lisboa, Rua Sá Nogueira, 1349-063 Lisboa, Portugal
e-mail: draposo@ipcb.pt

M. Figueira
e-mail: figueira.maria@edu.ulisboa.pt

J. Brandão
e-mail: joaoaranda@fa.ulisboa.pt

D. Raposo
ReThink – Centro de Investigação em Design para o Território & Polytechnic Institute of Castelo Branco, Av. Pedro Álvares Cabral, nº 12, 6000-084 Castelo Branco, Portugal

© The Author(s), under exclusive license to Springer Nature Switzerland AG 2025
D. Brandão et al. (eds.), *Perspectives on Design and Digital Communication V*, Springer Series in Design and Innovation 50, https://doi.org/10.1007/978-3-031-76156-0_8

it from other similar entities or competitors (Strunck 2007 [1], Raposo 2022 [2]). A Visual Identity System (VIS) is formed by the graphical-semantic correlation between the brand mark (logo, logotype and/or symbol), colors, typography, imagery, graphics and graphic compositions (Magalhães & Oliveira, 2023 [3]).

According to the model by Raposo et al. (2022) [4], a VIS is made up of the following elements: logo and typography, symbol, composition, scale/size, colour(s), texture/images and design style. This model stands out for exploring the possibilities in the relationship between the elements, allowing it to be applied to both the brand mark and the VIS.

For the same authors, the graphic-semantic correlation of the visual identity elements forms a language system with a certain tone or style that characterises the represented brand.

The visual language system results from the correlation established between the elements of the Visual Identity System (VIS), in other words, by the design principles, usage guidelines and standards that establish the possible combinations that determine the style, coherence and cohesion of the VI system (Lorenz, 2021 [5]). In the same sense, VIS flexibility is determined by the type of possibilities and resources that allow adaptability to a vast number of situations, applications, and contexts.

In Kreutz's thesis (2001) [6], Flexible Visual Identity (the author uses the term Metaphorical Identity) emerged as a new form of communication and branding strategy, arbitrary, flexible and dynamic to adjust to the requirements and characteristics of contemporary society. Kreutz (2001) [6] referred to systems in which the shape, colour or typography of the brand mark changes depending on a programme or concept, as opposed to what he called Conventional Stereotyped Visual Identity.

In the same vein, van Nes' theory (2012) [7] established a correlation between technologies and Flexible Visual Identity (the author uses the term Dynamic Identities) and, like Kreutz (2001) [6], refers above all to the graphic alteration of the Brand mark, proposing six categories of possible formal alteration.

It is undeniable how the technological evolution of recent decades has helped to mould the social, cultural, political, and economic landscape, as well as the way we communicate and inform ourselves. In this sense, technological advances have an impact on the design of visual identities, their structure and operation. However, there have been cases of Flexible Visual Identity Systems since at least the 1950s, a time when more structured, complex, and standardised Visual Identity systems were being consolidated. Flexible VI systems gained momentum in the 1980s with the personal computer popularising the graphic interface and on television with MTV. Later, along with digital printing, the internet and social networks gave new impetus, better technical and financial conditions and greater notoriety to Flexible Visual Identity Systems (Fonte et al., 2023 [8]).

In this way, we can see that Flexible Visual Identity Systems are not a new liquid possibility that is opposed to a more conventional, more inflexible one. However, despite the increased interest in flexible systems, there seems to be little knowledge on this topic, particularly in terms of their durability, communicational effectiveness, visual coherence, ease of perception and memorisation or semantic articulation with the brand.

Visual coherence is observed in the correlation and similarity between components observed on different supports, media and at different times (Peón, 2001 [9]).

Symbolic coherence refers to the compatibility or alignment between what the brand means and what the brand looks like (what it is and how it is designed). This alignment between brand and VI requires a clarification of the brand concept (purpose, values, objectives, mission and personality) and its graphic expression or tone of voice in a given market, materialised by the SIV (Gernsheimer, 2008 [10], Wheeler, 2009 [11]).

The quality of the graphic form of the brand mark is also related to its contrast or legibility, which conditions the perception, memorisation, recognition and understanding of its meaning (Gernsheimer, 2008 [10]). The graphic style of the brand mark is related to its longevity, which is intended to last, as well as its uniqueness (Gernsheimer, 2008 [10]).

Finally, flexibility refers to the set of characteristics that allow an VI to adapt to a vast number of situations without losing graphic and co-semantic coherence and cohesion (Peón, 2001 [9], Wheeler, 2009 [11]).

In this context, an investigative process was designed with the aim of deepening knowledge about the flexibility of Flexible Visual Identity Systems (FVIS) in the face of the multiplicity of contemporary media, focusing on the case of FVIS design for the Ílhavo Maritime Museum (ÍMM) in Portugal.

In this context, the following research question was defined:

How can flexible visual identity systems contribute to the communication of museums, especially the Ílhavo Maritime Museum?

Considering the research question, the following objectives were defined:

- Study the design of flexible visual identity systems.
- Study the visual identity systems of museums.
- Design a flexible visual identity system.

The research includes a Literature Review to delve deeper into the subject and provide a theoretical framework for this study, namely the concept of flexibility in VIS and its relevance to the communication of museums and other cultural institutions. Descriptive case studies of identities and flexible visual systems were carried out. Next, an exploratory case study was carried out looking at a Flexible Visual Identity System for the Ílhavo Maritime Museum. Direct observation and interviews were also used to obtain information about the object of study.

2 Theoretical Framework of the Study on Flexible Visual Identity Systems

The review of the literature shows that the study of this problem has come up against a considerable number of terms proposed for this type of visual identity system. The terms stand out: "mutant", "dynamic" and "flexible". Authors such as van Nes (2012)

[7], Jochum (2013) [12], Murdock (2016) [13] and Martins et al. (2019) [14] use the term "dynamic visual identity". For their part, Felsing (2010) [15], Hollington (2011) [16] and Lorenz (2021 [5] and 2016 [17]) prefer to use the expression "flexible visual identity" and Kreutz (2001 [6], 2007 [18] and 2012 [19]) "changing visual identity". However, the meaning they attribute to the expression is similar.

According to Martins et al. [14], a dynamic visual identity refers to an identity whose elements vary (Martins et al., 2019 [14]). Hollington (2011) [16] reinforces the existence of constant elements and elements that vary: the former are responsible for ensuring brand recognition and the latter for making it vary and adapt to the most diverse situations. Kreutz (2007, p. 3) [18] characterises these systems as more expressive, open, subjective and innovative because it's closer to a game with an aesthetic sense. Lorenz [17] argues that a visual identity that is not flexible, i.e. does not contain elements that vary, will not be able to adapt to the new demands of today (Lorenz, 2016 [17]).

This possibility for the system to vary some of its elements guarantees it great flexibility and expressive capacity. With this definition in mind, a flexible visual identity system is, according to Lorenz (2016) [17] it's a visual language code that is suitably versatile and adaptable to different situations, which can be customised or adapted for different audiences and media, while maintaining visual coherence as an integrated group (Lorenz, 2021, p. 4 [5]). As there is no consensus among the scientific community, the choice of the term "flexible" resulted from the syntactic analysis of the various words. While the term dynamic refers to movement, and the term mutant to profound change, the term flexible can broadly define the versatility of the VIS we are trying to refer to.

In order to better understand the concept of flexibility and its importance in VIS, we analysed the proposals and models of authors who have contributed to the subject: van Nes (2012) [7], Leitão (2014) [20], Martins et al. (2019) [14] and Lorenz (2021 [5] and 2016 [17]).

Van Nes (2012) [7]

Van Nes (2012) [7] takes an in-depth look at the elements that make up an IVS and how they can give rise to "dynamic visual identities" by creating their own categorisation (geared towards the brand mark). There are 6 categories created by the author:

1. Container—The brand mark is thought of as a container within which you can change the characteristics of various components such as colour, typography, graphic elements, etc. (van Nes, 2012 [7]).
2. Wallpaper—changing the elements in the background, considering that the logo is in the foreground (van Nes, 2012 [7]).
3. DNA—development of modules whose combination creates a language of its own (van Nes, 2012 [7]).
4. Formula—the use of specific rules governing the behaviour of the elements that define the visual identity and therefore the system (van Nes, 2012 [7]).

5. Customised—the participation of individuals, most often the general public, to create elements such as text, drawings, patterns, etc. (van Nes, 2012 [7]).
6. Generative—using algorithms to create the visual identity, allowing it to interact with external data.

Given the date of publication of the book (2012) [7] it is not surprising that time has influenced the categorisation. The evolution of the current panorama has revealed new IV possibilities that are not embraced by van Nes' categorisation, or on the other hand, the existence of very specific categories (such as the "Container" category) and others that are broader (for example, the "Formula" category).

Despite this, the Literature Review revealed that van Nes [7] is one of the most frequently referenced authors with regard to the type of VI under study. The author's synthesised view of the composition of an VIS and the variation of its components proved indispensable. The work of van Nes [7] instigated the study of the subject and gave rise to new perspectives such as those of Felsing (2010) [15], Jochum (2013) [12], Murdock (2016) [13] and Martins et al. (2019) [14].

Martins et al. (2019) [14]

In order to resolve what they consider to be subjective in van Nes' proposal (2012) [7], Martins et al.'s perspective (2019) [14] aims for greater objectivity by not relying on categories. The proposal has three parameters. Firstly, the authors try to understand whether the "dynamic" happens at the level of the brand mark or the system. Next, they explore how the elements can be related and varied by defining eight variation mechanisms: colour variation, combination, content variation, position, repetition, rotation, scale and shape transformation. Finally, they consider a set of seven characteristics that can be attributed to a visual identity or system based on the way they have been developed and their behaviour: flexible, fluid, informative, generative, participative, relative and unlimited.

The perspective of Martins et al. (2019) [14] manages to be more comprehensive than that of van Nes (2012) [7] since it addresses "dynamism" focussed on both the brand mark and the visual identity system. In turn, the association of characteristics independently, without limits (avoiding the existence of exclusive categorisations) proves to be significant. The work carried out by the authors in classifying various "dynamic" identities and systems also made it possible to analyse the frequency of the mechanisms of variation of the elements throughout the various characteristics. Thus, taking into account the design project, it is possible to use specific mechanisms in order to achieve desirable characteristics in the identity or visual system. For example, the authors concluded, taking into account the sample analysed, that a flexible system tends to use the mechanisms "content variation" and "colour variation" (Martins et al., 2019 [14]).

The authors also highlighted the growing use of "dynamic visual systems" in recent times, which puts the brand mark on the same level as the other elements of the system in terms of its recognisability (Martins et al., 2019 [14]).

Lorenz (2021 [5] **and 2016** [17]**)**

In his book "Flexible Visual Systems", Lorenz (2021) [5] focuses on the study of VIS as a whole and the search for a comprehensive categorisation based on formal characteristics. In this work, the author takes an inclusive perspective by making sure that the very definition of the model is itself flexible.

Lorenz (2021) [5] shares van Nes' point of view (2012) [7] with regard to the existence of variable and constant elements, explaining that there must be a balance so that recognition and, at the same time, change and adaptation to the context are possible. According to the author, there are two types of systems: form-based and transformation-based. The first uses geometric shapes as input, to which properties (such as colour) are associated and then combined with each other. The second type of system uses any type of input that undergoes changes and transformations, which will consequently be the distinctive element that allows recognition.

VISs can also be considered open or closed. The former allows for the addition and creation of new inputs, as well as the editing of existing inputs. The latter are characterised by the opposite, using only predefined components (Lorenz, 2016 [17]). The author also emphasises the importance of the system's responsiveness.

Lorenz's vision [17] meets the essential characteristics of an VIS. For example, an open system is more likely to last over time, allowing changes to its components when necessary. On the other hand, the responsiveness of the output contributes to the coherence and readability of the system.

Lorenz's model [17] is undoubtedly comprehensive in terms of the possibilities it offers. The focus on the process, i.e. the practical and design aspect, plays in its favour, as it does not restrict visual systems to categories or elements to specific transformations. In addition to all this, the in-depth study of VIS stands out from the rest, showing that the future requires flexibility, and VIS could be the answer.

Leitão (2014) [20]

Leitão (2014) [20] differs from the other authors by studying the flexibility involved in the presence of visual identity in various media. The author proposes four Principles that should guide the creation of both static and dynamic visual identities, based on the study by Elizete Kreutz (Leitão, 2014 [20]). These principles should be followed so that the brand has a strong and coherent presence in various media—an essential condition these days.

7. Principle of Morphology—refers to the structure of the visual identity: elements such as space, composition, proportion, and scale. The author warns of the importance of using a grid to orientate the elements.
8. Principle of Syntax—refers to the importance of exploring characteristics such as shape, colour, and texture.
9. Narrative Principle—refers to the concept, the story that the brand wants to tell. The author considers the existence of variables that classify the narrative: time and interactivity with the user.
10. Principle of Experience—refers to valuing the experience and emotion that the brand will generate in its audience.

Creating a set of principles capable of encompassing any brand to guarantee its success in various media in a world governed by technological evolution is both visionary and challenging. In fact, there is some disparity in the level of abstraction of the various Principles: The Morphological Principle and the Syntax Principle are more objective than, for example, the Narrative Principle and the Experience Principle. However, this is justifiable. While the first two Principles use specific design elements and notions such as the grid, shape, and colour, the latter two are more complex and don't use such tangible notions. The latter seek to go further by deepening and enriching the value of the brand through the story it wants to tell and the experience it wants to leave its audience with. However, given the current economy of mass customisation, it is increasingly important for designers to understand that their work goes beyond design practice; they must be empathetic. In addition, they must see technological evolution as an ally, for example in the Narrative Principle, by telling the story that the brand wants to convey, the designer can explore new ways of relating to the public by creating enriching interactions in all media.

2.1 Comparative Analysis of FVIS Models

Regarding the focus of the perspectives, it was possible to verify that the models reflect the evolution in the face of current needs. The van Nes (2012) [7] model, although designed to include dynamic visual identity systems, ends up using dynamic examples for the brand mark. The model by Martins et al. (2019) [14] applies to both systems and graphic brands, with the former gaining great interest in the face of today's challenges. Lorenz's model (2021) [5] is exclusively dedicated to systems and their ability to vary visually and adapt to various media and communication objects.

As for the variation of the elements that make up the visual system, van Nes' (2012) [7] perspective does not specify how the elements vary, but she does create very specific categories that turn out to be exclusive. In order to avoid the specificity inherent in the categories, Martins et al. (2019) [14] sought to analyse identities and visual systems in a more objective way, managing to specify how elements can relate and vary through eight mechanisms of variation. Lorenz's model (2021) [5] is quite comprehensive. The author doesn't specify how the elements vary (giving just a few examples) but creates two categories regarding the process of creating a visual identity system. Table 1 shows the occurrence of the Martins et al. variation mechanisms [14] in the various categories of the other authors.

As you can see, all the variation mechanisms can occur in any of Lorenz's (2021) [5] and van Nes's (2012) [7] categories, and in some there are transformations that always occur, such as the "content variation" mechanism in van Nes's "Container" category [7]. It is also possible to associate the "transformation of form" mechanism with systems based on Lorenz transformation. The "combination" mechanism, on the other hand, has a high probability of being present in form-based systems. Despite the definition of eight variation mechanisms, the Martins et al. model [14] is not

Table 1 Occurrence of the variation mechanisms of Martins et al. [14] in the various categories of van Nes (2012) [7] and Lorenz (2021) [5]

		van Nes (2012) [7]						Lorenz (2021) [5]	
		Container	Wallpaper	DNA	Formula	Customized	Generative	Flexible Systems based in shape	Flexible systems based on transformation
Martins et al. (2019) [14]	Color variation	V	V	V	V	V	V	V	V
	Combination	V	V	X	V	V	V	X	V
	Content variation	X	X	V	V	V	V	V	V
	Position	V	V	V	V	V	V	V	V
	Repetition	V	V	X	V	V	V	X	V
	Rotation	V	V	V	V	V	V	V	V
	Scale	V	V	V	V	V	V	V	V
	Shape transformation	V	V	V	V	V	V	V	X

X occurs | V may occur

limiting, as it allows for the use of various mechanisms at both the brand mark and system level.

Finally, the perspectives of Martins et al. (2019) [14] and Lorenz (2021) [5] show a concern to include the ability of the system or visual identity to adapt to various media and communication objects, in addition to its ability to vary graphically. Martins et al. (2019) [14] goes further by trying to understand which variation mechanisms are capable of contributing to adaptation to various contexts and contents. These two perceptions are in line with those of Leitão (2014) [20].

Each model makes contributions to the creation of VISs that can reinvent themselves and adapting to the most varied contexts and content. While van Nes [7] contributed to clarifying concepts regarding the ability of visual identity to vary, Martins et al. [14] explore how it can do so and open the door to identities and systems that can take on various characteristics. In turn, Lorenz [5] delves into the increasingly desirable capabilities of VIS in the face of today's challenges, seeking to reinforce their expressive freedom and adaptability. The latter is the focus of study by Leitão [20] who contributes through Principles that guide the designer throughout the project and complement the creation of flexible visual identities and systems.

The flexibility of a visual identity system gives it greater potential for variation and graphic expressiveness, as well as making it possible to bring customisation closer to the audience profile (Earle, 2021), while at the same time making it possible to reach broad audiences, creating emotional connections with different groups (Kreutz, 2007 [18]). In the same vein, Martins et al. (2019) [14] point out that FVISs make it possible to adapt the visual language to various media and diverse communication objects, going as far as animation and the use of algorithms, making it easier to change the sub-components over time or depending on the context, without compromising identification and coherence (Hollington, 2011 [16]).

3 Case Study

To complement the literature review, a descriptive case study was carried out to collect data on the practice of design with FVIS.

The selection of case studies aimed to include different types of FVIS and similarities with the characteristics of the Ílhavo Maritime Museum (mission, scope, objectives or organisational characteristics):

City of Bologna, Philadelphia Museum of Art, Swedish History Museum, National Gallery of Canada, Moscow Design Museum and the City Museum.

The cases were analysed according to the same structure and parameters: the context in which the project arose, the objectives, the concept, the capabilities, the applications, the creation and (where possible) implementation process, as well as its contribution and results. The parameters were analysed by applying Raposo's (2022) analysis model, as shown in Table 2, answering six questions that made it possible to understand how dynamics and/or flexibility occur and to interpret the

Table 2 Parameters for analysing flexible visual identity systems

Parameters	Analysis model by Raposo (2022) [2]
Variables	1. What are the visual variables (what changes and what is stable)?
Volumetry	2. Is it two-dimensional or does it have volume?
Animation/ transformation	3. Is it animated or does it change any components? How does this transformation take place and with what criteria?
Composition	4. Changes to the logotype/typography, the composition, the scale/size, the colours, the texture, the images, the design style or the symbol? How do the components combine and what possibilities are there in their relative position?
Focus	5. Is the dynamic happening at the level of the graphic brand or visual identity system, and is it visible in the language and means of communication?
Communication media	6. How do the communication media relate visually based on the elements of visual identity (coherence and consistency)?

projects according to the authors analysed previously: van Nes (2012) [7], Leitão (2014) [20], Martins et al. (2019) [14] and Lorenz (2021) [5].

3.1 Results of the Case Study

It was possible to conclude that only two of the organisations studied did not have a pre-existing IR. The remaining cases were rebranding's resulting from the search to revitalise the institution (Sweedish History Museum and City Museum), to renew the institution's identity (National Gallery of Canada) or to solve communication problems (Philadelphia Museum of Art).

As you might expect, all the concepts of the brands analysed reflect the objectives set for the IVSs created. As far as the development of the VI or VIS is concerned, the visual identity for the City of Bologna stands out. To create a detailed briefing, in-depth quantitative and qualitative research was carried out. As for implementation, all the cases involved an immediate, complete, and non-progressive change. There was a concern to make the public aware of the new brands as well as their concept associated with the identity of the institutions they represent.

In the implementation phase, the new systems and visual identities were supported through the creation of marketing plans (Philadelphia Museum of Art), the organisation of open sessions with the designers (City Museum) or structures to coordinate communication (Bologna City).

The systems or visual identities were applied to various communication media, the most common being posters, websites, social networks, merchandise (bags, cloth bags, etc.), flyers and mupis.

Five capabilities were detected when analysing the systems and visual identities studied, which guarantee a degree of flexibility. Diversity, most often associated with the variety of content made available by the institution, is found in the visual identities of the City of Bologna, the Philadelphia Museum of Art and the Sweedish History Museum. The latter two and the City Museum also have systems or visual identities that allow them to be constantly updated. It was also possible to conclude that the cases analysed which are flexible visual systems enjoy greater design freedom and ease of application (The National Gallery of Canada, Moscow Design Museum and City Museum). In the specific case of the City Museum, its ability to adapt to objects and communication media was more readily apparent.

Finally, it proved more difficult to evaluate the contribution of each FVIS, due to the lack of studies among the public. However, most of the visual identity systems studied were still in use at the time of this analysis. The City Museum ended up changing its visual identity and name, adopting its own typeface and a less dynamic and less expressive system. In the case of the Sweedish History Museum and the Philadelphia Museum of Art, the new IVF led to an increase in the number of visitors.

4 Interviews, Graphic Analysis of VIS and Direct Observation

To complement the reference case study, we analysed the Visual Identity Systems, particularly the brand mark, of 37 museums and 5 aquariums/oceanariums from 20 different countries: Germany (1), Denmark (3), Spain (3), France (1), Netherlands (3), England (4), Ireland (1), Iceland (1), Norway (2), Poland (1), Portugal (5), Sweden (1), Canada (2), Chile (1), United States of America (8), China (1), South Korea (1), Japan (1), Australia (1) and New Zealand (1).

This graphic analysis was carried out using an adaptation of the Competitor Map proposed by Raposo et al. (2020) [21] and Viera et al. (2023) [22], with the following analysis parameters: brand mark (Architecture, Type of brand); semantics (what is represented, analysis of the name); syntactics (anatomy of the brand mark, variants, typography, filling, contour, volumetry, colours), imagery.

The data indicates a predominance of corporate brands with monistic architecture, followed by endorsed brands. Most of the symbols allude to maritime elements or fishing, followed by abstract approaches and representations of the headquarters building or the concept of grandeur. The names are mainly descriptive, although there are metaphorical cases.

Syntactically, there is a predominance of cases with one or two variants of the brand mark, tending to be symbol plus logo, almost always with the symbol to the left of the logo. The majority use versalette or uppercase, bold or medium capitalisation.

The symbols are mainly curvilinear, schematized, with fill. In colour terms, blue predominates, followed by black, green, and orange.

Two semi-structured interviews were then conducted with the MMÍ's management to better characterize the museum's Corporate Identity, find out about any problems with the current IR and define a project briefing, as well as gain a deeper understanding of the Museum's history and operations, audiences, counterparts, and internal and external communication needs.

The interviews took place separately, allowing us to learn that the Ílhavo Maritime Museum is made up of three museum spaces (Bacalhaus Museum and Aquarium, Maritime Religiosity Centre and Santo André Ship-Museum), whose mission is "to preserve, study and disseminate in relation to their communities everything that involves maritime culture" (N. Costa, personal communication, June 21, 2022, Appendix C), working with the transversal community that identifies with the maritime theme. The management highlighted the disparity in visual language across the various physical spaces as the main communication problem and reinforced the importance of investing in brand activation.

The Museum's program is very wide-ranging and caters to a very diverse public, mostly Portuguese over the age of 18, but there are projects to interact with younger audiences, especially in conjunction with schools.

As far as communication channels are concerned, the director warned of the evolution and linear progression towards digital. At the time of the interview, there was no merchandising, although this was part of the institution's plans.

Finally, regarding the importance of ÍMM's visual identity, the importance of flexibility, plasticity and adaptability of the graphic media aimed at both young and more conservative audiences was mentioned.

Using the "Direct Observation" method, the ÍMM's visual communication supports in the various museum spaces were analyzed, and it was concluded that there is no globally coherent identity. They are visually coherent, with greater problems in the Cod Museum and Aquarium. Gaps were detected in terms of orientation systems, merchandising and support materials, as well as between printed and digital media. In general, there was an opportunity to increase the impact and flexibility of the ÍMM's communication through a FVIS.

5 Active Research. The Exploratory Case of FVIS Design for the Ílhavo Maritime Museum

Based on the above information and analysis, and in line with Lorenz's (2021) proposal [5], the design process began with the development of the visual identity system (graphic symbols, colours, typography, imagery) and the design of the brand mark, as well as the respective principles of use and standardization.

Graphic Symbols

Twenty-nine symbols were created to visually represent the narrative of the Museum's physical spaces. The graphic elements are intended to be a factor in the flexibility of the IVS, making it, according to Lorenz (2016) [17], an open system, in that new symbols can be created and added.

It was considered appropriate to use a rectilinear design, defining a grid based on the shape of the region's typical boats.

The symbols are highly schematic without being abstract, making them easy to apply and adapt to modules.

The symbols are applied and combined in a square grid, in which the symbols can appear in solid colours, textures or photographs. The repetition of the symbols—net, pattern of fishermen's shirts, sea, mesh, and rope—makes it possible to create continuous patterns (Fig. 1).

Colour Palette

The color of the ÍMM is blue, shared with the Cod Museum and Aquarium, unlike the other subunits:

Purple for the Center for Maritime Religiosity;
Orange for the Santo André Ship-Museum;
Green for CIEMar-Ílhavo.

Typography

Two typefaces were used: Centrales Sans and Flecha M. The first for the logo (Centrale Sans Bold) and for long texts, complemented by the Flecha M font for titles and short notes.

Images

The imagery is made up of symbols and photographs in black and white or color, to which a grain filter is added.

Brand Mark

The concept of the brand mark is based on the preposition "de" in the ÍMM's name, which refers to the sense of belonging to the city of "Ílhavo".

The concept consists of a symbolic and graphic representation of the museum's content in place of the preposition "de", giving a total of 9 possible symbols, to which others can be added.

On the other hand, in addition to the different symbol possibilities, the relative position between symbol and logo can take on three arrangements that differ in the number of lines in a grid and the justification of the content to the right/left (Fig. 2).

Graphic Applications

It was planned to design some communication media and apply the proposed visual identity system, namely: stationary, posters, flyers, flags, mupi, social networks, roll-up, website, credentials, brochure, merchandising (Fig. 3).

Fig. 1 Origin and construction grid of graphic symbols (Maria Figueira, 2023 [23])

6 Conclusions

Through this research process, it was possible to deepen our knowledge of FVIS, seeking to contribute to the adoption of a more explicit term, the identification of the principles that give them flexibility and coherence, and design methods.

Fig. 2 Examples of graphic media using the FVIS designed for the ÍMM [23])

Case studies of visual identities and flexible visual identity systems of a cultural nature were analysed, considering the perspectives studied. The knowledge acquired was put into practice through an exploratory case for the FVIS for the Ílhavo Maritime Museum.

The FVIS faithfully represents the entity, its narrative and variety of themes. The research thus proved to be productive, meeting the objectives and answering the main question "How can flexible visual identity systems contribute to the communication of museums, in particular the Ílhavo Maritime Museum?".

The visual identity system developed is dynamic in terms of the brand mark, with flexible characteristics, particularly expressiveness. The design of the ÍMM brand mark followed the principles proposed by Leitão [20], giving it coherence in different media and communication objects. On the other hand, the proposed FVIS is an open system that allows for the introduction of new symbols, which enables it to be managed and updated to meet new narrative and functional needs, contributing to its longevity. It is an FVI that is applicable to both the brand mark and the entire visual communication system and media.

Fig. 3 Examples of graphic artifacts using the SIFV designed for the ÍMM (Maria Figueira, 2023 [23])

In general, both the non-interventionist and active research components establish a correlation between the flexibility of visual identity systems and expressive freedom for the designer, the ability to adapt across media and communication objects, and versatility in terms of updating over time.

Acknowledgements This article is results from a Master's dissertation in Communication Design at the Faculty of Architecture of the University of Lisbon, defended in July 2023, entitled Sistemas de Identidade Visual Flexíveis em Instituições Culturais: O Caso do Museu Marítimo de Ílhavo, under the supervision of Professors João Brandão and Daniel Raposo [22].

References

1. Strunck, G. L. (2007). Como criar identidades visuais para marcas de sucesso. Rio de Janeiro: Rio Books.
2. Raposo, D.: Definição do Sistema de Identidade e Linguagem Visual da Marca. Manuscrito em preparação.
3. Magalhães, A., & Oliveira, F. (2023). Visual synthesis languages of the DNA of the Star Michelin gastronomic brands: Comparative Case Studies. Convergences—Journal of Research and Arts Education, 13(26), 149–165. https://doi.org/10.53681/c1514225187514391s.26.52
4. Raposo, D., Silva, F., Correia, R., Ribeiro, R., Neves, J., & Silva, J. (2022). Brand Marks examination. Empirical study of graphic parts in their relation to contrast, recognition, and memorization. Ergonomics in Design, 47, 574–582. https://doi.org/10.54941/ahfe1001985
5. Lorenz, M. (2021). Flexible Visual Systems (2nd ed.). Slanted Publishers.
6. Kreutz, E. (2001). As Principais Estratégias de Construção da Identidade Visual Corporativa. Universidade Católica do Rio Grande do Sul, Porto Alegre.
7. van Nes, I. (2012). Dynamic Identities: How to Create a Living Brand. Amsterdam, The Netherlands: BIS Publishers.
8. Fonte, P., Martins, N., Raposo, D., Pereira, L. (2023). Dynamic Visual Identities: Fundamental Principles of Their Design. In: Martins, N., Raposo, D. (eds) Communication Design and Branding. Springer Series in Design and Innovation, vol 32. Springer, Cham. https://doi.org/10.1007/978-3-031-35385-7_3
9. Peón, M. L. (2001). Sistemas de identidade visual. Rio de Janeiro: 2AB.
10. Gernsheimer, J. (2008). Designing logos: the process of creating symbols that endure. Allworth Press.
11. Wheeler, A. (2009). Designing Brand Identity (3rd ed.). John Wiley & Sons.
12. Jochum, E. (2013). Dynamic Branding: How flexible design systems turn brands into dynamic visual identities. Zurich University of the Arts, Zurich, Switzerland.
13. Murdock, J. E. (2016). Fluid Identity: History & Practice of Dynamic Visual Identity Design.
14. Martins, T., Cunha, J., Bicker, J., & Machado, P. (2019). Dynamic Visual Identities: From a Survey of the State-Of-The-Art to a Model of Features and Mechanisms. Visible Language. 53. 4–35. https://doi.org/10.34314/vl.v53i2.4649.
15. Felsing, U. (2010). Dynamic Identities in Cultural and Public Contexts. Lars Müller Publishers.
16. Hollington, S. (2011). Flexible visual identity systems. MA in Communication Design, Kingston University.
17. Lorenz, M. (2016). Sistemas visuales en identidades dinámicas [Universitat de Barcelona]. Disponível em: http://diposit.ub.edu/dspace/handle/2445/96603%0A, http://hdl.handle.net/2445/96603
18. Kreutz, E. (2007). Identidade Visual Corporativa Mutante: uma estratégia comunicacional contemporânea. In XXX Congresso Brasileiro de Ciências da Comunicação.
19. Kreutz, E. (2012). Construindo Marcas Mutantes. Chasqui. Revista Latinoamericana de Comunicación, 0(119), 61–65.
20. Leitão, S. (2014). Princípios estruturantes e orientadores da identidade visual de marcas em ambientes multimeios. Universidade de Aveiro. http://hdl.handle.net/10773/15166.
21. Raposo, D., Ribeiro, R., Amaral, M., da Silva, F.M., Martin Sanromán, J.R. (2020). The Brand Mark Competitors Map as Visual Research Tool. Using Graphic and Symbolic Data in the Brand Visual Identity Project. In: Rebelo, F., Soares, M. (eds) Advances in Ergonomics in Design. AHFE 2019. Advances in Intelligent Systems and Computing, vol 955. Springer, Cham. https://doi.org/10.1007/978-3-030-20227-9_9
22. Vieira, A., Brandão, J., Raposo, D., Martins, N. (2023). Principles for the Design of Brand Marks. In: Martins, N., Raposo, D. (eds) Communication Design and Branding. Springer Series in Design and Innovation, vol 32. Springer, Cham. https://doi.org/10.1007/978-3-031-35385-7_2
23. Figueira, M. (2023)—Sistemas de Identidade Visual Flexíveis em Instituições Culturais: O Caso do Museu Marítimo de Ílhavo. Faculdade de Arquitetura da Universidade de Lisboa

Fondazione Italiana Tipoteca and Museo Bodoniano: The Spill-Over of Digitisation of Typographic Collections into the Museum's Digital and Physical Realm

Emanuela F. Bonini Lessing

Abstract The paper focuses on the digitisation of typographic collections in two Italian museums: Tipoteca Italiana Fondazione, Museo Bodoniano. An earlier survey allowed us to understand the processes of acquisition of digital photographs, the organisation of documents in databases, and the availability of direct access to them by staff and external users in different Italian typographic museums. The research reported here brings a further dimension to the earlier survey by looking at the physical museum spaces from which digitisations originate, including the observation of relationships between real and virtual equipment and devices. It also examines whether the two museums can be considered hubs for the development of typographic culture, both in a virtual and in a real sense. It verifies whether documents, artefacts, together with people's living knowledge and experience contribute to the realisation of a true ecology of knowledge. The methods adopted included a review of the answers from the previous survey, an interview with the designer responsible for the concept of the institutional websites, an analysis of the websites and a visit to both museum spaces.

Keywords Typographic digital heritage · Italian printing museums · Hybrid museums

1 Survey on the Digitisation of Printing Collections in Italy

Previous research on Italian typographic museums (Bonini Lessing 2024) highlighted the dispersion of analog typographic artefacts in the country, due to various reasons. Currently, most holdings are difficult to identify, as they can be found in libraries, in non-specialised archives, in various other museum categories—e.g. those of science

E. F. Bonini Lessing (✉)
Università Iuav di Venezia, Venezia, Italy
e-mail: ebonini@iuav.it

© The Author(s), under exclusive license to Springer Nature Switzerland AG 2025
D. Brandão et al. (eds.), *Perspectives on Design and Digital Communication V*, Springer Series in Design and Innovation 50, https://doi.org/10.1007/978-3-031-76156-0_9

and technology—, as well as being present in presumably numerous private collections that are only partially open to the public, making research complex and a precise estimate of what is available impossible.

In this context, AIMSC—Associazione Italiana Musei della Stampa e della Carta (Italian Association of Printing and Paper Museums) (https://aimsc.it/)—a non-profit organisation founded in Italy in 2005—constitutes the only aggregated and explicit reference for printing museums in the country (Bonini Lessing 2024).

An assessment of the state of digitisation of the typographic collections held by AIMSC associated museums revealed the absence of shared models and procedures (Bonini Lessing 2024).[1] Thus, in 2022 a methodology was specifically developed to assess the state of digitisation of artefacts, consisting of a quantitative and a qualitative questionnaire applied to museum directors/curators. The questionnaire not only allowed for an initial estimation of the purposes and use of digital collection, but also aimed to verify the availability of the catalogued items to external users through various tools, such as databases, websites, and digital query devices in museum exhibitions. The research highlighted the existence of two important institutions in Italy, Tipoteca Italiana Fondazione and Museo Bodoniano,[2] which, not being part of AIMSC,[3] had not been investigated.

This paper intends to fill this gap, extending the survey method previously developed and described to these two institutions. The research reported here also investigates the relationship between information on collections available on the website and those available in the exhibition spaces of the two surveyed museums. To achieve this objective, the methodology includes a review of the answers regarding this topic gathered in the survey, an interview with the designer responsible for the concept of the institutional websites of TIF and MB, the observation of their websites, and a visit to both museum spaces.

Unlike studies that focus on the processes of digitisation and virtual collaboration, the research reported here is also interested in the physical museum spaces from which the digitisations originate, considering that those are key assets for carrying out activities related to contemporary print culture. We were therefore also interested in the relationship between real and virtual equipment and devices, between website and exhibition, and in how these tools contribute to fostering knowledge (Bollini and Borsotti 2023).

This paper examines whether TIF and MB can be considered hubs for the development of typographic culture, both in the virtual and the real sense. That is to say, it intends to verify whether documents and artefacts, combined with museum staff and visitor's expertise and experience contribute to the realisation of a true ecology of knowledge, in which the opposition between old and new is overcome, concepts such as those of loss and obsolescence are abandoned in favour of others such as

[1] A similar concern was also found among AEMP—Association of European Printing Museums (https://www.aepm.eu/).

[2] From now on Tipoteca Fondazione Italiana will be referred to as TIF and Museo Bodoniano as MB.

[3] In the meantime, TIF has joined AIMSC.

Fig. 1 Location map of the museums examined

reuse, renewal and new productions, inspired by different forms of knowledge and experience (Cameron 2021) (Fig. 1).

2 Saving, Digitising, and Carrying the Digital into the Physical Museum

The presence of publicly available typographic collections in Italy is due to the work carried out over time by some public institutions, such as museums and libraries, which collected, systematised and displayed materials whose historical or social value was already recognised long before the transition from analogue to digital was evident with all its consequences. Researchers in the field of Italian design heritage have already documented and discussed the rather silent practice of rescuing various typographic assets—printing presses, typefaces, punches, papers, inks, etc.—carried out also by individual enthusiasts since the 1990s, in contrast to the logic of discarding old technologies in favour of newer ones (Passerini 2014; Bonini Lessing et al. 2020).

A number of studies have shown how this first phase of rescue—which is still ongoing, even though much technical equipment has now been definitively lost—has been followed by another aimed at safeguarding artefacts not only physically but also through digital scanning or photography, by placing them in digital memories. This is the first transition to digital of elements produced and used in the analogue world (Cameron 2021). This activity was often conducted in an amateur manner by practitioners, who generally used unspecialised systems for acquiring, saving and possibly sharing data, with no real classificatory, let alone museum or exhibition purpose.[4]

Parallel to these safeguard actions, other opportunities have arisen in more recent typographic practice. On the one hand, the production of typefaces designed, developed and used only in the digital medium, has increased. On the other hand, analogue typefaces have been designed, developed and produced using digital tools and machines. These are sometimes aimed at supplementing incomplete original typographic sets in order to ensure their use in letterpress printing again, juxtaposing old types with new ones (Beckloff 2022). Sometimes, on the other hand, the aim is to explore new pre-digital printing potentials using complete typographic sets designed and produced with digital systems (Caccamo and Vendetti 2019; Vendetti 2019). Between these two lines of activity lies a vast and difficult to classify production of digital typefaces based on, or merely inspired by, historical sources (Cooper et al. 2014; Olocco and Patané 2022; Jury 2019; Shaw 2017).

These activities imply new questions about the possibility of collecting and valorising recent production, perhaps even "musealising" it, as much as their analogue-only predecessors (Amado et al. 2022). What role can typography museums play in current developments in research and design practice? Which artefacts and documents are to be saved and how can they be made available to the public? Who is the museum aimed at: specialised scholars or also amateurs, practitioners and design professionals? Is the museum a place of preservation or also of design theory and practice?

This paper highlights the events behind the digitisation processes of typographic collections in two Italian museums, TIF and MB. Furthermore, it intends to verify whether digitisation has generated something more than the preservation of materials through a migration of information from analogue to digital system (Bollini and Guida 2023; Resmini and Rosati 2011). That is, whether digital repositories have enabled new forms of storytelling and narratives that were previously unimaginable and unrealisable, and whether such archives and narratives are proposed in relation to other counterparts, constituting an open network of knowledge (Schnapp 2015; Dal Falco and Vassos 2017; Bulegato and Scotti 2024; Ceconello 2022).

The concept of an open, living archive (Collavizza 2019) presupposes two essential conditions (Bosco et al. 2023). First, the very evolution of the concept of archive from a private repository of documents to a platform for online content sharing. Second, the accessibility and practicability of contents in such an archive, that is now no longer available only the archive owner or experts, but also to a variety of users and content producers.

When this condition is realised, the promoting institution shares in a 'diffuse' way the authority, the expertise and even the capacity to generate content, along with partners that are accredited from time to time in a continuous process of knowledge

[4] In Italy, alongside these practices, however, there are also a variety of operations initiated by public institutions and private companies aimed at creating digital copies of analogue documents, entrusting tasks to international experts, through contracts and technical-scientific protocols. See e.g. the digitisation of the Venice State Archive in the framework of the Venice Time Machine project lead by EPFL https://www.epfl.ch/research/domains/venice-time-machine/.

generation (Cook 2013; Bonini Lessing 2022). This implies that the archive—which in the two cases presented here also coincides with the museum—goes beyond an analogue and digital repository of artefacts available to a restricted circle of experts, becoming the node of a network of relations between different stakeholders, of which the archive/museum is only one among many (Hazan 2013).

3 Object of the Investigation: Tipoteca Italiana Fondazione, Museo Bodoniano

Tipoteca Italiana Fondazione, known as Tipoteca, (Crocetta del Montello, Treviso) (https://www.tipoteca.it/en/) and Museo Bodoniano (Parma) are two Italian institutions dedicated to typography: the first with a focus on Italian and Veneto region typography, the second with a specific emphasis on the production of one of the most important Italian typographers of the past, Giambattista Bodoni.

TIF is a private, non-profit foundation established in 1995 and promoted by the Antiga brothers, owners of the printing and publishing company Grafiche Antiga. The Foundation's aim is to highlight and enhance the value of the Italian type and printing heritage, and it includes a museum, archive, library, print shop and auditorium. TIF is a member of AEPM (Association of European Printing Museums) and since 2023, of AIMSC (Associazione Italiana Musei della Stampa e della Carta).

MB claims to be the oldest printing museum in Italy, opened in 1963. It is located inside Palazzo della Pilotta, a monumental building that also hosts the Farnese Theatre, the National Gallery of Parma and the National Archaeological Museum. Its foundation coincided with the 150th anniversary of the death of Giambattista Bodoni, the typographer from the Piemonte region who made Parma the world capital of printing in the second half of the eighteenth century. MB is a member of AEPM, but not of AIMSC.

Both institutions are relevant for the breadth of the collections conserved and for their role in the preservation of historical memory. They are, however, two very different realities from a statutory point of view—the first is a private foundation, the second is a public museum—, this difference greatly influences their mission, operation and relationship with other public and private entities.

While taking these factors into account, the homogeneity of the materials in TIF and MB compared to the other museums in AIMSC makes the application of the methods adopted in the earlier survey (Bonini Lessing 2024) possible and consistent.

4 Application of Quantitative and Qualitative Survey Methods

A double questionnaire, aimed mainly at estimating the extent of digitised typography collections and the use museums make of what they acquire digitally, was developed in 2022 (Bonini Lessing 2024).

Before explaining the characteristics of the survey methods in more detail, it is necessary to recall the understanding of the term "digitisation" and "typographic collection".

In the context of the research reported here, the term "typographic collection" encompasses a variety of tools and artefacts, ranging from various types of printing presses, sets of movable type in different sizes and materials (wood, metal), printing papers, inks and binding tools, as well as their outputs such as posters, books, type specimens and documents detailing the profiles of entrepreneurs and/or previous business activities.

The term "digitisation" is understood here in a very broad sense, evidencing the existence of any of the following services: (a) acquisition of digital photographs of typographic collections, (b) photographic scanning or two/three-dimensional digital reproductions of the artefacts, (c) organisation of data related to documents in databases, (d) possibility of direct access to databases by museum staff or external users (scholars, designers, amateurs).

Similarly to the previous study, the first four questions posed to the directors/curators of TIF and MB assume yes/no answers and aim to determine an initial overview of digitisation practices. In line with the expanded objective of the investigation reported here, a last question was added about the presence of a printing workshop area within the museum space (Table 1).

Table 1 Preliminary questionnaire

	Tipoteca Italiana Fondazione	Museo Bodoniano
Acquisition of digital photographs of various typographical items	Yes	Yes
Photographic scanning or two/three-dimensional digital reproductions of the same	Yes	Yes
Organisation of the digital collections in the form of databases	Yes	Yes
Possibility of direct access to the digitised items by museum staff or by external users (scholars, designers, amateurs)	Yes, to museum staff only	Yes, to museum staff only
Availability of a printing workshop or a workroom for related activities	Yes	No

Table 2 Qualitative questionnaire

	Tipoteca Italiana Fondazione	Museo Bodoniano
Approximately what percentage of the collection is photographed or digitised with respect to the number of items owned by the institution?	20%	100%
How did you carry out these operations (e.g. by outsourcing to specialised companies or were they done in-house, etc.)?	They were done in-house	They were done with external assignments
For what purposes are the photographic images or digitisations utilised (e.g. website, printed catalogues, databases, etc.)?	They are mainly used for communication media (the website, the social networks) and for printed matter, at the request of third parties too	Printed publications (monographs or articles), study reasons (theses or other), commercial reasons (websites, our gadgets)
Does the museum have multimedia facilities within the exhibition spaces?	We have videos. The provision of audio guides with a web app is planned	There is a large touchscreen table (possibility of use by 4 users simultaneously) in an exhibition room of the museum
What audiences is the content addressed to?	The target audience is mostly schools of all levels. People interested in the field of communication design, typography and editorial design	Different: pupils, tourists, graphics/typography enthusiasts/professionals. Mostly non-experts
How often are the multimedia contents updated/implemented/replaced?	Unfortunately, contents are not updated	No replacement is currently planned
Approximately how many items are on display in the museum premises compared to those held in storage?	Approximately 30% of the materials owned are on display	In the new museum layout, much less than in the old one, because of smaller spaces: about 5%

This series of questions was followed by a qualitative questionnaire, offering the possibility of open-ended answers, concerning the way in which the acquisitions took place and the use the institution makes of the digitised collection, both in the virtual (e.g. use for the website, videos) and analogue (e.g. for catalogue publications, etc.) realms (Table 2).

5 Main Findings of the Survey

The percentage of items photographed or digitised by the two institutions is quite different: TIF claims to have digitised about 20% of its holdings, MB the totality. Diametrically opposed is the way in which the acquisition of the collection was carried out: at TIF through operators within the institution, and at MB through external professional commissions. Both institutions use databases to organise acquired data, which however is available only to in-house operators. The websites have minimal showcase functions, and do not serve as open archives.

Concerning the display of collections within the museum spaces, TIF shows about 30% of what it holds (and has acquired about 20%), MB displays only 5% (but has digitised 100% of the holdings related to the typographic assets).[5]

The majority of the public visiting the two museums are schoolchildren, who visit in large and scheduled groups. Amateurs and professionals in the design field are also an important part of the public, as are tourists—but almost exclusively in the case of the MB, which is located in the multifunctional monumental complex of the Pilotta, in the city of Parma. While schoolchildren and tourists generally visit museums only once, amateurs and professionals are perhaps the only ones who would maintain a continuous consultation of the website and eventually visit the museum again. This part of the public is potentially interested in the cultural offer consisting of various events and would be willing to return several times.

Concerning the dissemination of digitised collections, both institutions stated that they use the photos and scans to describe their holdings via the website and to produce institutional printed matter.

TIF also employs this material in the museum layout, illustrating the functioning of the printing presses by placing videos next to them (Fig. 2). Nevertheless, audio is not switched on because the exhibition was not designed to accommodate so many visitors at the same time, who would now be annoyed by the volume of the narration, as no specific sound stations are available. MB has employed digital tools and media to make ancient printed artefacts virtually browsable through a touch screen table in the museum[6] (Fig. 2). However, neither the videos nor the touchscreen table were updated after being put on display.

Further considerations can be made by comparing the answers provided by TIF and MB with those provided by other AIMSC members during the previous study.

Regarding the percentage of photographed or digitised collections, it is difficult to make comparisons, because the answers given by respondents differ greatly from each other. However, it can be said that TIF is in line with the majority of museums, i.e. they have digitised only a part (less than half) of their holdings, whereas MB is on a par with only three museums that claim to have digitised the entirety of their collection. TIF's practice of relying on in-house staff to make digital photographs

[5] The difference between the two institutions relates to the quantity of assets, the type of collection and their physical dimensions: TIF collects mainly working tools (punches, typefaces, as well as printing presses of various eras and technologies), MB mainly the outputs of typographic processing, i.e. printed artefacts. Another relevant difference relates, of course, to the extension of exhibition space available.

[6] Conversations between the author of the study and the museum staff revealed that an extensive digitisation campaign between 2008 and 2011 made it possible to digitally acquire many historic books, now available in the current 13 volumes that can be browsed in full on the touchscreen table. For further information on the digitisation purposes see: De Pasquale, A. (2010). I progetti di digitalizzazione del Museo Bodoniano di Parma. DigItalia, 5(2), 135–143.

Fig. 2 Scheme of the museum set-up of the two case studies. In orange: original documents and machinery. In light blue: digital exhibition equipment. The image above depicts the visitor's experience at Museo Bodoniano: a large interactive table at the end of the exhibition route allows visitors to browse the scanned books. The bottom picture shows the visitor's experience at Tipoteca Italiana Fondazione: the videos illustrate the functioning of the different machineries on display

or scans is similar to 60% of the other surveyed museums, while the rest of AIMSC members used external experts. All of the interviewed museums, including TIF and MB, use a part of the digitisations on printed matter and the website.

In addition, TIF's stated practice of including films based on the digitised materials on display in the museum layout is also common in 80% of the other museums. MB makes digitisations available by means of a touch screen table, as most other surveyed institutions claim to do. What emerges, however, is that while most of

AIMSC members adopt a combination of technologies—video and simple databases to be queried—on display, TIF and MB choose only one. The answer given by TIF and MB regarding the updating of media content in the exhibition is the same as that of the other interviewees: once made, they were no longer updated or increased. As far as exhibition design is concerned, the responses provided by TIF and MB confirm the general ability of all institutions to show a very small part of the collection held in storage—with the exception of two AIMSC museums interviewed previously which claimed to be able to show everything.

6 Genesis of the Institutional Websites and Their Relationship with the Museum Exhibition

The methodologically new part of this study includes an interview conducted with designer Damiano Fraccaro of Otium Studio, who developed both TIF's and MB's websites: the former commissioned in 2015, the latter in 2017, both of which went online about a year after being commissioned.[7]

The interview provided in-depth information on the print collections available digitally online on the websites and those available in the museum exhibition spaces.

In both cases, the website development brief also included a review of the visual identity of the museum. TIF and MB already had web pages, but both of them were rather outdated in terms of content and technology (e.g. neither was responsive) (Figs. 3 and 4).

As far as the museum layout is concerned, at the time of the development of the website, TIF had a visitor itinerary open to the public for more than a decade, which has remained essentially the same until today.[8]

At the time the new website was being commissioned, MB was housed on the third floor of the Pilotta building, only to be relocated to the ground floor and reopened at the end of 2022, after being closed for about a year and a half. Due to the smaller space available, the new exhibit consists of fewer display cases, a necessity that has given the impetus for a second phase of digitisation of many books, which can now be consulted thanks to the touch screen table.[9]

Damiano Fraccaro was asked the same questions regarding the work done for the two museums. The questions focus on aspects of website design and the relationship

[7] For an interview with Damiano Fraccaro on the launch of the MB website see https://www.frizzifrizzi.it/2019/02/01/il-museo-bodoniano-di-parma-ha-rinnovato-sito-e-identita-visiva/.

[8] For an extended discussion on the funding of TIF, the museum set-up and the relevance of the institution at the international level, see: Berra, S. (2006). Una storia di carattere. Dieci anni di Tipoteca Italiana; Berra, S., & Facchin, L. (Eds.). (2018). Tipoteca: una storia italiana. Antiga edizioni.

[9] For an extended discussioin on MB before the new opening, see: Ciavarella, A. (1968). Catalogo del Museo bodoniano di Parma. Museo Bodoniano, Parma; Museo Bodoniano (2005). I quarant'anni del Museo Bodoni 1963–2003. Museo Bodoniano, Parma.

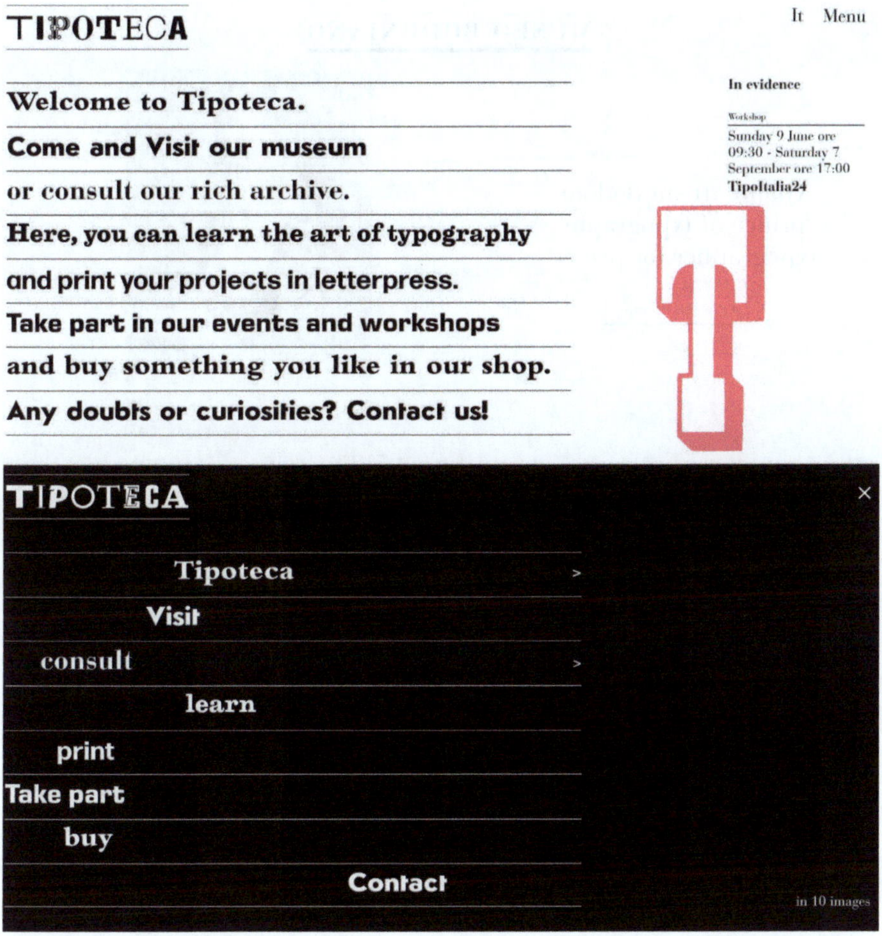

Fig. 3 Tipoteca landing page and menu. Design by Damiano Fraccaro—Otium studio

between website and exhibition, i.e. the relationship between real and virtual visits (Table 3).

7 Conclusions and Future Research

The research on TIF and MB contributed to the objective of completing the survey on digitisation processes in typographic museums, previously conducted with at the time members of AIMSC (Bonini Lessing 2024). It is now possible to define the state of digitisation of the collections owned by each of the museums, to compare them with the other museums examined, so as to constitute a mapping on the subject.

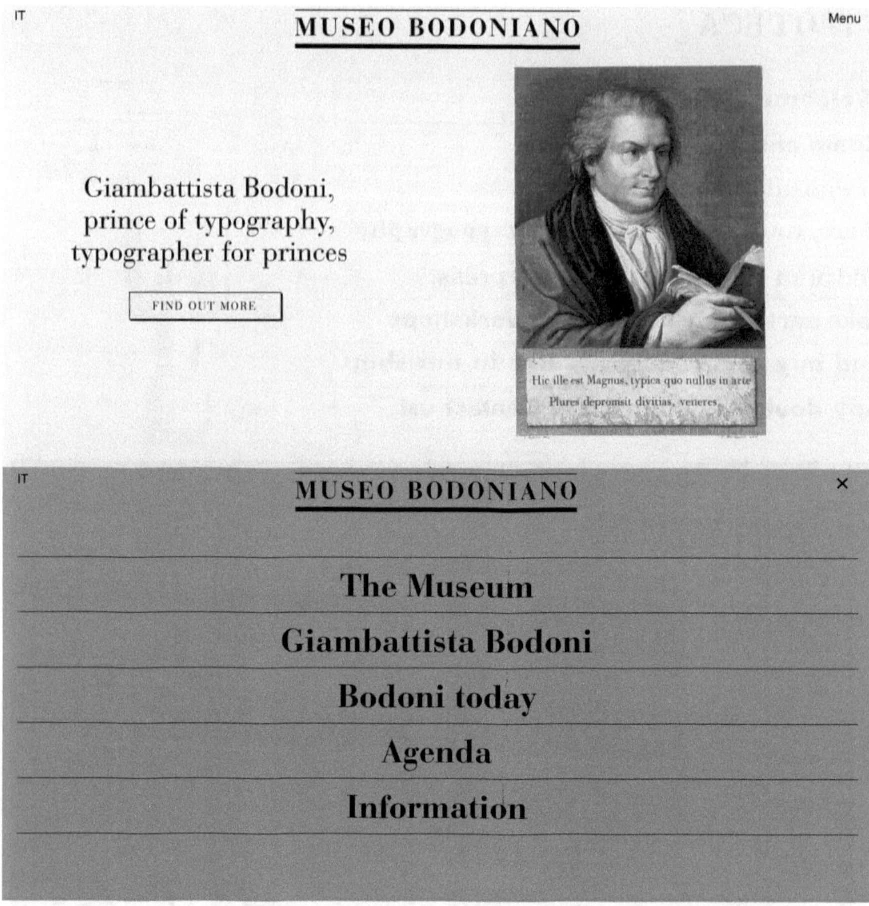

Fig. 4 Museo Bodoniano landing page and menu. Design by Damiano Fraccaro—Otium studio

The first part of the paper discusses the availability and accessibility by visitors of the digitised collection compared to the collection physically present in the museum display.

The interview with the websites designer allowed for the verification of how digitisations were used both to create the institutional websites and how they were poured into the exhibition.

It can be stated that the desired transformation of the two archives from repository of documents to platform for on-line sharing has yet to be completed, for TIF as well as MB. In fact, the two websites serve the essential function of showcases, enunciating certain documents and activities to be found on site. They provide very partial information on the print collections, having chosen to digitise and show only a few sample documents compared to the vastness of those held in the physical archive.

Table 3 Interview with Damiano Fraccaro, designer of Tipoteca Italiana Fondazione (TIF) and Museo Bodoniano (MB) websites. Answers refers to the corresponding working experience with each institution

Which professionals within the museum did you deal with for the development of the website?	
TIF With practically all of them (there aren't many), each in his or her role (who leads the educational part, who the print shop, who the events, etc.) as far as content is concerned, clearly the owner for approval of everything	**MB** Mainly with the museum manager
Were other external professionals involved, e.g. a curator, archivist, etc.?	
TIF Just to check some specific historical/educational notions. Then of course a website programmer, also to enhance the photographic part according to the website's settings	**MB** In the "Bodoni today" section, many professionals were involved: for the "Type Test" section, various type designers described the characteristics of typefaces inspired by Bodoni and provided font licences for online trials; in the "Bodoni news" section graphic designers, editorial designers, archives, testified to the use of Bodoni in their productions, some of which are considered iconic today (e.g. Vignelli Centre). And then a website programmer, also to fine-tune the photographic selection according to the website's settings
Given that you were asked to develop the website in parallel with the revision of the museum's visual identity, did you modify/agree with the brief you were given?	
TIF Together, we decided to dedicate pages that would best describe the articulation of their activities: museum, didactics, archives, print shop, events, etc. Together we also decided to feature specific pages about certain typefaces originating in the archive. This way, the website is not only a translation of the physical space, but also a translation of TIF's role on the Italian and international scene	**MB** I suggested expanding the website on the theme of Bodoni today, to also recount what Bodoni's legacy is today—or at any rate since his death. The proposal was received with interest: I took care to structure the content and the relationship with the external entities involved
Has the website been implemented over time/successively? If so, with what functions, sections, etc.?	
TIF It has not been changed, and is now almost 9 years old. It is very rare for a website to remain active for so long and still perform so well	**MB** Structurally not so much. Some menu headings have been changed and an ad hoc section was created after the Museum's recent change of location. Now the section "The Museum" is divided into several parts, including New Museum Bodoniano and Museum 1963–2022
To create the new website, were materials scanned specifically to make them available online?	
TIF A large part of the digital photos on the website were made ad hoc on this occasion, especially those concerning typefaces, while others that had previously been used for publications, mainly concerning certain historical documents, were reused	**MB** Most of the images on the website were produced specifically for this occasion, especially those concerning typefaces, while others were images that had already been used for publications, mainly concerning some historical documents

(continued)

Table 3 (continued)

Which professionals within the museum did you deal with for the development of the website?	
Did you address the issue of the relationship between the website and the existing analogue collection or the itinerary of the museum display?	
TIF Yes, the tour path of the website retraces the physical tour. The online navigation mirrors the on-site navigation step by step	**MB** In the section presenting the museum and the collection, the tour path is followed step by step. The "Today" section—note the colour change in the pages—is deliberately detached from the relationship with the physical place; it aims to be an expansion of what is on display in the museum
Is there any connection between the website and any digitally searchable material on site in the exhibition space—such as databases with more detailed information, interactive tables, etc.?	
TIF The museum layout dates back to 2002. So it has no interaction with the website. They are working on creating an app that will allow more dialogue between physical and digital space	**MB** At the time of my assignment, the original 1960s layout had no digital interaction. The new exhibition space offers a large interactive table with which you can navigate the website and digitally browse through some of Bodoni's important works
Does the website have direct links to other websites/databases/museums/archives related to the same topic?	
TIF Yes, to Grafiche Antiga—the company that owns the Fondazione Tipoteca Italiana, to other international museums and/or associations the museum belongs to	**MB** Yes, to the Pilotta, the museum's headquarters, to the Foundation, and to other international museums and/or associations the museum belongs to—see website footer
Would you like to add anything relevant to this assignment?	
TIF The website was designed to use 6 different typefaces, the 6 fonts also adopted for Tipoteca's visual identity. This feature is quite distinctive and complex to implement, both in terms of identity and web development. The entire website was in fact designed ad hoc	**MB** I think the "Type Test" and "Bodoni in Use" sections are very useful on an educational level, as well as allowing the museum (which is mainly known by insiders) to be able to relate internationally. The feedback and dialogue with the masters of contemporary typography has been exciting

However, MB's website includes a section dedicated to content beyond the museum collection: "Bodoni today" constitutes an interpretation of the functions a website can offer, an innovation compared to TIF's, which precedes it in time. It therefore represents a kind of membrane, a core platform for the exchange of information with external users—at the moment only a small selection of interlocutors. This section also presents an original curatorial and narrative interpretation, closely linking historical sources with the contemporary. The toolkit it provides allows for a certain possibility of interaction by designers and expert users.

As the interview with the web-designer and the observation of the website itself demonstrate, the two institutions do not present themselves in a particularly open and relational manner towards other archives or museums either, limiting the relationship to a restricted set of direct links to external subjects.

As previously detailed, the website and visual identity came about as a response to the need for a cultural repositioning of TIF and MB, as well as the need for a technological upgrade of earlier devices. On this occasion, a selection of artefacts was digitally photographed and then "displayed" virtually. Although functions and information available online are limited, the website gives preliminary insights into the historic collection of the institution and is easy for non-experts to navigate as well.[10]

With respect to the connection between equipment and devices, both virtual and real, and to the relationship between the website and the exhibition, the study highlights how each new task was considered separately, with no particular coordination between them. The website gives an account of the exhibition route, not vice versa, using a linear logic—the following tool includes information conveyed by the previous one and not a circular one, where the tools are part of a unique system, real and virtual. Obviously, it is much more agile to update a website than an actual exhibition layout. However, there seems to be a recent awareness at TIF, not so much of the advantages of reciprocity in outreach tools, but of the need to make the individual visitor's experience more in-depth and interactive than is now possible, relying only on captions placed next to the artefacts and videos without sound.

At present, in the two museums, technologies are not drivers of the knowledge ecology described in the introduction. However, this is achieved in part at TIF, thanks to a set of other "analogue factors". These include the articulation of the institution's spaces, divided into areas dedicated to temporary exhibitions, an auditorium, a library, but above all a place for complementary study and project activities, such as bookbinding workshops, calligraphy, etc., and a letterpress printing room equipped with two machines and all the necessary tools—from typefaces to inks and compatible papers. All this would be mere inert matter without the technical and passionate input of the staff who work there on a daily basis, bringing the diverse functions into being. Together with the online information, this makes TIF an attractive place for different targets, from schoolchildren to practitioners, designers, scholars, who together make up a community that is both local and international.

Lastly, since the Italian association of printing and paper museums is by vocation open to new members, future research could have the main task of extending the mapping on the digitisation of new museums' collections by applying the questionnaires presented here to new members. Further research could verify the relationship between the digitised collection and the exhibit on display, as has already been done for TIF and MB. The tools of analysis used in the study are simple and basic enough to be extended to other museums belonging to the same category, or to be applied to other museum groupings.

---

[10] This unfortunately places the two museums in the same position as many other Italian archives, which have poorly digitised and shared examples of their holdings online. For further knowledge on this topic see Chiesa, R., Filippini, A. (2022), Suggerire nuove storie dai documenti: l'Archivio Vico Magistretti/Suggesting New Stories from Documents: The Vico Magistretti Archive, Officina 38, pp. 62–65.

Acknowledgments I express my gratitude to Caterina Silva/Fondazione Museo Bodoniano and Sandro Berra/Tipoteca Italiana Fondazione for the information they provided, far beyond the mere answer to the survey.

References

Amado, P., Silva, A. C., Quelhas, V.: Post digital letterpress printing: Research, education and practice. Routledge, London (2022).

Beckloff, E.: Digital fabrication: Expanding access to and preservation of letterpress printing. In P. Amado, A. C. Silva, & V. Quelhas (Eds.), Post digital letterpress printing: Research, education and practice, pp. 95–103. Routledge, London (2022).

Bollini, L., Borsotti, M.: Exhibitions as Hybrid Environments. Exploring Situated & Embodied Interaction in Cultural Heritage. Diid Disegno Industriale Industrial Design, p. 426 (2023).

Bollini, L., Guida, F.: Digital Memories: What future for the past? What past for the future?. Pad Journal (15), pp. 6–19 (2023).

Bonini Lessing, E.: A Survey of the Digitisation of Collections in Italian Typographic Museums. In: Advances in Design and Digital Communication IV. Proceedings of the 7th International Conference on Design and Digital Communication, Digicom 2023, November 9–11, 2023, Barcelos, pp. 371–380. Springer Nature, Portugal (2024).

Bonini Lessing, E.: Patrimoni tipografici, digitalizzazione, community di utenti/Typographical Heritage, Digitization, User Community. Officina (38), pp. 22–28 (2022).

Bonini Lessing, E. Bulegato, F., Farias, P.: Italian typographic heritage. A contribution to its recognition and interpretation as part of design heritage. In: Lessons to Learn? Past Design Experiences and Contemporary Design Practices. Proceedings of the ICDHS 12th International Conference on Design History and Design Studies, Vol. 1, pp. 293–305. UPI2M Books, Zagreb (2020).

Bosco, A., Gasparotto, S., Bulegato, F.: The Digital Archive as an Inclusive Tool for Knowledge Construction Through Design Practices. Diid Disegno Industriale Industrial Design (2023).

Bulegato, F., Scotti, M.: Exhibiting Design as a Process. In: International Conference Design! OPEN: Objects, Processes, Experiences and Narratives, pp. 275–284. Springer Nature, Switzerland (2024).

Caccamo, A., Vendetti, A.: Revert to type. La stampa letterpress fra tradizione, pratica odierna e nuovi scenari. MDJournal 7 New Craft, pp. 118–131 (2019).

Cameron, F.R.: The Future of Digital Data, Heritage and Curation. In: a More-than-Human World (1st ed.). Routledge, London (2021).

Ceconello, M.: Design storytelling through archive materials. CONVERGÊNCIAS (16), pp 1–5 (2022).

Collavizza, I.: La vita di un carattere attraverso il racconto d'archivio: il Griffo. In: Bonini Lessing, E., Bulegato, F., D'Uonno, M., Marotta, N.A., Rita, F. (eds) Editoria e innovazione tra analogico e digitale, pp. 13–36. Università Iuav di Venezia, Venice (2019).

Cook, S.: Online Activity and Offline Community: Cultural Institutions and New Media Art. In: Fiona Cameron, and Sarah Kenderdine (eds), Theorizing Digital Cultural Heritage: A Critical Discourse (Cambridge, MA, 2007; online edn, MIT Press Scholarship Online, 22 Aug. 2013), https://doi.org/10.7551/mitpress/9780262033534.003.0007, accessed 21 March 2024.

Cooper, A., Gridneff, R., Haslam, A.: Letterpress: looking backward to look forward. In: Visible Language, vol. 47, n. 3, 2014, pp. 52–72 (2019).

Dal Falco, F., Vassos, S.: Museum Experience Design: A Modern Storytelling Methodology. The Design Journal (20), pp. S3975–S3983 (2017).

Hazan, S.: A Crisis of Authority: New Lamps for Old. In: Cameron, F., Kenderdine, S., (eds) Theorizing Digital Cultural Heritage: A Critical Discourse (Cambridge, MA, 2007; online edn, MIT Press Scholarship Online, 22 Aug. 2013), https://doi.org/10.7551/mitpress/9780262033534.003.0008, accessed 1 March 2024.

Jury, D.: Reinventing Print. Bloomsbury, London (2019).

Olocco, R., Patané, M.: Designing type revivals: handbook for a historical approach to typeface design. Lazy Dog, Milan (2022).

Passerini, L.: I predatori dei tipi perduti. Progetto grafico (26), pp 32–41 (2014).

Resmini, A., Rosati, L.: Pervasive Information Architecture. Designing Cross-Channel User Experiences. Morgan Kaufmann, Burlington (2011).

Schnapp, J., Mattei, M. G.: Digital humanities. Meet the media guru. Egea, Milano (2015).

Shaw, P.: Revival type: digital typefaces inspired by the past. Yale University Press, New Haven (2017).

Vendetti, A.: The contemporary production of movable types: Research perspectives for letterpress printing between typographic culture and digital craftsmanship. In: Bisson, M. (eds) Proceedings of IIIrd International Conference on Environmental Design, Mediterranean Design Association, pp. 321–327. Palermo University Press, Palermo (2019).

Beyond the Gaze: Decoding Behavioral Dynamics in Sans Serif Fonts Through Eye-Tracking Exploration

Ana Rita Teixeira, Sónia Brito-Costa, Hugo de Almeida, Sílvia Espada, and Fernanda Antunes

Abstract Typefaces play a crucial role in shaping the reader's response while the framework and emotional responses influence the readers' engagement. Understanding these dynamics will help in creating text content that can increase the effectiveness of communication. This study aims to analyze the interaction between typography, emotional framework and reader engagement through eye-tracking measures in 27 participants with an average age of 18. By comparing affirmations and questions in three emotional categories (positive, negative, and neutral) and three fonts (Open, Quick, and Tenor), we explored how the choice of sources and emotional content influence patterns of revisiting and fixing. Using an eye tracking system (Gazepoint GP3HD), the data collection facilitated the examination of presentations with 18

A. R. Teixeira (✉) · S. Brito-Costa (✉) · S. Espada · F. Antunes
Polytechnic of Coimbra, Higher School of Education, Coimbra, Portugal
e-mail: anateixeira@esec.pt

S. Brito-Costa
e-mail: sonya.b.costa@gmail.com

S. Espada
e-mail: silviaespada@esec.pt

F. Antunes
e-mail: fernandantunes@esec.pt

A. R. Teixeira
Aveiro University, IEETA, Aveiro, Portugal

A. R. Teixeira · S. Brito-Costa
INED—Center for Research and Innovation in Education, Polytechnic Institute of Coimbra, Coimbra, Portugal

S. Brito-Costa
Polytechnic Institute of Coimbra, Applied Research Institute, Coimbra, Portugal

H. de Almeida
CNL-Consumer Neuroscience Lab, University of Aveiro, Aveiro, Portugal

Imagine for Life - A Neuroscience Enterprise, Aveiro, Portugal

H. de Almeida
e-mail: hugodealmeida123@gmail.com

© The Author(s), under exclusive license to Springer Nature Switzerland AG 2025
D. Brandão et al. (eds.), *Perspectives on Design and Digital Communication V*, Springer Series in Design and Innovation 50, https://doi.org/10.1007/978-3-031-76156-0_10

expressions related to emotions, each infused with different emotional tones, and all participants read at their own pace, with sentences displayed randomly in font style for 3 s each. Significant differences in revisiting and fixing behaviors were found, with positive emotional signals triggering higher revisiting rates. The results also revealed the impact of sources on reading understanding, for affirmations with negative or neutral feelings. These results underline the importance of typography and emotional framework in communication design providing insights for creating more engaging text content.

Keywords Eye tracking · Typography · Open sans · Quicksand · Tenor sans

1 Introduction

The emotional response to typeface has been studied in various research papers. The studies have interrelated typefaces with specific visual characteristics with specific emotional effects [1].

The importance of positive and negative emotions in visual attention has been explored through eye-tracking studies. Positive emotions tend to widen attention to encompass global information, while negative emotions lead to more focused attention. This intricate interaction between emotions and visual processing underlines its impact on visual perception and its crucial role in understanding the mechanisms of emotional processing [2–5]. Moreover, recent research has investigated how the emotional tone of an image forms visual perception and human attention, revealing an emotional priority effect, by which emotional content initially captures attention strongly, but this advantage diminishes after initial fixation [6]. Although many neuroimaging and behavioral studies have investigated how emotional stimuli affect attention, few computer vision studies have addressed this issue, partly due to the lack of an eye tracking data set that includes emotional stimulations. Progress has been made in terms of semantics and attention, but much remains to be discovered about how image feeling relates to visual highlighting [6–9].

A recent review of studies on how the processes of visual attention bias and eye movements are related to individual responses to positive and negative stimuli highlights the selectivity of individuals' attention to environmental stimuli, which is linked to the autonomous defense mechanisms associated with survival [10]. These processes vary according to individual characteristics, including psychological well-being during attention shifts. Individuals with anxiety-related disorders or depression tend to be more susceptible to threatening stimuli. The eye tracking methodology is fundamental to detecting and characterizing individual differences in these processes [11], providing valuable insights for the detection and treatment of psychological disorders, as well as other psycho-physiological conditions, such as visual and cognitive fatigue, that can influence attention bias [10].

To address psychological issues of human behavior and understand how stimuli impact a user's emotion, eye tracking technology is crucial [12–14]. There are surveys that employ data on the location and size of the pupil, based on evidence with eye tracking. Although some devices can even synchronize eye tracking data (gaze) with pupil behavior data to simplify visualization, the study on pupil dilation and contraction behaviors, known as pupillometry, can be carried out with some eye-tracking systems [15].

Regarding readers' understanding of emotions, by presenting short stories and evaluating their responses to misaligned emotional situations, one study found that when the described emotional state did not coincide with the context of the story, readers took more time to process the information, indicating a focus on generic emotional representations rather than specific terms [16]. Subsequently, another research showed that emotionally engaging during reading improves understanding through a study with Persian-speaking students, those who discussed their feelings during reading performed better in understanding tests, highlighting the beneficial influence of emotional involvement in the understanding of literary texts, emphasizing the importance of Emotional Engagement in facilitating understanding and interpretation during reading [17].

About textual understanding and memorization in adults, the impact of valence (positive, negative, neutral) and emotional intensity (low, medium, high), revealing that emotional valence had a significant effect on understanding, with positive and neutral texts obtaining higher scores, and average emotional intensity facilitated understanding, while high intensity benefited positive texts, but damaged the negative ones. In terms of memorization, participants remembered more emotional words, especially positive texts, highlighting the crucial role of emotions in information processing [18].

Text may be interpreted when it is legible, but readability goes one step further and combines the emotional impact of design with the effort required to read [19]. Thus, improper use of a font can negatively affect the emotional state of participants, making them less tolerant and more critical, which can be avoided by ensuring that the megafonts used are readable and appropriate in personality and use. In addition, the emotional impact of the font type can affect the ethos of a person [20].

It is thus believed that studies that combine both cognitive and physiological processes (eye and body movements through sensors) will be crucial tools to better understand their interactions in the processing of emotional information [18, 21, 22].

To evoke distinct emotional responses through typographic work, designers must grasp the intricate connections between emotions and typography. Explorations into this relationship have highlighted how design elements influence emotional reactions [23]. Fawcett–Tang (2007) delineates typographic categories such as "type as image", "type as form", "type as experiment", and "type in motion" sorting typography based on its functions and forms [24–26]. Hillner (2009) contends that the visual arrangement of textual elements in multimedia does not merely dictate spatial organization but also influences the aesthetic quality, priming recipients for content assimilation [27]. Designers strategically time transitions during reading to guide or empower users' cognitive processes. Through such meticulous considerations, typographers wield typography to communicate nuanced emotions and sentiments, making emotional provocation a cornerstone of their practice [25].

Designers tactfully manipulate various characteristics—colour, shape, texture, and imagery—to enhance audience engagement and elicit emotional responses. Consequently, typographic designs are conceived as embodiments of "emotion in typeface" [25]. Designers themselves are not immune to the emotional impact of their environment, which influences their selection of design elements. This, in turn, shapes users' emotional engagement with the final design output [1].

Every typeface has a different personality—some shout and others whisper. The challenge is to recognize their personality and make appropriate use of it [28]. Also, the ability of a typeface to convey different feelings, messages or moods stating that typeface can evoke strength, elegance, agitation, and other feelings [1, 25, 28, 29].

Typefaces, as visual messengers, convey personality and evoke emotions through specific visual cues such as colour, shape, texture, and imagery [5, 29]. For instance, curvilinear shapes and open-faced letterforms often exude a sense of friendliness, formality, or informality, depending on contextual factors. Likewise, significant contrasts in stroke widths and proportions can evoke feelings of intrigue, attractiveness, or aggression. Consistency and simplicity in shapes often lend an air of professionalism and reliability, though they risk appearing dull if overused. Thus, the interplay of visual elements in typography shapes not only aesthetic appeal but also emotional resonance, underscoring the profound role of emotions in typographic design [1].

Neither serif nor sans serif typefaces are recommended based on an overview of experimental research data. Most of the time, there is no discernible difference in the data, and when there is, there are equally as many studies supporting the sans serif as there are supporting the serif [30].

The legibility of the typefaces and their formal characteristics must be considered. Typefaces with curvilinear forms and open letter shapes are generally perceived as "friendly" but can also be seen as "formal" or "informal" depending on other factors. Typefaces with large contrasts in stroke widths, cap height, and aspect ratio are generally considered "interesting" but can also be seen as "attractive" or "aggressive." Low-variety and low-contrast forms are generally associated with a "professional" feel but can also be seen as "reliable" or "boring". The relationship between emotional response and typography is an area of ongoing research, with studies exploring the potential contribution of user-centred design and emotion studies to typography [5, 31].

In the academic legibility and readability research, we can see that a significant number of relevant scientific studies have been carried out over the years, researchers have employed various methodologies, including eye-tracking studies, reading speed tests, and comprehension assessments, to investigate the differences between serif and sans serif fonts, and other typography characteristics [5, 15, 26, 32–36].

Readability is the level of comprehension and visual comfort when reading typeset material. It is affected by the way the type is arranged, including the choice of typeface, size to measure, inter-character spacing and leading [32–34, 36, 37]. The challenge was to recognize the typeface's legibility, readability and personality and make the right choice.

In this sense, our study was designed to analyze the readability of sans serif typefaces on screen and the emotional behavior of the participants' while reading phrases with different connotations, such as positive, neutral and negative so the choice of the typefaces for screen reading was carefully selected.

Our first selection focused on selecting open-source sans serif fonts, as there is a greater tendency for users to select these, and then fonts with different attributes to analyze the distinct emotional reactions. For this task, we used the Google Fonts site. From the variety of sans serif fonts presented, three were selected by a group of students: Open sans, Quick sans, and Tenor sans. The original purpose of the typeface was to enhance legibility on computer screens, rendering it highly suitable for web design. As the need for responsive design and compatibility across different platforms increased, Open Sans gained significant traction in a wide range of digital mediums [38].

Subsequently, its exceptional readability and adaptability led to its adoption in print media as well. Open Sans is Quicksand is a display sans-serif designed by Andrew Paglinawan. Quicksand has a geometric design, with uniform stroke widths and rounded letterforms, giving it a friendly and approachable feel. It is designed for display purposes but kept legible enough to use in small sizes as well. Quicksand works well in both small and large sizes, making it suitable for body text as well as headlines and titles [39]. Strizver (2013) states that "Display typefaces, also known as headline typefaces, tend to be stronger in personality, sometimes trading legibility at smaller sizes for a more powerful feeling." (p. 65) Tenor Sans Font is a humanist sans-serif typeface designed by Denis Masharov. A readable typeface is often described as a Humanist Sans Serif [30], Tenor Sans has a subtle stroke contrast that confers a visual interest that maintains a sense of warmth and approachability and optimized for print and web, its letterforms have excellent legibility characteristics [30, 40–43].

2 Materials and Methods

2.1 Environment and Equipment

This study focuses on the usability of sans-serif sources and extended for a duration of approximately two to three months and was developed in the laboratory of institutional usability, required by the restricted portability of the required device.

Within a controlled environment and the appropriate seating, we have gathered all the resources necessary to administer experiments to a cohort of participants, namely the standard equipment, such as monitors and computers equipped with the necessary software, we integrated an eye tracking system, specifically the model Gazepoint GP3 HD. Remarkable features of this eye tracker include a 150 Hz update rate and a repertoire of data presentation modalities, including thermal maps, eye fixing paths, screenshots, images, videos, web-based multi-user data aggregations, high-thinking voice recordings, webcam images, and dynamic areas of interest (AOIs). The resulting data has been systematically exported in various formats, including images, videos and statistical analyses.

2.2 Data Collection and Participants

The data collection sessions were divided into two segments, with a cumulative duration of approximately five hours, during which we evaluated 27 participants of both sexes aged between 18 and 54. Unfortunately, due to data storage anomalies, the information of three participants was irrevocably lost, resulting in analytical data from a total of 24 participants.

In the process of selecting fonts for analytical purposes, our emphasis was on accessibility, leading us to opt for fonts available through Google Fonts. This decision was supported by the ease of acquisition and the commendable quality of the sources offered on the platform, all of which are licensed for commercial use without restrictions.

2.3 Analyzed Fonts

- Open Sans fountain, characterized by a vertically oriented design with perpendicular terminals and tip cuts, classified in the Grotesque category.
- Quick Sand, distinguished by a more rounded shape with rounded terminals and asparagus, typifying a bowl-shaped structure and classified as Geometric.
- Sans tenor, notable for its varied thickness, perpendicular terminals, and wider stems in selected letters, classifiable under the humanist category due to its distinctive amalgamation of characteristics.

2.4 Experimental Protocol

To fulfil our research objectives, we designed a presentation with affirmations and questions related to mental health, each impregnated with different connotations: positive, neutral and negative.

A total of three phrases were presented per category, resulting in 18 distinct expressions. Each screen displayed the same content three times, although using different sources.

All text fonts were presented in standard low fonts, except for the initial font, and were standardized with a 30-point font size.

The presentation, comprehended 37 screens, lasted 94 s, intersecting the sentences with control screens with a central cross. The initial and final control screens lasted 3 s each, whereas the interventionist screen lasted 2 s. Each sentence screened visibility for 3 s. Both the presentation sequence and the assignment of typography styles were random for each participant.

During the testing phase, participants were provided with contextual information. They were informed that they could read the text at their preferred pace. Additionally, it was clarified that three phrases would be displayed on the screen simultaneously, without any specified reading order. Furthermore, participants were alerted that certain phrases would address the topic of bullying.

3 Results

We calculated the main and significant differences between the fundamental categories in that sense, comparing Baseline Features-Affirmations versus Questions. We considered three levels of elicited categorical emotions (positive, negative, and neutral) and three levels of typographic typefaces (Open, Quick, and Tenor).

The data from the procedure has been extracted through two eye tracking measures: revisitation and fixation. Firstly, Table 1 presents the number of revisitations and fixations.

The drop between the base-line variables measures by visual return sweeps as be observed, Affirmations = 467, Questions = 386.

Further analysis reveals that positive questions lead with revisits = 147, closely followed by negative questions = 134, and neutrally framed questions = 105 revisits. This suggests a preference for content featuring positive inquiries, although negative questions also garner significant attention. Similarly, positive framing emerges as the leader within affirmations, revisits = 166. Negative affirmations follow revisits = 148, while neutral affirmations record revisits = 143. This trend mirrors the findings in questions, indicating that positively framed content tends to attract more revisits compared to negative or neutral content.

The first and the second empirical studies by order, revisitations and fixations investigates the different of performance in visual cues. To gain valid parameters of visualization, we first illustrated by means of a comprehensive boxplot analysis, the distributions of revisitations and fixations are visually presented for each combination of typeface and emotions categories, offering insights into how typography influences reading behaviors and cognitive processing, as we show above.

3.1 *Revisitations Performance*

The boxplot in Fig. 1 illustrates the distribution of revisitations across various typeface samples used in the experiment. Each boxplot represents the revisitation performance for a specific typeface, providing insight into the variability and central tendency of revisitation behaviors considering questions (left) and affirmations (right).

Furthermore, data show, making use of the Wilcoxon signed-rank test, valuable in-sights into the influence of typefaces on revisitation patterns during eye-tracking

Table 1 Number of revisitations and fixations considering the experiment

Revisitations																	
Questions									Affirmations								
386									467								
Positive			Negative			Neutral			Positive			Negative			Neutral		
147			134			105			166			158			143		
Open	Quick	Tenor	Open	Quick	Tenor	Open	Quick	Tenor	Open	Quick	Tenor	Open	Quick	Tenor	Open	Quick	Tenor
26	112	9	22	55	57	20	54	31	40	62	64	37	82	39	33	81	29
Fixations (X 10^3)																	
Questions									Affirmations								
1414									1061.6								
Positive			Negative			Neutral			Positive			Negative			Neutral		
394			432			588			380			391			290.6		
Open	Quick	Tenor	Open	Quick	Tenor	Open	Quick	Tenor	Open	Quick	Tenor	Open	Quick	Tenor	Open	Quick	Tenor
142	228	24	16	136	280	204	272	112	83	172	125	53	198	140	112	101.6	77

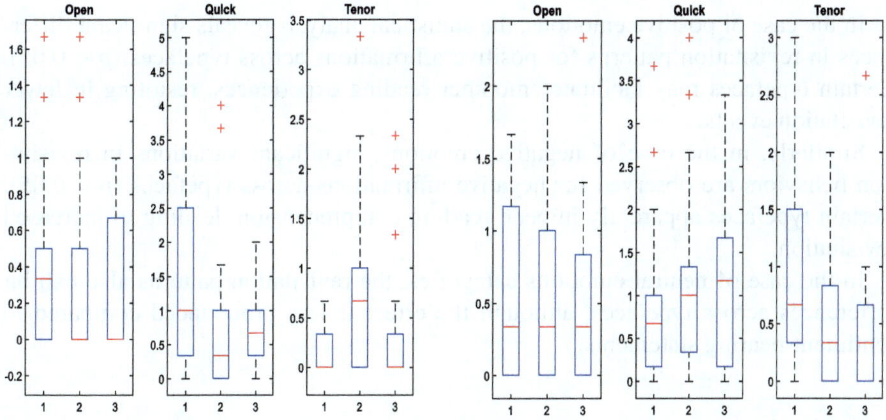

Fig. 1 Revisitations Performance considering questions (left) and affirmations (right). 1—Positive; 2—Negative; 3—Neutral

tasks involving affirmations and questions of changing emotional categories (Tables 2 and 3).

Table 2 Revisitations: statically performance considering the positive, negative and neutral affirmations

		Quick			Open		
		AP	AN	Aneutral	AP	AN	Aneutral
Tenor	AP	0.8997			0.0967		
	AN		0.0085			0.8168	
	Aneutral			0.0054			0.6951
Quick	AP	1			0.1239		
	AN		1			0.0114	
	Aneutral			1			0.0061

Table 3 Revisitations: statically performance considering the positive, negative and neutral questions

		Quick			Open		
		QP	QN	Qneutral	QP	QN	Qneutral
Tenor	QP	0.0001			0.0081		
	QN		0.9191			0.0047	
	Qneutral			0.0761			0.3151
Quick	QP	1			0.0012		
	QN		1			0.0730	
	Qneutral			1			0.0005

In the case of positive emotions, the statistical analysis reveals significant differences in revisitation patterns for positive affirmations across typefaces ($p < 0.05$). Certain typefaces may facilitate smoother reading experiences, resulting in fewer revisitation events.

Similarly, in the case of negative emotions, significant variations in revisitation behaviors are observed for negative affirmations across typefaces ($p < 0.05$). Certain typefaces apparently impede reading comprehension, leading to increased revisitation.

In the case of neutral emotions categories, the revisitation patterns also exhibit differences across typefaces, although the effect is less pronounced compared to sentiment-bearing statements.

3.2 *Fixations Performance*

The boxplot in Fig. 2 illustrates the distribution of fixation across various typeface samples used in the experiment. Each boxplot represents the fixation performance for a specific typeface, providing insight into the variability and central tendency of revisitation behaviors considering questions (left) and affirmations (right).

Based on the provided statistical analysis results using the Wilcoxon test, we are able to interpret the significance of differences in fixation performance across typefaces and sentiment categories (Tables 4 and 5).

For affirmations, there are significant differences in fixation performance between Quick and Open typefaces, particularly for affirmations with negative sentiment and neutral sentiment. However, for affirmations with positive emotions, the difference in fixation performance between the two other typefaces are not significant. These findings suggest that the choice of typeface significantly influences fixation patterns during the reading of affirmations, particularly when the content carries negative or neutral emotions. The lack of significant differences in fixation performance for

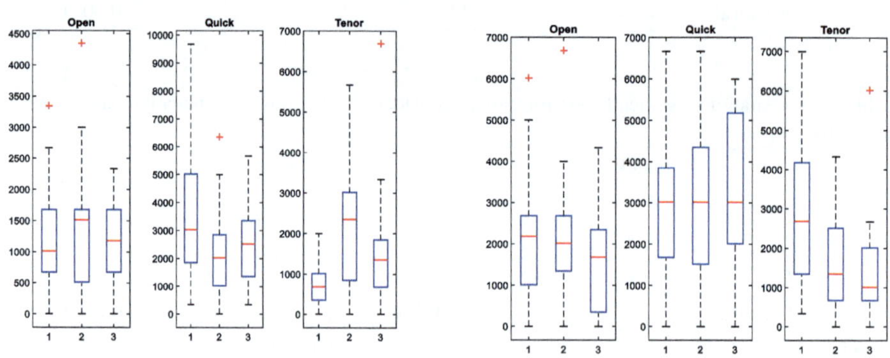

Fig. 2 Fixations performance considering questions (left) and affirmations (right). 1—Positive; 2—Negative; 3—Neutral

Table 4 Fixations: statically performance considering the positive, negative and neutral affirmations

		Quick			Open		
		AP	AN	Aneutral	AP	AN	Aneutral
Tenor	AP	0.7070			0.0477		
	AN		0.0002			0.0359	
	Aneutral			0.0000			0.4702
Quick	AP	1			0.0120		
	AN		1			0.0120	
	Aneutral			1			0.0003

Table 5 Fixations: statically performance considering the positive, negative and neutral questions

		Quick			Open		
		QP	QN	Qneutral	QP	QN	Qneutral
Tenor	QP	0			0.0592		
	QN		0.9499			0.0597	
	Qneutral			0.0156			0.0795
Quick	QP	1			0.0525		
	QN		1			0.9001	
	Qneutral			1			0.0644

affirmations with positive sentiment indicates that typeface choice may have less impact on fixation behavior in such cases (Table 5).

The results from Table 5 indicate that the choice of typeface can influence fixation patterns during the reading of questions, especially when the content carries neutral emotion. On the other hand, for questions with positive or negative elicit emotion, the typeface choice appears to have less impact on fixation behavior, as no significant differences were observed between the Quick and Open typefaces.

The results highlight the influence of typefaces on sentiment perception, particularly in affirmations categorized as positive or negative. Certain typefaces may convey emotions more effectively, impacting the overall tone and interpretation of textual content. However, the effect of typefaces on neutral statements appears to be less pronounced, suggesting that typography plays a relatively minor role in shaping neutral sentiment perception.

4 Discussion

The findings of this study reveal intriguing insights into the intricate interplay between typography, emotional framing, and reader engagement in the context of reading comprehension. By examining eye-tracking measures, specifically revisitation and fixation patterns, we gain a nuanced understanding of how these variables influence cognitive processing and interpretation of textual content.

One of the key observations is the differential impact of emotional framing on revisitation behaviors. Positive inquiries elicited the highest revisitation rates, followed closely by negative questions [44], indicating a preference for content featuring positive emotional cues. This suggests that readers are more inclined to engage with content that evokes positive emotions, underscoring the importance of emotional resonance in communication design. Moreover, the similarity in revisitation patterns between affirmations and questions across emotional categories underscores the robustness of these findings.

Furthermore, the analysis of typeface effects on revisitation and fixation behaviors provides valuable insights into the role of typography in shaping reader response. Significant differences were observed in revisitation patterns across typefaces, particularly for affirmations and questions with negative or neutral emotional content. Certain typefaces were found to facilitate smoother reading experiences, while others impeded comprehension, highlighting the importance of font selection in optimizing text readability and comprehension [5, 28, 40, 41, 45, 46]. These findings underscore the need for careful consideration of typographic elements in communication design to enhance reader engagement and comprehension [31].

The implications of these findings extend beyond theoretical considerations to practical applications in communication design and marketing. Designers and content creators can leverage the insights gained from this study to craft more effective textual content that resonates with target audiences. By strategically selecting typefaces [5, 36, 40] and framing content in emotionally compelling ways [23], communicators can maximize reader engagement and comprehension, ultimately enhancing the overall effectiveness of their messages [32, 47–49].

However, it is important to acknowledge certain limitations of this study. The controlled experimental setting may not fully capture the complexity of real-world reading contexts, and the generalizability of the findings may be limited to specific populations or text genres. Further research could explore additional factors, such as font size, color, and layout, to improve understanding of their influence on reading behaviors and cognitive processing, which will contribute to a deeper understanding of the effectiveness of sanserif sources and provide valuable insights to design accessible text content that improves understanding and engagement [50].

5 Conclusion

In conclusion, this study advances our understanding of how typography and emotional framing influence reader engagement and comprehension. By integrating insights from eye-tracking measures, designers and content creators can refine their communication strategies to effectively convey their messages and connect with their audiences on a deeper level. To better understand how font size, color, and layout affect reading habits and cognitive processing, more research could examine these and other factors. This would lead to a better understanding of the efficacy of sanserif sources and offer insightful advice on how to create accessible text content that increases comprehension and engagement.

The selection of size, color, and typography significantly shapes how we perceive and understand information while reading, directly impacting our reading habits and cognitive functions. Thoughtful consideration of these elements can evoke various emotions and establish a particular emotional ambiance in conveying the message. By meticulously choosing typography and designing these elements, one can notably enhance reading habits and cognitive processing, facilitating easier absorption and comprehension of content. Through deliberate design choices, designers can craft reading experiences that not only inform but also captivate and excite readers.

References

1. Amare, N., Manning, A.: Seeing typeface personality: Emotional responses to form as tone. In: IEEE International Professional Communication Conference (2012). https://doi.org/10.1109/IPCC.2012.6408605.
2. Huddleston, P., Behe, B.K., Minahan, S., Fernandez, R.T.: Seeking attention: An eye tracking study of in-store merchandise displays. International Journal of Retail and Distribution Management. 43 (2015). https://doi.org/10.1108/IJRDM-06-2013-0120.
3. Bueno, A.P.A., Sato, J.R., Hornberger, M.: Eye tracking—The overlooked method to measure cognition in neurodegeneration? (2019). https://doi.org/10.1016/j.neuropsychologia.2019.107191.
4. Wadlinger, H.A., Isaacowitz, D.M.: Positive mood broadens visual attention to positive stimuli (2006). https://doi.org/10.1007/s11031-006-9021-1.
5. Teixeira, A.R., Brito-Costa, S., Espada, S., Antunes, M.F.: Brain Computer Interface: Behavioral Differences in the Calmness Level and Reading Time, Considering Screen or Paper, Serif or Sans Serif Typefaces. In: Springer Series in Design and Innovation (2024). https://doi.org/10.1007/978-3-031-47281-7_3.
6. Fan, S., Shen, Z., Jiang, M., Koenig, B.L., Xu, J., Kankanhalli, M.S., Zhao, Q.: Emotional Attention: A Study of Image Sentiment and Visual Attention. In: Proceedings of the IEEE Computer Society Conference on Computer Vision and Pattern Recognition (2018). https://doi.org/10.1109/CVPR.2018.00785.
7. Öhman, A., Flykt, A., Esteves, F.: Emotion drives attention: Detecting the snake in the grass. J Exp Psychol Gen. 130 (2001). https://doi.org/10.1037/0096-3445.130.3.466.
8. Compton, R.J.: The interface between emotion and attention: a review of evidence from psychology and neuroscience (2003). https://doi.org/10.1177/1534582303002002003.
9. Gupta, R.: Commentary: Neural control of vascular reactions: Impact of emotion and attention (2016). https://doi.org/10.3389/fpsyg.2016.01613.

10. Efeturk, O.A., Turgut, G., Dereshgi, H.A., Yilmaz, A.: A Review of Visual Attention Research Using Eye-Tracking Technologies. Review Paper Journal of Smart Systems Research. 3 (2022).
11. de Almeida, H.M.R., Bem-Haja, P., Albergaria, J., Felizardo, S., Alberty, A.: Healthy but good: Using eye tracking technology in context of marketing to measure the impact of the description of a healthy product on its acceptance and desirability. Espacios. 38 (2017).
12. Baharom, N.H., Jayabalan, N., Amin, M.K.M., Wibirama, S.: Positive emotion recognition through eye tracking technology. Journal of Advanced Manufacturing Technology. 13 (2019).
13. Liu, S., Li, Z., Tao, X.: Emotion recognition research of eye-movement feature extraction classification network in online video learning environment. Presented at the (2023). https://doi.org/10.1117/12.2667404.
14. Abreu, C., de Almeida, H., Lucchese, F., Donado Briegas, M.J.J., Sanchez Iglesias, A.I., Castro, F. vicente, Brito-Costa, S.: The importance of brandy equity in natural human behavior: A study with eyetracking. Confinia Cephalalgica. 30 (2020).
15. Timm Barros, S.E., Diniz Teixeira, H., Merlotti Rodas, C., Borsetti Gregorio Vidotti, S.A., Vesu Alves, R.C.: Eye tracking e reações da pupila em estudos de User Experience. Brazilian Journal of Information Science: Research Trends. 15 (2021). https://doi.org/10.36311/1981-1640.2021.v15.e02113.
16. Gernsbacher, M.A., Goldsmith, H.H., Robertson, R.R.W.: Do Readers Mentally Represent Characters' Emotional States? Cogn Emot. 6 (1992). https://doi.org/10.1080/02699939208411061.
17. Afzali, K.: The Role of Emotions in Reading Literary Texts: Fact or Fiction? The Iranian EFL Journal. 9 (2013).
18. Megalakaki, O., Ballenghein, U., Baccino, T.: Effects of valence and emotional intensity on the comprehension and memorization of texts. Front Psychol. 10 (2019). https://doi.org/10.3389/fpsyg.2019.00179.
19. Jason Santa Maria: How We Read (2014).
20. Shaikh, A.D.: Psychology of Onscreen type: Investigations Regarding Typeface personality, Appropriateness and impact on document perception (2007).
21. Scherer, K.R.: What are emotions? And how can they be measured? (2005). https://doi.org/10.1177/0539018405058216.
22. Gygax, P., Garnham, A., Oakhill, J.: Inferring characters' emotional states: Can readers infer specific emotions? Lang Cogn Process. 19 (2004). https://doi.org/10.1080/01690960444000016.
23. Koch, Beth E.: Emotion in Typographic Design: An Empirical Examination. Visible Lang. 46 (2012).
24. Cumpston, C.: New Typographic Design (review). Journal of Scholarly Publishing. 39 (2008). https://doi.org/10.1353/scp.2008.0000.
25. Ho, A.G.: Typography Today : Emotion Recognition in Typography. Proceedings of 5th International Association of Societies of Design Research, Vols. 1+2 (pp. 5573–5582). Tokyo. Japan: Japanese Society for the Science of Design (JSSD) (2013).
26. De Almeida, H.M.R., Brito-Costa, S., Bem-Haja, P., Briegas, J.J.M.: Colour usage in the lettering and in background manipulation on logotypes: Eyetracking evidences. Confinia Cephalalgica et Neurologica. 32 (2022).
27. Hillner, M.: "Virtual Typography": Time Perception in Relation to Digital Communication. Leonardo Electronic Almanac. 14 (2006).
28. Svaiko, G.: Font Psychology: Here's Everything You Need to Know About Fonts.
29. Koch, B.E.: Emotion in typography design: An empirical examination.
30. Beier, S.: Designing legible fonts for distance reading. In: Digital Fonts and Reading (2016). https://doi.org/10.1142/9789814759540_0005.
31. The non-designer's presentation book: principles for effective presentation design. Choice Reviews Online. 47 (2010). https://doi.org/10.5860/choice.47-4466.
32. Espada, S., Teixeira, A., Antunes, M., Brito-Costa, S.: Natural and artificial lighting: Influence on readability. In: Human Dynamics and Design for the Development of Contemporary Societies (2023). https://doi.org/10.54941/ahfe1003538.

33. Teixeira, A., Brito-Costa, S., Espada, S., Antunes, M.: Tonal Contrast: Influence of Text Background Color on the Comfort and Time of Reading. In: 5ª Euromediterranean Conference for Enviromental Integration, Italy (2023).
34. Teixeira, A.R. o, Brito-Costa, S., Antunes, M., Espada, S.: The Influence of Line Length: A Pilot Study. In: Proceedings of the 9th World Congress on Electrical Engineering and Computer Systems and Science. Avestia Publishing (2023). https://doi.org/10.11159/mhci23.107.
35. Dogusoy, B., Cicek, F., Cagiltay, K.: How serif and sans serif typefaces influence reading on screen: An eye tracking study. In: Lecture Notes in Computer Science (including subseries Lecture Notes in Artificial Intelligence and Lecture Notes in Bioinformatics) (2016). https://doi.org/10.1007/978-3-319-40355-7_55.
36. Teixeira, A.R., Sónia, S., Antunes, M., Espada, S.: Behavioral Differences And Impact Of Lowercase And Uppercase Letters On Reading Performance. In: Proceedings of the 9th World Congress on Electrical Engineering and Computer Systems and Science (2023). https://doi.org/10.11159/mhci23.110.
37. Hojjati, N., Muniandy, B.: The Effects of Font Type and Spacing of Text for Online Readability and Performance. (2014).
38. Amert, K.: From Gutenberg to Opentype: An Illustrated History of Type from the Earliest Letterforms to the Latest Digital Fonts . Robin Dodd . The Papers of the Bibliographical Society of America. 102 (2008). https://doi.org/10.1086/pbsa.102.3.24293630.
39. Strizver, I.: Type rules! : the designer's guide to professional typography. Wiley (2006).
40. Bigelow, C.: Typeface features and legibility research. Vision Res. 165 (2019). https://doi.org/10.1016/j.visres.2019.05.003.
41. Legge, G.E., Bigelow, C.A.: Does print size matter for reading? A review of findings from vision science and typography. J Vis. 11 (2011). https://doi.org/10.1167/11.5.1.
42. Vignon, V.: Reading Letters. Designing for Legibility Sofie Beier, Amsterdam, Bis Publishers, 2012. Communication & langages. 2012 (2012). https://doi.org/10.4074/s0336150012014111.
43. Beier, S.: Typeface Legibility: Towards defining familiarity. (2009).
44. de los Santos, T.M., Nabi, R.L.: Emotionally Charged: Exploring the Role of Emotion in Online News Information Seeking and Processing. J Broadcast Electron Media. 63 (2019). https://doi.org/10.1080/08838151.2019.1566861.
45. Grunberg, N.E., McManigle, J.E., Barry, E.S.: Using Social Psychology Principles to Develop Emotionally Intelligent Healthcare Leaders. Front Psychol. 11 (2020). https://doi.org/10.3389/fpsyg.2020.01917.
46. Ramsay, C.M., Sperling, R.A.: Designating reader perspective to increase comprehension and interest. Contemp Educ Psychol. 35 (2010). https://doi.org/10.1016/j.cedpsych.2010.04.005.
47. Kim, S., Jung, A.R., Kim, Y.: The effects of typefaces on ad effectiveness considering psychological perception and perceived communicator's power. Journal of Marketing Communications. 27 (2021). https://doi.org/10.1080/13527266.2020.1765407.
48. Teixeira, A.R., Gomes, A.: An Experimental Study of Typography Using EEG Signal Parameters. In: Lecture Notes in Computer Science (including subseries Lecture Notes in Artificial Intelligence and Lecture Notes in Bioinformatics) (2020). https://doi.org/10.1007/978-3-030-49059-1_34.
49. Teixeira, A.R., Gomes, A.: Analysis of Visual Patterns Through the EEG Signal: Color Study. Presented at the (2023). https://doi.org/10.1007/978-3-031-35017-7_4.
50. Singer, L.M., Alexander, P.A.: Reading on Paper and Digitally: What the Past Decades of Empirical Research Reveal. Rev Educ Res. 87 (2017). https://doi.org/10.3102/0034654317722961.

Design Methodologies and Innovation

Design by Listening: How Do Children Draw Music? The First Stage of a Participatory Design Project

Ines P. Antunes, Carlos Rosa, and Flávio Almeida

Abstract Formal musical notation is considered a 'universal language', known and played worldwide by everyone from basic learners to orchestra musicians. However, when it comes to teaching it to younger children, accessibility concerns arise, such as economic and socio-cultural background or the adaptability of the formal notation to children's developmental characteristics. During the last century, artists, pedagogues, and composers have developed alternative notations, offering different paths to represent music visually. Considering both children's development and previous data on children's alternative notation, we will guide the reader through the first stage of a participatory design project with first-grade children. This project aims to create an alternative graphic system for musical literacy, demonstrating that Graphic Design and Participatory Design can be used to develop more democratic access to musical literacy. The first stage of the research involved asking children to imagine they were the first-ever inventors of musical notation, aiming to visually translate the nursery rhyme "*Twinkle, Twinkle, Little Star*". From this activity, individual notations were created by the participants, resulting in five different groups: Linear/Wave Notations, Mixed Notations, Shape-Code Notations, Abstract Notations, and Pictographic Notations. By the end of this chapter, we will highlight how children draw music, the symbols or figures they choose to express the intentions behind the visual transcription of a melody, if there are matching features between children's notations to be carefully analysed, and the connections between children's and other exploratory notations.

Keywords Graphic design · Participatory design · Children's musical notations

I. P. Antunes (✉) · C. Rosa
UNIDCOM/IADE, IADE—Universidade Europeia, Lisboa, Portugal
e-mail: inesp.antunes@gmail.com

C. Rosa
e-mail: carlos.rosa@universidadeeuropeia.pt

F. Almeida
IAD Labcom-Communication and Arts, University of Beira Interior, Covilhã, Portugal
e-mail: flavio.almeida@ubi.pt

© The Author(s), under exclusive license to Springer Nature Switzerland AG 2025

D. Brandão et al. (eds.), *Perspectives on Design and Digital Communication V*, Springer Series in Design and Innovation 50, https://doi.org/10.1007/978-3-031-76156-0_11

1 Introduction

Formal music notation arose from the need to supplement the continuous oral tradition and ensure quality during the performance of choir or instrumental melodies. Considering this, it is evident that the Western diagrammatic system did not consider learning and pedagogical concerns when it was created due to its oral transmission characteristics. Mainly during the 20th century, several authors developed their graphical notations as alternative or complementary systems. Researchers have explored the mark-making of young children (6–7 years old) to understand how they visually translate sounds and melodies. These background details were fundamental for the development of the main research project, of which the initial stage is detailed in this chapter. With the research question, 'How can graphic design support the development of an alternative method of music notation accessible to children?' as a starting point, this research project engages a participatory design methodology, promoting an environment of co-creation throughout its development. It is important to state that this research does not intend to substitute formal musical notation (considered a universal language) but to use Visual Design to create an alternative symbolic system that could engage children in their first contact with musical reading notation and learning basic musical notions through a simpler solution based on abstraction and graphic simplification. The first stage of the project, involved field research with 33 children from two different schools in Lisbon (Portugal), aged 6 and 7, attending their first year of basic education. These children worked together with the researcher and with the full support of the responsible music teacher to create their musical notations individually. By the end of this chapter, the results of this experimental activity will be provided, along with information about common features in children-created notations.

2 Music, Notations and Design

Music has been part of human life since ancient times, with knowledge of different melodies and songs passed down through generations by oral transmission. The need to create formal visual notations for individual guidance and memory purposes only arose with the performance of music in churches. From '*neumes*'—the first known symbols for music learning and interpretation in the Middle Ages—to the five-line stave (pentagram), several centuries passed, and the visual characteristics of the notation evolved. According to Grout and Palisca (2007), the '*neumes*' were written without a staff lines structure, being harder to translate without previous contact [6]. Several authors and creators used graphic design guidelines and methods to develop graphic music compositions, not to change the Western diagrammatic system for musical notation but to create complementary systems. According to McKay (2021), the patterns in visual structures, built from visual qualities such as shape, density, and the relation between dark and white space, were key to developing several open notations [9]. For this research, we are focused on co-creation with children to reach the symbolic system due to the need to adapt it to their learning and understanding level. Although universal, the formal musical system was not created with pedagogical concerns and, despite its proven effectiveness, is indeed complex to learn. By analysing and working with the children, it will be possible to create an alternative and simpler system for basic learning that answers both children's visual thinking and stage of development.

2.1 Graphic Musical Compositions

As stated, several graphic musical compositions were created as alternative notations to support a more immediate and intuitive reading. Others were naturally developed over centuries or were experienced by artists and designers. We have chosen five authors whose graphic musical compositions provide a theoretical context for the notation in development and guide the empirical study with the target audience. These authors are Wassily Kandinsky, Anestis Logothetis, Iánnis Xenakis, Pedro Rebelo, and Will Redman.

Wassily Kandinsky—synesthesia, rhythmic paintings and design

Kandinsky (1866–1944) was a Russian modern artist, painter, and designer believed to suffer from synesthesia, a rare neurological phenomenon which according to Murray (2021) ‹‹*(...) can be defined as a subjective phenomenon in which an individual may experience a "mixing" of sensory modalities*›› [11]. Kandinsky is known for saying he could listen to colourful sounds, fitting the description of Grapheme-Color Synesthesia. He created several abstract paintings based on specific music, and companies such as Google (*Chrome Music Lab*) now engage the public in digital activities where one can make digital graphic marks on a whiteboard and listen to the melody created by digitally translating the visual components.

Besides these paintings, Kandinsky is also known for his book '*Point. Line. Shape*' [7], in which he translated excerpts of Mozart music sheets using only dots and lines, managing to visually represent higher and lower notes, pitch, and melody (Fig. 1).

Anestis Logothetis

Logothetis (1921–1994) was a Greek composer who explored how symbols and shapes could represent sound, by adding sound features to his scores and freely creating compositions that represented musical information and had aesthetic value giving white space a purpose: ‹‹*Logothetis describes the physical paper as a space of interaction and music creation where the symbols become independent sonic entities ready to be performed.*›› (Karpodini & Michailidis, 2022) [8]. His work is considered a high point in the evolution of musical notation due to the redefinition of the roles of composer, performer, and audience.

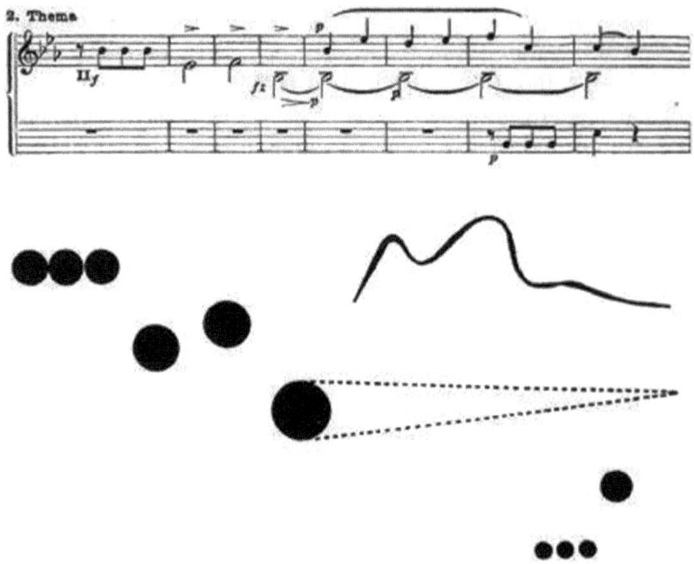

Fig. 1 Point and line to plan (1947), Kandinsky [7]

His graphic work, such as '*Graphic Score Odysee*' (Fig. 2), is considered a strong reference since its characteristic of *polymorphism* is mentioned as a structural innovation; nowadays, *polymorphism* is used in programming and code, allowing abstract group references to guide the behaviour of concrete classes, resulting in a simplifying construction and a clearer and more homogeneous code.

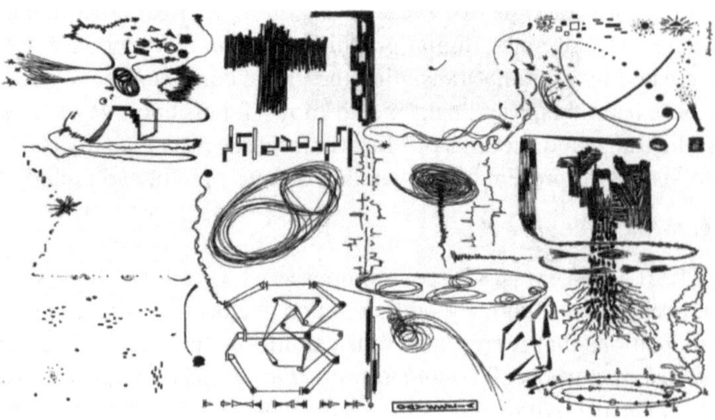

Fig. 2 Graphic score Odysee (1963), Anestis Logothetis [8]

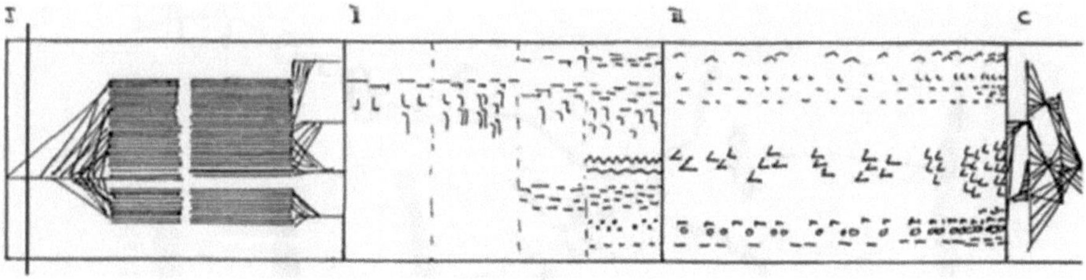

Fig. 3 I. '*Metastaseis*' (1954), Iánnis Xenakis [16]

Iánnis Xenakis—digital and architectural music notation

Born in Greece, Xenakis (1922–2001) was a naturalised French engineer, architect, and composer. With the development of his computer, The UPIC, in 1977, Xenakis' work is well known for its visual notation created digitally, capturing several marks to translate complex melodies, such as '*Metastaseis*' (Fig. 3). Combining an architectural and geometrical structure, to a figurative language, Xenakis notation built an analogy between shape and sounds.

Xenakis applied structural principles from both music and architecture into his work, creating a method based on mathematical principles and geometric construction. This method, which involved metaphorical visual graphics that needed translation to be understood as a musical composition (Felix & Elsamahy, 2021) [5], allowed the music business to expand and inspired several artists and electronic music.

Pedro Rebelo—sound and visual performance graphics

Pedro Rebelo (1972–) is a Portuguese researcher, composer, performer, and sound artist. He is a Professor and Director of Research at the Sonic Arts Research Centre (SARC) at Queen's University Belfast and leads participatory projects with local communities. Rebelo believes that a score as a roadmap becomes essential for music making, as the performer provides meaning and intention while translating the score. With his work '*Cypher Series*' (2015) [12], which he characterises as a collection of graphic scores that support temporal structure to both audience and performance at a live act, by translating the sound into graphics, it can provide a visual mapping that traces de differences and the common ground between the melody created and the melody that is being played for the audience.

In the example we share (Fig. 4), the abstract result from one of the graphic compositions, you can almost sense a division of the track in two different, but at the same time performed, sound variations; it is also possible to understand some matching shapes with symbols from a formal musical sheet. The study based on black lines and white space, allows us to focus only on the abstract figures, which can be addressed by the viewer, either as each form individually or as a complete work.

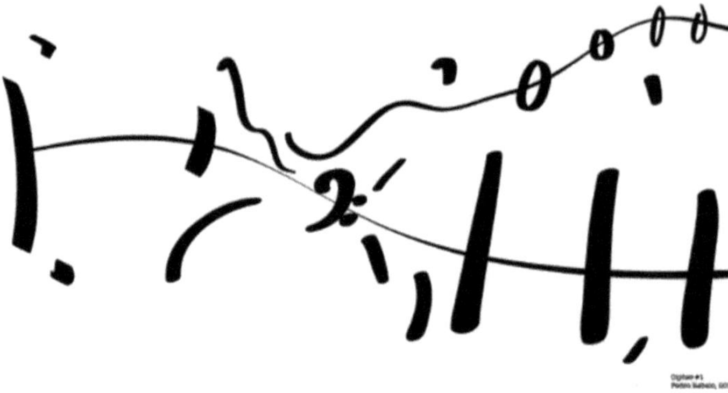

Fig. 4 Cipher series, Page 1 (2010), Pedro Rebelo [12]

Will Redman—unsystematic notation

North-American composer, percussionist and educator, Redman (1975–) is known for his adaptations of traditional music notation into expanded and alternative visual versions. According to Molly Sheridan (2011) [13], Redman considered his '*unsystematic notation*' as a way to answer the battle between graphic elements and the sound they are supposed to represent.

In his work '*Book*' (Fig. 5), he represented a musical notation adapting the formal five-stave musical sheet, and giving it movement by adding several lines, and abstract figures and by moving parts of the five-stave around, adding pieces and altering the degrees to which it is drawn, captivating authors such as McKay (2021) [9] who recently study open notations and mention the consistency expected in the interpretation of abstract notations, using Redman's work as one of the examples.

As we can acknowledge from these examples, musical notation is quite complex (either in its formal form or any graphical alternative form), containing information such as notes, pitch, melody, tempo, etc. Even though musical notations have a rich detailed character, having all the information we anticipate when thinking of a song is almost impossible; features such as intention and meaning are more individually interpreted than representable. Artists, creators, pedagogues, and composers such as Zoltán Kodály, Carl Orff, Émile Jaques-Dalcroze, Shinichi Suzuki, Edgar Willems, Murray Schafer, Orff Schulwerk and Keith Swanwick, among others, developed alternative notations for music. There are several researches on how children listen, think and interact with music and we will look at two of these studies, to better context our participatory project.

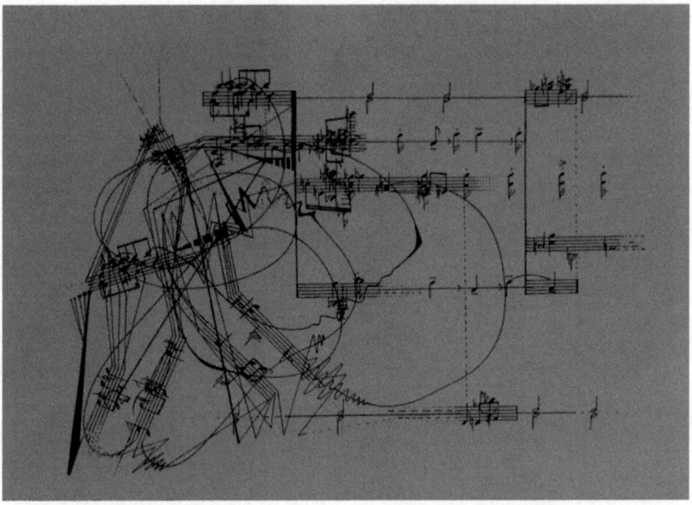

Fig. 5 Book (2006), Will Redman [9]

2.2 *Children Made Notations—Previous Studies*

Especially during the second half of the 20th century, the evolution of music led several authors to explore new ways of visually representing music to facilitate musical literacy. Considering learning, it is relevant to ensure that when formal musical notation was created, it wasn't invented with children's musical literacy as a primary concern. This is the key feature to understand why so many authors study this adaptation and try to develop alternative notations directed at early years. From Caroline Meggit and Tina Brune's (2015) [10] perspectives, children naturally develop the understanding that their mark-making can translate to specific meanings and when children realise this, they tend to invest quite some time in their symbolic language abilities, enhancing their imagination and thinking flow with fewer boundaries and insecurities than any adult could. Although children start mark-making at an early age, it is only later, during a stage of development when words also start to have intention and meaning, that children begin associating their thoughts and intentions with their drawings.

The understanding of musical notations made by children has been a matter of study for some decades. Several authors have explored how children draw and visually think about music compositions. Their previous studies provide fundamental guidance for the development of this research. One of the researchers we need to consider is Margaret S. Barrett, a professor interested in children's musical development and pedagogical engagement, she conducted several studies on children's understanding and exploration of music (Fig. 6), and how their mark-making could translated into sound, stating in one of her studies that *‹‹children have an immediate interest in their own compositions, as they evolve from their own experience.*

Fig. 6 Belinda's (1997), Margaret S. Barrett [1]

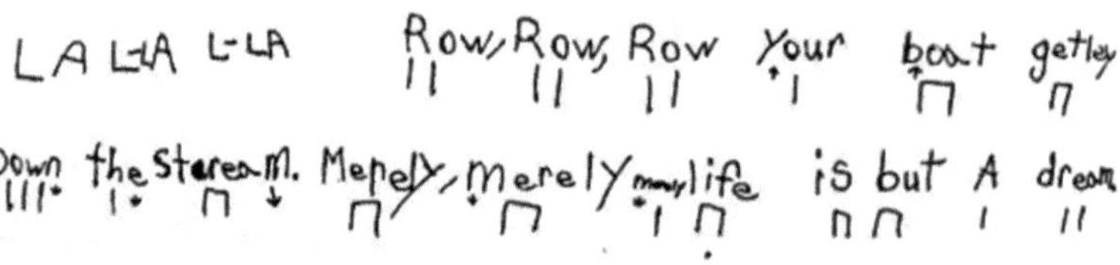

Fig. 7 Mary's (2012), Davidson and Scripp [4]

Furthermore, such works are directly revealing of children's musical understanding and ability to use the materials of music›› (Barrett, 1997) [1].

From Barrett's later studies (2006) [2], we can also understand that children have an immediate interest in their mark-making, giving them sense and creating instructions for their symbols to the sounds they intend to translate. In Davidson and Scripp's (2012) [4] research on children's musical notation, they observed that the notations created by children from 5 to 7 years old became more sophisticated over time, gaining more information and gathering more combinations between symbols and intentions (Fig. 7)

In addition to these studies, it is also important to consider details on children's visual perception and development. We chose these two examples because both were studies developed with the same age group in mind: first-year, first-grade children (aged 5–7 years). By this stage of development, children can engage in meaningful conversations, naming their feelings and experiences, and explaining their thoughts and creative results. This developmental milestone is crucial for achieving meaningful project outcomes. Additionally, children at this age are learning the alphabet and numbers, which makes their minds captivated by shapes and figures associated with purpose and meaning. Simultaneously, they are ready to explore mark-making, understanding given tasks, and creating not randomly but intentionally. Lev Vygotsky (1896–1934), a Russian psychologist renowned for several studies on children's visual perception and creative work, noted in one of his studies on child development that ‹‹(...) *the most important transformation that marks this transition is the shift from non-verbal perception and a lack of meaning to an objective perception characterised by meaning and the intervention of language*›› (Vygotsky, 2007, *Trans.*) [15]. He argued that this transition to a new form of internal perception represents an advanced stage in mental perception and activity, enabling learning, acquiring new perspectives, and initiating critical thinking. This reveals their ability to comprehend processes and seek innovative solutions to familiar tasks and novel approaches in ways to do things.

3 Design by Listening—How Do Children Draw Music

If we aim to design for children, they must be actively involved in creating new designs. This principle is fundamental in the guidelines for creating a '*design that matters*'. As designers, our responsibility lies in crafting solutions that effectively address public needs. Clay Spinuzzi (2005) [14] emphasised in his work that disregarding the public and assuming what works for them can lead to unexpected results in the usability of the design product. Therefore, the research methodology of participatory design is crucial for achieving co-creative solutions. Given the project's focus on accessibility, involving children in creating the 'artefact' was an immediate decision.

To substantiate our choice for a participatory design approach, it is important to revisit the origins of this research methodology: Participatory Design emerged in the 1970s–80s in Scandinavian countries, initially addressing the needs and rights of factory workers. According to Spinuzzi (2005) [14], *‹‹(…) this avowedly political research aimed to form partnerships with labour unions that would allow workers to determine the shape and scope of new technologies introduced into the workplace››*. As society evolved, Participatory Design adapted to cater to various groups and individuals, promoting project guidelines that foster positive partnerships between designers and the public/users.

Considering that children constitute the primary audience of our research project, it is crucial to discuss Design Thinking and its implications for children's learning. This discussion reinforces our decision to focus on children in their first year of first grade, typically aged 6–7 years old, aligning children's developmental stages with foundational principles of visual thinking.

3.1 The Project: Context, Public, Stages and Results

For the development of this project, a partnership was created with two local schools—Colégio Alfragide and Real Colégio Portugal, in Lisbon. With this partnership, we defined timetables with the responsible teachers to develop the participatory design activities. The teacher responsible for each group at the time of the activities was always present in the classroom, following the dynamic and granting children pedagogical support throughout the development of the research activities.

Context

Each activity had a duration of ninety (90) minutes. The participatory definition of this research project is fundamental for the quality of its results. By gathering children's insights on musical and visual thinking, the alternative system will be developed and tested by and with the public it intends to work for. Children will be considered at all the phases of development of the alternative graphic system.

Public

This project is being developed with a total universe of thirty-three (33) children, from first year—first grade, between 6 and 7 years old. Children had already had previous contact with formal musical notation due to musical lessons offered by the schools' curriculum.

The project explained

The full research project is developed in four stages: phase zero (development of free notations by children), phase 1 (learning and first trials of the alternative iconographic system), phase 2 (application of the iconographic system in melodies learning), and phase 3 (testing learning, memory and interpretation of melodies created by pairs). In this chapter, we will focus on the results from phase zero.

At this stage, we allow children to draw their notations individually. This way, we could understand better how children process their visual thinking by transferring what they hear onto paper. The song listened for the exercise was "*Twinkle, Twinkle, Little Star*" a nursery rhyme (well known by children), on its simple single-hand piano version. This way, and with prior knowledge of the melody, children could focus on the main goal of the exercise: explore how they draw music.

The first stage of the project—how was it guided

As an introduction, we did a small presentation activity: children said their name, age and favourite colour, and the researcher in place did the same. This way it was easier to carry on with the activities knowing children's names and working as an ice-breaking activity.

After this introduction, a short PowerPoint was presented to the groups. This way, they could see the formal five-staff notation. they're already learning at school and, at the same time, getting to know different visual ways to represent music: colour-coded notation, form notation, Kodaly, Kandinsky and Xenakis. Through these examples, children could get inspired and understand other ways—rather than formal pentagram notation—to represent music.

After this small presentation, we engaged the children by asking: "*what about you, how do you draw music?*"; this simple question on the board reinforced their imagination with a world where both music notation, alphabet and numbers have not been created, how would they teach visually "*Twinkle, Twinkle, Little Star*" (Fig. 8) to someone who didn't knew that song. The piano version of the music (one hand) was played in the classroom while the activities took place.

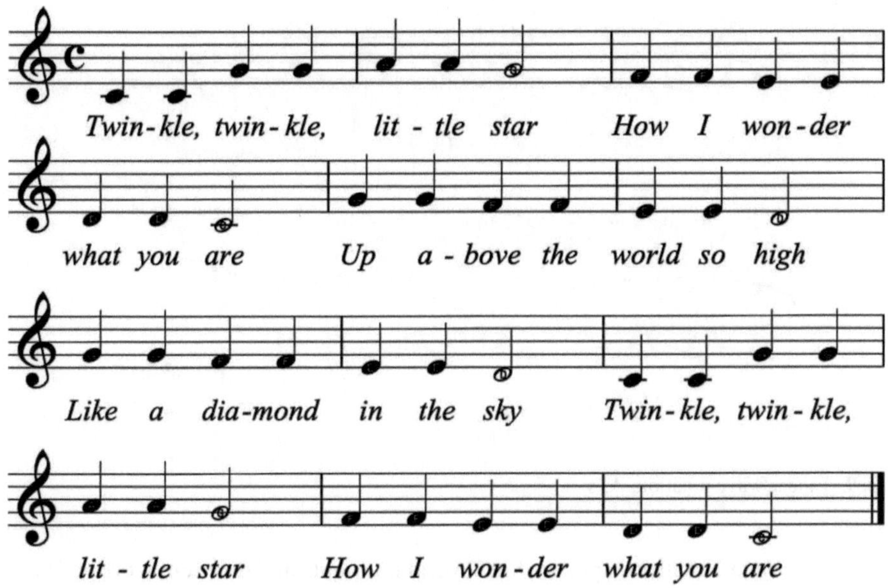

Fig. 8 '*Twinkle, Twinkle, Little Star*' (2022) Wouter Bruinsma—Formal Music Sheet [3]

At the end of the activities, children had the opportunity to share their work and talk about their notation and visual thinking, and how their notation would work and be explained. The first activity involved a group of 10 children (Group A) and the second group consisted of a larger group of 19 children (Group B). Additionally, and recognising the significance of understanding individual children's thinking and their visual application of music, we carry out an individual activity. This approach mirrored the dynamics used with Group A to ensure consistency in the activities' organisation and presentation, thereby minimising potential differences that could impact the final results at this stage.

Results

From these field activities, we could collect a total of twenty-nine (29) different notations. Some children had a harder time feeling confident in starting the task due to feeling less confident and afraid to fail the expected results. Once the researcher explained to the children it was a creative task and there were no right or wrong answers, their ideas started to flow. From children's notations, we discovered several diverse ways to represent visually the same melody, pitch, and intentions. While some children adhered to formal musical shapes they had learned in school or associated with the alphabet, others took a figurative approach, creating symbols such as stars, pianos, or people. However, the majority employed visual notations that we categorised into five main characteristics: Linear/Wave Notations, Mixed Notations, Shape-Code Notations, Abstract Notations, and Pictographic Notations.

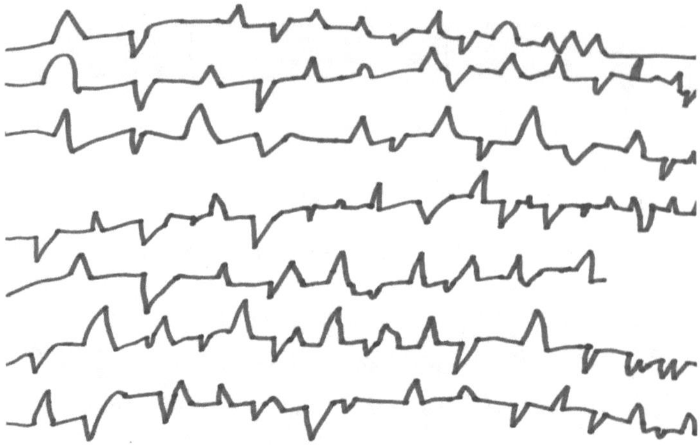

Fig. 9 Linear/wave notation, A.'s

Linear/Wave Notations appeared in several moments and different works of both groups. In the example (Fig. 9), A. drew different lines and shared that it should work as the melody, moving up and down, and each line should be read at once, from left to right and from top to bottom. Some children represented the lines and round waves, by simply drawing the path of the notes in the song from highs to lows in a consistent visual bit and shapes.

From the mark-making developed by the children from both groups, we could also identify consistent Mixed Notations, between more simple shapes (geometric or not) and some details from formal musical notation. The five-line stave (or pentagram) was represented in its full version by most of the children who chose this notation, but some opted to make it with only four lines or extend the lines and make a path similar to a line notebook. In the example shared above, S. (Fig. 10) which is learning to play the piano, decided to represent similar claves with (G and D), one for each hand following the formal notation guidelines; however, on this notation, the five-lines stave, would contain both claves in the beginning, with the upper four lines being used for the right-hand notes and the underline used for the left hand. To distinguish higher notes from lower notes, S. decided to draw arrows pointing up or down depending on the intention of the melody.

Another consistent option made by the participant children was what we called "Shape-Code Notations"; in this case, children decided to connect a shape (mostly geometrical, but also some pictographic or stain shapes); as highlighted by this example from K. (Fig. 11), when following this option children wrote down or next to each symbol what note should correspond to each shape, making their instructions clear.

Another approach utilised by children in their creations was Abstract Notations. Using multiple or single colours, predominantly composed of simple figurative results interspersed with various lines and movements intended to convey the

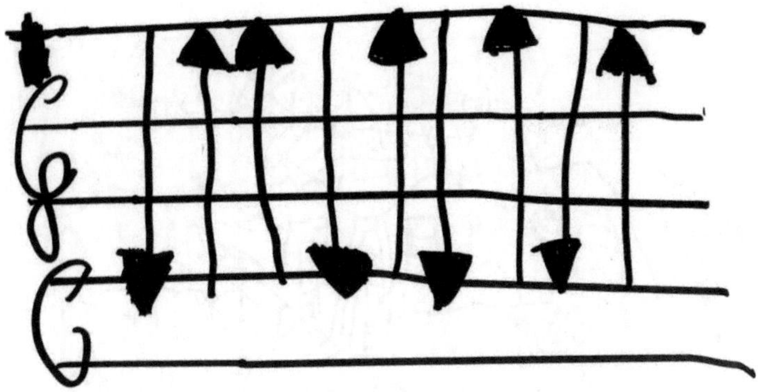

Fig. 10 Mixed notation, S.'s

Fig. 11 Shape-code notation, K.'s

melody they were listening to, this option was selected by approximately a third of all participants in the research. In the abstract notation depicted above (Fig. 12), B. highlighted which symbol signified the beginning of this notation, expressing pride in the figurative diamond shape denoting the conclusion, and indicating that stars represented key elements for understanding the song. Shapes resembling stairs represented fluctuations in the melody's pitch, whether ascending or descending.

Across all created notations, most children articulated clear instructions for different shapes, clearly communicating their intentions regarding which shapes represented higher and lower notes in their visual compositions. It was particularly intriguing to observe the majority of these notations featured pictographic elements introduced by their creators to signify specific notes, the beginning of compositions, or instances where the song was repeated. This type of marking appeared consistently in ninety per cent of the children's notations. Importantly, these shapes emerged without prior conditioning or collaboration among the children, suggesting compelling evidence that such shapes can effectively translate sound into visual representations.

However, some children opted to only use Pictographic Notations in their creation, just like M. in this example (Fig. 13). Such as other children, M. gave the smaller and rounder shape intending to be the higher note of the melody represented in his notation; and the larger shape, which takes a bigger area of the designed shapes to the lower note. The shapes represented in this notation having round waves on their continuation, represent longer notes with a clear intention of visually representing the melody path. Most of the information gathered about the visual notations was freely

Fig. 12 Abstract notation, B.'s

provided by each child. The researcher specifically questioned each child about the representation of higher and lower notes in their creations. This inquiry was crucial to comprehending the significance children attributed to the shapes they created and ensuring clarity and consistency in their intentions. These insights formed the foundation for further participatory research.

Fig. 13 Pictographic notation, M's

4 Conclusions and Next Steps

In this chapter, we aimed to guide the reader through the first stage of a participatory design project with first-grade children (6–7 years old), intending to understand their visual interpretation of music by leading an activity where they could draw their notation to translate the nursery rhyme '*Twinkle, Twinkle, Little Star*'. All participants in the activities had previous exposure to formal music notation through their school's curriculum, where music classes were included. Additionally, at least one child was receiving piano lessons outside of school and enthusiastically discussed her experience learning to play the instrument, mentioning she was currently focusing on practicing the right hand, indicating she was in the beginner stage of her learning.

As discussed throughout this chapter, most children demonstrated clear intentions in their notations, while others chose to explore more figurative representations related to the selected song. Some recurring characteristics included smaller and rounder shapes representing higher notes, and larger or square/rectangular shapes indicating lower notes in their visual representations. Although the task initially focused on notes and pitch, some children expanded beyond these parameters by incorporating additional elements. For instance, they incorporated figures with specific intentions such as indicating repetitions or marking the song's beginning. These additional shapes revealed that children created their notations with clear intentions, providing instructions and clarifications as needed. Even though the activity was developed by using only one song, we captured several notations with different characteristics which allowed us to group them in five different nomenclatures: Linear/Wave Notations (characterised by expressing melody changes through linear representations); Mixed Notations (which incorporate both features from formal musical notation and new shapes); Shape-Code Notations (in which children would set a shape for each musical note); Abstract Notations (by using several shapes, lines and figures that visually combined set the notation); and Pictographic Notations (where the use of shapes with pictographic characteristics define different notes or intentions). It is also an important conclusion to state we found some matching characteristics between the notations drawn by children and the work presented by different authors: for example, mixed notations drawn by children with Rebelo and Redman's works which also use visual settings from formal musical notation and add up exploratory figures and shapes to translate the melody; or how Line/Wave Notations explored by children, or the heaviness and lightness of the shapes meaning, accordingly heavy or higher notes, have connections with point and line work from Kandinsky. Following this stage, we explored the common elements in the notations freely created by children. This allowed us to evaluate the notations further and develop three graphic systems over three months. The next steps will involve a detailed analysis of the tests already conducted on these three graphic systems with six groups of children. This analysis will provide insights and information to understand the efficiency of these systems, which will be thoroughly explained in a new article.

References

1. Barrett, M. S. Invented notations: A view of young children's musical thinking. Research Studies in Music Education, 8(1), 2–14 (1997). https://doi.org/10.1177/1321103X9700800102.
2. Barrett, M. S. Inventing songs, inventing worlds: The 'genesis' of creative thought and activity in young children's lives. International Journal of Early Years Education, 14(3), 201–220 (2006). https://doi.org/10.1080/09669760600879920
3. Bruinsma, W. (2022) Twinkle, Twinkle, Little Star'.
4. Davidson, L., & Scripp, L. (2012). Young children's musical representations: windows on music cognition. In *Generative Processes in Music the Psychology of Performance, Improvisation, and Composition* (pp. 195–230). https://doi.org/10.1093/acprof:oso/9780198508465.003.0009
5. Felix, M. N., & Elsamahy, E. M. (2016). Visualizing Music Compositions in Architectural Conceptual Design. *Architecture and Planning Journal, 23*(2). https://www.researchgate.net/publication/298405364
6. Grout, D. J. & Palisca, C. V. (2007). História da Música Ocidental. Gradiva Publicações.
7. Kandinsky, W. Point and Line to Plan. The Solomon R. Guggenheim Foundation New York (1947).
8. Karpodini, C.; Michailidis, T. Making graphical scores mores accessible: a case of study. School of Computing and Digital Technology, Birmingham (2022).
9. McKay, T. (2021). A Semiotic Approach to Open Notations. Cambridge Elements—Music Since 1945.
10. Meggitt, C., & Bruce, T.. *NCFE CACHE Level 3 Child Care and Education (Early Years Educator).* Hodder Education (2015)
11. Murray, R. (2021). A review of synesthesia: Historical and current perspectives. *Murray UWL Journal of Undergraduate Research XXIV*.
12. Rebelo, P. (2015). Composing With Graphics: Revealing the Compositional Process Through Performance. *Proceedings of the 1st International Conference on Technologies for Music Notation and Representation TENOR-2015*, 5.
13. Sheridan, M. (2011) Will Redman: Graphic Ideas In Sound. NEWMUSICBOX. Retrieved from: https://newmusicusa.org/nmbx/will-redman-graphic-ideas-in-sound/. Last accessed on 2024/03/24
14. Spinuzzi, C. (2005). The methodology of participatory design. *Technical Communication, 52*(2), 163–174. https://www.researchgate.net/publication/233564945_The_Methodology_of_Participatory_Design
15. Vygotsky, L. (2007). Pensamento e Linguagem.
16. Xenakis, I. '*Metastaseis*'. Retrieved from: https://www.elbphilharmonie.de/en/mediatheque/iannis-xenakis-architect-of-sound/287

From Words to Icons. Advancements in Prompting Text-to-Image Models for Logo Design with Artificial Intelligence

Carlos Sena Caires

Abstract This paper presents an extensive review and empirical analysis of text-to-image models, focusing on their application in logo design and visual generation. Beginning with the seminal work by Goodfellow et al. on Generative Adversarial Networks in 2014, the paper traces the evolution of text-to-image technology through subsequent developments such as Generative Adversarial Text-to-Image Synthesis and Creative Adversarial Networks. The study explores the effectiveness of prompt engineering in guiding AI models towards desired outputs, showcasing the potential of prompt-based texting in enhancing creativity and generating logo visual content. Furthermore, the paper presents empirical research through a targeted questionnaire distributed to design and artistic communities. The questionnaire evaluates the effectiveness of AI-driven prompting text-to-image models in logo design, providing insights into the generated logos' perception and quality. The findings underscore the potential of AI as a valuable tool in logo design while highlighting areas for further refinement and development.

Keywords Text-to-image · Logo design · Prompt engineering · Generative artificial intelligence · AI-driven logo generation · Knowledge

1 Introduction

Text-to-image models have emerged as a promising way to enhance creativity, efficiency, and innovation in logo design. These models leverage artificial intelligence (AI) to interpret textual descriptions and generate visually compelling logos. This approach streamlines the design process, facilitating rapid concept generation and iteration while maintaining some creative control. Moreover, prompting text-to-image models enables designers to explore diverse design possibilities and iterate on logo concepts more efficiently. In this context, exploring the role of prompting

C. S. Caires (✉)
University of Saint Joseph, Macau, Estrada Marginal da Ilha Verde, 14-17, Macau, China
e-mail: carlos.caires@usj.edu.mo

© The Author(s), under exclusive license to Springer Nature Switzerland AG 2025

D. Brandão et al. (eds.), *Perspectives on Design and Digital Communication V*, Springer Series in Design and Innovation 50, https://doi.org/10.1007/978-3-031-76156-0_12

text-to-image models in logo generation holds significant implications for the design field. The research seeks to inquire deeper into this topic, investigating the impact of prompting text-to-image models on logo generation and strategies to achieve confident results.

The proliferation of logo generators across the web, including platforms such as *Wix Logo Maker*, *Fiverr Logo Maker*, *Logomakr*, *Looka*, *Logomaster*, *Free Logo Design*, *Logo AI*, and *Brandmark*, has democratized the process of logo creation, enabling users to generate visually appealing images within minutes. This exit from the traditional prolonged waiting period for a designer's final solution marks a significant shift in the design paradigm. However, while these web-driven solutions offer practicality, they have limitations and drawbacks. Among these limitations is the emerging stage of the field, which often translates into a need for more comprehensive support. Additionally, users may encounter registration costs, template constraints, and fixed design solutions, which can obstruct customization and creative expression. The generation process is largely 'template-based' whereby a fixed number of visual elements, such as icons, fonts, and colours, are combined in predetermined ways. Moreover, the uniformity and lack of originality inherent in some generated logos challenge achieving a distinct and professional brand identity. While web-logo generators excel at quickly producing logos, they may need to catch up in capturing the broader brand narrative and thematic elements that are integral to a cohesive brand identity.

Numerous bloggers are addressing the topic of AI's role in logo design, each offering varying degrees of depth in their arguments and speculation about the future trajectory of this field. Titles such as "*The Role of AI in Logo Design: Future Trends and Current Practices*" (source: https://blog.emb.global/role-of-ai-in-logo-design/), or "*Revolutionizing Logo Design: The Creative Power of AI*" (source: https://www.cademix.org/revolutionizing-logo-design-the-creative-power-of-ai/), and "*The Future of Logo Design with Artificial Intelligence*" (source: https://kreafolk.com/blogs/articles/logo-design-artificial-intelligence), populate the web, engaging in discourse on the subject. While the authors exhibit a positive outlook on AI's potential impact, we observe a deficiency of scientific rigour and empirical evidence in their discussions. Real-world case studies or concrete examples to substantiate their conclusions need to be improved, raising concerns about their claims' validity. Professional design input remains invaluable for creating a cohesive and impactful brand identity that resonates with audiences and distinguishes itself in a competitive market landscape.

2 Overview of Text-to-Image Models for Visual Generation

In 2014, Goodfellow et al. [1], proposed a new framework for estimating generative models via an adversarial process called GANs. The Generative Adversarial Networks (GANs) are a class of deep learning models consisting of two neural networks, a generator (G) and a discriminator (D), which are trained together in a competitive manner. The authors defined a generative model G that captures the data distribution, and a discriminative model D that estimates the probability that a sample came from the training data rather than G. The training procedure for G is to maximize the probability of D making a mistake. Since then, GANs have been widely used for image generation tasks, including text-to-image synthesis and visualization. Two years later, Reed et al. [2] published the Generative Adversarial Text to Image Synthesis research, where they develop a novel deep architecture and GAN formulation to effectively bridge the advances in automatic synthesis of realistic images from text. The authors demonstrate the capability of the new model to generate plausible images of birds and flowers from detailed text descriptions. In 2017, Elgammal et al. [3], proposed a new system, built over GANs for generating art. The system, called CAN (Creative Adversarial Networks) generates artistic images by looking at art references and learning about different styles, and becoming a creative network by increasing the arousal potential of the generated art by deviating it from the learned styles. It incorporates creativity constraints to encourage the generation of diverse and novel visual outputs. One year later, in 2018, Zhang et al. [4], proposed the Stacked Generative Adversarial Networks (StackGAN++), aimed at generating high-resolution photo-realistic images. It consists of a two-stage GAN where the first stage generates a low-resolution image from text, and the second stage refines the image to higher resolution. StackGAN++ has been used for various text-to-image synthesis tasks. According to the authors, although GANs have shown remarkable success in various tasks, they still face challenges in generating high quality images. With StackGAN++, the researchers were able to demonstrate that their method can significantly improve the state of the art in image generation tasks.

2.1 Prompt Engineering in AI-Based Image Generation

Prompt engineering involves structuring text to be interpreted by a generative AI model [5], where a prompt describes the task for the AI. This can range from requests like "*What is the size of the Universe?*" to "*Write a poem in the style of Edgar Allan Poe about leaves falling*" [6] or more elaborate instructions including context like "*Describe a scenery where a young woman, on a long white dress, (...)waiting for the arrival of her loved one, (...)as the gentle breeze carries the scent of salt and the sound of seagulls echoing in the distance.*" Additionally, the process of prompt engineering may entail phrasing specifying styles, providing background, or assigning roles to the AI, such as "*Write a song as a native Spanish speaker.*" Also, prompts may include examples (as images) for reference, enabling the model to learn from limited instances.

As studied by Caires et al. [7], text prompts typically describe the desired output, such as "imagine *a bus in the shape of a banana*" or "*draw a stool in wood material with four legs, 60 cm height*". Prompting these models involves manipulating words to achieve desired subjects, styles, layouts, lighting, and aesthetics. Prompt engineering, as investigated in this paper, is recognized as a novel creative skill for generating prompt-based Logo design. In an investigation into the creative skill of prompt Engineering, Oppenlaender et al. [8] define 'skill in prompt engineering' as the ability to effectively use language and prior knowledge to craft prompts that guide generative models towards desired outputs. Text prompts serve as instructions to enforce rules, define styles, automate processes, and ensure specific qualities and quantities of generated output, essentially acting as a form of programming to customize interactions with the model. As machines advance rapidly, there is debate over whether prompt engineering will become obsolete with newer models, but it remains a learned skill requiring expertise and practice. Branwen [9], suggested that prompt engineering models could become a new paradigm for interaction where users need only to figure out how to prompt a model to elicit the specific knowledge and abstractions necessary for completing downstream tasks.

In their recent analysis, Jindong Gu et al. [10], aim to provide a comprehensive survey of cutting-edge research in prompt engineering, focusing on its application across different types of vision-language models. Specifically, they examine multimodal-to-text generation models, image-text matching models, and text-to-image generation models, as used in Stable Diffusion (https://stability.ai/news/stable-diffusion-3) or Midjourney.ai (https://www.midjourney.com/home). One significant finding underscores the versatility and applicability of prompt engineering techniques across these diverse models. By employing prompt engineering strategies, one can achieve notable performance improvements in vision-language models, even in the absence of extensive labelled data. The overall impact and significance of prompt engineering on enhancing the capabilities of vision-language foundation models are underscored, with implications for advancing AI research and fostering innovation in various application domains.

2.2 *Previous Studies on Prompting for Text-to-Image Generation*

Previous studies on text-to-image generation have explored various aspects of prompting optimization, model behaviour, and design principles. Hao et al. [11] focused on optimizing prompts for text-to-image generation, proposing methods to improve the quality and relevance of generated images. The authors propose the concept of "prompt-adaptation", a general framework that automatically adapts original user input to model-preferred prompts. The research show that prompt adaptation and optimization can outperforms human prompt engineering. For instance, the Midjourney.ai Prompt Generator application [12] has incorporated the "Optimize" button option where users can let the AI-generator improve their prompt. In "Prompt design and engineering: introduction and advanced methods" [13], Xavier Amatriain [14], highlights advanced methods for guiding AI models in image generation tasks. The study features the concept of "Chain-of-thoughts" capitalizing on the premise that large language models excel at predicting sequences, but their design does not inherently facilitate explicit reasoning processes. Li et al. [15] addressed the issue of image content suppression in text-to-image diffusion models, proposing techniques to control the generation process and ensure desired outputs. The analysis aims to understand how to manipulate the text prompt embeddings and remove unwanted content from the generated image. On the other hand, Liu and Chilton [16] outlined design guidelines for prompt engineering in text-to-image generative models, emphasizing the importance of clear and informative prompts. The research focused on exploring what prompt keywords and model hyperparameters can help produce coherent outputs, investigating success and failures modes of prompting. Some of the conclusions pointed out that prompts should focus on subject and style keywords instead of connecting words and long sentences; And when generating, users should generate between 3 and 9 different seeds to get a representative idea of what a prompt can return (conditions we will find useful for our research). In a different study, Smith et al. [17] explored applying text-to-image models to inform the design of physical artefacts, demonstrating how AI-generated images can inspire and enhance creative processes beyond digital realms. Recently, Caires et al. [7] proposed combining design thinking methodologies with text-to-image artificial intelligence. The research confirmed that incorporating prompt-based text-to-image tools in the design thinking process has the potential to support students and teachers in generating creative solutions. It can also enable them to generate more visual representation in less time, and get feedback from peers and users, and prospective clients. Yang et al. [18] propose the term "Prompt tuning" as a technique used in natural language processing and machine learning that involves fine-tuning the language model using prompts. They state that "prompt tuning leverages human-provided prompts to tailor the behaviour of the model towards specific tasks or objectives." In other words, by providing carefully crafted prompts, designers can influence the outputs of the language model, steering it towards generating text that aligns with desired criteria such as style, genre, mood, or specific content.

3 Prompting Text-to-Image for Logo Design

Early research laid the groundwork for text-to-image technology, with seminal works such as Goodfellow et al.'s development of GANs in 2014 [1, 19]. Since then, researchers have made significant steps in refining these models for design applications [7, 15–17]. One notable advancement is the introduction of models like DALL-E (Distributed Automated Language Learning Encoder) by Radford et al. from OpenAI in 2021 or Midjourney.ai, founded in 2022 by David Holz. These applications showcase the potential of text-to-image models, demonstrating the ability to generate diverse and contextually relevant images based on natural language descriptions called prompts.

But can AI generate truly original logos? Christiaens and Haerens [20], initiated an exploration into the potential of AI to create original logos. Their endeavour, centred around developing a logo generator based on DALL-E, prompts the question of AI's capacity for true originality. Despite employing a relatively small model and dataset, the authors express confidence in the eventual realization of an AI-driven logo generator. They highlight the rapid evolution and learning capabilities of AI demonstrated in their work. However, they acknowledge limitations in their model, notably the absence of a defined design language and a scoring mechanism to differentiate between good and bad logos. To address these shortcomings, evaluating and rating outputs generated from text-to-image prompts, assessing the relevance of the prompts, and soliciting feedback on overall satisfaction could prove instrumental in advancing this nascent field and filling it with more scientific rigor.

On their research, Wernersson and Persson [21], offer valuable insights into the way in which AI is anticipated to shape the future of design, and specifically graphic design. They conclude that the design field is increasingly intrigued by the potential of AI for graphic content creation. AI can expedite and enhance design processes while equipping designers with innovative tools to augment creativity. Nevertheless, to leverage AI effectively in visual content creation, designers must stay abreast of the latest industry advancements. It is imperative to grasp the advantages and limitations of employing AI as a graphic content creator. Additionally, evaluating the potential influence on the quality and uniqueness of design outputs generated by AI-driven software and applications is vital. In logo design, text-to-image technology offers several advantages, including faster ideation, more rapid concept generation, increased design variation, and improved solutions. Designers should leverage these AI-powered tools to explore broader design possibilities and iterate on logo concepts more efficiently.

3.1 The Text-to-Image Model

We understand the limitations and benefits of formulating text prompts with AI, mainly using the Midjourney.ai bot (Caires et al. [7]). In previous research, we delved into the best possible formulation for creating compelling and precise prompts for generating images for stools and chairs. We know the bot understands (very appropriately) the given textual instructions. Simple ideas, such as "*draw a stool*" or "*sketch a stool*" were generated accurately. Also, by providing more details, such as "*design a stool with three wooden legs and a seat made of transparent acrylic*", we acknowledge that the generated result is accurately aligned with the requested prompt.

For the current research, the text-to-image model used is as follows: starting from more straightforward instructions as

> *"imagine a letter mark of a 'Z' word"* to more complex instructions as
>
> *"design an emblem of a store 'X' for a group 'Y' with a style 'W', excluding 'this' or 'that', with the following parameters for 'style', 'quality', 'lightning', and 'aspect ratio,' etc.",*

we tested the Midjourney.ai bot on the text prompting accuracy. In Fig. 1, we considered systematically structuring the prompt text according to a simplified model for

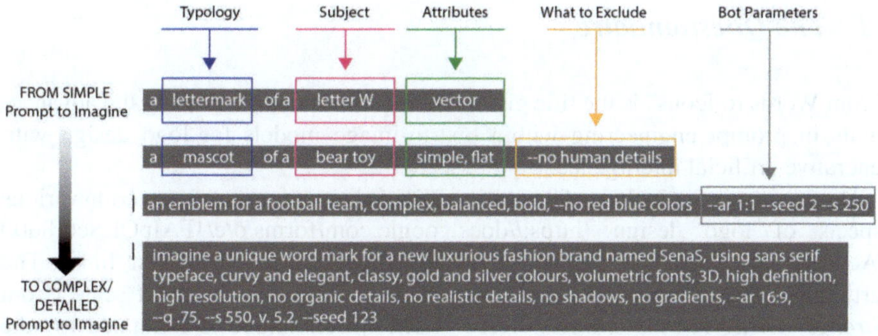

Fig. 1 Text-to-image model progression from simple to complex sentence structures

increasingly complex ones. Including in the simplest prompts the type of logo we want to generate, the subject, and some attributes. In the more complex text prompts, we added more instructions, such as what we want to exclude from the generated image and the specific parameters of the Midjourney.ai bot we use. The parameters helped define specifics such as the weight of each phrase or word ('X'::value), the quality of the generated image (q.0.1 to q.1.0), or, for example, the style (from 0 to 750). We also used the 'Seed' parameter whenever we wanted to diverge from the previous results, assigning a new 'Seed' (i.e., –seed 0, –seed 126) to each generation of a new logo.

4 Research Method

The research methodology involved the distribution of a questionnaire to specific groups within the design and artistic communities. Emails were sent to students, teachers, and professionals in these fields to gather diverse perspectives and insights. Students from the bachelor programs of Design, Architectural Studies, and Communication and Media at the University of Saint Joseph in Macao were specifically targeted to ensure a focused sample. In order to incorporate international perspectives, the survey was also extended to others, such as students and teachers in Vietnam, Finland, and Portugal. In total, 114 valid responses were collected from these various groups. Subsequently, the data was analysed and summarised in Chap. 5 to draw meaningful conclusions regarding the effectiveness of AI-driven text-to-image models for logo design. We used the Midjourney.ai bot to prompt text-to-image and generate corresponding visual representations for letter marks, symbols, word marks, emblems, mascots, icons, and badges. The bot leverages advanced natural language processing and image generation techniques to understand and translate text descriptions into graphical elements. By analysing participants' responses and feedback, the questionnaire aims to evaluate the effectiveness and potential of these AI-driven text-to-image models for logo design.

4.1 The Questionnaire

"From Words to Icons" is the title given to the questionnaire exploring the advancements in prompt engineering within text-to-image models for logo design with generative artificial intelligence.

The questionnaire includes 69 questions divided into ten sections covering various aspects of logo design (https://docs.google.com/forms/d/e/1FAIpQLSe6r8d00YAc4ctwka0Kvwlio2fjtHmMe-OFQj3cPheBiT3qgw/viewform?usp=sf_link). The participants are asked to rate their agreement on a five-point Likert scale (from '*Strongly Disagree*' to '*Strongly Agree*'). The questionnaire is estimated to take around 20 min to complete. The ten sections cover different types of logos, including Letter Marks (7 questions), Symbols (6 questions), Word Marks (4 questions), Emblems (6 questions), Mascots (6 questions), Icons (6 questions), Badges (5 questions), and Visual Appeal (15 questions). Additionally, the questionnaire explores the respondents' overall perception regarding the authenticity and quality of logos generated from text prompts (8 questions) and a final section with six questions for final considerations on future uses of text prompts and AI-driven logo generation. It is essential to note that all logos included in this study were created by the Midjourney.ai bot, except the eight logos on the Overall Perception section, which were designed by the author of this study (logos inside the pink box at the bottom of the list, see Fig. 2).

4.2 Metrics for Evaluation

The questionnaire employed several metrics to evaluate the effectiveness of text-to-image AI-generated logos. (I) Accuracy of Logo Representation: This metric assessed how closely the generated logos matched the textual prompts provided. It evaluated the fidelity of the generated logo to the specified instructions (7 sections for Letter Marks, Symbols, Word Marks, Emblems, Mascots, Icons and Badges, comprising 40 questions). (II) Visual Appeal Assessment: This metric focused on the aesthetic quality of the logos, evaluating factors such as colour scheme, typography, and overall design coherence to determine visual attractiveness (section on Visual Appeal comprising 15 questions). (III) Relevance to Text Prompt Evaluation: It examined the extent to which the logos aligned with the content and intent of the text prompts. It assessed whether the logos effectively conveyed the desired message or image specified in the prompts (Questions 7, 13, 18, 24, 30, 36, 41). (IV) Creativity and Uniqueness: This metric analysed the level of innovation and uniqueness demonstrated in the generated logos. (V) Brand Identity Alignment Assessment: This metric determined how well the logos reflected the brand identity and values specified in the text prompts. It assessed whether the logos accurately represented the brand's personality and positioning (6 questions). (VI) Overall Satisfaction Ratings: Participants rated their satisfaction with the generated logos. This metric encompassed their

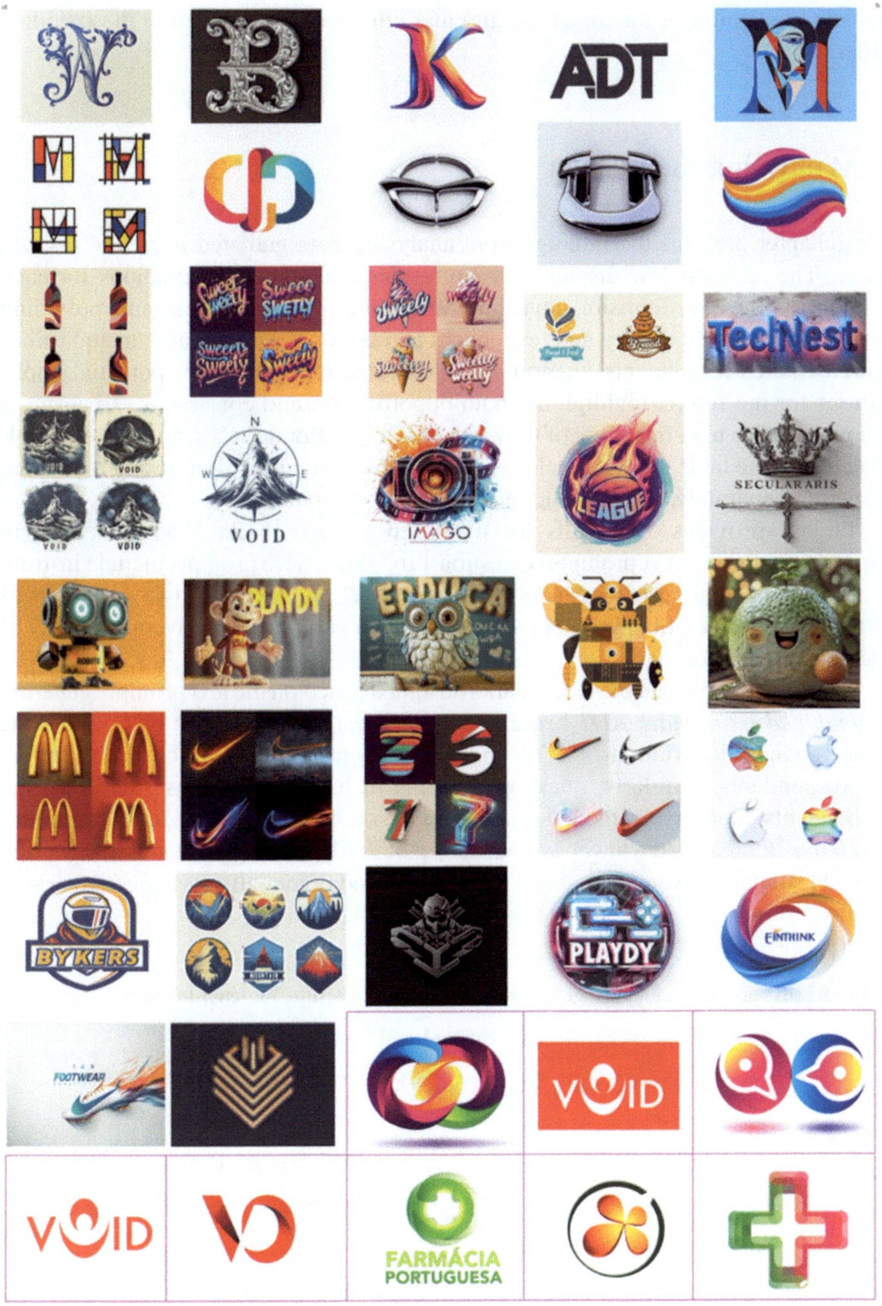

Fig. 2 Logos used in the questionnaire

holistic perception of the logos' quality and effectiveness in meeting the specified criteria.

5 Analysing the Results

This chapter presents the findings from analysing data gathered from 114 respondents. The tables below display average ratings and standard deviations for each section of the questionnaire, revealing variations in effectiveness and providing insights into design quality and respondent perceptions. Additionally, the questionnaire explores respondents' views on AI-generated logos and their potential implications for the future, highlighting both opportunities and constraints. To ensure a comprehensive understanding of the results each questionnaire's sections are consolidated into one table, offering a clearer perspective compared to analysing individual questions separately, which could lead to misinterpretations.

Table 1 provides the results for six different letter marks, each generated in response to distinct text prompts (Question 1 to Q.6). These prompts include instructions such as creating letter Marks for letters *W*, *B*, *K*, *ADT*, and two variations of letter *M*. The table offers valuable insights into the variability and average quality of the generated letter marks.

The results show that the letter marks designed based on the text prompt "*generate a combined letter mark ADT*" received the highest average rating of 4.51 and the lowest standard deviation of 0.74, indicating high quality and consensus among the respondents. Similarly, question 3 seems to have gotten consensus from the respondents. Conversely, the letter marks based on the prompt "*create a letter mark of a letter W*" received a lower average rating of 2.90 and a higher standard deviation of 1.18, suggesting some variability in opinions and potentially less effective design results.

Table 1 Text prompts with average and standard deviation results for letter marks

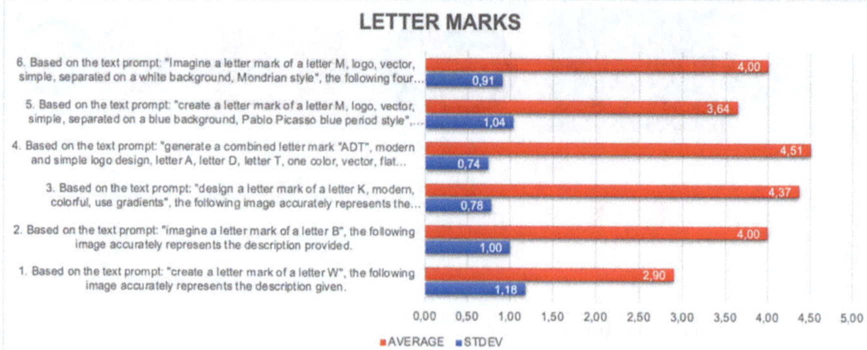

Table 2 provides the results for five different symbols, each generated in response to distinct text prompts (Q.8 to Q.12). These prompts include instructions such as creating symbols for a wine brand, an ice cream store, a new car brand, and a new company called *CLIP*.

The provided data presents standard deviation values ranging from 1.05 to 1.28, indicating a high level of perception variability among each symbol's ratings. Meanwhile, the average ratings of Q.8 to Q.12 range from 2.62 to 3.60, providing an overall measure of the symbols' effectiveness in meeting the specified design criteria. Overall, the results for Symbols are less convincing when compared with the letter Marks values in Table 1, showing a higher variability of opinions when interpreting the given text prompts and the generated images. Nevertheless, average results from questions 9 and 12, 3.28 and 3.60, respectively, could indicate some consensus on the generated results.

Table 3 summarizes the average ratings and the standard deviation for various Word Marks created in response to different text prompts. These word marks encompass a range of design specifications and attributes, including typography, flat design, colour schemes, and specific thematic elements, such as psychedelic Art and futuristic neon. The data shows that the average ratings range from 2.18 to 3.32, indicating variability in the perceived quality of the designs. Word Marks 14 and 17 received the highest average ratings of 3.32 and 3.28, respectively, suggesting their text prompts and visuals were more efficient. In contrast, word Mark 15 received the lowest average rating of 2.18 and the highest standard deviation of 1.52 indicating that it was less favoured among the designs. Overall, the analysis highlights the subjective nature of design evaluation and the importance of considering various design elements and textual descriptions in creating valuable word Marks from text prompts.

Table 4 presents evaluations of Emblem designs created in response to various text prompts (Q.19 to Q.23). The average ratings range from 3.36 to 3.89, indicating a positive reception across the respondents. Emblem 20 received the highest average rating of 3.89, suggesting that it resonated particularly well with the respondents as a representation of the outdoor adventure brand *VOID*. Conversely, emblem 21 received

Table 2 Text prompts with average and standard deviation results for symbols

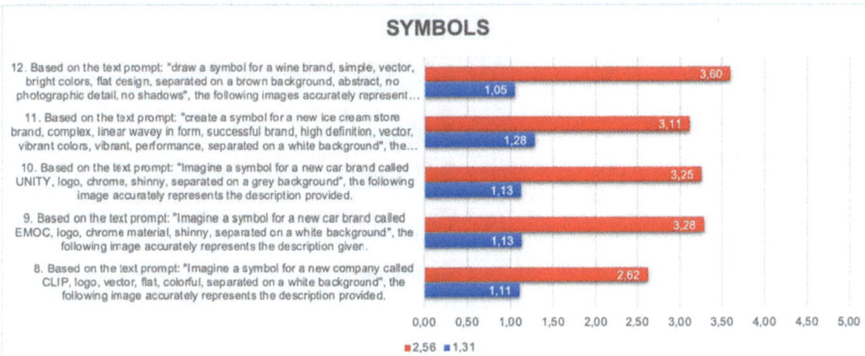

Table 3 Text prompts with average and standard deviation results for word marks

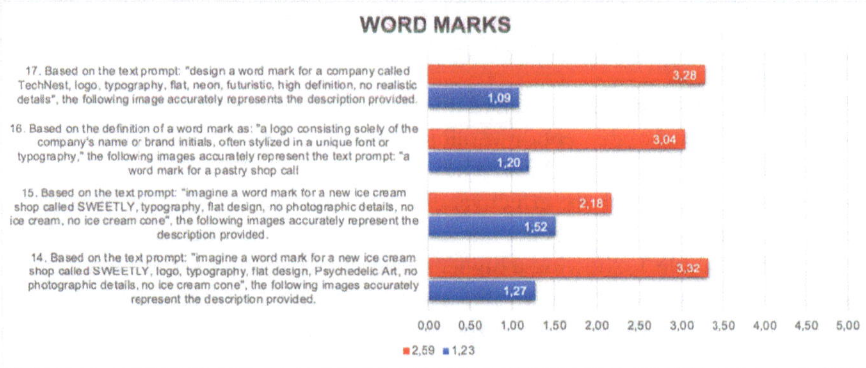

the lowest average rating of 3.36, indicating a slightly less favourable response, albeit still above the mean. The standard deviations range from 1.01 to 1.22, reflecting some variability in the ratings for each design.

The data for Table 5 is the evaluation of Mascot character designs tailored to diverse brand identities and based on different text prompts (Q.25 to Q.29). Mascots serve as iconic representatives, embodying the essence and values of the entities they symbolize. From a quirky robot for a technology company to a playful monkey for a children's entertainment brand or a smiling bee for an environmental conservation organization, each generated design incorporates the subjects given, characteristics and styles on the text prompts.

The average ratings for the mascot designs range from 2.92 (Q.29) to 4.21 (Q.25), indicating varying levels of success in meeting the specified criteria. A higher average rating on text prompt 25 suggests that the result resonates well with the intended brand identity and target audience. The text prompt for question 29 has a lower rating that may indicate areas for improvement or divergence from the desired text

Table 4 Text prompts with average and standard deviation results for emblems

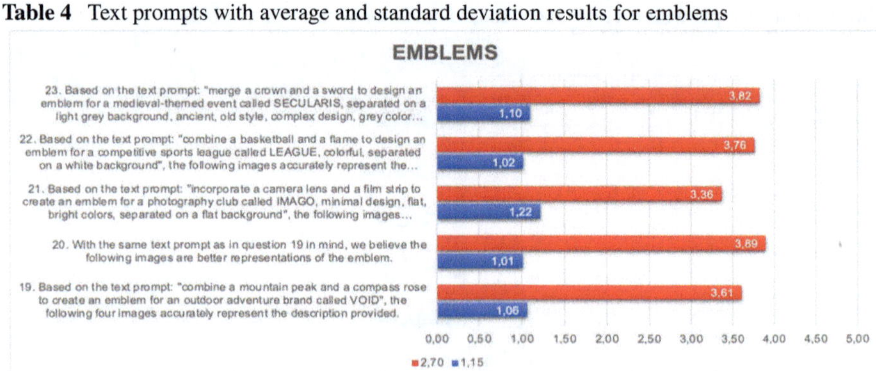

Table 5 Text prompts with average and standard deviation results for Mascots

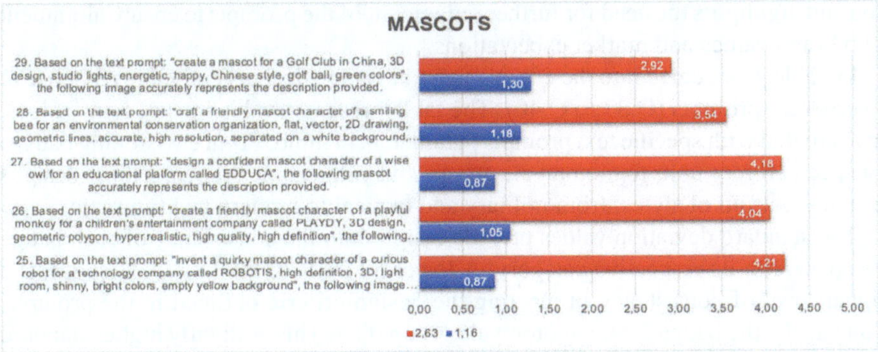

prompt attributes. Furthermore, question 25 has a lower standard deviation of 0.87, suggesting a higher level of agreement among the respondents.

Table 6 presents evaluations of newly designed Icons aimed at redefining and future-proofing iconic brands (Q.31 to Q.35). Through the given text prompts, the bot generated several icons for brands like *McDonald's*, *NIKE*, *SEVEN-ELEVEN*, and *APPLE*, envisioning their futures on various backgrounds to ensure versatility and visual impact.

The average ratings range from 2.04 (Q.34) to 3.10 (Q.35), indicating a low to moderate level of success in meeting the objectives outlined in the text prompts. Icons associated with *NIKE* (Q.32) and *APPLE* (Q. 35) received relatively higher average ratings, suggesting that they effectively captured the essence of these brands and resonated well with the respondents. Conversely, the *NIKE* brand icon (Q. 34) received a lower average rating, indicating potential challenges in aligning with the brand's identity and future direction. The standard deviations, ranging from 1.15 (Q.33) to 1.33 (Q.34), reflect higher variability in respondents' perceptions of the

Table 6 Text prompts with average and standard deviation results for icons

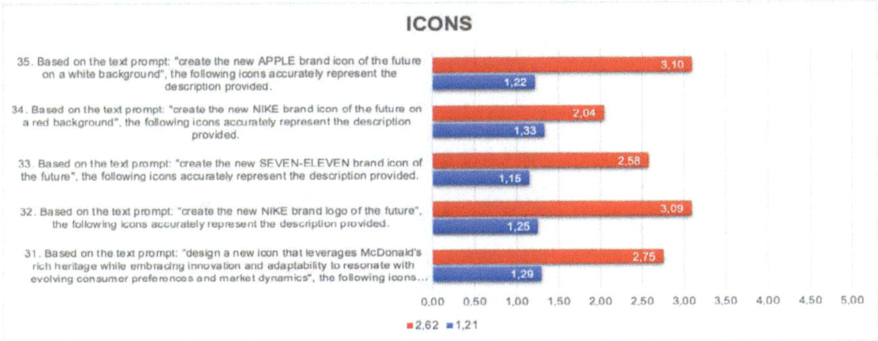

icons' effectiveness. This variance underscores the subjective nature of design evaluation and highlights the need for further refinement of the prompts to ensure alignment with brand values and market expectations.

In Table 7, we delve into the effectiveness of Badge designs crafted in response to diverse text prompts (Q.37 to Q.40). The table presents evaluations of four badges, each created with specific text prompts parameters in mind. From envisioning badges for special forces units to motorcycle groups and video game branding, these designs span a spectrum of styles, from military and tactical to modern and futuristic.

The standard deviation values provide insight into the consistency of each badge design within its respective category. A lower STDEV of 0.93 on Q.37 suggests a higher level of consistency in meeting the design criteria outlined in the prompts. Conversely, the badge for the motorcycle group (Q.40) has a slightly higher standard deviation of 1.07, suggesting a somewhat more significant variability in design execution and perception by the respondents. The average ratings (above the median of 3.00) further indicate the perceived effectiveness of each badge, with higher average scores reflecting better alignment with the given prompts, 3.79 on Q.38 for the *BYKERS* badge.

Table 8 provides insights into the impact of different text prompts on the quality of design outcomes (Questions 7, 13, 18, 24, 30, 36, and Q.41). Each question represents a pair of text prompts, with one prompt hypothesized to generate better results than the other. For instance, Prompt 7 suggests that simpler instructions to create a letter mark of a letter "X" will lead to better outcomes than a more detailed directive. Similarly, other prompts explore specificity, complexity, and stylistic preference variations.

Based on the results obtained and their averages, most respondents believe that the more descriptive and detailed a prompt text is, the more likely it is to achieve better results. However, the relatively high standard deviation in almost all responses, ranging from 1.16 to 1.33, indicates significant variability in the answers. Thus, we cannot conclusively confirm these results. Nevertheless, it suggests a trend that values description over the simplicity of the prompt text.

Table 7 Text prompts with average and standard deviation results for badges

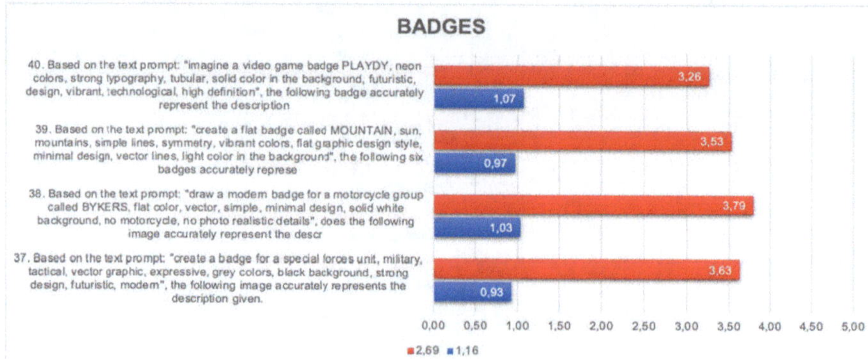

Table 8 Impact of text prompts and quality of design

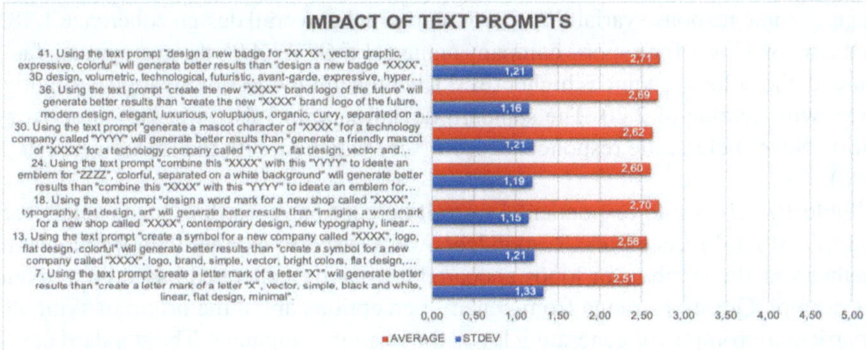

Table 9 presents the assessment of visual appeal across various design aspects for different logo concepts generated in response to specific text prompts (15 questions, from 42.1 to 43.6). In the first section, represented by questions 42.1 to 42.6, respondents considered a text prompt requesting a dynamic logo for a finance company called '*FINTHINK*'. The questions cover typography, colour scheme, overall visual appearance, design coherence, uniqueness, and satisfaction with the generated image. Similarly, the second section, questions 43.1 to 43.6, explores visual appeal in response to a prompt for a creative logo for a sports company named '*FOOTWEAR*'. This comparative analysis provides valuable feedback on the effectiveness of different design elements in capturing visual appeal across distinct brand identities.

Comparing the two logos generated, we observe some interesting trends. In the first logo section, which evaluates the visual appeal of a finance company logo called '*FINTHINK*', the average scores range from 2.23 to 3.31, indicating moderate satisfaction levels across different aspects. Furthermore, the standard deviation values,

Table 9 Text prompts and visual appeal results

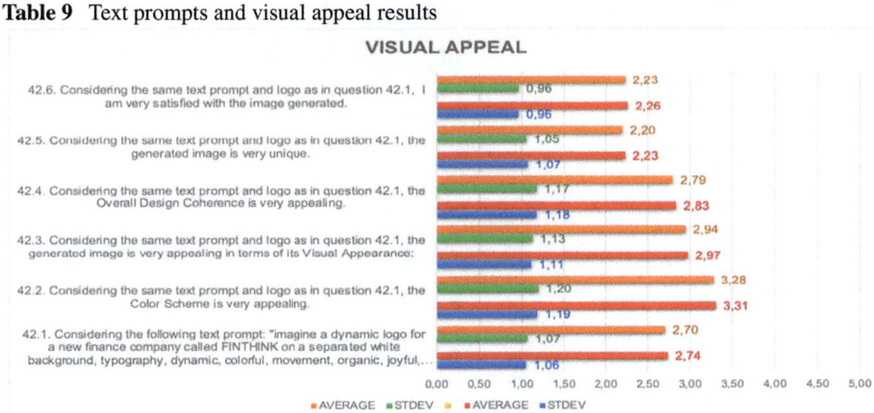

ranging from 0.96 (for satisfaction), could be conclusive. 1.19 (for colour scheme) suggests some response variability, particularly in the overall design coherence 1.18. On the second logo, for a sports company named '*FOOTWEAR*', the average satisfaction with the colour scheme is higher (3.31), but the uniqueness of the logo is slightly lower, with a value of 2.20. The standard deviation value also suggests some variability. Nevertheless, the respondents seem very satisfied with the image generated (0.96).

Table 10 delves into respondents' overall perceptions regarding logos generated by artificial intelligence bots. Respondents were asked to express their opinions on whether specific symbols or logos appeared artificially generated based on a given text prompt. Questions range from general perceptions about the origin of symbols to particular prompts for generating logos for various companies. The standard deviation values, ranging from 1.10 to 1.24, reflect the variability in responses, indicating differing levels of certainty in participants' perceptions.

Meanwhile, the average scores, ranging from 2.79 to 3.83, provide insights into respondents' overall perception regarding the artificial nature of the generated logos. Firstly, respondents have a relatively high consensus regarding certain logos' artificial generation, reflected in high average scores and low standard deviations. For example, in question 45, the average score is notably high at 3.83, suggesting a solid consensus that the symbol appears to be generated by artificial intelligence. The standard deviation of 1.10 indicates relatively low response variability, further supporting this trend.

Conversely, other questions display more variability in respondents' perceptions. Question 46 exhibits a lower average score of 2.85, indicating a less unanimous agreement among respondents. Additionally, the standard deviation of 1.24 suggests more significant variability in responses, with some participants likely perceiving the

Table 10 Overall perception of generated logos from text prompts results

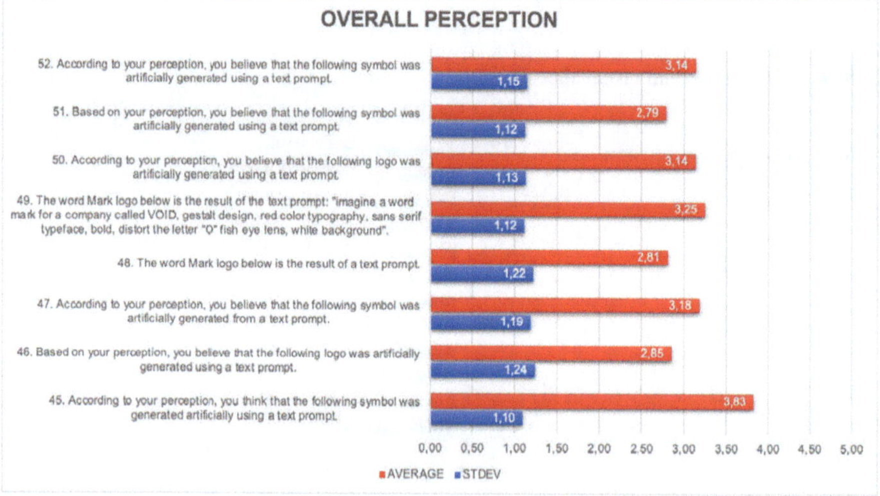

logo as artificially generated while others may not. Comparing questions 49 and 51 provides further insight into trends regarding specific prompts. Question 49 yields an average score of 3.25. This suggests a relatively high consensus among respondents that the logo appears artificially generated based on the provided prompt. In contrast, question 52 has a lower average score of 3.14 and a slightly higher standard deviation of 1.15, indicating more variability in respondents' perceptions.

All the logos from this table (Overall Perception, Q.45 to Q.52) are created by a human designer (the author) rather than generated by an artificial intelligence bot. This information was not provided to the respondents. From the data, it becomes evident that respondents' perceptions of the logos presented in the study suggest a level of uncertainty regarding their origin; the respondents' perceptions varied considerably. Some logos garnered relatively high average scores, indicating a consensus among respondents that they appeared to be artificially generated. However, these perceptions contrast with the actual origin of the logos, highlighting the potential for AI-generated logos to create designs that mimic the logos generated by designers. Conversely, logos that received lower average scores and higher standard deviations suggest a less unanimous agreement among respondents, indicating more significant variability in perceptions. These findings underscore the importance of considering human biases and expectations when interpreting perceptions of design origin, especially in contexts where AI-generated designs are increasingly prevalent.

Table 11 explore some final considerations regarding using text prompts for generating logos (Q.53 to Q.59). Respondents provided insights into their perceptions of logos created through this method compared to those crafted by professional designers. The analysis delves into logos' effectiveness, quality, accuracy, and satisfaction levels generated from text prompts. Additionally, the respondents shared their future intentions regarding using AI-driven tools for logo design creation.

The results indicate a generally positive perception of logos generated from text prompts, with an average rating of 2.74 (Q.53, effectiveness) to 3.74 (Q.59, valuable tools) across various considerations. Despite some variability, as indicated by the

Table 11 Final consideration on generating logos from text prompts

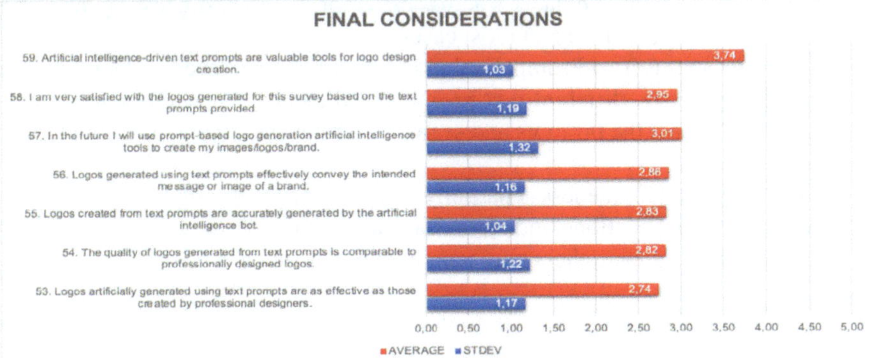

standard deviation ranging from 1.03 (Q.59) to 1.32 (Q.57, future uses), the overall sentiment suggests that participants view these AI-generated logos as adequate, comparable to professionally designed ones, they are "valuable tools for logo design creation" (3.74). Moreover, respondents expressed a lower satisfaction (rating of 2.95) with some of the logos generated but indicated a willingness to use AI-driven text prompts for future logo design creation. These findings highlight the potential of AI as a valuable tool in logo design, offering efficiency and creative solutions. Nevertheless, it seems respondents believe these digital tools are less effective than designers.

6 Discussion

The questionnaire findings reflect on the advancement of prompting text-to-image models, highlighting design opportunities and challenges. By analysing the effectiveness of textual prompts in generating AI-driven logos, designers and researchers can refine prompt engineering strategies to enhance design outcomes. The findings highlight the importance of developing tailored prompts that effectively capture specific design requirements and brand attributes (i.e. applying prompt parameters and commands more accurately). Moreover, understanding the role of prompt specificity, complexity, and stylistic preferences can inform the development of more sophisticated text-to-image models that better align with user expectations and design goals. Based on the metrics used to evaluate the effectiveness of text-to-image AI-generated logos, the following results are to be considered:

(I) The Accuracy of Prompts to Logo Representation: Achieved. The generated logos matched very closely the textual prompts provided as indicated by the highest average ratings and low standard deviation for Letter Marks (e.g. Q.4), Symbols (e.g. Q.12) and Mascots (e.g. Q.25) designed based on accurate text prompts.

(II) The Visual Appeal Assessment: Can be achieved, with varying levels of success for colour schemes, and overall design coherence, indicated by the average ratings and standard deviations across different sections, suggesting moderate to high satisfaction levels in most cases.

(III) The Relevance to Text Prompt Evaluation is partially achieved, as there is some variability across different text prompts, indicating that while some results effectively meet the prompts and seem to be relevant, others may not align as closely.

(IV) Creativity and Uniqueness is partially achieved, with varying levels of success across different sections, indicating that while some designs are perceived as creative and unique, others may not stand out as much.

(V) Brand Identity Alignment Assessment is partially achieved, with some designs effectively resonating with the brand identities they represent (e.g. *Nike*), while others may struggle to align with brand values and essence (e.g. *SEVEN ELEVEN*).

(VI) Overall Satisfaction Ratings is partially achieved, with respondents expressing varying levels of satisfaction with logos generated from text prompts, suggesting that while some find them effective and valuable tools, others may still prefer professionally designed logos.

While the questionnaire provides valuable findings, it is essential to acknowledge its limitations and identify areas for future research. Firstly, the sample size of 114 respondents does not fully represent the diverse/multiple perspectives within the design community. Conducting larger-scale questionnaires with broader demographics could yield more robust and generalizable results. Additionally, the research focused primarily on AI-generated logos and may overlook the nuances of human-designed logos. Future research could explore comparative studies between AI-generated and human-designed logos to provide deeper insights into design preferences and effectiveness. Furthermore, investigating the impact of cultural and contextual factors on logo perception could offer valuable cross-cultural perspectives.

7 Conclusion

The paper offers a comprehensive overview of text-to-image models' evolution and current state, particularly in logo design. Beginning with the foundational work on Generative Adversarial Networks (GANs) by Goodfellow et al. in 2014, the field has seen significant advancements, including developing new applications like DALL-E and Midjourney.ai among others. These models exemplify the potential of AI-driven text-to-image synthesis in generating diverse and contextually relevant visual representations based on natural language prompts. In this context, prompt engineering is a creative skill that allows users to effectively use language and prior knowledge to craft prompts that align with specific design objectives. Nowadays, researchers can achieve significant performance improvements in vision-language models by leveraging prompt engineering strategies.

Moreover, the research methodology employed in this study, including the targeted distribution of questionnaires to diverse groups of students and experts within the design community, yielded valuable insights into the effectiveness and potential of prompting text-to-image models for logo design. The analysis of the questionnaire responses provided nuanced perspectives on the variability in design quality, respondent perceptions, and the impact of different text prompts on logo design outcomes. From evaluating various aspects of logo design, including Letter Marks, Symbols, Word Marks, Emblems, Mascots, Icons, and Badges, to assessing overall perceptions and future intentions regarding AI-driven logo design tools, the study offers a holistic understanding of the strengths, limitations, and implications of AI in the design process. Overall, while AI-driven prompting text-to-image models demonstrate promising capabilities in logo design, challenges remain, such as ensuring accuracy, relevance, and brand consistency in generated images. Additionally, addressing concerns about the artificial nature of generated logos and effectively integrating AI-driven tools into the design workflow are crucial considerations for future research and practice. Nevertheless, the findings underscore the potential of AI as a valuable tool for enhancing creativity and efficiency in logo design, paving the way for innovation and exploration in this field.

References

1. Goodfellow, I. J., Mirza, M., Xu, B., Ozair, S., Courville, A., & Bengio, Y. (2014). Generative Adversarial Networks. ArXiv: https://arxiv.org/abs/1406.2661
2. Reed, S., Akata, Z., Yan, X., Logeswaran, L., Schiele, B., & Lee, H. (2016). Generative adversarial text-to-image synthesis. In Proceedings of the 33rd International Conference on Machine Learning (ICML) (Vol. 48, pp. 1060–1069).
3. Elgammal, A., Liu, B., Elhoseiny, M., & Mazzone, M. (2017). CAN: Creative Adversarial Networks, Generating "Art" by Learning About Styles and Deviating from Style Norms. ArXiv: https://arxiv.org/abs/1706.07068
4. Zhang, H., Xu, T., Li, H., Zhang, S., Wang, X., Huang, X., & Metaxas, D. (2017). StackGAN++: Realistic Image Synthesis with Stacked Generative Adversarial Networks. ArXiv: https://arxiv.org/abs/1710.10916
5. Ziegler A., Berryman, J. (2023). "A developer's guide to prompt engineering and LLMs - The GitHub Blog". github.blog in: https://github.blog/2023-07-17-prompt-engineering-guide-generative-ai-llms/
6. Reid, R. (2023). "How to write an effective GPT-3 or GPT-4 prompt". Zapier. Retrieved 2024–01–23, in: https://zapier.com/blog/gpt-prompt/
7. Caires, C.S., Estadieu, G., Olga Ng Ka Man, S. (2024). Design Thinking Methodology and Text-To-Image Artificial Intelligence: A Case Study in the Context of Furniture Design Education. In: Martins, N., Brandão, D., Fernandes-Marcos, A. (eds) Perspectives on Design and Digital Communication IV. Springer Series in Design and Innovation, vol. 33. Springer, Cham. https://doi.org/10.1007/978-3-031-41770-2_7
8. Oppenlaender, J., Linder, R., & Silvennoinen, J. (2023). Prompting AI Art: An Investigation into the Creative Skill of Prompt Engineering. ArXiv: https://arxiv.org/abs/2303.13534
9. Branwen, G. (2020–2023), GPT-3 Creative Fiction, in: https://gwern.net/gpt-3
10. Gu, J., Han, Z., Chen, S., Beirami, A., He, B., Zhang, G., Liao, R., Qin, Y., Tresp, V., & Torr, P. (2023). A Systematic Survey of Prompt Engineering on Vision-Language Foundation Models. ArXiv: https://arxiv.org/abs/2307.12980
11. Hao, Y., Chi, Z., Dong, L., & Wei, F. (2022). Optimizing Prompts for Text-to-Image Generation. ArXiv: https://arxiv.org/abs/2212.09611
12. https://promptfolder.com/midjourney-prompt-helper/
13. Amatriain, X. (2024). Prompt Design and Engineering: Introduction and Advanced Methods. ArXiv: https://arxiv.org/abs/2401.14423
14. https://amatriain.net/
15. Li, S., Hu, T., Khan, F. S., Hou, Q., Wang, Y., & Yang, J. (2024). Get What You Want, Not What You Don't: Image Content Suppression for Text-to-Image Diffusion Models. ArXiv: https://arxiv.org/abs/2402.05375
16. Liu, V., & Chilton, L. B. (2021). Design Guidelines for Prompt Engineering Text-to-Image Generative Models. ArXiv: https://arxiv.org/abs/2109.06977

17. Smith, A., Schroeder, H., Epstein, Z., Cook, M., Colton, S., & Lippman, A. (2023). Trash to Treasure: Using text-to-image models to inform the design of physical artefacts. ArXiv: https://arxiv.org/abs/2302.00561
18. Yang, H., Lin, J., Yang, A., Wang, P., Zhou, C., & Yang, H. (2022). Prompt Tuning for Generative Multimodal Pretrained Models. ArXiv: https://arxiv.org/abs/2208.02532
19. Goodfellow, I., Pouget-Abadie, J., Mirza, M., Xu, B., Warde-Farley, D., Ozair, S., Bengio, Y., et al. (2014). Generative adversarial nets. In Advances in neural information processing systems (pp. 2672–2680).
20. Christiaens, B., & Haerens, K. (2022). Can AI generate truly original logos? Retrieved 2024–02–12, in: https://www.ml6.eu/blogpost/can-ai-generate-truly-original-logos
21. Wernersson, J., & Persson, R. (2023). Exploring the Potential Impact of AI on the Role of Graphic Content Creators: Benefits, Challenges, and Collaborative Opportunities. http://hj.diva-portal.org/smash/get/diva2:1788167/FULLTEXT01.pdf

Design-Driven Branding: A Proposal for a Methodological Model for Strategic and Creative Brand Direction and Design of the Brand Visual Identity

Daniel Raposo

Abstract Over time, various methodological models have been proposed for Branding and/or Brand Visual Identity, sometimes confusing these concepts. On the other hand, there is still a lack of knowledge about key concepts, with authors entrenched in their areas of Management, Marketing, Communication or Design, without consulting the others. Using a mixed, non-interventionist methodology based on a literature review, some methodological models for Branding and/or Visual Brand Identity are broken down and compared. The findings result in a diagrammatic model defined in an exploratory approach resulting from active research, proposing methodologies and techniques, as well as a Design-driven branding action. The proposed model is characterised by being open (brand-world-market-people) and dynamic (as opposed to linear models), promoting co-design, testing and evaluation through design.

Keywords Design and branding · Brand visual identity · Brand image · Branding methodological model

1 Introduction

Branding, i.e. the process of creating brands, their design, attribution and their articulated management and strategy, has been the subject of study and publications in the areas of Management, Marketing, Corporate Reputation, Communication and Design. However, the literature and research in design tends to be confined to Visual Identity Design, in the definition of concepts and graphic representation of the graphic system.

D. Raposo (✉)
ReThink – Centro de Investigação em Design para o Território & Polytechnic Institute of Castelo Branco, Av. Pedro Álvares Cabral, nº 12, 6000-084 Castelo Branco, Portugal
e-mail: draposo@ipcb.pt

CIAUD, Lisbon School of Architecture, Universidade de Lisboa, Rua Sá Nogueira, 1349-063 Lisboa, Portugal

© The Author(s), under exclusive license to Springer Nature Switzerland AG 2025
D. Brandão et al. (eds.), *Perspectives on Design and Digital Communication V*, Springer Series in Design and Innovation 50, https://doi.org/10.1007/978-3-031-76156-0_13

The management, marketing and corporate reputation perspective seeks to articulate corporate image, market needs and opportunities with corporate capabilities and competitive and commercial advantages. The communication perspective proposed by DirCom, on the other hand, proposes the dilution of departmental barriers, dialogue and coordinated cooperation capable of generating a positive corporate image. In these proposals, design activity tends to be portrayed as a subordinate area, with importance in contrast and differentiation through the design of graphic signs as an identification system and brand language (Balmer, 2001; Olins, 1990, 2008; Costa, 2008; Johnson, 2019).

Organisations still don't have the mechanisms to assess the context or the corporate identity itself. On the other hand, methodological approaches tend to focus only on a few aspects such as product or brand management or the de-sign of visual identity, lacking articulation between tangible and tangible dimensions (Balmer, 2001).

On the other hand, the design perspective on branding has become entangled in the Corporate Identity concept, focusing too much on the concept and design of the brand mark as a sign of identification that obeys a meaning, on the design of the main visual communication artefacts and design principles or graphic standardization, without establishing relationships and relevance with management, marketing and communication (Raposo, 2008, 2012; Raposo et al., 2020b; Cassissi, 2023).

Under the concept of Corporate Identity, design developed normative programmes with a strategic purpose centred on the effectiveness of identification and persuasion that worked when communication was unidirectional. However, contemporary brands are organic systems that adapt, which cross the areas of management, marketing, design, communication, strategy, advertising, and technology, seeking to ensure that the brand experience is impactful, useful, relevant, and differentiating (Brea, 2020).

As Cameira (2020) points out, some design professionals consider branding to be about developing a broader and more complex visual identity, in a view that is considered incomplete because it does not include the brand dimension and its articulation with the other components of the organization and business.

Brands are above all symbolic systems to which organizations, products and services are linked. They should not be limited to commercial, graphic or product components or subsystems such as the business plan, communication, or communication plans (Brea, 2020).

From a systems theory perspective, branding is a supersystem with principles, predetermined by the brand personality, used to make sense of and correlate the management, strategic, communication and visual, material, and spatial, financial, and logistical, behavioural, sensory, and emotional subsystems (Oliveira, 2018).

The brand ecosystem is complex, integrating human systems, actions, and communication, with diverse internal and external participants (Neumeier, 2007) in a complex relationship between identity, organizations, marketing, management, technology, communication, design, culture, and society (Brea, 2020).

Brands today are managed symbolic systems (branding) in the correlation of internal and external communication (between message creators and consumers), in the design of contact interfaces and experiences that mediate to create value and a sense of belonging according to cultural standards and market requirements, needs and expectations. In this ontology of brand communication, corporate identity and culture are influenced by context, just as brand personality is determined by the need for differentiation and relevance to stakeholders in comparison to competitors or peers (Raposo, 2018).

A brand is a network of systems that must be created, managed, or studied considering its context, making it a "wicked problem" with multiple causes, effects, and characteristics. Branding is a chain for creating value and managing the brand image, acting on how to interpret, evaluate, create, communicate, and manage the brand in an integrated and sustainable way so that it succeeds in its context (Brea, 2020).

Although brands are created by groups, organizations, or corporations, they only exist when people are aware of them, when there is a mental perception of them, when there is a brand image (Costa, 2004; Neumeier, 2007) and their value is attributed by people (Aaker, 2001).

Over time, methodological models have emerged in the field of branding with the aim of presenting an organized roadmap for the construction, development, and effective management of a brand and/or its visual identity, based on the vision of the author proposing it. However, most of them end up focusing on one area or mainly on a few activities in the process (Johnson, 2019).

In this study, we proposed the study of methodological models on branding that detail the perspectives of visual identity design, with the aim of developing a more complete proposal from a design perspective.

A mixed methodology was adopted, with a non-interventional research phase based on a literature review, which aims to identify the phases, techniques, activities, and perspectives that are essential to a branding methodological model. In the active research phase, a dynamic methodological model was developed.

2 Theoretical Framework

The most referenced brand management models tend to be written from a business or marketing perspective, namely Keller (1998), Davis (2000), Aaker (2001), Kapferer (2008), and Balmer and Soenen (1999).

Costa (1977) was one of the pioneers to establish a correlation between design, communication, and brand, presenting visual identity as the system that structures and correlates the means of presentation and communication of the brand over time to generate a psycho-visual impact on memory, creating the brand image. According to Costa (1977), information about the market and culture should inform the brand project and its visual identity.

For Jenkins (1993) the process begins with creative research, which includes internal and external interviews and comparative analysis of competences in relation to competitors, as well as analysing competitors and gathering press reports; after a summary report, scenarios are defined and the creative and strategic proposal is validated; followed by Visual Identity Strategy Design, Communication Media; implementation and Continuous management and development.

Under the heading of Corporate Identity Design, Naples (1988) positions the visual system as a strategic interface for managing the brand image. The author's proposal begins with analysis of the brief, definition of concepts and strategy; approval and De-sign creation; Design developments; refinement of design; and implementation, proceeding to the necessary adjustments and design of visual standardisation (Naples, 1988).

Chaves (1988) proposal is structured around a semiotic relationship between reality, corporate identity, corporate communication, and corporate image or brand image. Chaves (1988) considers that the process begins with the analytical research phase and the identification of constraints, followed by the conception and design phase, the definition of strategy and the normative stage, consolidated by communication and intervention tactics.

From the perspective of organisational identity, Brun and Rasquinet (1996) propose the need to integrate departments, a strategic sense, the definition of a shared ideology and vision. The authors recommend that the process begins with a visual analysis and audit and concept definition; this is followed by conception; design and development of system applications, implementation, and standardisation.

Proposed as a complete method for designing brand identity, Wheeler's (2003) proposal begins with research in which objectives, competitors and the perspectives of different stakeholders are assessed; this is followed by the analysis and strategic definition of positioning, brand architecture, name and design; design takes care of vitalising the strategy; the media and visual identity design programme are developed; finally, the implementation plan is developed and applied.

The relationship between Brand Architecture, Brand Personality and Visual Identity is largely due to Olins (2008). His methodological proposal starts with Investigation, analysis, and strategic recommendations, considering competencies, opportunities, and market requirements; moving on to the definition of brand purpose and architecture, naming and visual style or tone of voice; the development and communication of the vision; the implementation of communication in various media and use in products and standardisation systems (Olins, 2008).

From a perspective focussed on graphic design, Peón (2009) considers that visual identity is a set of elements that identify and present the brand, functioning as an interface for corporate identity to condition the type of brand image generated. The system must be flexible in its use, differentiating and easy to memorise and identify. The author believes that the visual identity system must be globally integrated and informed by market research, which guides the conception and design and application of graphic solutions, which must be standardised and implemented in a coherent manner (Peón, 2009).

In de Slade-Brooking's (2016) proposal, the brand fulfils semiotic and symbolic functions that facilitate stakeholder choices. The process proposed by de Slade-Brooking (2016) is based on customer research and visual enquiry into brand chains, architecture and categories and their design; the concept and strategy establish the visual orientation and tone of the brand, which must be tested and validated, followed by implementation and evaluation of the results.

According to Johnson (2019), it is essential to carry out targeted research and ask the right questions when studying the positioning of competitors and the brand audit, studying the context or market in evolutionary terms and in the moment, clarifying corporate values and perceptions about the brand, balancing internal and external data, defining scenarios to align the brand with the market and the story and role of products or services; the strategy consists of defining a purpose and vision capable of positioning and differentiating, defining a brand personality and respective storytelling; then determining the brand architecture and naming; then designing toolkits or visual identity systems, correlating the brand mark with typography, imagery, colours, language and other graphics; implementation, which consists of putting the communication plan and specifications into practice, along with the standards manuals, segmenting, evaluating and correcting what is necessary; activation to increase the size of the brand in order to maintain alignment with the business, the longevity of the brand and the expansion of the brand (Johnson, 2019).

The proposal by Gautier and Roller (2019) focuses mainly on the visual identity system. However, the authors point out that the entire visual identity system must be informed by a positioning study, internal auditing, an inventory and analysis of graphic media and benchmarking; followed by ideation, sketches and selection and evaluation of proposals, development, and presentation to the client; validation and development of standardisation processes, consolidation of design principles, grids, styles, and standards; followed by development and application.

As Carmi (2020) points out, the brand determines the focus on identity and semantics articulated with normative principles that define the overall vision, strategy, actions and determine the parameters for evaluating results. According to this author, the Brand Design Strategy defines the brand architecture and overall strategy, and is determined by the principles, basic idea, and brand promise from which the Brand Design Language is developed, the applications in Digital Design, Packaging Design, Space Design, Editorial Design, articulated and managed by Brand Governance (Carmi, 2020).

According to Sher (2021), branding correlates management, marketing, and design to create a culture of co-operation and innovation, taking the brand as the interface for a relationship of trust and differentiation in the market. Sher (2021) mentions the importance of research into the context, namely competitors and audiences, along with an assessment of the brand's situation, purpose, and vision, resulting in a communication strategy and planning and visual identity standardisation systems. Sher (2021) presents the process as a spiral that stems from the purpose and opens to digital applications and physical media that share the same brand narrative.

In VMLY&R's (2023) proposal, the branding process results from a succession of divergent and convergent moments, where research evaluates the brand in its context, the brand's assets, interviews are carried out with key people and customers/users, trend research is carried out, opportunities, advantages, benefits and opportunities are identified and Personas are created; the definition of the brand is done collaboratively to characterise the purpose, culture, experience and brand strategy; ideation and concept follow; the basic visual identity elements are designed; then the system and standardisation; continuing with the communication and promotion elements for the launch and presentation (VMLY&R, 2023).

Brand Fusion is a concept used to refer to the crossing of multidisciplinary knowledge (vision, culture, and image) and integrating it into practice (alignment between purpose, positioning, and strategy) and applying it to brand strategy (brand experience, company interests/competences and services). In their proposal, Smith and Williams (2022) complement Brand Fusion with the concept of purpose-driven brand strategy, considering it to be a way of articulating the corporation's interests with those of its stakeholders, as well as aligning symbolic and intangible components with tangible ones, namely products and services.

The articulation between brand and stakeholders is often associated with the concepts of brand experience and emotions in brands, positioning the brand through emotional archetypes capable of stimulating a greater number of senses, creating more intense experiences, personifying, and engaging the different audiences. In this regard, Ghio (2019) states that brands must have a social dimension with truly rooted human values capable of dictating management choices.

Communication is no longer unidirectional, so contemporary corporations and brands must be open and have ways of collecting, interpreting, and dealing with feedback from outside the organisation. Corporate identity and philosophy are impacted by stakeholder interests and evaluation, and should inform strategy, brand promise, products, services, and communication channels. The purpose of the brand, it's positioning, the content, channels and tone of communication, products and services need to be articulated to the recipients through shared values (Minamiyama, 2007).

Table 1 summarises and compares the steps and procedures recommended by the authors consulted in this theoretical framework.

3 Procedures and Design-Driven Branding Model

Following the identification, comparison and analysis of the concepts involved and the stages proposed by Costa (1977), Jenkins (1993), Naples (1988), Chaves (1988), Brun and Rasquinet (1996), Olins (2008), Wheeler (2003), Peón (2009), Johnson (2019), Gautier and Roller (2019), Slade-Brooking (2016), Carmi and Ubertis (Carmi, 2020), Brea (2020), Sher (2021) and VMLY&R (2023), a proposal was drawn up.

Unlike the companies of previous centuries, organisations in the 21st century need to be open, interdepartmental, and multidisciplinary. The brand is an opportunity to make sense of analysing data about the context and determining action.

The proposals by Olins (1990), Johnson (2019), Carmi (2020), Sher (2021) and Wheeler (2003) represent some of the first forays to establish a correlation between design and branding, which we intend to take up and deepen.

The proposal for a model is based on ideas that are consensual with the proposals studied, namely that: the brand exists in a context and its characterisation must take

Table 1 A comparison between the stages of several methodological models for branding and/or visual identity design

Costa (1977)	Jenkins (1988)	Naples (1988)	Chaves (1988)	Brun and Rasquinet (1996)	Olins (2008)	Wheeler (2003)	Peón (2009)
Research on market – Corporate audit – Competitors audit – Audience mapping	Investigation – Specialized press – Interviews with top management, employees – Analysis of competitors and suppliers – Analysis of consumer needs and expectations		Company request Analytical phase: – Identification, Investigation and Diagnosis – Image policy in communication	Document analysis, visual audit, field study	Investigation, analysis, and strategic recommendations – Project conditions for success – Business divisions and economic situation – Corporate audit to visual design, communication, behavioral and positioning – Competitors audit and market analysis – Brand perception analysis – Audience and stakeholders mapping – Desk research, Interviews and workshops, presentation findings and core idea	Research and analysis – Clarify vision, strategies, and values – Research stakeholders needs and perceptions – Internal, competitive, technology and legal audit	

(continued)

Table 1 (continued)

Costa (1977)	Jenkins (1988)	Naples (1988)	Chaves (1988)	Brun and Rasquinet (1996)	Olins (2008)	Wheeler (2003)	Peón (2009)
Intended brand image – Institutional goals – Self-concept and corporate philosophy – Commercial goals – Analysis of the corporate visual and communication system	Inform – Report and summary of analysis and platform with creative paths for future	Briefing and requirements of visual Identity – Brand mark – Management requirements – Legal requirements – Value benefits	Intervention programme constraint	Diagnosis/ recommendations	Development of the identity or brand idea (look and feel) – Behavioural change, brand architecture – Name and style – Presentation and path selection – Design approaches on basic brand visual elements	Brand strategy – Synthesize learnings – Clarify brand strategy – Cocreate brand attributes – Present brand brief – Naming strategy	Prelaminar solution – Concept – Drafts and idea developments – Definition of requirements – First solution selection
	Presentation and decision on the strategy to be followed	Analysis of findings Presentation to the client and decision on the strategy to be followed	Normative phase – General intervention strategy – Intervention plan on image and communication – Parallel intervention programmes	Definition of the creative profile in the form of a concept Technical specifications for the design team		Design concept – Visualize the future – Design brand identity – Finalize brand architecture – Examine applicability – Present visual strategy	

(continued)

Table 1 (continued)

Costa (1977)	Jenkins (1988)	Naples (1988)	Chaves (1988)	Brun and Rasquinet (1996)	Olins (2008)	Wheeler (2003)	Peón (2009)
Definition of the communication strategy	Design creation and proposal presentation – Visual identity strategy design –Design of brand communication media	Design creation – Concise brief – Visual identity design – Proposal presentation	Normative phase – General intervention strategy – Intervention plan on image and communication – Parallel intervention programmes	Graphical creation – Exploration – Short list – Opting for a solution	Launch and introduction of the communication vision – Internal launch – Partner, distributor, and supplier launch – External launch	Brand expressions – Finalize identity solutions – Initiate trademark protection – Prioritize and design applications – Design identity program – Apply brand architecture	Solution – Definition of the visual identity requirements and characteristics and media selection

(continued)

Table 1 (continued)

Costa (1977)	Jenkins (1988)	Naples (1988)	Chaves (1988)	Brun and Rasquinet (1996)	Olins (2008)	Wheeler (2003)	Peón (2009)
Design	Design development – Nomination of the internal director for brand management – Regular meetings for discussion and agreement	Design developments – Development of visual identity applications and communication media – Mockups and testing – Presentation and refinement of design	Technical request technical request	Internal communication – Visual identity applications – Definition of the application programme – Design of applications – Visual identity implementation – Internal and external communication	Implementation – Brand guidelines – Brand centre (or intranet) – Brand guardianship – Brand book – Making change stick – Managing application – Formal and informal brand management systems and control mays – Design of communication materials – Products, packaging, signs, exhibitions, clothing's, – Digital, promotional, forms, publications, vehicles, advertising, others		Project development – Design of Visual Identity applications and pre-production and implementation plan – Communication plan – Brand identity manual

(continued)

Table 1 (continued)

Costa (1977)	Jenkins (1988)	Naples (1988)	Chaves (1988)	Brun and Rasquinet (1996)	Olins (2008)	Wheeler (2003)	Peón (2009)
Implementation of the identification system on the market – Signage – Workspaces – Stationary – Car fleet – Packaging – Industrial design – Editorial design – Public relations – Advertising	Continuous management and development	Implementation – Adjustments, design, and redesign – Visual Identity manual		Development of the visual identity standards manual		Managing assets – Build synergy around new brand – Develop launch strategy and plan – Launch internally first – Launch externally – Develop standards and guidelines – Nature brand champions	Implementation – Production and put into practice
Communication management among time							

(continued)

Table 1 (continued)

Johnson (2019)	Gautier and Roller (2019)	Slade-Brooking (2016)	Carmi and Ubertis 0.9 (Carmi, 2020)	Brea (2020)	Sher (2021)	VMLY&R (2023)
Investigation – Positioning analysis – Verbal audit – Visual audit – Behavioural audit – Competitors audit – Peer audit – Swot analysis – Past, present, future test – Interviews and meetings to balance internal designer and external reality on the brand	Analysis – Positioning study, inventory, brand audit – Comparative analysis and benchmarking	Customer research and visual enquiry – Consumer-profile boards – Focus group, observation, questionnaires, and interviews – Touching point analysis – Market sector analysis, product category analysis, competitors brand analysis or audit, visual research boards – Visual audit – Swot analysis – Discussion		Research	Analysis – Target audience – Positioning and competitor analysis – Self analysis, purpose, vision, mission, and values	Brand dive Market and big data analysis – Brand audit – Brand asset analysis – Trend mapping – Internal research – Key people interview – Customer/user research – Personas/journeys – Opportunities/threats map – Benefits and attributes value chart

(continued)

Table 1 (continued)

Johnson (2019)	Gautier and Roller (2019)	Slade-Brooking (2016)	Carmi and Ubertis 0.9 (Carmi, 2020)	Brea (2020)	Sher (2021)	VMLY&R (2023)
Strategy and narrative – Brand ambition levels – Brand identity – Alignment of the brand whit the target market – Brand manifest – Brand story – Brand personality	–	–	Brand design strategy – Analysis of brand perception/brand audit – Brand essence clarification – Brand positioning – Brand equity – Vision and mission – Brand proposition – Brand architecture – Legal checks	Discovery or clarification of the vision, purpose, values, market, culture, core business, future scenarios	– Briefing – Target audience – Brand Identity (re)definition – Brand, personality, tone, message, value proposition – Slogan Brand history/ manifesto – Elevator pitch – Playbook	Brand definition – Brand positioning pyramid – Brand story – Brand architecture – Brand core values – Brand purpose, workshop, brand tension exercise, brand metrics definition, brand experience strategy, and brand culture definition
Bridging the gap – Brand visual style criteria – Naming – Brand architecture – Design principles		Concept development – Brand strategy, naming and brand architecture – Inspiration, mood boards, tend boards, concept boards – Brainstorming – The big idea – Concept development, drafts and best concept selection – Brand standards	Brand design language – Definition of verbal and visual language and style (look and feel) of brand visual identity – Brand book – Brand manual – Design of brand communication media	Decide, target, promise, benefits, narrative, positioning, territories, and their integration		Brand exploring – Brand ideas map – Look and feel moodboards – Brand storyboard – Brand culture core assets – Trend convention/ disruption, looking sideways, brand ideas board, brand naming models, brand gym

(continued)

Table 1 (continued)

Johnson (2019)	Gautier and Roller (2019)	Slade-Brooking (2016)	Carmi and Ubertis 0.9 (Carmi, 2020)	Brea (2020)	Sher (2021)	VMLY&R (2023)
Design – Medium Strategy – Verbal and Visual Identity – Graphic design	Conception – Rupture or continuity – Definition of graphic principles and brand tone – Selection and design of visual identity elements	Design prototyping, development, refinements, presentation materials	Digital design – Web design, App design, UX design, motion design, social media network, augmented reality, software development Packaging design – Packaging and labeling design, line of products design, materials, and prices Space design – Retail and environmental design, exhibition design, signage systems, trade show design Editorial design – Journal, magazine, newsletters, catalogues, infographics, folders, ebooks, etc.	Creation and development of actions, discourses, languages, experiences, interfaces	Development – Development of communication/ strategic planning – Brand book summary – Style guide – Ideation – Concept drafts – Presentation and deliverables – Visual identity design system: brand mark, colours, typography – Marketing phase	Brand expressions – Brand idea core assets – Brand visual identity – Brand voice – Brand motion – Brand core applications (digital, print, product, place look and feel), brand mark design, typography, colour schemes, imagery, iconography, layout moods, core application mockups, manifesto, brand core headlines and baseline

(continued)

Table 1 (continued)

Johnson (2019)	Gautier and Roller (2019)	Slade-Brooking (2016)	Carmi and Ubertis 0.9 (Carmi, 2020)	Brea (2020)	Sher (2021)	VMLY&R (2023)
	Development – Main brand applications and brand standards – Visual identity language Applications – Stationary – Internal communication – External communication Signage systems Car fleet Events Graphic pre-production and production	Testing of design solutions in the market – Design of materials			Application – Basic visual identity media – UX and UI design – Social media – Ads – Brand identity standards	Brand system – Brand culture framework – Brand story book – Brand ID system book – Brand tools, branding workshop blueprint, brand training workshops, brand digital centre
Implementation – Adaptation of media and visual messages to the audience culture and market contexts – Brand identity manual and visual consistency	Implementation – Templates and monitoring Visual identity standards developed	Design implementation	Brand governance – Management and evaluation of brand design strategy implementation	Integration and adaptation, interaction management		Brand experience – Brand video – Stationary – PPT and/or work templates – Digital brochures – Advertising templates – Social media templates – Print materials – Merchandise – Interior design
Engage or revive – Feedback points – Evaluate and adjust design – Brand extensions			Brand communication	Managing consistency and adaptation over time and context		

into account problems, tensions, opportunities and shared values; that the branding process requires the creation of mechanisms for collecting, interpreting and valuing information about the context; that the brand is a way of giving meaning to all the dimensions of the organisation or business, articulating internal and external components, and intangible meanings with the user experience, products and services; that strategy is a way of aligning all departments, including different areas and seeking effectiveness; that visual identity is a language system that confers unity, differentiation and recognition; that implementation presupposes continuous monitoring, readjustment and evaluation.

In this sequence, it was possible to determine the ecosystem for a Design-driven branding model (Fig. 1), considering that the brand exists in an ecosystem, which includes the world, ways of life, the market with its requirements, opportunities for competitiveness, a culture, economic viability, and the social context.

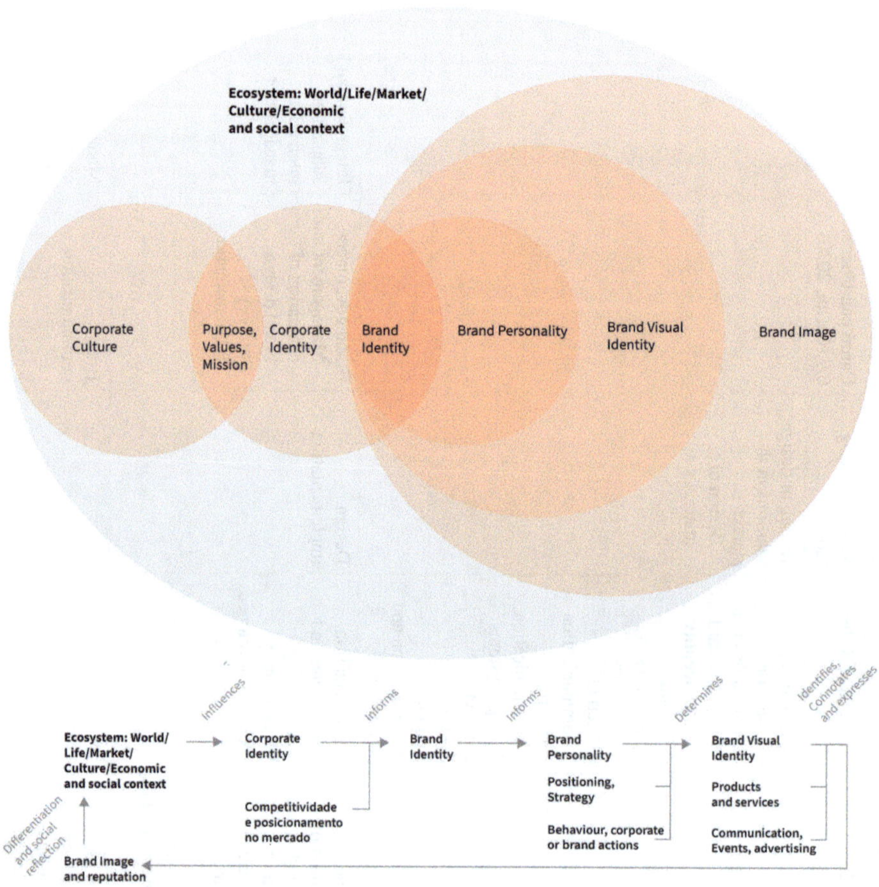

Fig. 1 Ecosystem of the design-driven branding

We now know that Corporate Identity is useful information for defining brand identity and brand personality, but that it is not a field of activity for design. Corporate identity is a set of beliefs and values that shape the identity of a group, organisation or department and determine its choices in a business environment (Raposo et al., 2020b; Lorenz, 2021).

There is a relationship between corporate identity and brand identity, in that the brand's DNA is the result of internal factors, such as Corporate Identity, and external factors such as market opportunities, the need to differentiate from competitors, the expectations and needs of the target audience, fashions and valued information, which determine the level of proximity between Corporate Identity and Brand Identity (Raposo et al., 2020b).

Therefore, Brand Identity is made up of the Purpose and Central Idea of the brand, its Mission, Vision; Brand Promise; Unique Characteristics and Brand Positioning, in a correlation that forms the brand's DNA.

Brand Personality is a way of personifying the brand and characterising the type of relationship and positioning it will have with its recipients, namely the experience it will provide (Olins, 2008; Oliveira, 2018). Brand Personality includes positioning and determines the general and communication strategy, serving as a guide for corporate or brand behaviour and respective actions.

As far as visual identity is concerned, it is an organised system that ensures brand identification and differentiation (Raposo, 2012) and acts as a language system (Oliveira, 2018), the glue that binds all the brand's means of communication, information, and persuasion (Costa, 1977). The visual identity system gives visible form to the brand and expresses its style and personality over time, most explicitly in advertising contexts, but also by aligning products and services (Raposo, 2012).

Corporate image or brand image arises even if it is not managed by the corporation or brand, by comparison, making value judgements based on the cultural repertoire of stakeholders in each time and context (Costa, 1977; Olins, 2008; Raposo, 2012). As well as the object of branding, brand image must therefore be an essential axis of brand characterisation and strategy.

The Design-driven branding proposal (Fig. 2) is made with the awareness that design and branding are different areas, still, considering the potential of design to systematise data in complex contexts, to integrate multidisciplinary knowledge through design, as well as in the construction of graphic-semantic systems. Design ends up being an axis of the whole process due to its integrating character of multi- and trans-disciplinary knowledge through design, its focus on life and the potential of design culture for the development and competitiveness of the brand.

The proposal is for the Design-driven branding model to be structured around five sequentially organised and numbered phases:

- Research (gathering data on the sector, competitors and understanding the company in all its aspects. Study of trends, fashions and social behaviour, as well as legislation);
- Analysis and Diagnosis (interpreting data, making the most of it and defining ways forward);

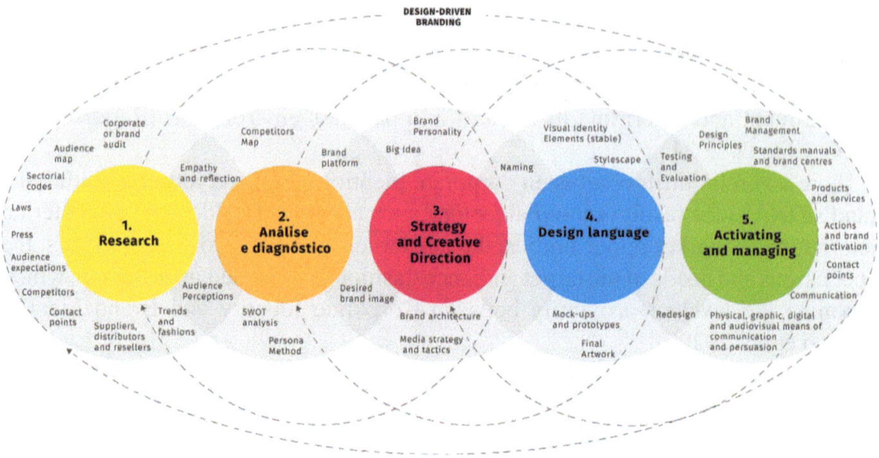

Fig. 2 Model of design-driven branding

- Strategy and Creative Direction (strategic and tactical decisions, positioning, characterisation of the brand's DNA and personality, design principles);
- Design and Language (conception, sketches, studies, prototypes, approval, development, and pre-production. Management of graphic and product processes);
- Activate and Manage (Production, implementation, constant evaluation, and monitoring. Implementation of awareness-raising actions and tools to support brand and visual identity management).

This model considers that there is no separation between brand, management, production, body-action, or business. This is an exception in the case of endorsed brands or multi-brands, where there should be no separation between management, business, and brand. The brand is the heart, the beginning, and the end of all activity.

The sequence of the stages contributes to the effectiveness of the proposal, but the process is not linear, it is dynamic, meaning that the activities of one stage are interlinked with those of the previous stages, being carried out as overlapping stages, and there may be a need to revisit, reassess, rethink, or redefine components. In addition, each phase includes activities of divergence (investigation and search for dispersed, diverse, and different types of data, exploratory development, discovery, innovation, and future scenarios, etc.) and convergence (interpretation and valuation of data/information, decision-making, organisation, system design, evaluation, strategy, management, etc.).

Another characteristic of the Design-driven branding model is that the activities in each stage create the conditions for collecting, interpreting, integrating, and evaluating data both internal and external to the organisation or brand, driven by the brand's design.

As this is a methodological model, it must be adapted to the time, requirements and conditions of each case, and this proposal is made for the desirable scenario.

Phase 1, Research, is a common denominator for a significant majority of the authors consulted and the proposals analysed, proposing the collection of external and internal data, as well as the ecosystem. This proposal puts forward methodologies and techniques for carrying out the activities in this phase.

The corporate/brand audit (Raposo, 2012a) is carried out by collecting internal and external data. Internally, the aim is to get to know and characterise the corporate identity, purpose, mission, values, vision, brand image, business situation, objectives, capabilities, and market, by collecting data through interviews and questionnaires with managers and key employees (especially those who have contact with the customer and decision-making power in day-to-day management decisions, production, product evaluation, services, delivery, and communications). A visual audit is carried out (analysis of the graphic-semantic quality of the visual identity elements and means of communication and alignment with the brand) and a name audit (brevity, verbalisation, capacity for expansion and internationalisation, suggestion, protection and registration, alignment with the brand). Externally, points of view, the real brand image, public expectations, and interests are identified. To this end, it is important to draw up an audience map, organising them by strategic and priority interest, by interest groups and behavioural profile. Customers, suppliers, and distributors are partners who must believe in the strength and value of the brand and who can help assess the existing brand image and draw a deviation curve from the desired brand image. Society includes stakeholders other than consumers and internal audiences, those who may benefit or be affected by the brand's actions and who therefore have an interest in the process, making it important to assess their perception of the brand. Something similar occurs with the written press, television, and social media, where it is important to assess whether the news and publications are favourable or critical of the brand. From the brand's ecosystem or context, it is also important to know the applicable legislation, perceptions about the brand and the profile of competitors, detect trends, fashions, signs that may gain importance in the future, identify good practices or actions and sectoral graphic codes that are important for characterising the brand and its visual identity system (Raposo, 2012a).

Along with cross-sectional reading and consulting scientific studies, benchmarking, trend-boards, and concept-boards are suitable ways of identifying signals, trends and fashions that can help evaluate the brand and design future scenarios.

The Analysis and Diagnosis activity consists of interpreting the data collected to assess perceptions about the brand, compare it with competitors and stakeholder expectations and create the foundations for strategy and ideation. Methods such as the competitor map, the brand platform, swot analysis, the persona method, canvas models, among others, can be used.

The competitor map is a technique for identifying sectoral graphic codes and characterising the graphic and semantic trends of visual identity systems and, above all, brand marks. The competitor map supports the selection and design of visual identity elements so that they are more coherent and distinctive in each market and cultural context (Raposo et al., 2020a, 2021; Raposo, 2022).

The brand platform defines or summarises the brand's AND: Purpose (reason for being, vision of the world that guides the actions, aspirations, inspirations it wants to leave in the world); Brand identity and principles (distinctive characteristics, convictions, beliefs, values and truths); Brand personality (values/way of thinking; archetype; way of being/attitudes/style/expression/tone of voice); Promise (contact or value proposition and mission in the market); and Positioning (unique characteristics and place in the market compared to others). The platform can be used to summarise broader information about the brand or to start characterising it.

The persona method and the user journey make it possible to synthesise and visualise common denominators of public groups or stakeholders, namely interests, expectations, behaviours, lifestyles and how to align them with the brand.

At the level of Creative Direction and Strategy, it is recommended to define the desired Brand Image or Brand Picture (Davis, 2000), with the aim of using it as a beacon for the brand and strategy, a guide for all dimensions of the brand, management, communication, and business.

Defining the Brand Picture means characterising the brand, defining its identity, and positioning. The brand is the result of defining a message and a process of communication and action to be maintained between the organisation, its public and stakeholders. The visual identity is the system of visual language and brand identification (Lorenz, 2021).

There are therefore activities that take place in this stage that are interdependent and may lead to revisiting or rethinking the previous ones. The brand's Core Idea is the basic concept that synthesises what the brand stands for, its purpose, values, and associations (Olins, 2008).

As Sinek (2009) argues, purpose is the brand's reason for existing, which defines its DNA and the entire branding process, which can be found using the Butterfly Method (proposed by Wolff Olins) also known as the Big Ideal (proposed by John Shaw and Colin Mitchell at Ogilvy), which consists of using a Venn-Euler diagram where two circles or ellipses intersect. The first circle/ellipse represents the cultural tension or problem and the second what the brand can do to mitigate/resolve this tension or problem, to find the purpose at the intersection.

Brand Personality (Olins, 2008; Raposo, 2012; Oliveira, 2018) is a process of brand personification that determines the identity, semantic and visual content of the brand, directly associated with positioning.

Brand Architecture is a way of organising and managing brands and sub-brands (of corporations, products, or services), determining different levels of symbolic and reputational proximity. The visual identity is determined by the Brand Architecture option because it plays the role of giving it visible form (Martín García, 2005).

It is at this stage that strategic and tactical choices are made about the type of media and actions that are most relevant, along with other management activities.

The Design and Language stage can begin with naming or renaming in conjunction with the Brand Personality.

The main elements of the brand's visual identity are defined (brand mark, colour, imagery, typography, textures, media, formats, and other graphics) as well as its language system (design principles, visual system, styles, layout, etc.) (Raposo, 2012; Magalhães & Oliveira, 2023).

Having the main elements of the brand's visual identity, Stylescape can be useful for exploring the language of the visual identity and getting it validated by the client, expert panels or focus groups.

At this stage, mock-ups, prototypes and resistance, use and perception tests are made, followed by development and final artwork for various media, communication, advertising, reinforcement, and expansion of the product range.

The activation and management stage corresponds to the moments of public contact with the visual identity, communication media and artefacts, products and services, locations, and types of actions, contact points. The implementation of the visual identity and means of communication, duly monitored, corrected, and evaluated, with the possibility of testing and redesign. Brand management is carried out across the entire organisational or brand dimension and is characterised by a culture of brand design.

Design principles are included in brand standards manuals and brand centres, ensuring that the brand is coherent over time, in different circumstances and print media, spaces, graphic, digital, and audio-visual artefacts, contributing to a coherent brand experience, aligned with the intended brand image and relevant to stakeholders.

As you can see, management and activation are connected to other stages and require constant work, with a strong link to research.

Figure 3 should be seen from the bottom to the top. From a brand management perspective, the brand's purpose, mission, values, and vision must be coherent with the corporate identity and based on market opportunities and stakeholder expectations so that they are positively evaluated, valued, and associated with socially relevant aspects.

Brand characterisation, brand personality and corporate behaviour must be coherent and strong enough to condition all management, production, action, and communication options.

The basic elements of the visual identity system are mainly graphic identifiers that are semantically loaded with the meaning of the brand. However, the brand mark connotes and expresses ideas that must be aligned with the brand concept.

The flexible elements of the system determine its flexibility of use and application, through the correlation between the visual variables (what changes and what is stable; is it two-dimensional or does it have volume? does it have animation or does any component change? How does the transformation take place and with what criteria?; Does it change logo/typography, composition, scale/size, colour(s), texture/images, design style or symbol?; How are the components combined and what possibilities are there in their relative position?; Does the dynamic take place at the level of the graphic brand or in the visual identity system, visible in the language and means of communication?; How are the communication media visually related based on the visual identity elements?

The visual identity system therefore determines recognition, differentiation, and coherence over time, contributing to memorisation as well as the effectiveness of communication and advertising.

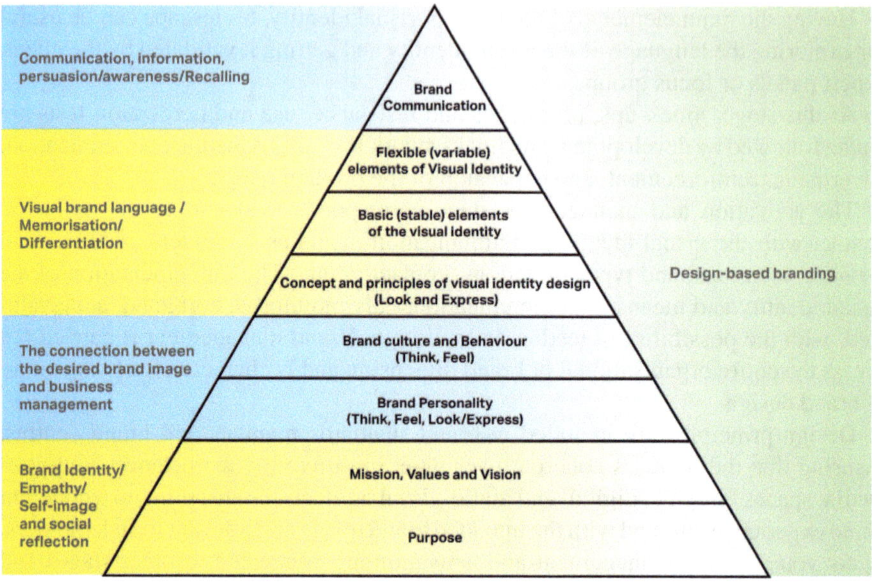

Fig. 3 Management following design-based branding

4 Conclusions

By proposing Design-Based Branding, the author hopes to contribute to bringing design, communication, management, marketing, and production closer together in the field of branding, as well as to a better understanding of some of the key concepts discussed here.

This Design-Based Branding model aims to offer a strategic, social, and integrated approach, considering the brand as a cultural interface in a market, time, and culture where there are other players. The brand becomes the result of a managed interaction between internal and external components, with design as an integrating and meaning-making process.

It proposes a systematised and dynamic process that guides the collection and interpretation of data, as well as supporting the selection and evaluation of decisions, fostering multidisciplinary thinking and an integrated visual identity, intrinsic to the management of a design culture.

In the model, the brand image acts as the guiding principle for management, considering the purpose and other aspects of the brand's DNA. On the other hand, brand personality is articulated with the visual identity design system, expressing the brand's purpose, and entering directly into the stakeholders' experience with the brand.

For internal employees, the Brand Identity and Personality end up binding people around the purpose and supporting decision-making. From the external perspective, the Brand Identity and Personality establish emotional bonds with people and express the ideas and visualised characteristics used in evaluating, positioning, and differentiating the brand.

The proposal can be implemented as part of brand creation or during the evaluation and monitoring process, as well as being used in part or in full. In each phase, some key components are pointed out that should be included in that phase, fostering the assertiveness of operations, and contributing to the correlation between internal and external factors, interests, needs, requirements, and opportunities.

References

Aaker, D. (2001). Criando e administrando marcas de sucesso. 3rd Ed. Futura.

Balmer, J. M., & Soenen, G. B. (1999). The acid test of corporate identity management. *Journal of Marketing Management, 15*(1–3), 69–92.

Balmer, J. (No. 3/4 de Vol. 35 de 2001). Corporate identity, corporate branding and corporate marketing—Seeing through the fog. European Journal of Marketing, pp. 248–291 https://doi.org/10.1108/03090560110694763.

Brea, G. (2020). Brand Book. Ideas sobre Marca y Diseño. Wolkowicz Editores.

Brun, M., Rasquinet, P. (1996). L'Identite Visuelle De L'Entreprise. Au-Dela Du Logo. Editions d'Organisation.

Cameira, S. R. (2020). Branding + Design. A Estratégia Na Criação De Identidades De Marca. Editora Senac.

Carmi, E. (2020). Branding Design Oriented. Fausto Lupetti Editore.

Cassissi, L. (2023). Identidad, identificación e imagen en branding. Obtido de Foroalfa: https://foroalfa.org/articulos/identidad-identificacion-e-imagen-en-branding

Chaves, N. (1988). La Imagen Corporativa Teoria e metodología de la identificación institucional. Editorial Gustavo Gili.

Costa, J. (1977). La Identidad Visual. Ediciones Club Master7.

Costa, J. (2004). La Imagen de Marca. Paidós Diseño.

Costa, J. (2008). El DirCom hoy. Dirección y gestión de la comunicación en la nueva economia.Costa Punto Com Editor.

Davis, S. M. (2000). Building the Brand Driven Business. Jossey Bass.

Gautier, D., Roller, F. (2019). Concevoir une identité visuele. Editions deux-cent-cinq.

Ghio, M. (2019). Oxitobrands: Marcas humanas para un mercado emocional. Experimenta.

Jenkins, N. (1993). La identidade visual de la empresa. Deusto.

Johnson, M. (2019). Branding in five and half steps. Thames & Hudson.

Kapferer, J. N. (2008). The New Strategic Brand Management. Creating and Sustaining Brand Equity Long Term. Kogan Page Limited.

Keller, K. L. (1998). Kevin Lane—Strategic brand management: building, measuring andm managing brand equity. Prentice Hall.

Lorenz, M. (2021). Flexible Visual Systems. The Design Manual for Contemporary Visual Identities. Slated.

Magalhães, A., & Oliveira, F. (2023). Visual synthesis languages of the DNA of the Star Michelin gastronomic brands: Comparative Case Studies. Convergences - Journal of Research and Arts Education, 13(26), 149–165. https://doi.org/10.53681/c1514225187514391s.26.52

Martín García, M. (2005). Arquitetura de Marcas. Modelo de construcción de Marcas y Gestión de sus Activos. ESIC Editorial.

Minamiyama, H. (ed. lit.) (2007). World Branding: Concept, Strategy and Design. Ginkgo Press.

Naples, V. (1988). Corporate Identity Design. John Wiley & Sons.

Neumeier, M. (2007). ZAG. The 1 Strategy of High-Performance Brands. AIGA/New Riders.

Olins, W. (1990). Making Business Strategy Visible Trough Design. Harvard Business School Press.
Olins, W. (2008). The brand Handbook. Gower publishing limited.
Oliveira, F. (2018). Brand's identity and Visual Culture. In Raposo, D. (Ed.), Communicating Visualy: The Graphic design of the brand (117–138). Cambridge Scholars Publishing.
Peón, M. L. (2009). Sistemas de Identidade Visual. 2AB.
Raposo, D. (2008). Design de identidade e imagem corporativa. Edições IPCB.
Raposo, D. (2012a). La letra como signo de identidad visual corporativa: codificación y descodificación visual del sistema de identidad [PhD in Design Thesis at Faculdade de Arquitetura. Universidade de Lisboa].
Raposo, D. (2012b). Definição, gestão e desenho da marca. Brand Trends Journal [Em Linha] ISSN: 2237–8529. VOL IV (3). Disponível em WWW:http://www.brandtrendsjournal.com
Raposo, D. (2018). Communicating Visually: The Graphic Design of the Brand. Cambridge Scholars Publishing.
Raposo, D. (2022). Análise de Marcas Gráficas: Marcas portuguesas de produtos alimentares destinados à exportação. Lisboa: Faculdade de Arquitetura. Universidade de Lisboa.
Raposo, D., Ribeiro, R., Amaral, M., Moreira Da Silva, F., Ramón Martin Sanromán, J. (2020a). The Brand Mark Competitors Map as Visual Research Tool. Using Graphic and Symbolic Data in the Brand Visual Identity Project. In: Rebelo F., Soares M. (eds) Advances in Ergonomics in Design. AHFE 2019. Advances in Intelligent Systems and Computing, vol 955.
Raposo, D., Oliveira, F., Farinha, L. (2020b). From Identity Into Brand Visual Identity: Finding and Defining the Intangible Brand DNA. In Farinha, L., & Raposo, D. (Ed.), Handbook of Research on Driving Industrial Competitiveness with Innovative Design Principles (pp. 66–85). IGI Global. http://https://doi.org/10.4018/978-1-7998-3628-5.ch005.
Raposo, D., da Silva, F.M., Neves, J., Silva, J., Ribeiro, R., Correia, R. (2021). Brand Marks Analysis. Criteria and Evaluation Components to an Analysis Tool. In: Markopoulos, E., Goonetilleke, R.S., Ho, A.G., Luximon, Y. (eds) Advances in Creativity, Innovation, Entrepreneurship and Communication of Design. AHFE 2021. Lecture Notes in Networks and Systems, vol 276. Springer, Cham. https://doi.org/10.1007/978-3-030-80094-9_52
Sher, P. (2021). Branding and the Visual Response. How a Brand turns into visual identity. Brand Guide Universe.
Sinek, S. (2009) The Golden Circle. TedTalks. https://www.youtube.com/watch?v=fMOlfsR7SMQ
Slade-Brooking, C. (2016). Creating a brand identity. A guide for designers. Laurence King Publishing.
Smith, T., Williams, T. (2022). Brand Fusion: Purpose-driven brand strategy. De Gruyter.
VMLY&R (2023). The Branding Process. VMLY&R.
Wheeler, A. (2003). Designing Brand Identity: An Essential Guide for the Whole Branding Team. John Wiley & Sons Inc.

Chandra-Padma: Design and Developing a Non-linear Narrative Based Augmented Reality (NNAR) Experience

Sajini Lankadari and Buddhika Rodrigo

Abstract The adoption of non-linear narrative techniques in storytelling has shown promise in enhancing the educational experience. With this in mind, the book "*Chandra-Padma*" was designed to cater to the non-linear storytelling experience for children (Lankadari & Rodrigo, 2024). In this context, Augmented Reality (AR) technology can enhance and enrich the traditional experience of reading a non-linear book. However, the dynamic nature of non-linear storytelling presents unique challenges in creating supportive AR applications. Moreover, designing and developing an AR application for children who have no prior experience with AR is also a challenge. Subsequently, the project suggests a model where a physical storyboard-based iterative process allows children to understand the AR concept and enjoy the non-linear story in the physical setting. This child participatory research approach emphasizes smooth transitions from a physical to a digital environment for a nonlinear narrative. After that, these data and insights that emerge during the test time are combined to develop an AR space to give a better storytelling experience for a non-linear story. The primary purpose is to find out the set of functionalities and features derived from this approach in order to build an NNAR (Non-linear Augmented Reality) application in the future. This continuous feedback loop and progressive learning make this model resilient and capable of evolving over time. A pilot test was carried out, particularly in the context of a group of Sri Lankan children (ages 7–14). The paper focuses on a participatory research methodology, involving children in the design and development process. Additionally, this approach provides valuable insights into children's preferences and behaviors. In addition to augmenting the reading and learning experience, this study will also serve as a model for future

The original version of the chapter has been revised: Typo in the chapter title has been updated. A correction to this chapter can be found at
https://doi.org/10.1007/978-3-031-76156-0_21

S. Lankadari (✉) · B. Rodrigo
Department of Integrated Design, University of Moratuwa, Moratuwa, Sri Lanka
e-mail: gpsajinil@gmail.com

B. Rodrigo
e-mail: buddhikar@uom.lk

© The Author(s), under exclusive license to Springer Nature Switzerland AG 2025, corrected publication 2025

D. Brandão et al. (eds.), *Perspectives on Design and Digital Communication V*, Springer Series in Design and Innovation 50, https://doi.org/10.1007/978-3-031-76156-0_14

designers to develop NNAR storytelling applications focusing on improving user experience with non-linear narratives.

Keywords Non-linear narratives · Augmented reality · Children's literature

1 Introduction

The way of storytelling has evolved over time since the cave paintings. Story-based education improves imagination and educates children while allowing them to fantasize about stories as they learn. For this purpose, there has been a space to adapt interactive design approaches. In this sense, using non-linearity as a narrative approach can enhance the user experience and allow the user to stay engaged and control the narrative (Huttner & Robra-Bissantz, 2017). Consequently, the previous research of '*Chandra-Padma*' book, and findings suggested that the use of a non-linear narrative structure can significantly enhance children's motivation to engage and react to the book in different ways. In the book '*Chandra-Padma*', the effectiveness of this non-linear narrative structure has been evaluated and can serve as a guide for future non-linear content creators on how to think outside the traditional structure of children's books and understand and apply non-linear narrative strategies. However, it will be a challenge for children to separate components in the '*Chandra-Padma*' Non-linear story, since this narrative aims to combine concepts that seem on opposite sides of the spectrum (see Fig. 1). With interactive technologies, storytelling becomes more and more interesting and intuitive in the sense of human–computer interaction (Zhou et al., 2004).

Fig. 1 Story-arc for the 'Chandra-Padma' non-linear book

Throughout history, storytelling tools have evolved as well. In this regard, AR technology has been used for illustrated storybooks for children in recent years and it has seen a rapid expansion in the field of children's books (Karaata & Yilmaz, 2023). When children are bored with reading and understanding non-linear books, AR apps can help them stay motivated because AR enhances the learning experience (Hung et al., 2016). Augmented Reality enables the telling of stories in 3D and allows the audience to dive into the experience. Children's AR applications are often improvised creations, as they are developed by educators with limited technological expertise or developers with limited knowledge of educational principles. However, the design of the next generation of AR experiences will be intentional and purposeful. With such a thoughtful AR system design, children will be able to have hands-on experiences and learn in the most effective ways (Billinghurst & Duenser, 2012).

In AR, the user (the subject) that enters the simulation (the story world) will emotionally respond, make decisions, and act consequently with these environmental entities. 'Tónandi', for instance, is designed to interact naturally with the sounds and creatures surrounding users. The AR headset connects the user to a luxurious sensory ecosystem that grows around them, transforming the environment around them (Calise, 2022; *Tónandi*, n.d.). These activities will influence the user to place objects in the scene, respond with judgment, and make crucial decisions (Meyer, 2016). Synchronization Techniques can be applied to coordinate and harmonize the actions of several participants (Zaman et al., 2023). Moreover, Children will most benefit from Augmented Reality if they are willing to read collaboratively and share ideas (Billinghurst et al., 2001). As an example, 'Sally & Molly' is a book with and it's AR application, giving an opportunity for single-play and cooperative multiplayer play mechanics in different play scenarios using the book. Additionally, integrating tangible elements and AR can have potential benefits in terms of non-linearity. The 'Living Paper' project, for example, creates immersive stories through digital objects with the tangibility of physical cues (Claudino Daffara et al., 2020). Subsequently, this study investigates a child participatory research approach between 'Reality' and 'Augmented Reality' to design and develop an immersive experience for the '*Chandra-Padma*' non-linear narrative book.

2 Methodology

Despite multiple studies that point to virtual environments as the most effective methods for telling non-linear stories, the process for creating immersive environments for non-linear books with two storylines such as '*Chandra-Padma*' is unclear. This project adopts a participatory research paradigm, since it has the ability to solve real-world challenges and allows for close observations at the ground level to improve the design (Zhou et al., 2004). Additionally, the participatory research employed creative and playful methods which produced rich and diverse data. Insights and data were supplemented by interviewing children either during or after their creative efforts or observing them during the data-provoking process (Sevón et al., n.d.).

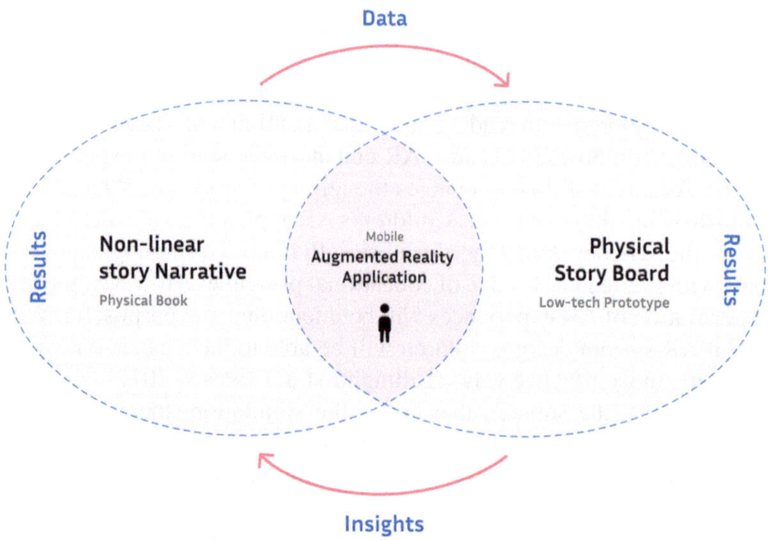

Fig. 2 Child participatory research model for design and developing an NNAR application

Figure 2 shows the child participatory research model that was used here for AR Strategy and Roadmap Development for this research. It has two main components: a storybook (*Chandra-Padma*) and a storyboard. Additionally, a basic AR application prototype was introduced since the children were not familiar with the Augmented Reality concept. This app, version 1.0, was also meant to serve as the base NNAR app for future enhancements during iterative cycles.

As a result of the first cycle of research, patterns, and themes were collected from the children. As part of this participatory research, thematic analysis was used, which is also a qualitative data analysis technique that involves identifying, analyzing, and interpreting patterns or themes within qualitative data sets. A Pilot test was conducted to derive themes to get a feature list to build the NNAR application and ensure it meets the expectations and requirements of its young audience (Druin, 1999; Dam, 2023; Szabó & Hercegfi, 2023). This pilot test was conducted with a small group of children aged 7–14. In the pilot test, positive outcomes were recorded, and potential areas for future development were identified and extracted through the existing research and case studies to cover the gap.

2.1 Participants

Despite the original target age range of the '*Chandra-Padma*' book being 8–10 years old, the researcher selected to test the model with a broader age group spanning from 7 to 14 years. Piaget classified children into various developmental stages, with ages 7–14 representing Concrete Operational and Formal Operational stages

(Jacko & Sears, 2002). Thus, this age group allowed for a more comprehensive understanding of the diverse ways to perceive and interact with the Augmented Reality experience, contributing valuable insights to the '*Chandra-Padma*' study. The group of 12 students for this research study was purposefully selected from a Saturday class called 'Creative Art and Science'. The children who are involved in this research already know each other and are familiar with the researcher and the classroom setting before the study begins. Children were thus given a voice so they could express their points of view without fear of disagreement with adults. Furthermore, it was important to select individuals with experience and knowledge of the creative context (Palinkas et al., 2015). The children had a basic understanding of design and were exposed to creative thinking as well, which made the research process easier. Children can be classified in the class as being either lower-middle or lower socioeconomic levels.

2.2 Materials

During the research, 3 materials were used to get data and insights to conduct the thematic analysis.

- Non-linear Book
- Physical Storyboard
- Test AR Application

Non-linear book. '*Chandra-Padma*' is a design intervention aimed at facilitating non-linear storytelling within a physical narrative. The book underwent testing with children aged 8–10, and the results indicated a positive impact on how children engage with and respond to the non-linear narrative presented in the book (Lankadari & Rodrigo, 2024). Both storylines of the Storybook of '*Chandra-Padma*' (see Fig. 3) begin with the main character hearing a song and becoming curious about the singer. Despite that, the combined story has been carefully constructed to avoid the complexity and confusion that can result. Throughout the book, poems, and dialogues constantly cross paths between the two storylines (see Fig. 4). Furthermore, time dilation theory is applied to calculate the duration of a period of time without harming the inter-stress of the story plot created for children, without resorting to any artificial means to estimate it (Kanai et al., 2006). The story's endpoint is in the middle of the book, which combines the two storylines in a meaningful way. The narrative structure that was used for designing this experimental non-linear narrative structure and the book can be found below chart.

- Storyline x, y: Story of character 1 (*Chandra*), Story of character 2 (*Padma*)
- Exposition x, y: A moon somewhere in the universe, The earth
- t1, t2: Time period character 1 unite with character 2 ($t1 >> t2$), Time period character 2 unitement with character 1 ($t2 << t1$).

Fig. 3 Chandra-Padma non-linear book

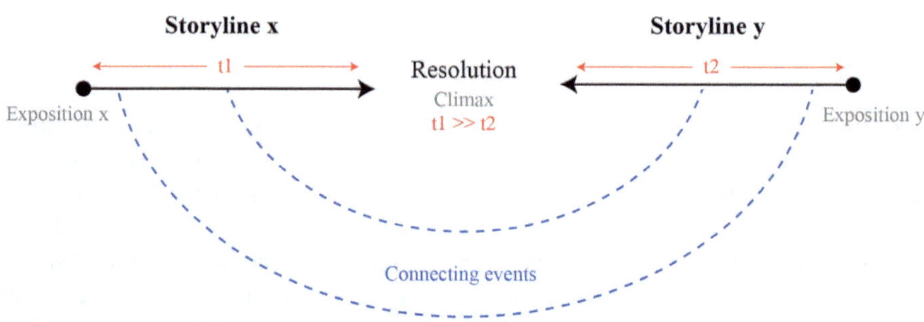

Fig. 4 Non-linear narrative structure in Chandra-Padma book

Physical Storyboard. The use of the physical storyboard generates a number of benefits (Billinghurst et al., 2001). The creation of a '*Chandra-Padma*' storyboard served as a pivotal step towards developing an AR non-linear application, especially for children with no experience with AR technology. The board was created on an A4-sized regiform board to align with the book cover surface, as it was the target image for the AR application. Since the book has two environments, this storyboard also visualizes these environments. Characters were created separately with their actions according to the book's story scenarios. Characters were also connected with a toothpick to easily grab and place on the board (see Fig. 5). This approach aimed to seamlessly integrate physical elements from reality with digital data from virtual

Fig. 5 Physical storyboard

environments. The data collected underwent thorough analysis through content and thematic analysis methodologies (Alhumaidan et al., 2018).

Test AR Application. Out of the various devices that facilitate AR technology the mobile AR category was selected for this study based on its availability and feasibility for working with children, as well as children's familiarity with mobile phones compared to other devices (Warr, 2018). Almost all the children in the participant group had no experience with, nor had they seen or heard about, AR storytelling. To address this, the initial mobile AR application was crafted to introduce the basic concept of augmented reality to children. This test AR application helped the children understand the fundamental technology, demonstrating that it uses a target image to build a virtual environment around it. This approach provided the children with a foundational understanding of how AR works, laying the groundwork for further engagement with the technology.

The mobile application, Chandra-Padma (V.1) Version 1.0 was created using Unity 3D, version 2017.3.1, to support Android platforms. The augmented reality tracking procedure was implemented using the Vuforia Engine. To ensure consistency, the same smartphone, a Huawei GR5, was used in all sessions. This approach allows for iterative enhancements, ensuring the app evolves effectively based on user feedback and technological advancements. Two target images were included in this test AR application: the front cover and the back cover of the book. When a child initiates the test AR application, the app begins by processing and identifying the target image. The app uses the camera to scan the environment, searching for the predefined target images. Once identified, the animated video (with voice) plays on the surface of the book. Additionally, extra elements such as stars and planets were added to the AR prototype, covering all XYZ nodes in 3D. However, the interface for the test AR app had not been built at this initial stage. It allows the children to experience an interactive AR environment while providing a foundation for further development

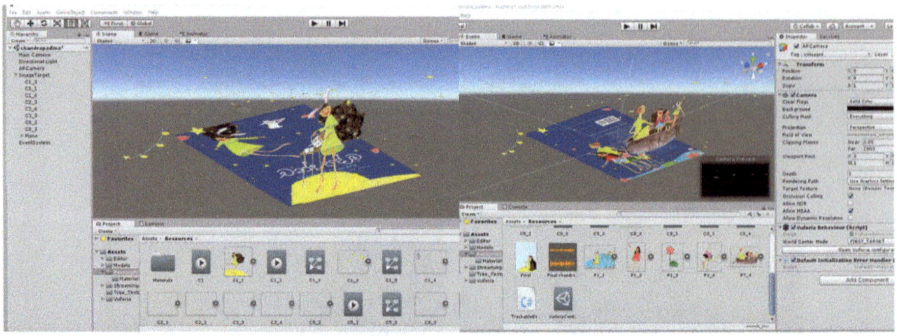

Fig. 6 Chandra-Padma V.1.0 test AR application

of the NNAR application (Kurutu Balitto (Sajini Lankadari), 2023; Lankadari, n.d.) (Fig. 6).

3 Model Testing

To test the design approach and the efficiency of the model (see Fig. 2) a pilot test was done by selecting a small group of children. This purposeful group of 12 children (age 7–14) from an 'Art and Science' Saturday class, were selected for this research study. Research sessions conducted over 3 Saturdays, (8.30 a.m.–9.30 a.m.). Some children got the chance to participate on all 3 days. Research session was introduced as part of the class for children as the 'Storytelling Time'. Researchers start the 'Storytelling Time' with a brief and friendly discussion with children related to the book title in order to provide prior knowledge about the story and make the environment comfortable for children. Throughout the study, the storybook, storyboard, and test AR application were introduced, and children were encouraged and had the freedom to ask questions and comment on the materials at any time. Participants chose to participate individually, or to be paired with someone and participate in the research activity; some children experienced it more than once.

First, the children read the '*Chandra-Padma*' non-linear book with the guidance of a trained adult research assistant. Afterward, they were invited to re-tell the story using the storyboard. Then children were invited to try the test AR application. Following this, an open-ended and general usability test was conducted. As part of the usability test, the children were instructed to open the test AR app and explore the story using the physical book. While the children completed this task, the researcher observed their behavior and listened for feedback. This approach allowed the researcher to gather insights into how the children interacted with both the physical world and the virtual world, noting any difficulties, reactions, or suggestions they had regarding the experience (Experience, n.d.). Nevertheless, not all the 12 children actively participated in testing this model. Some of them watched the process and gave feedback. All child participants were observed by the researcher throughout the research (during the reading non-linear book, while telling the story with the help of the storyboard and using a basic AR application (Justice et al., 2008). In addition to that, non-verbal behaviors were also noted. During the '*Storytelling Time*', the researcher observed children and took field notes of non-verbal responses (Mulyasari, 1993).

4 Data Analysis

The data analysis was open-ended and iteratively evolved during the research phase. (Duenser & Hornecker, 2007). Data were analyzed by using applied thematic analysis (inductive), which is used to analyze qualitative data and drive themes with methodological consistency as described by Creswell (2014), Lankadari and Rodrigo (2024). While the storytelling time was taking place, (Fig. 7) non-verbal behaviors and other actions were also observed. Total comments, questions, and other notes (interview transcripts and notes) were presented on the Miro board.

Research Phase

- Reading the '*Chandra-Padma*' non-linear book
- Re-telling the story with the help of the storyboard
- Using the test AR application

The analysis is more interactive than the hierarchical approach from the bottom to the top since the three stages in the analysis are interrelated (Creswell, 2014). Therefore, the collected data were analyzed by using a thematic analysis approach. After the 'Storytelling Time', thematic analysis sessions were conducted to identify each new category. Field notes on observation, videos, and recording scripts were

Fig. 7 The data and insights were identified during 3 steps

Fig. 8 The set-up for the thematic analysis map on the Miro board

analyzed to identify new codes and themes of children's responses. Codes were limited to provide categories or patterns that could be used and identified for the Augmented Reality component (Nowell et al., 2017). The manual thematic analysis was conducted using Miro Board and finalized 4 categories (Lankadari & Rodrigo, 2022).

Moreover, knowledge from existing research on AR books was also used to identify gaps in interaction patterns (Fernandes & Leite, 2024). Based on this approach and various case studies, a tech stack for the AR application was derived to implement design features and functions for future NNAR applications (Fig. 8).

5 Research Findings

As the children did not have any experience with AR technology, this study aimed to explore the possibilities of using child data and insights to develop NNAR (Non-Linear Narrative with Augmented Reality) applications for non-linear storybooks. First, the data were broken down into smaller segments, with each segment assigned a code and a corresponding meaning. This qualitative data was then categorized into four key themes. The themes were Non-linear story content, Responsive Characters, Different contexts within the physical world, and Engagement through gamification.

By considering these four themes, an NNAR application can be iteratively improved (Table 1).

6 Discussion: What Was the Lesson Learned?

By utilizing Mobile Augmented Reality technology, the study aimed to enhance '*Chandra-Padma*' narration for children and find solutions for the challenges when implementing non-linear stories with immersive experiences. To conduct this participatory research, the first step was to read *Chandra-Padma's* experimental book. Children find it more enjoyable and interesting to participate in the storyboarding process instead of worrying about the final outcome. Despite this, the non-linearity remains complex, and it appears that this was the children's first time reading a book with a non-linear narration structure with two stories. The second step is to create the same story in storyboards and gather insights to develop the AR application. However, the storyboard used was pre-marked with basic spatial tags like the moon and the earth. The researcher believes that these predefined tags limited the imagination and they tended to use the board only horizontally or vertically. The researcher suggests that providing a blank setting/space or building blocks and allowing the children to create it themselves would be more effective. This approach would enable a broader expression of their creativity and offer more valuable insights. Moreover, mobile AR and non-linear storytelling are relatively new in Sri Lanka (De Silva et al., 2020). It was found that the majority of children in this study had never used or heard of AR books before they participated in this study (see Fig. 9). There was only one girl who heard of it and saw an AR book at a book fair, but she never experienced it on her own. Thus, the initial AR application (*Chandra Padma* V.1.0) was also introduced for children to test.

Overall, the research model had positive outcomes. The children were happily engaged during the storytelling sessions and provided valuable feedback from three different perspectives. To extract AR features and functions, existing case studies and research were also utilized.

6.1 Theme 1: Non-linear Story Content

The main problem observed in the research's initial stage was that children tend to concentrate on one story at a time when recounting a narrative using the physical board. They failed to grasp the overall picture of the story (Fernandes & Leite, 2024). Thus, proper guidance needs to be given before starting. Even when reading the book and using storyboards, they recreated, retold, and memorized only one storyline, '*Chandra's story*', very well.

One boy (age 14) correctly identified the characters and elements for two different contexts, sky, and earth, and created a story path for each storyline before beginning

Table 1 Themes were derived from the analysis pilot test and existing studies

Themes	Categories	Design features and functions for NNAR
Non-linear story content	I want someone to guide me	Children needed guidance or tutorials within the app on how to navigate to see *Chandra's* world and *Padma's* world.
	I want to see existing storylines	Children used mental maps on where to put multiple storylines that separate the two stories and intersect in the story resolution. Children understood the branching point at the key moment/the climax (the place where *Chandra* and Padma finally meet after 76 years) to understand the resolution.
	I want to see the difference between the two contexts	Children expected to see two diverse story contexts in the book (Sky and Earth) to cater to various interests and preferences. Add context-related elements such as more stars for the sky in *Chandra's* story. Add more lotuses for *Padma's* story (Hughes, 2013).
	I want to see the characters' timeline for time dilation	Children knew *Chandra* had been waiting 76 years. They are curious about what happened to *Padma* during that time.
	I want to understand how poems and dialogs are connecting	Children wanted additional narrative elements such as poems and dialogues by overhearing conversations or interactions within the two worlds as an overlay.
Responsive characters	I want more live characters	Implement three-dimensional character models to enhance visual appeal and interaction. Select real dialogues instead of a third-person narrative to create a more authentic and engaging experience (Lambert & Butcher, 2018).
	I want character to feel me and respond to me	Enable user interaction by allowing characters to react to gestures or movements captured by the device's camera (Wonderscope—a Magical AR Storybook for Kids, 2020).
	I want the character to hear me and respond to me	Implement responsive characters. As an example, *Chandra* can hear the child's voice and respond accordingly (*Tőnandi*, n.d.).
	I want to hear other background sounds	Children wanted to hear background sound effects and also gave examples such as night cricket, comet entrances, or water splashing sounds to enhance immersion and create a dynamic environment.

(continued)

Table 1 (continued)

Themes	Categories	Design features and functions for NNAR
Creating different contexts within the physical world	I want to see the virtual world through my physical world	While some children used storyboards to show storylines horizontally, some children imagine the storyline is vertically, where *Chandra*, coming from the sky and *Padma* is on the earth. Thus, they expected to see scenario changes in response to specific movements detected by the AR camera, such as moving the mobile device vertically upward to trigger storyline A scenarios or vertically downward for storyline B scenarios. Implement characters who can respond to the physical world objects. (As an example, *Chandra* can move from the sky to earth without getting endangered by the physical objects in the room) (Wonderscope—a Magical AR Storybook for Kids, 2020).
Engagement through gamification	I want to play in this virtual world	When using the storyboard, children carefully moved characters without being endangered. Therefore, need to include gamification elements within the AR environment that correspond to tasks, such as mini games. Create a reward system that offers virtual rewards, achievements, or unlockable content to encourage users to complete tasks and engage with the app (Becker & Hornecker, 2021).
	I want to do collaborative storytelling with my friends	Some children paired up to present the story on the storyboard. Thus, implementing multiplayer functionality into the '*Chandra-Padma*' AR app will allow multiple users to connect and interact within the same virtual environment simultaneously (Becker & Hornecker, 2021).

the storytelling with the board (see Fig. 10 left). He also demonstrated how the characters should move on the board, using the example of a '*Dham*' board, a traditional Sri Lankan board game similar to a chessboard. He also explained how the comet (Comet Boy with the star kite) should appear in the AR app and pointed out the direction for it (Fig. 10 right). It seems like only the older children (ages 12, 13, and 14) understood the link between the poems and dialogs of storylines A and B, but they didn't put effort into showing it on the physical storyboard.

6.2 Theme 2: Responsive Characters

For the physical storyboard and AR app, 2D flat elements were used. During the storytelling time, children mentioned that they preferred 3D characters over 2D stickers since it would bring the characters to life. Moreover, since the physical storyboard provided some tangible sense, they wanted the same for the AR application. They wanted to touch the characters and elements in the virtual world and have them respond accordingly. For example, the younger audience, aged 7, 8, and 9, were frustrated when they couldn't touch the stars, which they saw inside the test AR application, even though the stars appeared to be on the table in front of

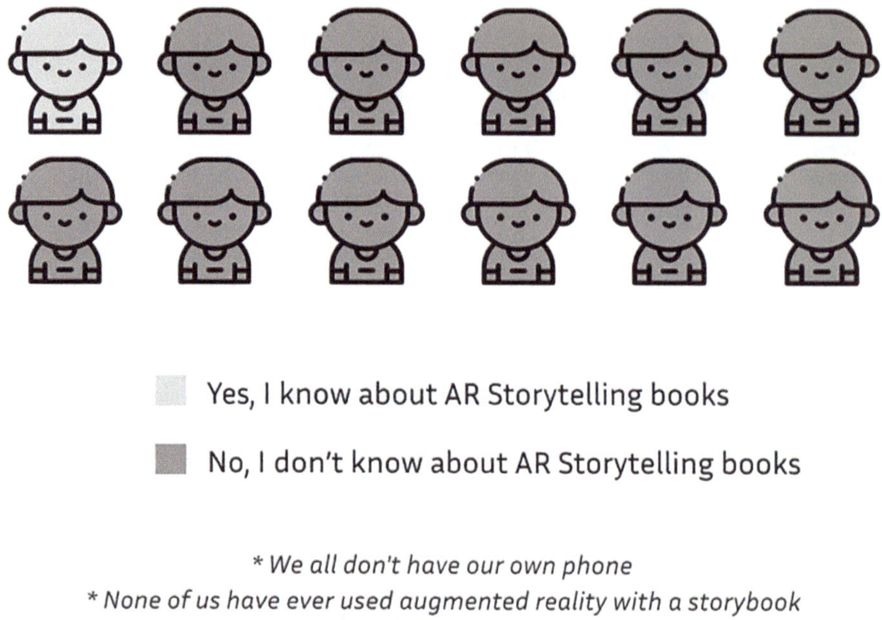

Fig. 9 Proficiency and familiarity with augmented reality technology of the participating group of 12 children aged (7–14)

Fig. 10 Creating story paths on board and giving their feedback on test AR application

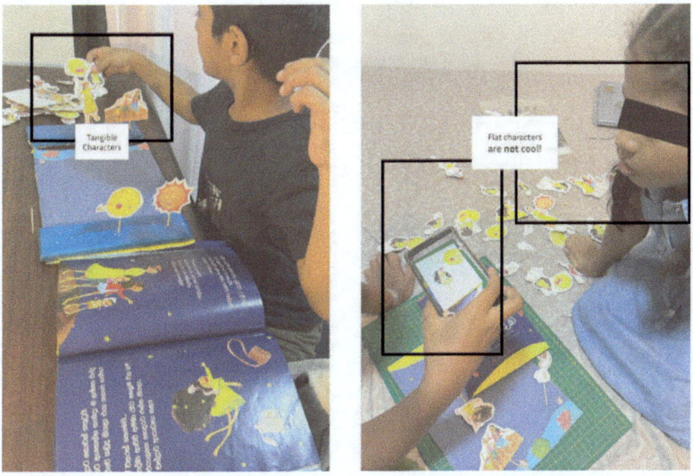

Fig. 11 Tangible characters and non-tangible characters in the pilot test

them. This disconnect between the virtual and physical experience was particularly disappointing for them (Fig. 11 right).

Within the test AR application, the pre-recorded audio was used to tell the story. Since the AR interface wasn't developed, the children couldn't control the voice. They recommended that the scene would be more realistic if they could control the scene and talk to the characters in real time. One girl (age 14) suggested it should be similar to Siri on an Apple phone. Moreover, one boy (age 7), even though he didn't read the book, moved the character (Comet boy with the star kite) with comet sounds he made from his mouth ('Suru sur sur…') on the tangible storyboard. He also rocked the board on the storyboard to give a realistic feeling (Fig. 11 left).

6.3 *Theme 3: Creating Different Context Within the Physical World*

A notable feature of the storyboard was the child's use of spatial tags to mark significant events and locations within the story environment, such as the climax of the story. A girl holds the character upside down to imitate the exact book character in the *Chandra-Padma* book. This provided the children with a holistic understanding of the narrative landscape and helped them understand the virtual landscape. A boy (age 12) held the two characters together to show the final resolution. According to his vision, the two main characters, *Chandra*, and *Padma*, meet in the middle of the board.

It was interesting to observe how physical environments influence children's interaction with characters on a storyboard. It was conducted in settings either at a table

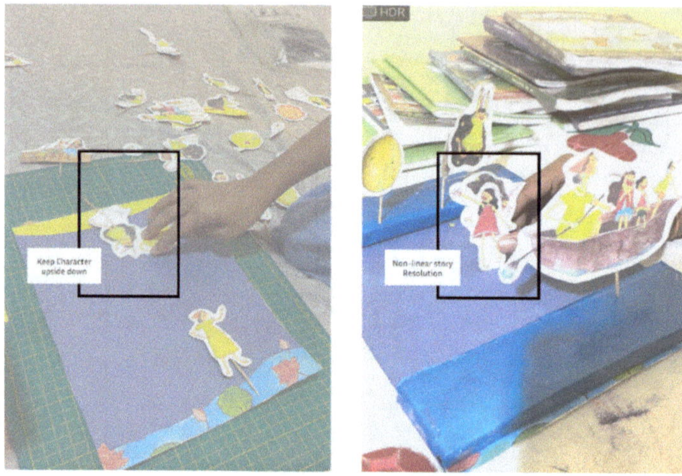

Fig. 12 Creating the spatial tag on the storyboard

with chairs or on the floor with a soft mattress. Children sitting on the soft mattress tended to engage with characters along a horizontal plane, primarily on the XY axis, likely due to the relaxed and unrestricted nature of their seating arrangement (Fig. 12 left). In contrast, children at the table interacted more vertically, utilizing all three axes (XYZ), possibly influenced by the structured and firm support of the table setting (Fig. 12 right). These findings highlight the significant roles played by both the physical setting and the solidity of the environment in shaping how children perceive and interact with AR content. Thus, NNAR application designers can use this understanding to customize storytelling planes and interaction modes based on the physical context, thereby enhancing user engagement and immersion in AR experiences.

6.4 Theme 4: Engagement Through Gamification

The non-linearity remains complex, and it appears that this was the children's first time reading a book with a non-linear narration structure with two stories. The two stories are flowing simultaneously and at first, children were not able to understand the concept. However, with adult guidance and explanation, they gradually begin to tell the story simultaneously and collaboratively. As an example, during the session, one girl suggested to another that she would handle one story while asking the other girl to handle the second story on the board. They then collaboratively worked on the storyboard to bring both narratives to life (Fig. 13 left). This insight inspired the incorporation of collaboration as an AR feature to allow multiple users to engage with stories and continue storytelling. Interacting within the same virtual environment

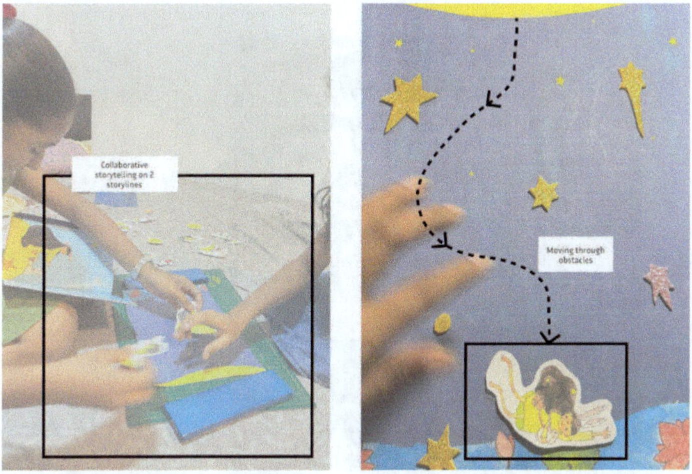

Fig. 13 Collaborative work on storyboard and gamification ideas

simultaneously and providing AR experiences to different users will ensure that all participants see the same elements and events within the shared space.

It was fascinating to observe one little girl (age 9) carefully moving characters on the storyboard, expressing concern about avoiding danger, such as hitting a dangerous comet. She had similar experience with basic mobile games (mini games) and suggested incorporating elements from those games into the non-linear story (Fig. 13 right). This insight stimulated the inclusion of gamification and AR features in the storytelling app, allowing children to engage with the stories through interactive gameplay. NNAR application designers can use this insight to incorporate gamification by offering small tasks or challenges to the child, with rewards promised upon completion.

7 Conclusion and Future Enhancement

In this study, a child participatory research approach took place to emphasize the transition from the physical world to the technological world flawlessly. After the pilot test of this model, a set of data and insights were gathered to develop an NNAR space to give a better storytelling experience for a non-linear story. The primary purpose is to find out the set of functionalities and features derived from this approach in order to build an NNAR application. In this approach, an end-to-end pipeline for creating an NNAR application for a non-linear narrative book was discussed. These experiences also suggest several enhancements for future technical work, in addition to the deployment and user study described above. This continuous feedback loop and progressive learning will make this NNAR application resilient and capable of evolving over time (Fig. 14).

Fig. 14 Envisioned NNAR app interface

Note. It should be noted that any kind of mobile device capable of supporting Augmented Reality applications or non-linear books, including fancy, attractive hard-cover books, are not available to this group of children. They come from lower-to-lower-middle socioeconomic backgrounds and are unable to afford books or devices of that kind.

8 Ethical Considerations

Including children in research projects like *Chandra-Padma* is crucial since they have unique insights adults often overlook. Their perspectives and experiences can provide valuable contributions to the design process that may not be apparent to adults. By actively involving children in research, we gained a deeper understanding of their needs, preferences, and behaviors, which ultimately enriches the project findings. All the data gathered from child participants had a significant impact on our project findings. The study adhered to ethical guidelines for research involving human subjects, ensuring informed consent from all participants, and safeguarding their privacy and confidentiality throughout the study. Also, written parental consent was obtained before children were used as test subjects, and permission was obtained for the recording of ethical behavior for the study to be conducted responsibly. Additionally, children were asked whether they would prefer to read the story or use the storyboard while I was taking pictures, videos or audio recordings.

Before involving children in the *Chandra-Padma* research project, ample information was provided to ensure they could give informed consent. However, it's important to note that the topic of non-linear storytelling with AR can pose challenges, particularly because children are still developing cognitively. This means their comprehension of what they are consenting to may be less than that of the average adult. Therefore, the implications of non-linear books, storyboards, and the test AR applications were explained to children in a fun way, facilitating their understanding of these complex narratives. After the explanations were provided, children had the opportunity to ask questions (Marney, n.d.). Above all, we encouraged children to unleash their creative ideas, and our primary aim was to ensure that their participation in this project was enjoyable and memorable.

Acknowledgements Our sincere gratitude goes out to all children and their parents who participate in the '*Kurutu Balitto*' Art and Science Class—Panagoda, Homagama, Sri Lanka for graciously allowing our research to take place. With the assistance of Thanuja Priyadarshani, a senior teacher with more than twenty years' experience working with children, this research was seamless and enjoyable. Using a participatory research model such as this would not have been possible without the creative and enthusiastic engagement of the children. I am deeply grateful to all of them for their involvement.

References

Alhumaidan, H., Lo, K. P. Y., & Selby, A. (2018). Co-designing with Children a Collaborative Augmented Reality Book Based on a Primary School Textbook. *International Journal of Child-Computer Interaction, 15*, 24–36. https://doi.org/10.1016/j.ijcci.2017.11.005

Becker, G., & Hornecker, E. (2021). *Sally&Molly: A Children's Book with Real-Time Multiplayer Mobile Augmented Reality* (p. 86). https://doi.org/10.1145/3450337.3483498

Billinghurst, M., & Duenser, A. (2012). Augmented Reality in the Classroom. *Computer, 45*, 56–63. https://doi.org/10.1109/MC.2012.111

Billinghurst, M., Kato, H., & Poupyrev, I. (2001). The MagicBook—Moving seamlessly between reality and virtuality. *IEEE Computer Graphics and Applications, 21*(3), 6–8. https://doi.org/10.1109/38.920621

Calise, A. (2022). *Mixed Reality: Frontiera dell'educazione museale. 6*, 199–221. https://doi.org/10.6092/issn.2531-9876/14308

Claudino Daffara, S., Brewer, A., Thoravi Kumaravel, B., & Hartmann, B. (2020). *Living Paper: Authoring AR Narratives Across Digital and Tangible Media* (p. 10). https://doi.org/10.1145/3334480.3383091

Creswell, Jhon. W. (2014). *Research Design*. SAGE Publications, Inc.

Dam, R. F. (2023, October 16). *The 5 Stages in the Design Thinking Process*. The Interaction Design Foundation. https://www.interaction-design.org/literature/article/5-stages-in-the-design-thinking-process

De Silva, W., Naranpanawa, P., Hettihewa, U., Liyanage, P., Samarakoon, U., & Amarasena, N. (2020). Science Zone: An Augmented Reality based Mobile Application for Science. *2020 2nd International Conference on Advancements in Computing (ICAC)*, *1*, 222–227. https://doi.org/10.1109/ICAC51239.2020.9357153

Druin, A. (1999). Cooperative Inquiry: Developing New Technologies for Children with Children. *Proceedings of the SIGCHI Conference on Human Factors in Computing Systems*, 592–599. https://doi.org/10.1145/302979.303166

Duenser, A., & Hornecker, E. (2007). *An Observational Study of Children Interacting with an Augmented Story Book* (Vol. 4469). https://doi.org/10.1007/978-3-540-73011-8_31

Experience, W. L. in R.-B. U. (n.d.). *Usability Testing 101*. Nielsen Norman Group. Retrieved July 10, 2024, from https://www.nngroup.com/articles/usability-testing-101/

Fernandes, A., & Leite, L. (2024). The Expanded Book—Various Perspectives in Augmented Reality. In N. Martins & D. Brandão (Eds.), *Advances in Design and Digital Communication IV* (pp. 224–237). Springer Nature Switzerland.

Hughes, H. (2013). *iSolar System: An Augmented Reality Book*. Carlton Books Ltd.

Hung, Y. -H, Chen, C. -H, & Huang, S. -W. (2016). Applying Augmented Reality to Enhance Learning: A Study of Different Teaching Materials. *Journal of Computer Assisted Learning*, *33*. https://doi.org/10.1111/jcal.12173

Huttner, J.-P., & Robra-Bissantz, S. (2017). *An Immersive Memory Palace: Supporting the Method of Loci with Virtual Reality*.

Jacko, J., & Sears, A. (2002). *The Human-Computer Interaction Handbook: Fundamentals, Evolving Technologies, and Emerging Applications* (p. 1312).

Justice, L., Pullen, P., & Pence Turnbull, K. (2008). Influence of Verbal and Nonverbal References to Print on Preschoolers' Visual Attention to Print During Storybook Reading. *Developmental Psychology*, *44*, 855–866. https://doi.org/10.1037/0012-1649.44.3.855

Kanai, R., Paffen, C., Hogendoorn, H., & Verstraten, F. (2006). Time Dilation in Dynamic Visual Display. *Journal of Vision*, *6*, 1421–1430. https://doi.org/10.1167/6.12.8

Karaata, E., & Yilmaz, N. (2023). Use of Augmented Reality in Illustrated Children's Books and An Application ExampleResimli Çocuk Kitaplarında Artırılmış Gerçeklik Kullanımı ve Bir Uygulama Örneği. *Medeniyet Sanat Dergisi*, *9*. https://doi.org/10.46641/medeniyetsanat.1279849

Kurutu Balitto (Sajini Lankadari) (Director). (2023, August 1). *Chandra Padma* (*චන්ද්‍ර පද්ම*) [Video recording]. https://www.youtube.com/watch?v=21qUHIF25VE

Lambert, N., & Butcher, R. (2018). *Little Red Riding Hood AR book*. https://www.youtube.com/watch?v=F2ieduC3wCI

Lankadari, S. (n.d.). *Chandra Padma* (*චන්ද්‍ර පද්ම*)*—YouTube*. Retrieved July 7, 2024, from https://www.youtube.com/

Lankadari, S., & Rodrigo, B. (2022). Storytelling for Preschool Children in Sri Lanka: Social and Emotional Development Between Linear and Non-linear Storytelling Approaches. In N. Martins & D. Brandão (Eds.), *Advances in Design and Digital Communication II* (pp. 452–465). Springer International Publishing.

Lankadari, S., & Rodrigo, B. (2024). Chandra-Padma: Identifying Motivations for Children to Respond and React to a Book with a Non-linear Narrative Structure. In N. Martins & D. Brandão (Eds.), *Advances in Design and Digital Communication IV* (pp. 732–750). Springer Nature Switzerland.

Marney, C., Jack. (n.d.). *Ethics | ChiCI - Child Computer Interaction*. Retrieved April 9, 2024, from https://chici.org/ethics/

Meyer, S. (2016). *Right, Left, High, Low Narrative Strategies for Non–linear Storytelling* (p. 335). https://doi.org/10.1007/978-3-319-48279-8_29

Mulyasari, E. (1993). Children Responses to Short Stories and Aloud. *Probst*.

Nowell, L., Norris, J., White, D., & Moules, N. (2017). Thematic Analysis: Striving to Meet the Trustworthiness Criteria. *International Journal of Qualitative*, *16*. https://doi.org/10.1177/1609406917733847

Palinkas, L. A., Horwitz, S. M., Green, C. A., Wisdom, J. P., Duan, N., & Hoagwood, K. (2015). Purposeful Sampling for Qualitative Data Collection and Analysis in Mixed Method Implementation Research. *Administration and Policy in Mental Health and Mental Health Services Research*, *42*(5), 533–544. https://doi.org/10.1007/s10488-013-0528-y

Sevón, E., Mustola, M., Siippainen, A., & Vlasov, J. (n.d.). Participatory research methods with young children: A systematic literature review. *Educational Review*, 1–19. https://doi.org/10.1080/00131911.2023.2215465

Szabó, B., & Hercegfi, K. (2023). User-centered approaches in software development processes: Qualitative research into the practice of Hungarian companies. *Journal of Software: Evolution and Process*, *35*(2), e2501. https://doi.org/10.1002/smr.2501

Tónandi. (n.d.). Magicleap. Retrieved April 6, 2024, from https://world.magicleap.com/en-us/details/com.magicleapstudios.tonandi

Warr, A. (2018). *Action Research into Mobile Augmented Reality for the Utility of Public Spaces*. https://doi.org/10.13140/RG.2.2.16354.43208

Wonderscope – a magical AR storybook for kids. (2020). Within Unlimited, Inc. https://www.tapsmart.com/apps/ar-apps/wonderscope-review/

Zaman, F., Anslow, C., Chalmers, A., & Rhee, T. (2023). MRMAC: Mixed Reality Multi-user Asymmetric Collaboration. *2023 IEEE International Symposium on Mixed and Augmented Reality (ISMAR)*, 591–600. https://doi.org/10.1109/ISMAR59233.2023.00074

Zhou, S., Cheok, A., Pan, J., & Li, Y. (2004). *An interactive 3D exploration narrative interface for storytelling*. 155–156. https://doi.org/10.1145/1017833.1017867

Alcântaras, o som é um sistema: Touch the Sound/Reach the Sound

Ramusyo Brasil and Cesário Alves

Abstract The region of Alcântara, Maranhão, Brazil, is a complex synthesis of a worldculture. Synthesis because it takes place in a microcosm, and complex because of the derivations and ramifications the clash of civilizations has generated as a culture. Reaching/touching a sound is an artistic, scientific and political effort by understanding sound as a world-system that connects everything, places sonic-visual thinking as a means of recognizing popular knowledge and a (trans)historical social critique of the (de)territorialization of Maranhão's black and indigenous peoples. What results from our phenomenological observation, are photographic and cinematographic records, texts and sound recordings. What results from our methodological construction and interpretation is a film-essay conceived as a score to a live sound performance. On a theoretical level, we have used concepts and observations from sonic and musical studies (Johnson, 2023; Nancy, 2011; Chion, 2010; Jenny, 2001), as well as from visual studies and technical images (Flusser, 2014; Català, 2005; Arnheim, 1998). We started from audiovisual anthropology, bringing it into tension with a vivid dimension of practice as research (Henriques & D´Aquino, 2023), based on the experience of the researchers with sound and visual arts. The results give rise not only to a reflection on the path taken so far, as well as the future challenges in further research, to reverberate the struggle of quilombola people of Alcântara and sense how climate, territory and nature forge sonic culture, translating into language, politics and representation.

Keywords Documentary photography · Experimental sound and cinema · Artistic practice as research

R. Brasil (✉)
Laboratório de Artes na Montanha – Graça Morais do Instituto Politécnico de Bragança, 5300-253 Bragança, Portugal
e-mail: ramusyo@ipb.pt

C. Alves
ID+, Escola Superior de Media Artes e Design do Politécnico do Porto, Rua D. Sancho I, 981 4480-876 Vila do Conde, Portugal
e-mail: cesarioalves@esmad.ipp.pt

© The Author(s), under exclusive license to Springer Nature Switzerland AG 2025
D. Brandão et al. (eds.), *Perspectives on Design and Digital Communication V*, Springer Series in Design and Innovation 50, https://doi.org/10.1007/978-3-031-76156-0_15

1 Alcântaras, Two Degrees South of the Equator

Alcântara is a city in the state of Maranhão, in north-eastern Brazil, in which there are more than 208 rural quilombola settlements, community lands of descendants of black populations enslaved by the Portuguese colonial process, in a region that also houses the Aerospace Launch Base of Brazil. The name, that also identifies cities or places in the Iberian Peninsula and Africa, carries traces of its origin in cultures and ancestral knowledge that can still be observed, with sonic and visual clarity, in the cultural, religious, and artistic manifestations in the region. Alcântara, meaning "stone bridge" in Arabic, alludes precisely to the idea of connections drawn between ethnic groups, creative processes, and the formation of new (aest)ethics based on the updating of ancestral knowledge applied to current technologies.

Just two degrees south of the equator, the sun seems closer and the heat at noon may be unbearable. We can observe its effects in the vibrance of colors in the landscape and the skin of human bodies, but also in the sounds travelling in the air. There's a sense of being touched or even caressed by the sounds carried and modulated by the wind and the heat. Sounds in general, but the electronically amplified ones especially, reflect off surfaces, faster or slower, according to distance and climate conditions. Since temperature affects the speed of sound and the winds are permanently blowing and changing directions in the hills of the peninsula of old Alcântara, the experience of environmental sounds is quite unique and seems to acquire an ever-changing spatiality and depth. If there's sunlight in Alcantara there's reggae music travelling through the winds, coming from a Radiola sound system, miles away or just next door, but never at the same time of the day.

In these pages, we are looking for a way of operating through what is aesthetically close to the artistic research project we are describing. In this way, the written text,

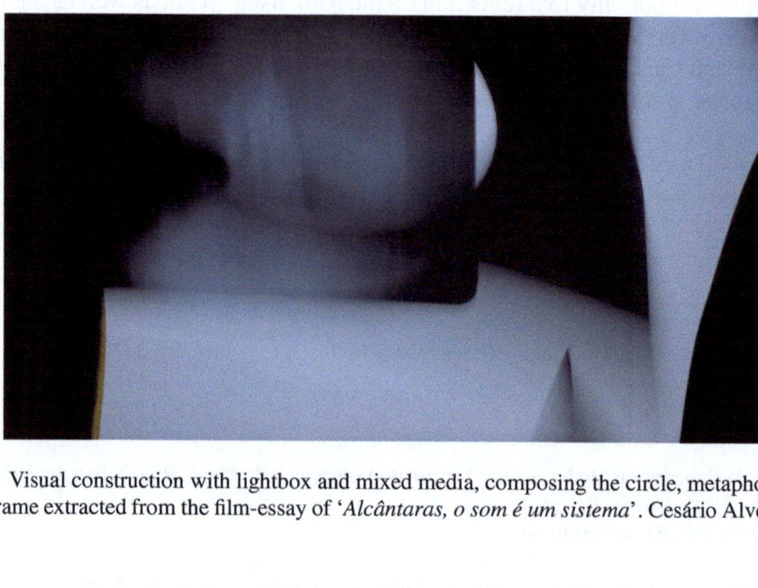

Fig. 1 Visual construction with lightbox and mixed media, composing the circle, metaphor of the sun. Frame extracted from the film-essay of '*Alcântaras, o som é um sistema*'. Cesário Alves, 2022

Fig. 2 Visual construction with lightbox and mixed media, composing the circle, metaphor of the sun. Frame extracted from the film-essay of '*Alcântaras, o som é um sistema*'. Cesário Alves, 2022

links to audiovisual materials and images to form the fabric of thought, in the manner of an essay. Thus, the images do not illustrate the written text, but make up the argument along with it. Seen in this way, writing (textual, visual, audiovisual) is here a procedure that develops ideas from lived aesthetic experiences, bringing from them considerations and reflections, doubts, and inferences.

The central questioning of 'Alcântaras' lies in the attempt to establish a fruitful balance and tension between documentary recording and experimental research in sound and visual arts, making the film-essay the audiovisual score of a sound expression that is in the process of becoming. At the same time, methodologically, the idea of "practice as research" as a means of touching reality is also a key to creation, by mixing community and collective processes with the subjective vision/hearing of the artists/researchers.

Visually, the film-essay is composed mainly of cinematographic images which ontologically presuppose the possibility of movement, but the camera stands still in most of them, since the scenes show moving subjects. On the other hand, in the only truly static photograph seen in the film, a photogram printed with light direct into silver salt paper, the camera moves gently over the details, revealing the hair of a girl, effectively fragmenting one photograph into many photographs/frames.

For the sake of coherence to the selection of images, but also as a deliberate constraint from the great amount of material produced, a decision was made to present here, only frames extracted from the film-essay, keeping its chronological order. The film reduced to only a few of its smallest fractions, photographs, static and imprisoned in time, a synthesis within a synthesis, a poem within a poem, a curatorial gesture. The photographs distributed in these pages are therefore a new gaze into this part of the work. We took this opportunity to experiment and see how movement could be represented photographically and silently in the printed page.

2 The Film as a Score

In the region of Alcântara, language and culture have a unique character, sculpted by the slow but permanent action of time. Our own experience of the places and events there, was highly sensorial and even transcendental, in a way that cannot be fairly described by any written account or contained within the limitations of the technical apparatuses we used to capture the waves of sound and light: photographs, films and audio recordings. These are subjective and fractional interpretations, but still vehicles of knowledge and memory which can be revisited repeatedly, even if representing something that is truly unrepeatable. Those limited mediums and spaces of representation offer their own opportunities for the synthesis of sounds, images, and ideas.

The reproducibility and repeatability of the recording mediums was therefore embraced in our process of research, as a useful device for the study and interpretation of past events or experiences. As creators and performers of our own events, we aimed at bringing to this work an element of contingency and uniqueness that emerges from the collaboration of multiple artists. Therefore, the crossing of different views and mediums includes stable and repeatable visual and sonic elements, but culminates with a unique live performance, which creates, adds, and subtracts new images and sounds to a film-essay, reacting to the moment in time and the environmental conditions of the place where it is presented.

The main component of the live performance is the film-essay [1], it needs to be projected in a room, in a scale and position that best allows it to be viewed by performers and the public. It includes stereophonic sound that needs to be amplified and matched with the dimensions of the room and the other equipment that supports the variety of instruments of the performers. The film, containing documentary footage made locally but also staged formal elements, recalling the circle

Fig. 3 Entrance of the bay of Alcântara, Maranhão, Brazil. Frame extracted from the film-essay of '*Alcântaras, o som é um sistema*'. Cesário Alves, 2019

Fig. 4 Radiola sound system MKW SOM in Alcântara, Maranhão, Brazil. Frame extracted from the film-essay of '*Alcântaras, o som é um sistema*'. Cesário Alves, 2019

shape of the sun (Fig. 1, 2, 3) and speaker boxes of sound systems (Radiolas), was edited so that it serves as an equivalent to a musical score. The editing timeline lays down a basis for the composition of the audiovisual elements and sets durations and marks for the incorporation of live sounds.

The sound creation performed live interacts with the film, which incorporates already a time structure, a periodic system [2] that emulates what we can observe in nature and our own physiological processes. The noises of machines are heard before any image appears, the bass guitar starts and creates the pace to suggest the continuous but arrhythmic vibrating pulses of the hearts of the drummers and dancers of Tambor de Crioula and other manifestations we can see onscreen, as well as the low frequency sounds of machines present in every contemporary urban landscape. Electronically synthesized white noise becomes the basis to evoke the memory of wind. The dub siren and the delay effect (Fig. 7) in modulated feedback and amplitude, reveal a hint of the presence of Jamaican music in the performance and in the film-essay. The tape loops of recorded sounds are rhythmically repeated as percussive textures and the conductive electrodes of modified synthesizers in contact with the skin of the performer, generates the sci-fi tones that attempt to reach beyond space and time, reminding us that from Alcântara we can also reach outer space.

3 Correlations Between Image and Sound

Our research deals with a limitation of another dimension, which is not one of representation, but of the nature of the materials we work with, which are the still image, the moving image and the medium of sound (the ones reproduced in the film and those we produce live in the performance). They are read by our cognitive apparatus, which involves not only a physiological operation, but also alludes to a logic of perception, which has to do with how our body translates the stimuli we receive. In visual studies, Català [3] talks about the levels of perception operated by human beings to deal with visual information, transforming it into meaning, this field of tension between signifier and signified.

The first frontier when we encounter a stimulus, in our case a potential image, is at the physiological level, through the organs of perception (sight, hearing, smell, touch, taste). The second level is ecological, through the universe of perception, both the being and the world in which it is inserted are nature, even if we sometimes don't perceive ourselves as something that belongs to nature. Through the first two levels, the physiological and the ecological, we can talk about the ontological being. In other words, first and foremost, the being 'is', considering the nature of reality and existence in which it is inserted. With the two ontological levels as the raw material of human existence, we arrive at the anthropological level of perceptive life, establishing the cultures of perception in the exchanges between humans and between social groups, being nature themselves. Hence the intrinsic relationship between nature and culture, in what we call the ecology of knowledges. Thus, on the fourth level we have the cognitive dimension, which deals with the forms of perception. The cognitive function of perception is therefore produced as a concrete act of seeing through certain determined parameters. This does not mean a hierarchy between the levels of perception, but rather the degrees of refinement that can occur from a body that feels, absorbs, reacts, and constructs, according to the biological and cultural instruments he finds.

We have, as a synthesis, the dyads that inform about human perception: organs/physiology, worlds/ecology, cultures/anthropology, forms/cognition. All these notions of the depth and source of human perception are articulated with the

Fig. 5 DJ from Radiola sound system MKW SOM in Alcântara, Maranhão, Brazil. Frame extracted from the film-essay of *'Alcântaras, o som é um sistema'*. Cesário Alves, 2019

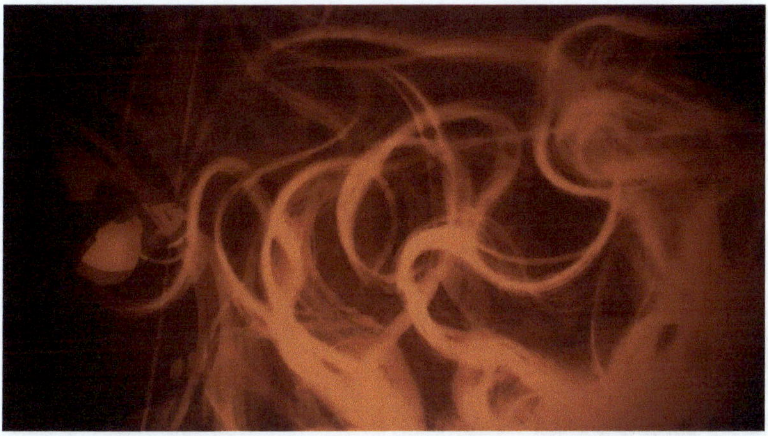

Fig. 6 Hair of a girl, photogram printed with light direct into silver salt paper. Made in Vila do Conde, Portugal. Frame extracted from the film-essay of '*Alcântaras, o som é um sistema*'. Cesário Alves, 2022

theory of form or the psychology of form (gestalt), which deals with the basic mechanisms of perception, which, based on certain conditions listed here, alter the ways of seeing [4].

Sound, on the other hand, has a different cognitive nature. There tends to be greater isomorphism between visualities and their conceptual manifestation. Firstly, because "morphé", "form", is implied in the word "isomorphism" and is immediately thought of in terms of the visual. Furthermore, sound carries form with it. It doesn't dissolve it in the representation, it enlarges it, gives it a thickness and a vibration whose drawing does nothing more than thicken the experience of listening. "The visual persists until it fades away, the sonorous appears and fades away even in its permanence" [5].

In this sense, sound in its form and content, in its production, reception and perception, is immanent. This means that sound exists in its own interiority, concretely, in contrast to the existence, real or fictitious, of a dimension external to itself. In other words, and still according to Nancy, the visual is more mimetic and the sonorous methesic. While the visual relates to the imaginary, the sonorous is in the order of the symbolic referral, both obviously not limited to these dimensions, but marked by them.

An example of the non-limitation of these dimensions is the use of voice in audiovisual discourse, which refers not only to a location but also to mental images constituted by them. Electronic mediation fixes the voice, making it repeatable, representable. Direct voice recording procedures in documentary contexts evoke a kind of resurgence of vocal energies, repressed for centuries in the cultures of Westernized societies [6].

One of the narrative lines in the film-essay is based on words led by the voices of two residents from Alcântara. Voices are vehicles of closeness, rather than of distance

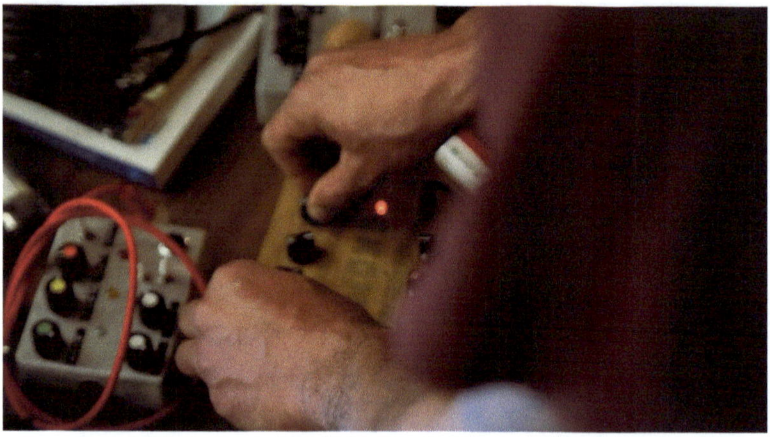

Fig. 7 Sound system builder and Reggae DJ in Aveiro, Portugal. Frame extracted from the film-essay of '*Alcântaras, o som é um sistema*'. Ramusyo Brasil, 2022

as they come from within the body, while images provide us with a more distanced or metaphorical analysis [7].

Following is a transcription of a small extract of both spoken testimonials, words of significant political content as presented in writing, but uniquely modulated and sensibly spoken in the recordings:

Cláudio do Espírito Santo (Camafeu): *Alcântara. Alcântara era uma cidade de muitos sofrimentos na época da escravatura. Foi muito sofrimento, muita tara.*[1]

Joralda Ramos Ribeiro: *Mas ainda assim há muita gente com racismo, os que são brancos, mais claros não quer chegar perto do negro. Além de não ser agradável a deus porque ninguém é melhor do que ninguém, todos somos descendentes desses três grupos.*[2]

The unique characteristics of each of these languages do not prevent them from correlating on some levels, establishing dialogues, counterpoints, confrontations, densifications, and attenuations. However, there are levels of materiality in both, which mean that when image and sound are combined, sound interferes more in the apprehension of an image than the other way around. And it is in this gap, between the visible and the audible, that we invest our creative thoughts, to make an image resonate with new or other meanings, as well as bringing to light a sound that reveals itself in an acoustic image, an image of thought, broadening the senses in the experience of multimedia language towards an Audio Vision [8]. Seeing the color of sound and listening to the sound vibrations of a still or moving image, diegetically or non-diegetically.

[1] Translation to English: Cláudio do Espírito Santo (Camafeu): Alcântara. Alcântara was a city of much suffering during the time of slavery. It was a lot of suffering, a lot of insanity.

[2] Translation to English: Joralda Ramos Ribeiro: But there are still a lot of people who are racist, those who are white don't want to get close to black people. Apart from the fact that it's not pleasing to God because no one is better than anyone else, we are all descendants of these three groups.

4 Threshold of Practice as Research

Listening and looking attentively at the cultural expressions of the people, as sine qua non knowledge and skills for taking Maranhão's popular culture to the place where it is found, was taken into consideration by the project's researchers, in what is currently called "practice as research", as a fundamental characteristic of what we do in the artistic field. The cultural practitioners/agents are those with the knowledge, know-how and experience at the heart of the scenes being researched. Practice as research is a departure from and a development of conventional research models such as participant observation and ethnomethodology. These methodologies, despite the researcher being immersed in the field, maintain a clear division between the researcher and the researched. Practice as research recognizes that knowledge is not exclusively epistemic, that is, defined in the traditional manner of the arts and humanities as a closed text. This methodology also recognizes that researchers' own creative practices can and do generate knowledge [9].

The research was based on audiovisual images produced in the field by Ramusyo Brasil at various cultural events in Maranhão throughout the 2010s, such as: the Tambor de Crioula at São Benedito festival in the city of Alcântara (Figs. 10 and 11); the Bambaê in the region of Penalva and Olinda Nova do Maranhão (Fig. 12), 'boi sotaque de Costa-de-Mão' from Cururupu, in the Baixada Maranhense (Fig. 8); 'Boi sotaque de Costa-de-Mão e Matraca', in São Pedro square, in São Luís, state of Maranhão (Fig. 9). These ethnographic images met the photographs of Radiolas (Fig. 4 and Fig 5) and 'carros de som' (sound vehicles) portraits, landscapes and soundscapes produced by Cesário Alves, in the context of the artistic residency held between August and September 2019, in Alcântara.

Fig. 8 Player of matraca (instrument) in largo de S. Pedro, S. Luís, Maranhão, Brazil. Frame extracted from the film-essay of '*Alcântaras, o som é um sistema*'. Ramusyo Brasil, 2017

Fig. 9 Player of pandeirão (instrument) in largo de S. Pedro, S. Luís, Maranhão, Brazil. Frame extracted from the film-essay of '*Alcântaras, o som é um sistema*'. Ramusyo Brasil, 2017

The first challenge was to establish a relationship between these images, so that at the same time as telling a story, they could serve as an opening for an aesthetic experience. Our choice was to work with the film-essay as the central piece, the place from which all the others derive, namely: the live sound-visual performance [10] alongside the film-essay, the photographic exhibition, the website [11], and the publication (zine) that emerge from it, bringing together documentation of the creative process and the results achieved. The film-essay is the space/time where audiovisual materials meet to produce a particular flow of meanings. This fluctuating visuality therefore establishes a process of reflection: hermeneutics does not stop at the images and sounds themselves, but starts from them, from their confrontations, without losing the potential of either language/medium, because one is completed by the other [12]. At this threshold, we find in the experience of sound construction that makes up the sound-visual performance a combination of the production of a document of culture (film-essay), with the rhizomatic possibilities [13] of connection, heterogeneity and multiplicity of meanings, based on a certain exogeny, characterized by the vanishing lines and the abstraction of the sound design made live.

Thus, each appearance of the sound-visual performance '*Alcântaras, o som é um sistema*' was uncertain, imprecise and contingent, because we are always at a certain distance from the event. Between the past, the now and what is to come, we work on processes of deterritorialization of what has been with the creative gesture of becoming, to do justice to the subjects and manifestations researched, as well as our predilections for experimentation, giving rise to an aesthetic reflection on the themes and narratives opened up by the film-essay, which concern the manifestations themselves, the ways of life of that place, and the structural racism that marks the constitution of social groups throughout history, as well as the ways of fighting that take place in different ways in these communities, including in the festivities. Feast time is revolutionary because it is diametrically opposed to work time, and when experienced in a genuine and Dionysian way, it profanes the order established by the constituted power and provides another way of sharing the sensible. Between us artists and the agents of popular culture, in the work '*Alcântaras, o som é um sistema*' a temporality proper to the arts regimes is established, in which a co-presence of heterogeneous temporalities is possible [14].

5 Composing a Multimedia Constellation

The circulation and public presentation of the results of this process are fundamental objectives of its creation and to achieve this it was necessary to start viewing and listening sessions, image and sound editing and sound creation, before looking for possible places and audiences to show it to. After fieldwork in Brazil, the territory of our experience in terms of meetings and rehearsals between participating artists was the cities of Bragança and Vila do Conde, in the north of Portugal, between the institutions where the two main researchers teach and develop their practices, with a first experimental presentation in Montemor-o-Novo, Portugal and a trip to Malaga, Spain with the leverage of support for internationalization from the Portuguese Government's Directorate General for the Arts.

The rehearsals that started the project took place in the second half of 2021, at the Laboratório de artes na Montanha—Graça Morais of the Polytechnic Institute of Bragança, and at the Black Box of the School of Media Arts and Design of the Polytechnic of Porto, in Vila do Conde. The first rehearsals took place with Cesário Alves, Ramusyo Brasil and Miguel Pipa, from which a first performance experience was made, as part of the ARCA—Arquivo e Cinema Festival, which took place in November 2021, in Montemor-o-Novo, Portugal. During these first steps, we used the projection of the film-essay, which includes a basic soundtrack (the score), the creation of noises from found objects, amplified electronically with contact microphones, plus the electric bass (with distortion, delay and loop effects), and the projection of silhouettes of leaves and other concrete objects with two overhead projectors. In this first moment, we discovered the sound and image ecology that permeates our enjoyment. So much so that, for us, some of the best experiences of sound and visual performance have been in these rehearsals and in their productive failures.

The performance on November 26, 2021, in Montemor-o-Novo, was presented by Cesário Alves and Ramusyo Brasil, at the Cine-Teatro Curvo Semedo. After this performance, we came to two conclusions: that two operators were too few to handle so many variables, and that image back-projection implied a level of weight in the production that would not facilitate the circulation of this work.

In January 2022, a successful submission of a project to DGArtes Internationalization Support Programme allowed for the circulation of '*Alcântaras, o som é um sistema*' to Malaga, Spain. At this moment the team included anthropologist, sound system builder and DJ Gustavo Pimenta and sound and visual artist Mariana Sardon, who, with extensive experience in building electronic instruments, also developed a

Fig. 10 Coreiros (choir men) of tambor de crioula (set of 3 drums) in Praça do Galo, church of Nossa Senhora do Rosário, Alcântara, Maranhão, Brazil. Frame extracted from the film-essay of '*Alcântaras, o som é um sistema*'. Ramusyo Brasil, 2019

community and participatory activity in the project's presentation and intervention venues, creating magnetic tape loops to be used as a tool for creating sound textures in performance. This collaborative growth allowed for the establishment of more varied and richer areas of sound intervention. Cesário Alves operated a modular synthesizer, with samples of voice excerpts and other concrete sounds from the field research. Mariana Sardon worked with tape loops and a crackle box with contact electrodes, a noise generator whose sound changes according to the tactile intervention of the operator, using rubber bands, leaves, staples and other objects to produce sounds, sometimes dissonant or noisy, trying to react to and integrate the acoustics of the space into the gestures. Gustavo Pimenta, in charge of the final sound mix, incorporated the sounds of a dub siren into the soundscape of the performance, processed by a delay effect and a drum machine, creating fat, watery rhythms in permanent distortion.

Ramusyo Brasil on electric bass, through delay and loop effects, provided the rhythmic and harmonic background, the bone structure of the sound creation.

From these essays and the work of reflection on the images produced, the sound-visual performance took place on June 9, 2022, at the Aula Magna of the Faculty of Communication Sciences of the University of Malaga, in Malaga, Spain, and the opening of the image graphic exhibition at the Galería Central of the same University, as a first derivation of the project in other media, giving the documentary work another way of presenting and reading it. The sound and visual performance at the Aula Magna took place with the four members of the group. The artists were free to perform more spontaneously, with greater exploration of silences, as well as the creation of more intense sound blocks. On July 1, 2022, the performed occurred at the Librería Suburbia in Malaga. A small bookshop in the center of the city, with a reduced and domesticated sound system with a smaller image projection, tailored to the space provided.

On this occasion, Cesário Alves, Ramusyo Brasil and Gustavo Pimenta performed, forcing a new synthesis of the relationship between images and sounds. The sound expression of the three performers sounded different, with a greater subtlety in the sound ecology, incorporating the acoustic conditions of the space, to work almost by punctuations and brushstrokes of sounds. On this day, the project launched another derivation of this investigation, in printed form, a zine that is configured as a graphic dimension of the work done. The printed publication was conceived as something that could be visual, tactile, literary, and documentary, that holds itself as a poetic statement and research document, contributing for an expanded view of the project.

At the same time, museologist Carolla Ramos, who was also responsible for managing the funding and production, set up the virtual exhibition of '*Alcântaras, o som é um sistema*' on the website of the Contemporary Art Museum of Maranhão—MUCA, creating a consolidated multimedia constellation of the project, which brings together some of its images and information, as well as links to the different cultural agents involved. In October 2022, there were two more performances of '*Alcântaras, o som é um sistema*', one on the 8th, in the micro-cine-theater of the VIC, Aveiro Arts House, in Aveiro, Portugal, in an experience of great proximity to the public, in terms of image projection and the placement of technical paraphernalia for sound creation, taking into account once more, the size and ambience of the place; another at the Ciclo Internacional de Transversalidades Artísticas—CITA, in the city of Bragança. The room provided was the micro-performance space at MINA—Coworking and Creative Hub, which offered a unique experience for audience and artists, due to its peculiar acoustic conditions resulting from the natural stone walls that characterize the building.

Fig. 11 Drummers of tambor de crioula (set of 3 drums) and coreira (choir woman) in Praça do Galo, church of Nossa Senhora do Rosário, Alcântara, Maranhão, Brazil. Frame extracted from the film-essay of '*Alcântaras, o som é um sistema*'. Ramusyo Brasil, 2019

On October 13, 2023, the performance was presented in the city of Alcântara, Maranhão, Brazil, at the eXperimental Film Festival—FeX, finally returning to the source that generated the whole process, giving back to the Alcântara audience the images and sound impressions that came from or inspired it. Only Ramusyo Brasil and Gustavo Pimenta were present, while Cesário Alves and Mariana Sardon performed asynchronously, in a recording made a few days earlier in the Black Box of the School of Media Arts and Design of the Polytechnic of Porto. The presentation consisted of two projections: one of the film-essay, as shown in previous moments, and another of Cesário Alves and Mariana Sardon, recorded for this purpose. For the first time we presented the performance in an open space under moonlight: the outdoor amphitheater of the Cinema de Alcântara, which completed a multimedia constellation of a film-essay, six sound-visual performances in three countries (Portugal, Spain and Brazil), a photographic exhibition, the publication of a printed zine, and a virtual exhibition. With '*Alcântaras, o som é um sistema*' coming to the city of Alcântara, the project closed, so to speak, a first cycle.

6 Proposing a Critical Constellation

Within the development of the project, the reflection that arose from it is also constituted by what is not in the work. What was left out is part of the whole experience, but it is still latent in the perception of the artists and in the dialogues resulting from the process. In this sense, the process of constructing a work of art is integrated with the technical and political dimensions of human labor, even the word 'ars' originally means technique, but also work. In classical antiquity, for example, there was no distinction between art and politics. Art was produced in the private sphere to be exhibited to the public, and then returned to the private sphere for further elaboration [15].

Our perceptions of the process are also motivated by what was left out of the final work. At the same time as the different languages give us tools to talk about something that touches us, they also demand certain ways of interacting with the form, synthesizing the content that comes from it. That said, we couldn't help but be affected by the quilombola struggle of the communities displaced by the construction and expansion of the Brazilian government's Alcântara Aerospace Base. A project coined in the late 1970s and 1980s, it affects communities of former slaves by removing them from centuries-old settlements and placing them in agro-villages, sometimes far from the sea, which is terrifying for communities that live from fishing, subsistence farming and extractivism. By dealing with issues of structural racism and the foundations of power in colonial Alcântara, which led to the deaths of many black people, in the audio testimonies of Camafeu (Cláudio do Espírito Santo) and Dona Joralda Ramos Ribeiro, an elderly lace maker, we touch on symbolic but fundamental parts of the history of political disputes in the city of Alcântara.

However, the political perspective of the institutional struggles of present-day history, in this case, the state versus society, has not escaped us, but could not find a

Fig. 12 Dancers of Bambaê (circular dance, singing and drumming by women), Penalva, Baixada Maranhense, Maranhão, Brazil. Frame extracted from the film-essay of '*Alcântaras, o som é um sistema*'. Ramusyo Brasil, 2011

place in the work for the time being. Of course, this struggle is not so dual, there are intersectional ties and negotiations that take place at the level of tensions between interest groups and lines of force. The low-ranking military jobs and military education of the quilombola youth of Alcântara have a major social impact, and there are those who feel cared for and welcomed by the presence of the Aerospace Base in the region, but this is far from unanimous.

It is notorious that the city's population suffers from the lack of piped water and the lack of quality transportation between Alcântara and the capital of the state of Maranhão, São Luís (in terms of the quantity and quality of the boats and the few daily trips), both of which are the result of political indecision at municipal and state level.

7 Final Considerations and Perspectives on the Future

By recognizing Maranhão culture as a mode of subjectivation and a mode of counter-hegemonic struggle, which constitutes a way of knowing how to do things in relation to the world, this implies, at the limit, a distinct, authentic form of force, which is observed in the construction of the artistic and cultural signs of these people, with which we try to show/listen and dialogue, from another artistic and cultural epistemology.

In this way, reaching a sound, touching a sound, is an artistic and aesthetic gesture, but also a scientific and political effort, which, by understanding sound as a world-system that connects everything, places sonic-visual thinking as a means of recognizing popular knowledge and a (trans)historical social critique of the (de)territorialization of Maranhão's black and indigenous peoples. Through an insight on the sonic and popular culture of Alcântara and other places of state of Maranhão, Brazil, comprised by a live audiovisual performance, installation piece, workshop, virtual exhibition, printed zine, and this piece of writing, we aim at raising awareness for political rights of the quilombola community and the cultural and environmental balance of the region.

If a new return to Alcântara and second cycle of research becomes possible in the future we wish to incorporate in our field research the technological means to measure the amplitudes and frequencies of sounds in selected locations of the region, collecting visual audio waveforms and audio data, as well as environmental data, variations in temperature and humidity, that we know by actual experience, changes the physiological behavior of our bodies as well as that of light and sound waves. We believe there's a myriad of scientific and technical information to be acquired that could complement and expand the sensitive approach of the first cycle of this endeavor.

New collaborations will need to be established and a whole new process of research initiated, for us to keep exploring new paths to understand how the topography and climate conditions in Alcântara, Brazil, favor a unique environment for a sonic experience framed by an ecology of the body and the land, that needs to survive the politics of power.

Acknowledgements Funding from Fundação de Amparo à Pesquisa e ao Desenvolvimento Científico e Tecnológico do Maranhão—FAPEMA (Process COOPI-07877/17) and, Direção Geral das Artes—DG Artes (Application 14831). Support from ID+, Escola Superior de Media Artes e Design, Politécnico do Porto.

References

1. Ramusyo Brasil Youtube Channel, https://www.youtube.com/watch?v=0-MuZJ8FxlA, last accessed 2024/03/31.
2. Jenny, H.: Cymatics—A Study of Wave Phenomena and Vibration. Macromedia Publishing, Newmarket USA (2001).
3. Català, J.: A forma do real: introdução aos estudos visuais. Summus Editorial, São Paulo (2011).
4. Arnheim, R.: Arte e percepção visual. Uma psicologia da visão criadora. Editora Pioneira, São Paulo (1998). Catalá, J.: Film-ensayo y vanguardia. In Cerdán, J. y Torreiro, C.: Documental y vanguardia, Cátedra, Madrid, 109–157 (2005).
5. Nancy, J.: À escuta. Chão de Praça, Belo Horizonte (2014). Deleuze, G., Guattari, F. Mil platôs 2: capitalismo e esquizofrenia. 2nd edn. Editora 34, São Paulo (2011).
6. Zumthor, P.: Performance, recepção, leitura. Cosac Naify, São Paulo, 18 (2014).
7. Johnson, B.: Earshot: perspectives on sound. Routledge, New York (2023). https://doi.org/10.4324/9781003042662
8. Chion, M. La description du son dans l'analyse áudio-visuelle, Homepage, http://michelchion.com/texts, last accessed 2024/03/10. Author, F.: Contribution title. In: 9th International Proceedings on Proceedings, pp. 1–2. Publisher, Location (2010).

9. Henriques, J., D'Aquino, B. Jamaican sound systems and knowledge systems: practice-based research (PBR) in popular culture. Performance Matters, 9.1–2, 316-335 (2023).
10. Museu Contemporâneo de Arte do Maranhão—MUCA Youtube Channel, https://www.youtube.com/watch?v=P12WqxE30_k, last accessed 2024/03/30.
11. Museu Contemporâneo de Arte do Maranhão—MUCA website, https://omuca.wordpress.com/alcantaras-o-som-e-um-sistema/, last accessed 2024/03/30.
12. Catalá, J.: Film-ensayo y vanguardia. In Cerdán, J. y Torreiro, C.: Documental y vanguardia, Cátedra, Madrid, 109–157 (2005).
13. Deleuze, G., Guattari, F. Mil platôs 2: capitalismo e esquizofrenia. 2nd edn. Editora 34, São Paulo (2011).
14. Rancière, J. A partilha do sensível: estética e política. Editora 34, São Paulo (2009).
15. Flusser, V.: Comunicologia: reflexões sobre o futuro. Martins Fontes, São Paulo, 172 (2014).

Design Research and Applications

Design Based Research as a Guide to Develop Didactical Strategies Using Podcasts

Elton Rubens Vieira da Silva and Pedro Beça

Abstract This chapter presents findings from a study exploring the use of Design-Based Research (DBR) in developing a pedagogical intervention using podcasts as an assessment tool to enhance student engagement levels. The research demonstrates the effectiveness of DBR planning in constructing the intervention in professional educational institutions. Through the investigation, the research objectives were addressed, emphasizing collaborative work, direct student interaction, and the application of diverse methods such as focus groups, interviews, questionnaires, document analysis, testing, and logbooks. The study contributes to expanding understanding of DBR and underscores the relevance of professional education, an area often overlooked in academic research. Practical implications suggest that other researchers can replicate the experience and explore new media in pedagogical interventions. However, study limitations, including time constraints and a primary focus on podcasts, may have constrained the potential for innovative findings. Future research is recommended to deepen DBR application in diverse educational contexts and focus on professional education to reduce dropout rates and increase student engagement, ultimately contributing to more effective and inclusive educational practices.

Keywords Design-based research · Podcast · Vocational school

1 Introduction

Scientific research in the field of education is complex. The school dynamics are shaped by various actors working with different areas of knowledge. The methodological approach of the research is yet another variable that directly influences the

E. R. V. da Silva (✉) · P. Beça
University of Aveiro, 3810-193 Aveiro, Portugal
e-mail: elton.vieira@ua.pt

P. Beça
e-mail: pedrobeca@ua.pt

© The Author(s), under exclusive license to Springer Nature Switzerland AG 2025

D. Brandão et al. (eds.), *Perspectives on Design and Digital Communication V*, Springer Series in Design and Innovation 50, https://doi.org/10.1007/978-3-031-76156-0_16

outcome of an investigation in this context. Developing research that produces a solid theory and innovative practical results is considered a significant challenge [1].

Researchers worldwide have developed methodological alternatives in education to create theoretical knowledge from practice [2–5]. In 2003, a collective of researchers introduced the Design-Based Research (DBR) methodology intending to conduct research in the field that has practical utility to address real challenges in a classroom [6].

The DBR methodology integrates theory and practice for the development and evaluation of relevant educational interventions. DBR acknowledges the complex nature of education, seeking a profound understanding of the teaching–learning process through a variety of approaches, methods, and research instruments [6]. DBR differs from traditional research methods in its focus on iterative cycles and the development of theories on learning and instructional design [4, 7].

The methodology has gained popularity, and several studies emphasize DBR's ability to assist teachers as creators of new learning environments [8]. Junior et al. [9] conducted a study using DBR to create and evaluate a technology-enhanced learning environment in high school mathematics, with positive results in student engagement and learning. Another study by McKenney and Reeves [10] applied DBR to develop and implement a professional development program for teachers, resulting in improved instructional practices and student learning in education science.

To better understand the potential of DBR from a practical study, this article describes the methodological journey of a research project aimed at developing a pedagogical intervention, that uses podcast creation as an evaluative activity for vocational education professors to increase student engagement levels.

The initial movement is to define research questions that will guide the development of this article. Thus, the research questions are:

RQ1: What are the main advantages of using DBR in an investigation involving new digital media, especially podcasts, and pedagogical strategies?
RQ2: How do the characteristics of the educational context influence the empirical study using DBR?
RQ1: What are the selected data collection methods and instruments, and what justifications underlie these choices?

To understand the impacts of DBR in this project, we need to comprehend the context and purpose of the empirical research.

2 Theoretical Foundation for Integrating Podcasts in Education

In the early 2000s, the podcast was defined as an audio file that was available for download from an RSS feed and, when downloaded, could be listened to whenever, wherever, and however the listener wanted [11]. Today, with the evolution of technology and the media itself, this description is no longer sufficient to describe what a podcast is. Researchers such as Rime et al. [12], Harrison et al. [13], and Bontempo [14] seek to understand podcast media based on content-based characteristics: Podcasting is an auditory or audiovisual experience of diverse content and formats. Primarily spoken, it is a media made available over the internet and can be consumed wherever, whenever, and however the user desires.

Due to the versatility in content creation and consumption methods, podcasts have become an ally in the teaching and learning process. The initial studies on podcasts and education focus on the increasing use of the tool in distance education [15, 16], but the media quickly finds its way into face-to-face classes and demonstrates the potential to transform social and entertainment spaces into learning environments [17]. Riddell et al. [18] argue that students perceive listening to educational podcasts as requiring less mental energy than other forms of study, as they deliver scientific content in summarized form and a more informal tone. Students who choose to listen to educational podcasts actively seek them out and tend to listen to episodes from beginning to end [15], demonstrating greater engagement with the content. However, listening is just one way to use podcasts in education.

Because of the ease of access to technologies for developing this media, education professionals are already using podcast creation as a didactic activity. Podcasts created by students can be understood as a synthesis of learning and as a platform for communicating scientific (or non-scientific) content to audiences internal or external to academia [19]. Students who create podcasts go through a process of assimilating and reflecting on the topics discussed in class, moving from followers of instructions to producers of knowledge [20]. Harris [21] states that through podcasts, students can develop interpretation and communication skills, engaging with topics that challenge expectations and normative perceptions.

Understanding podcast as a media format with educational potentialities yet to be explored, this article describes the proposal of a research project that aims to develop a pedagogical intervention to assist teachers and students in using the creation of their podcasts as a didactic activity. The objective is to understand the impact of this intervention on the levels of student engagement with their studies. This project is proposed as part of the Multimedia in Education doctoral program at the University of Aveiro, Portugal.

The Design-Based Research (DBR) methodology has been demonstrated to be the best alternative for investigating with empirical and interventionist characteristics. The term "pedagogical intervention" is used within the DBR approach proposed by McKenney and Reeves [10]. The authors constructed their DBR model based on surveys and analyses of existing models and frameworks (Fig. 1).

This model presents the main elements of a flexible process in 3 phases: Analysis/Exploration, Design/Construction, and Evaluation/Reflection. The phases also interact with actions of implementation and dissemination of the theoretical and practical findings of the research. The three main phases of the generic DBR model are versatile, interactive, and iterative. The complete study is conceived in cycles of activities: micro, meso, and macrocycles. Each phase of DBR, due to its own characteristics, represents a micro-cycle. A meso-cycle is formed by 2 or more micro-cycles, and the entire project is understood as the macro-cycle. Although appearing in Fig. 2

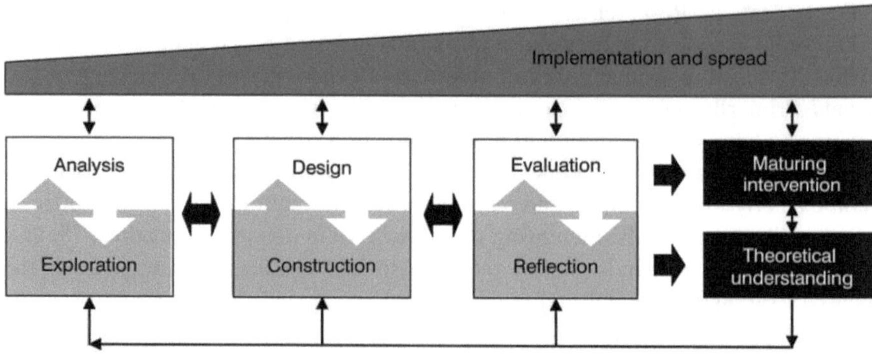

Fig. 1 Generic model for conducting DBR in education (McKenney and Reeves [10])

sequentially, cycles can occur in parallel. There is the possibility for research using DBR to have two or more macro-cycles; however, it should be contextualized with the characteristics of the research and the time available to the researchers.

At this point, the first adaptation of DBR to the research project addressed in this article is already established. The investigation is part of the construction of a doctoral thesis, which in turn has a deadline for its completion. A DBR project with numerous meso-cycles can take years to complete. Therefore, as recommended by the authors themselves, the doctoral project's investigation will execute the first three micro-cycles.

Having established the theoretical foundations and research objectives, we will seek to understand how DBR influenced the development of the investigation on the use of podcasts as a didactic activity. We will dedicate the next chapters to describing the phases of DBR and the planned and executed activities.

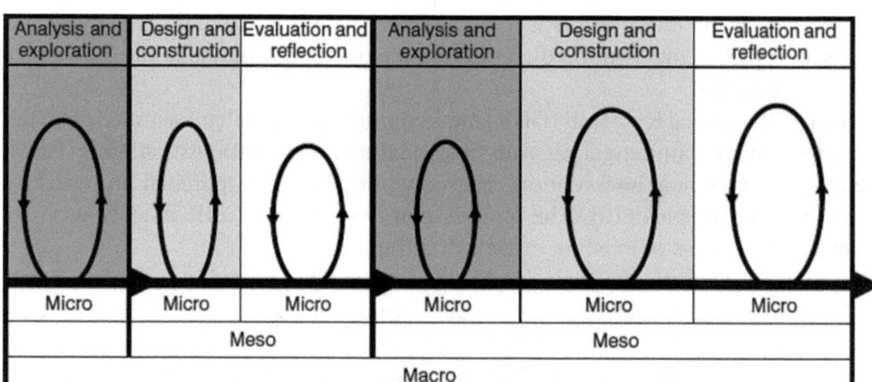

Fig. 2 Micro, meso, and macrocycles (McKenney and Reeves [10])

3 Planning and Design of Didactic Tool with Podcasts

It is common for research projects to begin with a perceived problem. The research is built to understand and develop solutions to this problem. However, in many cases, what is perceived is not the cause, but only one of the symptoms of a deeper and more complex problem. Acknowledging the value of comprehending the source of the problem, the first phase of DBR aims to immerse in the field and build cooperative relationships with stakeholders for a better understanding of the problem to be addressed [10].

The project described in this article proposes to initially use podcasts as a didactic instrument in the pursuit of student engagement. Employing DBR concepts, researchers will go to the field to understand if: (1) there is indeed a problem to be solved; (2) podcasts can address this potential problem; and (3) what is the best way to use podcasts to solve the problem.

Researchers working with DBR to construct a pedagogical intervention should be open to adjusting the research direction based on findings from the field. Following the generic DBR model, the following methodological steps have been proposed for this investigation (Fig. 3).

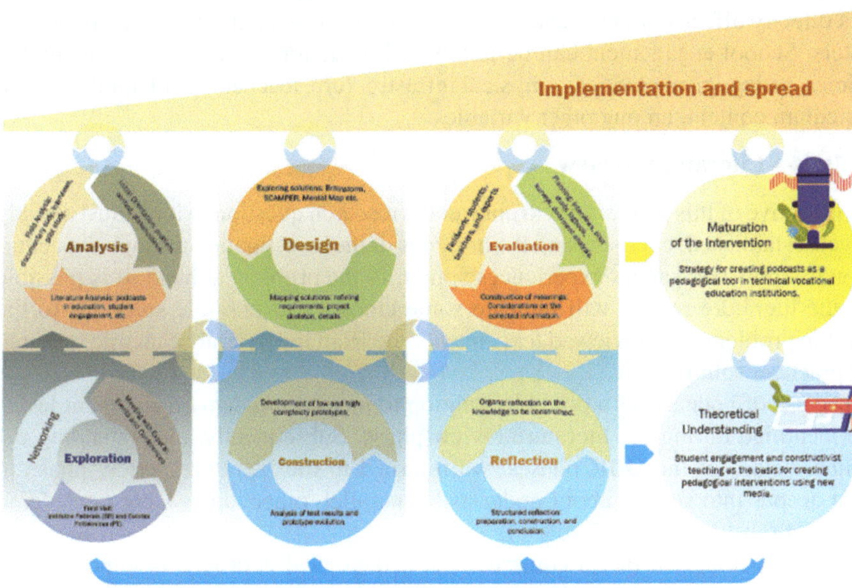

Fig. 3 DBR research steps

3.1 DBR—1st Phase: Analysis/exploration

Analysis—Initial Orientation

The idea of the research project described thus far begins with an assumption that innovative and engaging pedagogical practices are few and underutilized in the classroom. Therefore, questions are posed to guide the investigation: what alternative approaches are possible for current educational practices? How can these alternatives be established and sustained?

During the initial orientation phase, a draft of the problem definition is written. In the project described in this article, the issue that led to the development of the research was as follows: student engagement is low in vocational schools in Brazil and Portugal, which is one of the main causes of dropout rates. This phase discusses two dimensions of analysis: the problem and the context.

Problem: The dropout rate in vocational education is high, and several studies [22–24] indicate that student engagement is an important variable for understanding this problem.

Context: Although dropout rates in vocational education are recognized as a problem at various levels of education, they have characteristics due to the objective of this educational category and the target audience (authors on dropout rates). Dropout rates directly affect students, teachers, education professionals, parents, and policymakers. School engagement can be influenced by actions involving organizational policies, pedagogical practices, physical infrastructure, teachers' work methods, and curriculum content, among other variables.

Analysis—Literature Review

The objective of this phase is not to answer the research question, which must already be well-established, but to expand the horizons of the investigation through the acquisition of knowledge about experiences similar to the problem at hand. It is possible that the literature review will indicate some clues about possible solutions to the research problem. The reviewed texts may come from theoretical academic research and practical solutions.

The use of podcasts as a possible solution to increase student engagement levels was identified during the literature review phase. Subsequently, understanding the cyclical nature of the DBR phases, we returned to the literature review phase to delve deeper into studies about podcasts. In parallel, other topics were considered important for the research (Table 1).

The texts indicated that a constructivist pedagogical approach is important for greater student integration in the teaching–learning process, and consequently, an

Table 1 Literature review

Podcast	Podcast in education	Student engagement	Constructivism learning	Design-based research	Technical and vocational school

increase in student engagement levels. Thus, the constructivist approach becomes the cornerstone of the pedagogical discussion in the research project.

Analysis—Field-Based Investigations

This phase aims to identify and consolidate the definition of the problem, analyze the context, and research needs. McKenney [25] presents strategies that help advance this phase: policy synthesis, perception research, and field portrait.

Policy synthesis aims to understand the regulations governing the educational institution and how these regulations influence the teaching and learning process. Among the documents analyzed for this research project are the pedagogical strategic plan for the years 2023 and 2024, institutional protocols, curriculum of the disciplines, attendance records, grades, and the pedagogical plan of the curricular unit.

To understand the perception of all those involved in the problem, information about the context was gathered through data collection tools such as questionnaires, interviews, and focus groups. In the presented research project, information was also collected through testimonies and participation in pedagogical meetings with teachers, coordinators of curricular units, and the school board.

The field portrait was investigated through a pilot study with students from the Instituto Federal de Pernambuco (IFPE). The pilot study was developed to allow observations of the student's daily school life and how these students dealt with new challenges. It was also important to understand how teachers act in the face of a new dynamic. Based on the theoretical findings in the literature review phase, the pilot study suggested the use of podcasts as a didactic activity. The data collected during this phase are used as input for the next phases of DBR. Figure 4 presents the design of the pilot study.

The data collection process used the already validated questionnaires Utrecht Work Engagement Scale—Students [26] and Student Engagement in School—Four-Dimensional Scale [27] applied to students from educational institutions, with the active participation of teachers and other education professionals in engaging students with data collection instruments. From the analysis of the collected data, it is possible to construct a report that can be used by the doctoral research as well as by the educational institution itself in the development of pedagogical planning.

Exploration—Site Visits

The field visit phase is important for researchers to understand the problem in its real context. The Instituto Federal de Pernambuco (IFPE) and Escola Superior de Tecnologia e Gestão de Águeda (ESTGA) were the institutions chosen to be investigated. Photographs and notes are essential instruments for collecting information. This phase also aims to sensitize the actors involved in the research about the study. Researchers were allowed to participate in a pedagogical meeting at IFPE, where they could see discussions about didactic strategies and present the project to teachers, coordinators, and students participating in the meeting.

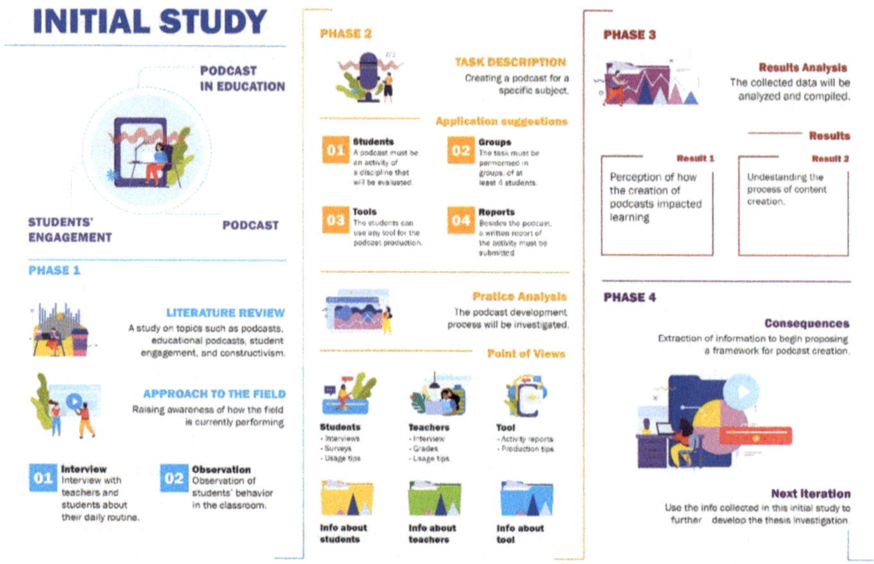

Fig. 4 Initial study design

Exploration—Meeting with Experts

Exchanging experiences with other experts in the field is a great opportunity to perceive innovative solutions to the problems faced. Participating in conferences and presenting your research to other professionals is also a good strategy to obtain qualified feedback. In the doctoral research, efforts were made to participate in all internal events related to the doctoral program. The project was also presented at important events in the field of Design and Educational Technology, as well as pedagogical events in vocational schools.

Exploration—Networking

Participating in events is a way to create a network of contacts. This network can generate opportunities for the continuation of research. It was through the researchers' network of contacts that it was possible to develop research in the classroom, contacting teachers from the selected educational institutions, namely IFPE and ESTGA.

As a result of the application of the first micro-cycle of DBR, this investigation arrives at a definition of the research problem, long-term goal, partial project requirements, and initial proposals (Table 2).

From this information, the design and construction phase of the problem begins. The organization of the information collected in this phase is important for the smooth progress of the subsequent phases.

Table 2 Problem definition, long-rage goal, partial design requirements, and initial design proposition

Problem definition	Engagement: students may achieve good grades in their assessments, but that does not determine the level of student engagement with their studies, courses, and/or educational institutions. School dropout rates increase when students do not identify with their studies and/or when students fail to see the real impact of their studies on their lives. Explanations include: – The curriculum of courses does not offer learning of theoretical and practical knowledge contextualized with the real world – Teachers' didactic strategies in the classroom do not engage the new generations of students with different demands and desires – Assessments of students' abilities are based solely on grades from traditional activities
Long-rage goal	Developing a pedagogical intervention that utilizes podcasts as a didactic activity to increase students' engagement levels with the instructional content
Partial design requirements	The pedagogical intervention should include a step-by-step guide for using podcasts as a didactic activity The intervention should be designed to be used by both teachers and students The intervention should include a technical guide for podcast development and a pedagogical guide on how to use podcasts as a didactic instrument
Initial design proposition	The step-by-step guide for podcast use can be divided into preparation, execution, and evaluation phases The intervention should have both a digital and a physical version Project conception involves a phase of proposal presentation and teacher training for tool usage

3.2 DBR—2nd Phase: Design/Construction

The process of designing and constructing a pedagogical intervention is systematic but demands creativity, application of emerging insights, and openness to chance [10]. During the project design, potential solutions are generated, mapped, prototyped, and tested. Creating a multidisciplinary team is important in the design/construction phase of a pedagogical intervention. The development team should consist primarily of stakeholders directly involved in the research. In our case, researchers, students, teachers, and other education professionals. Effective communication strategies and the use of various design tools, such as models, mock-ups, sketches, and storyboards, can help create an environment that stimulates creative thinking.

Following the dynamics of DBR, this phase is cyclical, interactive, and iterative. In other words, it can occur in parallel with other phases and evolve through testing and discarding alternatives.

Design—Exploring Solutions

The definition of the problem and the long-term objective describes the origins of the challenge. The requirements and initial propositions give us ideas on how to approach the challenge. In this phase, ideas are generated, considered, and analyzed.

Table 3 Creativity techniques

Idea generation	Lateral thinking, SCAMPER
Idea consideration	Mental map, strengths, and weakness
Idea checking	5 Whys, Cartoon story boards

According to Vieira [28], there are more than 300 techniques for generating alternatives that can be explored in various projects. The most common, and the basis for several others, is brainstorming. There are creativity techniques with different objectives; some aim to generate the greatest possible number of alternatives, others aim to map already generated alternatives, and others aim to select those with the greatest potential for development. Reinforcing the importance of teamwork, most alternative generation techniques are designed to be executed in groups.

For our project, traditional techniques for generating alternatives were used (Table 3).

Design—Mapping Solutions

From the generated alternatives and the cyclical analysis of project requirements and propositions, exercises of convergent thinking are employed. To identify which alternatives are worth the effort to be developed, information is gathered on what can be done and how the idea can be developed.

Creating a skeleton of the research project described in this article is important because it helps identify its main needs. McKenney and Reeves [10] recommend creating a skeleton that considers: materials/resources; activities/processes; and participation/implementation (Table 4).

The skeleton indicates the project scope and defines the preliminary terms of objectives, people, time, and budget. This tool is created to be flexible and subject to rewriting whenever necessary.

Once the skeleton is developed, it is possible to specify the aspects of the entire intervention. During this phase, models can be developed to help identify the procedural specifications necessary for the intervention's development.

Table 4 Main needs

Design task	Podcast as a didactic activity
Materials/resources	Worksheets Guidebook/deck Digital tutorials
Activities/processes	Teacher meetings In and out of class activities Workshops
Participation/implementation	Individuals and teams of teachers Teams of students Administrators

Table 5 Prototype characteristics

Product component (direct)	Artifact construction with information on how to develop a podcast
Process component (indirect)	Guide for teachers to outline plans and use new pedagogical tools in their classes

Construction—Prototype Creation

Prototypes are tools for iterative and cyclical refinement, built to assist developers in making the best decisions. Widely used in the fields of engineering and design, prototypes, when used in other areas, can be described as unfinished versions of the solution.

In the doctoral project, due to the nature of the defined pedagogical intervention, the prototypes had the following development nature (Table 5).

The prototypes developed in this phase were built with the collaboration of teachers, students, and other education professionals involved in the project. The maturity of the prototype evolved as test cycles occurred, ranging from low-complexity prototypes using paper mock-ups of some functions to high-complexity prototypes that were functional and included all components of the intervention.

Construction—Prototype Review

Prototypes are built to be tested. Feedback from users is collected and analyzed. Researchers must determine whether the data is sufficient to start developing the intervention or if the prototype needs to evolve for another round of testing. During this phase, the requirements, skeleton, and detailed project specifications are also analyzed.

The information collected from the testing rounds should be organized and critically analyzed. Redesigning the intervention proposal is a natural consequence of the interactive and iterative cycles of prototype use. At the end of this phase, the pedagogical intervention was functional and ready to be tested in real environments without the control of the development team.

3.3 3rd Phase: Evaluation/Reflection

Evaluation—Planning

The term "evaluation" is used in this context when there are empirical tests of the intervention that have been mapped and built. McKenney and Reeves [10] argue that an intervention developed through DBR should undergo three stages of empirical testing (alpha, beta, and gamma). Each of these stages generated data that was used for the evolution of the project. Therefore, this intervention was evaluated following the following steps (Table 6).

Table 6 Evaluation steps

Establish the focus	The doctoral research has two focal points of analysis: the pedagogical intervention that will assist teachers and students in using podcasts as an assessment method, and the impacts on the level of engagement in vocational students when this intervention is utilized
Frame guiding questions	Questions in the alpha test: how well-designed is the pedagogical intervention using podcast creation? What changes can be made to make podcast creation clearer for students? Questions in the beta test: How relevant is the pedagogical intervention in the use of podcasts as an assessment method for users? What are the characteristics of the intervention that are most effective? What intentional and unintentional processes are generated by the intervention? Questions in the gamma test: did the pedagogical intervention impact the level of engagement/involvement of vocational students? What is the long-term impact of using the pedagogical intervention? What are the characteristics of a classroom that may interfere with the successful use of the intervention?
Select basis strategies and determine specific methods	Utilize data collection instruments such as focus groups, interviews/ questionnaires, documentary analysis, and logbooks
Draft and revise a planning document	All methodological steps will be documented, from the planning process of intervention construction, through the testing phase, and ending in the dissemination of results
Choose participants	Project participants will be teachers, students, and other education professionals in vocational education in Brazil and Portugal
Collect and analyze the data	Data collection will be carried out using the instruments presented. Qualitative and quantitative data will be generated. The data will be critically interpreted to design the conclusion of the study
Report the study	The research will be reported based on the development of the doctoral thesis. Furthermore, the knowledge generated by the research will be transformed into articles and book chapters. The pedagogical intervention will also be made available to the public

Evaluation—Fieldwork

Drawing upon the studies by Plomp [29] and based on the research by Mafumiko [30], the following actors have been proposed for the development of field investigation (Table 7).

Organic Reflection

The reflection phase is important for aligning the results of empirical research, based on the collected data, with the production of a new theoretical understanding of the context. The processes of reflection are guided by rational thinking; however, in educational research, creativity is an important characteristic in the process of reflecting on the obtained results.

Table 7 Research actors

Students from technical and vocational education institutions in Portugal	2 classes
Students from technical and vocational education institutions in Brazil	2 classes
Teachers from technical and vocational education institutions in Portugal	2 professors
Teachers from technical and vocational education institutions in Brazil	2 professors
Podcast producers in Portugal	5 producers
Podcast producers in Brazil	5 producers

Table 8 Prototype characteristics

Preparation	Compile the main facts/observations gathered during the classroom investigation, in addition to participation in pedagogical meetings, considering empirical and theoretical aspects
Image forming	Select and synthesize the most relevant aspects for the investigation
Conclusion drawing	Use the results of the last two steps to build the final considerations on the research and establish future activities

Organic reflection occurs outside of working hours and is generally promoted for cases where the research schedule is tight. McKenney and Reeves [10] point out that organic reflection can be exercised during breaks in research work, interacting with people who have different viewpoints, or working on parallel projects. All these strategies aim to reduce the cognitive load on researchers and promote the formulation of new ideas based on contact with other realities.

Structured Reflection

Structured reflection is part of the knowledge construction process based on the information gathered during evaluation activities. Among the reflection activities are (Table 8).

A single cycle of evaluation and reflection can lead to new discoveries, hypotheses, and conjectures that aid in the theoretical construction of knowledge.

3.4 DBR—Implementation/Spread

Implementation

In parallel with the mesocycle defined in DBR, forms of implementation in the field and dissemination of the pedagogical intervention are investigated. These phases aim to analyze and build relevance for the project within the academic/school community.

The implementation stage seeks to understand the actions necessary for the pedagogical intervention to be put into practice. For the pedagogical intervention to be implemented in a real environment, teachers and education professionals must understand the didactic potential of the intervention and undergo training to guide the use of podcasts as an assessment tool. Supporting materials in text and audiovisual formats were also developed.

Creating means for the use of the pedagogical intervention to become sustainable and recurrent is the result of a well-planned educational process.

Spread

Developing impactful interventions is important, but if the intervention is not used by the target audience, no matter how innovative and revolutionary the idea is, the impact of the idea in the classroom becomes insignificant. McKenney and Reeves [10] state that the propagation process occurs in the form of dissemination and diffusion. Dissemination makes information about the intervention accessible to the public through courses, workshops, publications, and other media. Diffusion occurs when the target audience, through interactions with others or pedagogical policies, begins to spread the impacts of using the pedagogical intervention.

It is part of the objective of this project to integrate the pedagogical intervention into the pedagogical strategies of educational institutions. Additionally, workshops were conducted with teachers for presentation and initial monitoring of the application process of the intervention in the classroom.

4 Reflections on DBR and the Construction of a Pedagogical Intervention Using Podcasts

Despite DBR presenting well-defined methodological steps, your interactive and iterative nature makes it a versatile methodology that can be easily adapted to the research context. During DBR, data are produced that serve as a basis for constructing a pedagogical theoretical framework and practical didactic interventions.

Building a relevant didactic intervention that focuses on podcasts, would indeed require a methodology that could adapt to the constant evolution of new media. The active participation of stakeholders in the intervention is another important characteristic of the DBR process. The Design and Construction phase proposes collaborative construction among researchers, teachers, students, and other education professionals. In this way, different perspectives on the use of podcasts, whether only as consumers or as content producers, are considered. From this information, it is possible to develop an intervention that is valuable, easy to use, compatible with the context of the curriculum/institution, and tolerant of the everyday challenges of school life. These are strategic advantages that aid the research development process and help answer the RQ1 proposed in this article.

Social interaction in the pedagogical intervention development process is a critical point of the DBR methodology. The needs of the research team and stakeholders must be aligned. Teachers and education professionals are actors who should be involved from the beginning, as they need to believe in the positive impact of the intervention before it is put into practice. Podcasting is already a popular medium, but it should be introduced to this audience based on its educational potential. Once convinced, collaborative work becomes easier for the development of the pedagogical intervention.

However, students have another dynamic. They are the most important actors in the research, the main ones affected by the intervention. It is crucial that they can contribute to knowledge construction during the research. In our investigation, students are part of higher education courses in vocational training. Investigating courses in higher education makes this interaction more direct and conscious on the part of the students. Bringing a study using a new medium is a strategy to arouse curiosity and involvement among teachers.

Vocational education is guided by the teaching of technical practice, so the intervention must be developed as part of the students' technical learning. The project thus becomes more challenging due to the technical characteristics of podcasts. Through the DBR phases and the constant presence in the field required in the intervention construction methodology, this challenge is faced collectively by all actors involved. Time in the field is guided by the workload and duration of the curriculum units under investigation. DBR, due to the cyclical nature of micro cycles, can efficiently extract relevant data for research in the four-month blocks of classes per semester of the curriculum units.

These characteristics of vocational education influence the planning of research using DBR, and in this scenario, it was possible to answer the second research question of this article.

With DBR, it is preferable to develop qualitative-based research, but one that also has quantifiable data. The main difference from other research methodologies is that in DBR, these data are extracted to construct a practical and applicable project in real classrooms. Adapting to the context of the pedagogical intervention project using podcasts, the following data collection tools were selected (Table 9).

Table 9 Data collection tools

Focus group	After teachers and students used the developed intervention, they were invited to participate in a group discussion about the tool's characteristics. The discussion was recorded and analyzed
Interviews/ surveys	Teachers and students were interviewed or responded to questionnaires to collect their impressions about the developed intervention and how it influenced student engagement
Document analysis	Documents that recorded the level of student engagement after using the intervention were analyzed. Examples included attendance logs and grades
Tests	Teachers and students used the intervention in an introductory manner. The objective was to sensitize the actors to the tool and collect initial impressions
Logbook	Students were asked to report their experiences using the developed intervention in diary form

All data collection tools are supported by the DBR methodology and contribute to the construction of meaning in field investigation. The dynamics of a classroom are difficult to investigate, which is why different data collection techniques are necessary, analyzing the diverse perspectives of the actors both inside and outside the classroom.

These reflections on data collection tools directly address RQ3 and make us more aware of the project's complexity.

The intervention developed using DBR seeks to create a solution that will be actively used in classrooms, and adaptable to different curricular units, courses, or vocational education institutions. The educational context is surrounded by a bureaucratic system of action already defined, especially when we consider vocational education as defined by the institutions under investigation, namely IFPE, and ESTGA. Research and subsequently, pedagogical intervention must find a balance with this educational system to achieve its goals. Choosing the podcast as the focus of the intervention is a way to limit the possible variables impacted by pedagogical intervention, increasing the possibility of carrying out an effective intervention and making the project feasible within the time and space available for research.

Reducing challenges by focusing on the podcast is supported by the DBR methodology and advised in the process of constructing a doctoral thesis.

5 Conclusion

This article demonstrated the planning of a Design-Based Research (DBR) for the construction of an innovative pedagogical intervention, focusing on the use of podcasts as a teaching tool. The framework developed by McKenney and Reeves [10] employs well-structured phases, emphasizing practical results based on solid theoretical knowledge. The adaptation of the DBR methodology for studies in vocational education institutions was evidenced, highlighting the meticulous description of the necessary steps and justification for the choices made during the research development.

The results of this study satisfactorily addressed the objectives proposed in the construction of this article. It demonstrated the potential of collaborative work in building a pedagogical intervention, the methodological flexibility of DBR in developing solutions for problems in vocational education institutions, the direct and conscious interaction of students in the construction of a tool they will use themselves, and the challenge of using podcasts as an ally to technical learning. The use of different data collection methods, such as focus groups, interviews/questionnaires, document analysis, testing, and logbooks, is part of the necessary steps for the DBR application and provides a broader view of the research context.

Contribution to the field: DBR is a relatively new methodology, and the description of its use in diverse contexts strengthens the theoretical framework of the methodology. Furthermore, vocational education is often neglected in research, and along with the growing relevance of podcasts in education, the importance of exploring and describing research that uses new media, such as podcasts, in the teaching and learning process in vocational education institutions is highlighted.

The practical implications of this study can be considered relevant considering the description of this project. Other researchers can replicate the experience of building a pedagogical intervention using new media, based on the actions and justification of the choices made during the investigation.

This research is limited by the time imposed to produce the doctoral thesis, i.e., it is not possible to carry out successive macrocycles to test the pedagogical intervention developed. Focusing on the use of podcasts as the main tool in building the pedagogical intervention may lead to the loss of opportunities for unexpected and innovative solutions. However, knowing the innovation potential of podcasts themselves, it is a risk worth taking.

Therefore, it is suggested that future studies deepen the use of DBR in various contexts and explore the potential of new media in vocational education. Developing projects that use student preferences can generate relevant and impactful results for educational practice, aiming to improve engagement and learning in the classroom.

This study highlights the importance of exploring new methodological and technological approaches in educational research, emphasizing the need for studies that bring tangible benefits to the school environment and student education.

References

1. Phillips, D. C., Dolle, J. R. From Plato to Brown and beyond: Theory, practice, and the promise of design experiments. In L. Verschaffel, F. Dochy, M. Boekaerts & S. Vosniadou (Eds.), Instructional psychology: Past, present and future trends. Sixteen essays in honour of Erik De Corte (pp. 277–292). Oxford, UK: Elsevier Science Ltd. (2006).
2. Brown, A. L. Design experiments: Theoretical and methodological challenges in creating complex interventions in classroom settings. Journal of the Learning Sciences, 2(2), 141–178. (1992).
3. Lagemann, E. C. An elusive science: The troubling history of education research. Chicago, IL: University of Chicago Press. (2002).
4. García-González JR, Sánchez-Sánchez PA. Theoretical design of research: Methodological instructions for the development of scientific research proposals and projects. Inf Tecnol.; 31(6):159–170. (2021).
5. Aguirre, J. S., & López, M. L. El diseño como motor de productividad. Revista 180, (37). (2016).
6. Design-Based Research Collective. Design-based research: An emerging paradigm for educational inquiry. Educational Researcher, 32(1), 5–8. (2003).
7. Bakker, A. Design research in education: A practical guide for early career researchers. Routledge. (2018).
8. Tinoca, L., Piedade, J., Santos, S., Pedro, A., & Gomes, S. Design-based research in the educational field: a systematic literature review. Education Sciences, 12(6), 410. (2022).
9. Junior, V. F., Ceci, F., Woszezenki, C. R., & Gonçalves, A. Design Science Research Methodology Enquanto Estratégia Metodológica para a Pesquisa Tecnológica. Revistas Espacios 38 (6), 25. (2017).
10. McKenney, S., & Reeves, T. Conducting educational design research. Routledge. (2018).

11. Berry, R. Will the iPod Kill the Radio Star? Profiling Podcasting as Radio. Convergence: The International Journal of Research into New Media Technologies, 12(2), 143–162. https://doi.org/10.1177/1354856506066522. (2006).
12. Rime, J., Pike, C., & Collins, T. What is a podcast? Considering innovations in podcasting through the six-tensions framework. Convergence: The International Journal of Research into New Media Technologies, 28(5), 1260–1282. https://doi.org/10.1177/13548565221104444. (2022).
13. Harrison, J., Archer-Boyd, A. W., Francombe, J., Pike, C., & Murphy, D. T. The relationship between environmental context and attentional engagement in podcast listening experiences. Frontiers in Psychology, 13. https://doi.org/10.3389/fpsyg.2022.1074320. (2023).
14. Bontempo, R. Podcast Descomplicado: Crie podcasts impossíveis de serem ignorados (2nd ed., Vol. 1). Bicho de Goiaba. (2020).
15. Drew, C. Educational podcasts: A genre analysis. E-Learning and Digital Media, 14(4), 201–211. https://doi.org/10.1177/2042753017736177. (2017).
16. Liu, L., Huguet, M.-P., & Haley, T. Work in progress - SAGES: Podcast, wikis and emerging technologies in the engineering classroom. 2008 38th Annual Frontiers in Education Conference, S3J-13–S3J-14. https://doi.org/10.1109/FIE.2008.4720614. (2008).
17. Ng'ambi, D., & Lombe, A. Using Podcasting to Facilitate Student Learning: A Constructivist Perspective. Journal of Educational Technology & Society, 15(4), 181–192. (2012).
18. Riddell, J., Robins, L., Brown, A., Sherbino, J., Lin, M., & Ilgen, J. S. Independent and Interwoven. Academic Medicine, 95(1), 89–96. https://doi.org/10.1097/ACM.0000000000002984. (2020).
19. Moore, T. Pedagogy, Podcasts, and Politics: What Role Does Podcasting Have in Planning Education? Journal of Planning Education and Research, 0739456X2211063. https://doi.org/10.1177/0739456X221106327. (2022).
20. Kendall, R. Podcasting and Pedagogy (pp. 41–57). https://doi.org/10.4018/978-1-4666-4333-8.ch003. (2014).
21. Harris, J. Podcast Talk and Public Sociology: Teaching Critical Race Discourse Participation through Podcast Production. About Campus: Enriching the Student Learning Experience, 24(3), 16–20. https://doi.org/10.1177/1086482219880845. (2019).
22. Hong, J. C., Zhang, H. L., Ye, J. H., & Ye, J. N. The effects of academic self-efficacy on vocational students behavioral engagement at school and at firm internships: A model of engagement-value of achievement motivation. Education Sciences, 11(8), 387. (2021).
23. Keijzer, R., van Schooten, E., van der Rijst, R., & Admiraal, W. Individual characteristics of students in vocational education moderating the relationship between school engagement and vocational identity. European Journal of Psychology of Education, 37(4), 1255–1283. (2022).
24. Nouwen, W., & Clycq, N. Assessing the added value of the self-system model of motivational development in explaining school engagement among students at risk of early leaving from education and training. European Journal of Psychology of Education, 36, 243–261. (2021).
25. McKenney, S. Computer based support for science education materials developers in Africa: Exploring potentials. University of Twente, Enschede, The Netherlands. Retrieved from http://doc.utwente.nl/75705/ Author, F.: Article title. Journal 2(5), 99–110 (2016).
26. Schaufeli, W. B. & A. B. Bakker. UWES: Utrecht Work Engagement Scale. Preliminary Manual. OccupationalHealth Psychology Unit: Utrecht University, The Netherlands. (2003).
27. Veiga, F. H. Assessing student Engagement in School: Development and validation of a four-dimensional scale. Procedia-Social and Behavioral Sciences, 217, 813–819. (2016).
28. Vieira, E. R. Construçao do guia de padroes de criatividade para desenvolvedores de software. In Congresso Brasileiro de Pesquisa e Desenvolvimento em Design (Vol. 11, pp. 3154–3164). (2014).
29. Plomp, T. Educational Design Research: an Introduction. In Educational design research - Part A: an Introduction (pp. 10–51). Enschede, the Netherlands: SLO. (2013).
30. Mafumiko, F. S. M. Micro-scale experimentation as a catalyst for improving the chemistry curriculum in Tanzania, University of Twente, Enschede, (2006).

Antecedents of Loyalty in Online Retail Stores in Customer Service

Pedro Manuel do Espírito Santo, Patrícia Azinheira Cardoso, and Alzira Maria Ascensão Marques

Abstract Competition with retailers has intensified, leading organisations to look for new strategies to defend their reasonable improvement in products and services. The quality of customer service is seen as a crucial role for companies due to its impact on the link with consumers, making it important to analyze the factors that influence and the results of customer service quality. Thus, this investigation pointed to the customization of customer service and the advertising of customer service as factors that precede the quality of customer service. Satisfaction, trust and loyalty were identified as outcomes of customer service quality. The research, with a sample of 176 consumers from online electronics shops, used the PLS-PM (structural equations modeling) methodology to test the hypotheses. It was found that the customer service quality helps online satisfaction and online trust, leading to consumer loyalty to the online shop. In addition, it is recommended that brands personalize the service enabling to buyer first choice and invest in advertising the service.

Keywords Loyalty · Customer service · Online satisfaction · Online trust · Retail stores

1 Introduction

In recent years, researchers have dedicated themselves to studying service quality in different socio-demographic contexts and sectors of activity, such as retail, clothing brands, tourism, among others [1, 2].

P. M. do Espírito Santo (✉) · A. M. A. Marques
Centre of Applied Research in Management and Economics (CARME), Polytechnic University of Leiria, Campus 2 - Morro do Lena, Alto do Vieiro, Apt 4163, 2411-901 Leiria, Portugal
e-mail: pedro.m.santo@ipleiria.pt

A. M. A. Marques
e-mail: alzira.marques@ipleiria.pt

P. A. Cardoso
Polytechnic University of Coimbra – ESEC, Rua Dom João III, 3030-329 Coimbra, Portugal
e-mail: pmcardoso@esec.pt

© The Author(s), under exclusive license to Springer Nature Switzerland AG 2025
D. Brandão et al. (eds.), *Perspectives on Design and Digital Communication V*, Springer Series in Design and Innovation 50, https://doi.org/10.1007/978-3-031-76156-0_17

However, in the retail sector it is crucial to continually focus on the quality of service offered to satisfy customer needs [3]. Blut [3] explains that to offer superior service quality, it is crucial to understand how customers perceive and evaluate the service. The literature therefore focuses on analysing the various variables associated with quality as a way of boosting business and finding solutions to offer each customer a better online shopping experience [3].

According to [4] consumer retention is the key to long-term sustainable relationships. This relationship is maintained through three types of communication:

- Interactive—One-way messages from the organization to the consumer, of an informative nature;
- Communicational—Bidirectional messages, informing and being informed;
- Dialogue—Two-way messages between consumers and organizations.

In this context, consumers are becoming increasingly aware and demanding when it comes to providing their personal information to organisations, which is intensifying the competition between online retail companies to win over these consumers. This scenario stems from organisations' interest in developing products and services that meet consumers' needs, moving towards more personalised marketing in their offer, with the aim of retaining and building loyalty [5, 6]. Therefore, it's crucial to examine service quality in retail companies and how it affects customer satisfaction and loyalty. Perceptions and opinions about products and/or services, with/among consumers can be reached through social networks, virtual communities (forums), chat rooms (twitch) and text messages (email and/or sms). In the case of adapting customer service, this arises from an external process, where consumers assess how well the organisation relates to them and/or how well it can meet their needs [7].

Organisations need to adapt to collecting, collecting and publishing facts from buyers, adapting their offerings to their needs and changing the organisational culture and focus on consumer relations [8]. It is therefore vital for any company to continue offering quality customer service to increase sales, appeal and remember consumers, guaranteeing their satisfaction, trust and loyalty [9, 10].

Nowadays, new ways of reaching consumers are needed. In recent years, organizations have aimed to gather more data about their customers and potential customers to better define and comprehend their profiles or consumer types, intending to provide a tailored service [11]. Anshari et al. [12] suggests that new trends in marketing allow for adapted communication to expand the better customer support. The personalisation of help and communication is essential to customer relations.

Therefore, comprehending the significance of customer service quality within the organization sphere becomes crucial to enhance organizations' competitiveness in attracting their clientele [13]. This research endeavors to uncover insights regarding the impact of support service quality on the bond between consumers and organizations, while also scrutinizing personalization as a key element of support customer service quality.

2 Literature Review

2.1 Customer Service

Associations are decided to offer customers more competitive procedures [7]. The quality of a benefit is made conceivable by the advancement of the collection and examination of customer information, such as their individual interface, encounters and other data around their day by day lives, through the organisation's stages of choice [7].

The quality of service provided by the organisation should be implemented continuously, as it aims to satisfy consumers. Ensuring the quality of the process as a whole, in terms of its production and delivery. In this sense, quality customer service has turn into a crucial deal for organisations [13], reflecting the consumer's personal judgement of service and interaction with a website and the extent to which the service meets their needs [14, 15].

Consumers are not just in pursuit of high-quality products; they also demand superior services. Concurrently, organizations are dedicated to providing more valuable and competitive offerings to consumers [7]. Enhancing service quality has become feasible through advanced methodologies for collecting and analyzing consumer data, encompassing personal interests, experiences, and additional facets of their everyday lives.

Barbosa and Minciotti [16] stated that it is essential to offer excellence in service, because if there is a failure in the combination of consumer expectations and needs, this will lead to dissatisfaction with a given product and/or service; leading organisations to look at and think about service quality through a holistic view, under its performance, under the emotion experienced and under the affective response achieved, in order to build customer loyalty [16].

2.2 Advertising Messages and Customization of Service

Nowadays, marketing communications are undoubtedly a very important part of organisations, as their success or failure will depend on how they are transmitted and implemented.

Barreto [8] comment that promoting messages are portion of a promoting handle, caught on as a social prepare, overseeing the trade of data and boosts between an association and its different gatherings of people. This handle points to advance both the association and the shopper, with the shopper being the target of all the organisation's promoting endeavors.

Therefore, organisations' advertising messages are going through a new phase in which marketing professionals are being forced out of their comfort zone, having to review and recreate new concepts, rethink the organisation's true values and develop new methodologies for implementing strategy [7].

In this context, when a consumer obtains relevant information about a product and/or service in an advertisement, they will be more satisfied and more likely to buy that product and/or service. It is therefore possible to conclude that advertising has a positive and beneficial impact, creating behavioural intentions such as purchasing, creating loyalty and word-of-mouth [13].

To increase the effectiveness of advertising messages, many organisations resort to personalising advertising messages [17]. This personalisation is done through marketing mix and the collection of information about consumers [18]. According to Arora et al. [18], the personalisation of marketing communications is correlated to the distinctive preferences of each consumer.

All advertising messages must be multichannel and controlled, because in order to build long-term and profitable relationships, we must invest in various advertising channels. An example of this is the use of personalised messages, sent to a specific target audience using different channels, in order to broaden contacts with the organisation. There should therefore be a certain amount of use of certain communication channels (and not all of them) and the alignment of these channels with consumer preferences and the organization's target. Only then will there be a positive response from consumers to the messages sent [19].

Many organisations personalise their advertising messages [17], using marketing strategies and gathering data from clients and consumers [18]. This personalisation is tailored to the person choices, and it is believed [20] that organisations can use several channels to transmit their messages, thus demonstrating their commitment to customer relations.

Thus, the personalisation of marketing messages aims to gain value for the buyer, thereby influencing their perception of the quality of services [21, 22]. Thus, this investigation examine the next hypothesis:

H1: The personalisation of marketing messages has a positive effect on customer service.

2.3 *Customer Service Customization*

Confronted with forceful competition and key openings in quality of benefit, associations are challenged to discover the foremost viable technique to improve their client benefit additionally to convey esteem that separates themselves from other suppliers of the same benefit [13].

The authors Roy et al. [23] state that customer service adaptation is defined by the time and effort saved by consumers: when looking for the service, while using the service and after-sales service (if any). According to Roberts et al. [24], client benefit adjustment is an adjustment that tends to progress the consumer's seen relationship with the association, driving them to talk well of it and prescribe it to their companions and family.

Some authors [23] define the personalisation of customer service as saving consumers time and effort: in the search for the service, during the use of the service and after-sales (if any). Agreeing to Roberts et al. [24], personalised client benefit is an adjustment that tends to progress the consumer's discernment of their relationship with the association, driving them to talk well of it and prescribe it to companions and family. In this setting, we consider it critical to allot a profile to each buyer, taking into consideration their needs.

The implementation of a good customer service fit is perceived by the consumer as a degree of fairness in the consumer-organisation relationship, i.e. consumers believe that the organisation has anticipated their needs correctly and treated them fairly [23]. This leads consumers to feel that the relationship they have with the organisation is worth the time spent and, most importantly, they know that their investments were not unreasonable [23].

Thus, if the customer service strategy is well implemented, it will reduce the organisation's costs, while creating attractive experiences for the consumer and keeping them [13].

Based on these insights, we propose the following hypothesis:

H2: Personalised client benefit incorporates a positive affect on client benefit quality.

2.4 Online Satisfaction

According to Song et al. [25], the conceptualisation of satisfaction has changed in recent years. Strong competition and rapid development in different sectors has created a need for organisations to expand and defend their market share by reaching the largest number of consumers. To achieve this goal, organisations need to create consumer satisfaction [26].

Satisfying relationships over the long term is the goal of any organisation that wants to stay in business [27]. Consumer satisfaction is a priority in the growth of any organisation, and satisfaction can appear after several opinions and/or beliefs [28]. Consequently, every organization must strive for customer satisfaction to ensure its survival, aligning its business and marketing endeavors accordingly.

In marketing-orientated businesses, achieving consumer satisfaction is a primary goal, which can stem from various perceptions and expectations [29]. Organisations must therefore prioritise consumer satisfaction by targeting their business and marketing strategies to succeed.

In this context, satisfaction is important for perpetuating the retail business [26], as satisfaction is the collection of an arrangement of encounters with the item and benefit of a specific association, coming about from the consumer-organisation association over time. Buyer satisfaction is characterised by sentiments of satisfaction or disappointment that emerge when comparing the genuine execution of a acquired item with already set up desires [30].

According to the authors Peña and Reis [31], the most conscientious organisations are those that provide a quality service and are concerned with consumer satisfaction, because they know that in this way they will survive, grow and generate profit in the market in which they operate. In this way, satisfaction is fundamental to business success [26]. It is the result of accumulated experiences with a product or service provided by an organisation, built up through the continuous relationship between the consumer and the organisation over time.

Organisations that provide greater value to their consumers tend to satisfy them and exceed their expectations, establishing themselves as more reliable in the eyes of their customers [4, 13].

Quality customer service makes it easier to achieve customer satisfaction [19]. An organisation that consistently and incrementally improves the quality of its services over the long term [24] is likely to increase customer satisfaction.

Thus, the following hypothesis will be examined:

H3: The quality of service has a positive affect on consumer satisfaction.

2.5 *Online Trust*

These days, getting a consumer to fully trust an organisation becomes a very complicated task, as we have witnessed a large number of top organisations committing extremely serious transgressions.

Thus, the great challenge for companies will be to restore the trust of their consumers by standing out for their differences and sharing their dreams at the same time [30].

Trust involves a feeling of security, influenced by an organisation's positive and supportive actions, which motivate and guide individual consumer behaviour [25]. Agustin and Singh [32] states that online trust can be defined as the consumer's belief in the equilibrium between the perceived advantages and drawbacks of maintaining a relationship with the organization.

An organisation is considered trustworthy when it consistently delivers on its ability of value to its consumers [33]. This trust is cultivated through various aspects, including product development, production methods, advertising strategies, sales processes, in-store services, and after-sales support. Thus, we intend to explore the following:

H4: The quality of service positively influences trust.
H5: Satisfaction positively affects trust.

2.6 *Loyalty*

Consumers have altered their interaction dynamics with brands and organizations. Online consumer loyalty is influenced by a multitude of factors, such as consumer satisfaction and the depth of the relationship with the organization [34].

In markets characterized by intense competition, volatility, and diminishing product differentiation factors, the primary aim of marketing strategies is to cultivate and sustain consumer loyalty [35], this entails fostering enduring relationships with consumers, leading to the establishment of a resilient organization or a resilient brand [30].

The authors Mabkhot and Shaari [35] comment that acquiring new consumers can become quite costly for organisations, so consumer loyalty is the way forward. The authors also add that brand loyalty is the pillar for profitable and lasting growth, as the awareness acquired over time leads to brand recognition, increased sales and higher profit margins [36]. It should be emphasised that a consumer who is loyal to a particular brand, regardless of any situation, will not be swayed by an opposing marketing strategy [35].

Loyal consumers are those who continue to buy for a number of personal reasons, affordability, accessibility and location, and may also show affection for the organisation/brand [25].

The essential function of marketing strategies is to cultivate and preserve consumer loyalty, particularly in highly competitive market environments where product differentiation is becoming increasingly uncertain and reduced [35]. The focus is on forming lasting relationships with consumers, contributing to the strength of organisations and brands [25].

The approach of consumers interaction with brands and organisations has evolved. Several elements influence consumer loyalty in the online environment, including consumer online satisfaction, online trust and the degree of involvement with the organisation [6].

In this way, satisfaction is both a determining factor and a result of loyalty. Trust also plays a significant role in loyalty, as Ercis et al. [26] indicates that it forms a crucial link in the relationship between organisation and consumer, encompassing the products and/or services offered and intense engagement. On this point of view, this research sets out to analyse the following:

H6: Online Satisfaction influences positively online loyalty.
H7: Online Trust influences positively online loyalty.

3 Methodology

In arrange to realize the investigate destinations and assess the proposed demonstrate, a quantitative study was carried out within the setting of online retail. In this way, in arrange to test the proposed inquire about speculations inside a hypothetical system, a quantitative technique was selected via a cross-sectional study, as quantitative methods offer a more transparent and objective analysis of information, especially for testing research models and hypotheses. Data were gathered through a self-administered online survey, and participants were recruited via social media platforms.

Information collection was established on an internet survey planned particularly for this reason, to get a bigger test. A survey was in this manner drawn up on the Google Shapes stage, with things adjusted from other thinks about. Thus, for the customization of client benefit publicizing, we adjusted 3 things from Shanahan et al. [37], for customized support service, we employed the three items outlined by Bock et al. [38]. In assessing customer service quality, we utilized the four items from Shanahan et al. [37]. Furthermore, for trust evaluation, we referred to the five items from Song et al. [25] while for satisfaction and loyalty measurement, we adopted the three items each from the same study.

3.1 *Description of Sample*

The sample comprised 176 users and consumers from specialized online retail shops in Portugal. Demographic analysis revealed that 56.3% of the sample consisted of female consumers, with the majority being under the age of 30 (61.4% of cases). Most of respondents had secondary education (48.9%) and higher education (49.4%).

4 Results

Previously, multicollinearity was assessed by analysing the VIF coefficient and it was found that the VIF value is less than 5 and does not bias the results obtained [39]. The SMARTPLS software version 3 was used to validate and test the model proposed in this study. The investigation employing estimation is divided into two stages: examining the measurement model and scrutinizing the structural model.

4.1 *Structural Equation Measurement Model*

The primary stage of the investigation utilizing PLS is the investigation of the estimation show, which looks for to evaluate the capacity of the things to degree the develops, especially in terms of unwavering quality and legitimacy.

Convergent reliability and validity were examined using the Average Variance Extracted (AVE) and Composite Reliability (CR). Table 1 shows that the AVE (ranging from 0.64 to 0.73) and CR (ranging from 0.84 to 0.92) are above the threshold values (AVE > 0.5; CR > 0.7). In expansion, we examined unwavering quality utilizing Cronbach's α and ρA and all the values are over the suggested values ($\alpha > 0.5$; $\rho A > 0.7$). In expansion, we inspected the standardized loadings (λ) and all of them are over the suggested esteem ($\lambda > 0.7$).

In Table 2, we present Fornell and Larcker's criteria [40] for evaluating discriminant validity. Our findings indicate that all the Average Variance Extracted (AVE) values (located on the diagonal of the table) surpass the squared interconstruct correlation estimates. In addition, we analysed the HTMT correlation ratio over suggestion of Henseler et al. [40] and the results are shown in Table 3.

Table 1 Measurement model

	Items	λ	*t values*	α	ρA	CR	AVE
Customized customer service	CCS1	0.846	26,884	0.77	0.78	0.87	0.69
	CCS2	0.841	22,696				
	CCS3	0.804	16,827				
Trust	TRT1	0.796	18,646	0.88	0.88	0.91	0.67
	TRT2	0.852	19,255				
	TRT3	0.778	21,998				
	TRT4	0.795	18,053				
	TRT5	0.868	32,481				
Satisfaction	SAT1	0.744	13,927	0.73	0.78	0.84	0.64
	SAT2	0.789	20,717				
	SAT3	0.859	46,527				
Loyalty	LOY1	0.805	22,927	0.81	0.81	0.89	0.73
	LOY2	0.887	40,926				
	LOY3	0.863	27,263				
Customer service advertising	CSA1	0.792	11,620	0.76	0.79	0.86	0.67
	CSA2	0.875	20,667				
	CSA3	0.783	12,024				
Customer service quality	CSQ1	0.860	29,423	0.88	0.89	0.92	0.73
	CSQ2	0.796	18,004				
	CSQ3	0.908	43,785				
	CSQ4	0.855	28,921				

Table 2 Fornell and Larcker criterion—discriminant validity

	TRT	CSA	CCS	LOY	CSQ	SAT
Trust (TRT)	0.82					
Customer service advertising (CSA)	0.36*	0.82				
Customized customer service (CCS)	0.48*	0.40*	0.83			
Loyalty (LOY)	0.68*	0.29*	0.36*	0.85		
Customer service quality (CSQ)	0.62*	0.30*	0.46*	0.62*	0.86	
Satisfaction (SAT)	0.76*	0.25*	0.45*	0.64*	0.56*	0.80

* Correlations are significant at level 0.05

4.2 *Structural Model*

The next step involves evaluating the relationships within the structural model. This assessment aims to confirm the validity of the proposed hypotheses by examining the path coefficients and their corresponding significance levels. To determine the

Table 3 HTMT ratio—discriminant validity

	TRT	CSA	CCS	LOY	CSQ	SAT
Trust (TRT)						
Customer service advertising (CSA)	0.43					
Customized customer service (CCS)	0.58	0.53				
Loyalty (LOY)	0.80	0.36	0.45			
Customer service quality (CSQ)	0.70	0.35	0.55	0.72		
Satisfaction (SAT)	0.90	0.32	0.60	0.78	0.65	

Table 4 Conceptual model—hypothesis analysis

Hypothesis		β	*t values*	95% confidence interval		*p values*	*Result*
				2.5%	97.5%		
H1	CSA → CSQ	0.140	1.976	0.009	0.287	0.048	Supported
H2	CCS → CSQ	0.405	4.512	0.223	0.574	0.000	Supported
H3	CSQ → SAT	0.558	11.372	0.463	0.654	0.000	Supported
H4	CSQ → TRT	0.293	3.945	0.143	0.430	0.000	Supported
H5	SAT → TRT	0.591	11.129	0.489	0.696	0.000	Supported
H6	SAT → LOY	0.297	2.740	0.078	0.503	0.006	Supported
H7	TRT → LOY	0.454	3.944	0.227	0.678	0.000	Supported

statistical significance of each coefficient, a non-parametric technique known as bootstrapping was employed. This method involves the creation of new sub-samples through a series of resampling procedures. For this specific study, 5,000 samples were generated using the bootstrapping technique, as recommended by the statistical software, to obtain more reliable and stable results. The findings of the hypothesis testing are presented in Table 4 [39]. Table 4 shows the hypothesis test.

5 Discussion and Conclusions

The results also demonstrate that customer service quality is positively influenced by customer service advertising ($\beta_{CCS \rightarrow CSQ} = 0.405$; $p < 0.01$) ($\beta_{CSA \rightarrow CSQ} = 0.140$; $p < 0.05$).

In this context, based on the literature reviewed, personalization and advertising contribute to creating value for the consumer and altering the consumer's perception of the online shop. Consequently, we deem it crucial to assign a profile to each consumer, ensuring that individual preferences and needs are duly considered.

The adaptation of customer service should be so that each consumer can have a different experience, according to their interests and needs. This is also very convenient, as it will facilitate the relationship between consumer satisfaction and purchase intention [19].

According to literature, personalising advertising messages according to the individual preferences of each consumer will undoubtedly offer a better quality of service. By clearly and objectively targeting organisations, personalisation becomes a competitive advantage, as well as a sign of higher profits and margins. Therefore, the more personalised the messages to consumers, the higher service provided, as it meets the needs of consumers.

According to Roy et al. [23], the more an organisation adapts its customer service to the customer's preferences, expectations, needs and even after-sales service, the higher the quality of the service it provides, as it meets all the parameters required and expected by the consumer.

Hence, as a practical recommendation, we propose that online shops provide options for personalized consumer profiles tailored to their individual needs. Additionally, it is advised that online shops effectively communicate their value proposition to enhance the quality of customer service [3, 38].

Quality customer service yields valuable outcomes for online shops, notably enhanced satisfaction ($\beta_{CSQ \rightarrow SAT} = 0.558$; $p < 0.01$) and improved trust in the online shop ($\beta_{CSQ \rightarrow TRT} = 0.293$; $p < 0.01$). Our study therefore suggests that strong customer service improves satisfaction [26, 32] and facilitates trust in the online shop [41].

This study follows literature, who state that in order for quality to exist in a given service within an organisation, it is necessary for this quality process to be implemented continuously, producing consumer satisfaction. Guaranteeing the quality of the process, in terms of its production and delivery. In addition, it is essential to offer quality customer service, because if there is a failure in the combination of consumer expectations and needs, this will lead to dissatisfaction with a given product and/or service [16].

According to the authors Pasharibu et al. [41], trust is all about the knowledge acquired by the consumer, i.e. the opinion they have of each organisation, an opinion they have formed over the time they have interacted with each one.

Consequently, we firmly advocate for online shops to prioritize the quality of service delivered to their customers. Moreover, this research posits that satisfaction serves as the foundation of trust ($\beta_{SAT \rightarrow TRT} = 0.591$; $p < 0.01$), so online shops should focus on customer satisfaction.

According to the authors Pasharibu et al. [41], trust is all about the knowledge acquired by the consumer, i.e. the opinion they have of each organization, an opinion they have formed over the time they have interacted with each one.

Loyalty emerges as a pivotal variable in our study, exerting a direct influence on satisfaction ($\beta_{SAT \rightarrow LOY} = 0.297; p < 0.01$) and trust ($\beta_{TRT \rightarrow LOY} = 0.454; p < 0.01$).

This results follows the work of Song et al. [25] who conclude that satisfaction is a prerequisite for achieving loyalty, as increased satisfaction results in increased loyalty. Furthermore, the authors Kotler and Keller [30] add that a consumer's loyalty is the extent of a consumer's satisfaction. Thus, this study corroborates that the greater a consumer's satisfaction, the more loyal they will be to a particular service.

Following on from the work of Song et al. [25], it shows that it is trust that sustains long-term relationships between consumers and organisations,

These results suggest that as long as an organisation remains trustworthy and delivers on its promise, consumers will speak highly of it and actively continue to buy from the same organisation (product and/or service). It follows that consumers who are sure that the organisation meets their preferences will be more loyal.

This study focused on the importance of customer service quality in building customer loyalty for online shops. It examined the impact of customer service advertising, personalized service, and overall service quality on loyalty and satisfaction within specialized online retailers. However, e-marketing aspects and the broader consumer experience in online shops were not included in the analysis. While this research offers valuable insights into customer service quality, the sample primarily consisted of young online shoppers, suggesting the need for future studies with more diverse demographics.

Acknowledgements This work is financed by national funds through FCT—Fundação para a Ciência e a Tecnologia, I.P., under the project UIDB/04928/2020.

References

1. Loureiro, S. M. C., Cavallero, L., and Miranda, F. J., "Fashion brands on retail websites: Customer performance expectancy and e-word-of-mouth," *Journal of Retailing and Consumer Services,* vol. 41, pp. 131–141, 2018/03/01/ 2018.
2. Rita, P., Oliveira, T., and Farisa, A., "The impact of e-service quality and customer satisfaction on customer behavior in online shopping," *Heliyon,* vol. 5, p. e02690, 2019/10/01/ 2019.
3. Blut, M., "E-Service Quality: Development of a Hierarchical Model," *Journal of Retailing,* vol. 92, pp. 500–517, 2016/12/01/ 2016.
4. Srihadi, T. F. and Setiawan, D., "The Influence of Different Level of Service Characteristics and Personal Involvement towards Consumer Relational Response Behaviors," *Procedia - Social and Behavioral Sciences,* vol. 210, pp. 378–387, 2015/12/02/ 2015.
5. Ferreira, S., Santos, S., and Santo, P. E., "How Creativity and Celebrity Trust Promotes Intention to Visit a Destination," in *Springer Series in Design and Innovation,* vol. 19, ed, 2022, pp. 689–700.
6. Santo, P. E. and Marques, A. M. A., "Determinants of the online purchase intention: hedonic motivations, prices, information and trust," *Baltic Journal of Management,* vol. 17, pp. 56–71, 2022.
7. Jung, A. R., "The influence of perceived ad relevance on social media advertising: An empirical examination of a mediating role of privacy concern," *Computers in Human Behavior,* vol. 70, pp. 303–309, 2017/05/01/ 2017.

8. Barreto, I. F., Crescitelli, E., and Figueiredo, J. C. B., "Resultados de marketing de relacionamento: Proposição de modelo por meio de mapeamento cognitivo," *Revista Brasileira de Gestao de Negocios,* vol. 17, pp. 1371–1389, 2015.
9. Espírito Santo, P., da Cruz, S. M., Fortes, N., and Cardoso, P. A., "Antecedents of Engagement on Social Media: Fatigue and Anxiety," in *Springer Series in Design and Innovation.* vol. 27, ed, 2023, pp. 115–124.
10. do Espírito Santo, P. M. and Trigo, A., "Influence of Website Design on E-Trust and Positive Word of Mouth Intentions in E-Commerce Fashion Websites," in *Lecture Notes in Business Information Processing* vol. 402, ed, 2020, pp. 316–330.
11. Ellsworth, P. C., "Confusion, concentration, and other emotions of interest: Commentary on Rozin and Cohen (2003)," *Emotion,* vol. 3, pp. 81–85, 2003.
12. Anshari, M., Almunawar, M. N., Lim, S. A., and Al-Mudimigh, A., "Customer relationship management and big data enabled: Personalization & customization of services," *Applied Computing and Informatics,* vol. 15, pp. 94–101, 2019/07/01/ 2019.
13. Scheidt, S. and Chung, Q. B., "Making a case for speech analytics to improve customer service quality: Vision, implementation, and evaluation," *International Journal of Information Management,* vol. 45, pp. 223–232, 2019/04/01/ 2019.
14. Santo, P. E. and Cardoso, P., *Employer Branding e Marketing Interno: Uma mudança nas organizações*: Independently published, 2021.
15. Santo, P. E. and Cardoso, P., *500 Brand and Marketing Definitions: For researchers and professionals.* : Independently published, 2021.
16. Barbosa, T. A. C. and Minciotti, S., "Serviço de atendimento ao cliente terceirizado ou próprio? Uma análise da satisfação do cliente usuário," vol. 9, pp. 81–95, 01/01 2007.
17. Bleier, A. and Eisenbeiss, M., "Personalized online advertising effectiveness: The interplay of what, when, and where," *Marketing Science,* vol. 34, pp. 669–688, 2015.
18. Arora, N., Dreze, X., Ghose, A., Hess, J. D., Iyengar, R., Jing, B., *et al.*, "Putting one-to-one marketing to work: Personalization, customization, and choice," *Marketing Letters,* vol. 19, p. 305, 2008/09/16 2008.
19. Seiders, K., Voss, G. B., Grewal, D., and Godfrey, A. L., "Do Satisfied Customers Buy More? Examining Moderating Influences in a Retailing Context," *Journal of Marketing,* vol. 69, pp. 26–43, 2005.
20. Do Espírito Santo, P. M. and Santos, S., "Sponsorship congruity and attitude towards advertising in music festivals: The role of trust and social media engagement," in *Multi Conference on Computer Science and Information Systems, MCCSIS 2019 - Proceedings of the International Conferences on ICT, Society and Human Beings 2019, Connected Smart Cities 2019 and Web Based Communities and Social Media 2019*, 2019, pp. 309–316.
21. Ferreira, V. H. S., Marques, A. M. A., Santo, P. M. D. E., and da Silva, S. F., "The influence of knowledge management on the result of innovation of companies in the mold industries," in *Proceedings of the European Conference on Knowledge Management, ECKM*, 2021, pp. 283–291.
22. Santo, P. M. D. E., Ferreira, V. H. S., and Marques, A. M. A., "How knowledge sharing mediates the effects of internal marketing on customer orientation," in *Proceedings of the European Conference on Knowledge Management, ECKM*, 2021, pp. 657–665.
23. Roy, S. K., Shekhar, V., Lassar, W. M., and Chen, T., "Customer engagement behaviors: The role of service convenience, fairness and quality," *Journal of Retailing and Consumer Services,* vol. 44, pp. 293–304, 2018/09/01/ 2018.
24. Roberts, K., Varki, S., and Brodie, R., "Measuring the quality of relationships in consumer services: an empirical study," *European Journal of Marketing,* vol. 37, pp. 169–196, 2003.
25. Song, H., Wang, J., and Han, H., "Effect of image, satisfaction, trust, love, and respect on loyalty formation for name-brand coffee shops," *International Journal of Hospitality Management,* vol. 79, pp. 50–59, 2019/05/01/ 2019.
26. Erciş, A., Ünal, S., Candan, F. B., and Yıldırım, H., "The Effect of Brand Satisfaction, Trust and Brand Commitment on Loyalty and Repurchase Intentions," *Procedia - Social and Behavioral Sciences,* vol. 58, pp. 1395–1404, 2012/10/12/ 2012.

27. Miswanto, M. and Angelia, Y., "The Influence of Service Quality and Store Atmosphere on Customer Satisfaction," *Jurnal Manajemen dan Kewirausahaan,* vol. 19, 09/01 2017.
28. Vk, H., "A Study on the Mediation Role of Customer Satisfaction on Customer Impulse and Involvement to Word of Mouth and Repurchase Intention," 10/01 2013.
29. Augusto, L., Santos, S., and Santo, P. M. D. E., "Usability and sophistication of websites: A path to satisfaction in online retail," *RISTI - Revista Iberica de Sistemas e Tecnologias de Informacao,* vol. 2020, pp. 542–556, 2020.
30. Kotler, P. and Keller, K. L., *Marketing Management*: Pearson Prentice Hall, 2009.
31. Peña, L. and Reis, D., "Linking customer satisfaction, quality, and strategic planning," *RAE - Revista de Administração de Empresas,* vol. 40, pp. 42–46, 03/01 2000.
32. Agustin, C. and Singh, J., "Curvilinear Effects of Consumer Loyalty Determinants in Relational Exchanges," *Journal of Marketing Research,* vol. 42, pp. 96–108, 2005.
33. Sahin, A., Zehir, C., and Kitapçı, H., "The Effects of Brand Experiences, Trust and Satisfaction on Building Brand Loyalty; An Empirical Research On Global Brands," *Procedia - Social and Behavioral Sciences,* vol. 24, pp. 1288–1301, 2011/01/01/ 2011.
34. Cheng, F.-F., Wu, C.-S., and Chen, Y.-C., "Creating customer loyalty in online brand communities," *Computers in Human Behavior,* vol. 107, p. 105752, 2020/06/01/ 2020.
35. Mabkhot, H. A. and Salleh, S. M., "The influence of brand image and brand personality on brand loyalty, mediating by brand trust: An empirical study," *Jurnal Pengurusan,* vol. 50, 2017.
36. Dunn, L. and Hoegg, J., "The Impact of Fear on Emotional Brand Attachment," *Journal of Consumer Research,* vol. 41, pp. 152–168, 2014.
37. Shanahan, T., Tran, T. P., and Taylor, E. C., "Getting to know you: Social media personalization as a means of enhancing brand loyalty and perceived quality," *Journal of Retailing and Consumer Services,* vol. 47, pp. 57–65, 2019/03/01/ 2019.
38. Bock, D. E., Mangus, S. M., and Folse, J. A. G., "The road to customer loyalty paved with service customization," *Journal of Business Research,* vol. 69, pp. 3923–3932, 2016.
39. Hair, J. F., Black, W. C., Babin, B. J., and Anderson, R. E., *Multivariate Data Analysis*: Pearson Education Limited, 2018.
40. Henseler, J., Ringle, C. M., and Sarstedt, M., "A new criterion for assessing discriminant validity in variance-based structural equation modeling," *Journal of the Academy of Marketing Science,* vol. 43, pp. 115–135, 2015/01/01 2015.
41. Pasharibu, Y., Lidia Paramita, E., and Febrianto, S., "Price, service quality and trust on online transportation towards customer satisfaction," *Jurnal Ekonomi dan Bisnis,* vol. 21, pp. 241–266, 10/31 2018.

Stuck! Stalling in Computer Games

Pedro Cardoso and Miguel Carvalhais

Abstract Games are commonly designed to assist players in their progression, maintaining their attention and motivation until they achieve closure while presenting challenges that need to be overcome to progress. But not all games are designed with this in mind, and players do not always play to progress. When that happens, we call it *stalling*. In computer games, stalling is when players or the game system try to maintain a particular state, impeding player progression and the game from developing. This chapter explores stalling as an act of players and, alternatively, as an act of the game itself that can be designed or result from emergent behaviours. It presents a model composed of two axes—Player/Game and Transitory/Permanent—that generate four types of stalling: Squandering, Casting-off, Lingering, and Taunting. This model leads to the conclusion that stalling is a legitimate playing tactic and versatile strategy for the design of games.

Keywords Game design · Stalling · Aesthetic friction · Computer games

1 Introduction

Games usually develop through players' actions. They present challenges that players try to overcome to achieve closure. In this, game systems assume an ambivalent stance as they are simultaneously designed to incite players to progress while presenting obstacles and challenges to overcome as compulsory requisites for such progression. In simpler terms, game systems both incite and impede players from progressing. With this in mind, one may say that games establish a relationship with players that is simultaneously *dialectical* (Cardoso, 2016) and *adversarial* (Crawford, 1984) as well

P. Cardoso (✉)
University of Aveiro/DigiMedia, Aveiro, Portugal
e-mail: pedroccardoso@ua.pt

M. Carvalhais
i2ADS & Faculty of Fine Arts of the University of Porto, Porto, Portugal
e-mail: mcarvalhais@fba.up.pt

© The Author(s), under exclusive license to Springer Nature Switzerland AG 2025
D. Brandão et al. (eds.), *Perspectives on Design and Digital Communication V*, Springer Series in Design and Innovation 50, https://doi.org/10.1007/978-3-031-76156-0_18

as *provocative* since they tease players to move forward while acting in opposition to that.

But what if players do not respond to such provocations? What if they play not to progress in the game but instead to impede its progress and bring it to a halt? Players typically play *against* the game but *towards* the game's goals, with victory and defeat being conditions that both parties—players and games—agree to (Frasca, 2007). What if players play in opposition to those goals? This is what we call *stalling*.

Stalling can be construed as anti-game behaviour, a *spoil-sport* behaviour, to put it in Huizinga's terms (1950/2016), and is typically seen as an act of players. However, stalling can also be seen as a design strategy to make players get stuck in a given part of the game, experiencing a game state of sameness, therefore, an act of the machine.

Enthralling in this state of sameness, either because of player or game actions, is an expression of what we call *aesthetic friction* (Carvalhais et al., 2019), a countering of the positive feedback hedonistic loop that states of flow usually entail (Csíkszentmihályi, 1990/2008) and that most games are designed to support, elicit and ultimately commodify (Soderman, 2021). Aesthetic friction prioritises the construction of meaning to the experience of plain fun and comfort (Cardoso et al., 2019; Monteiro & Carvalhais, 2023), as usually happens with entertainment games (Arjoranta, 2022). It confronts players with the need to make an effort to step outside their comfort zones, of what is already known to them and what they are already competent in and understand (Carvalhais, 2023). It thus forces players to stop and reflect before they act (Sicart, 2023). This stands in opposition to flow states in which players do not need to stop and think, where they plainly and simply act.

This chapter discusses stalling as an act of the player, as an act of the game, and as a design strategy. It examines its transience and, consequently, presents four types of stalling that result from this framework.

2 Stalling as an Act of the Player

Stalling is usually seen as an act of players, most commonly in multiplayer games, where it describes behaviours that avoid all conflict or that resort to actions and strategies to "waste time".[1] However, contrary to what this common definition may seem to suggest, stalling is not always easy. To be successful at stalling, players may need to be agile, knowledgeable, and skilful enough so that they manage to traverse the game space dexterously and safely. Avoiding conflict in a game can be more difficult, laborious or burdensome than playing it conventionally, with the intent to progress in the game and to face any challenges and conflicts one may be driven to. However, to stall, players often have to assume defensive and non-offensive or evasive stances simultaneously. This means that they may have to deal with continuously spawning threats that have the potential to increasingly overcrowd

[1] Stalling has been a quite common term within the gamer community to name any tactic that impedes a game from progressing, for the most diverse intents and purposes, or even none.

the game space, as players are not focused on eliminating threats but rather on evading them, which may develop into a positive feedback loop of progressively troublesome situations that are harder to endure or escape from.[2]

Some techniques of player stalling consist of running away or diverting, planking, and creating infinite chains.[3] Running away or diverting is quite self-explanatory. It implies that players avoid sources of damage without attacking them, as any attack is also a potential threat to the player. This is not akin to what stealth games typically propose because stealth as a strategy contributes to players' success and, ultimately, to their progression in the game. Running away or diverting players are not only refusing to engage in the conflict the game proposes. They are also renouncing the opportunities to progress in the game such engagement would offer. Planking consists of abusing the properties of a certain space or object in a game that gives players momentary intangibility, i.e. making them immune to damage as a consequence. An example of this can be found in consecutively balancing on stage ledges in *Super Smash Bros.* (1999). Grabbing a ledge in this game and some of its sequels makes players temporarily intangible and impervious to any attacks. Due to the interaction of this with other game mechanics, some techniques may allow players to repeatedly grab and let go of ledges to continuously, and potentially infinitely, refresh that intangibility.[4] An infinite chain is an action or technique that can be maintained for an indefinite period of time. This can be achieved through skill or, sometimes, because of a glitch, and can be used for offensive or defensive purposes. In the case of stalling, as we've defined, an infinite chain can be used to halt the game indefinitely.

Stalling is frequently employed to win by time out or to tease and provoke other players. In competitive settings, such as tournaments, this behaviour may be banned as it can unnecessarily prolong events, make the game unplayable, or even be seen as trolling, a behaviour that is commonly frowned upon. Stalling may also result from inherent asymmetries in the game that players may exploit or react against (Neto et al., 2023).

Stalling differs from other related behaviours, like camping,[5] at a fundamental level. For example, while stalling, players refrain from engaging in conflict and frequently move around the game space to avoid it. On the other hand, camping players rarely move but intend to fight. A camping player is usually in a relatively stable and safe place, waiting for an opportunity to emerge and only then take action. For example, camping in action games with battle royale mechanics allows players

---

[2] As an example, in *Streets of Rage* (1991) it is commonly easier to eliminate enemies as they appear on screen without moving forward in the level, since if not so, enemies will accumulate in a larger group that the player will have to deal with simultaneously.

[3] Diverting, planking, and infinite chains are common terms employed in the slang or jargon within the gamer community to address such behaviours.

[4] This is a technique that players nicknamed "ledgestall". More info at https://www.ssbwiki.com/Ledgestall. Last accessed on 2024/07/08.

[5] Camping is a common term within the gamer community to name a very usual tactic in which players stand still waiting in a static position in the game world to gain some kind of advantage over their adversaries, eventually to eliminate them without being detected.

to minimise effort and risk when holding to safe and advantageous positions from where they may capture or take down opponents without exposing themselves.

3 Stalling as an Act of the Game

Stalling is commonly seen as an act of players, but can it also be an act of the game, something that is executed by the system, perhaps even conceived by its designer? To explore this possibility, we need to expand our definition of stalling and of its goals, much beyond those of conflict avoidance. To grasp the essence of stalling, we need to descend onto a more abstract layer and try to understand it at the level of the game system. If games develop through some sort of conflict (Crawford, 1984) and players may avoid conflict to stall the game, one might say that to stall is to halt the game's progression. It is, in essence, to prevent the game from changing its state. Therefore, at the more abstract level of the game system, to stall is to maintain the game state; it is to pursue homeostasis and to maintain a stable equilibrium.

Therefore, be it with the intent to prolong the playing time of a game or to achieve dramatic or narrative tension, designers may develop techniques to stall players and keep them stuck in a particular game state. In this sense, stalling is not a behaviour of the player but a construct, a design mechanic that manifests as a behaviour of the game system.

An example of this can be found in the boss fight with The End in *Metal Gear Solid 3: Snake Eater* (2004). Although there are other paths the player can follow, the one in which they need to wait about a week for their opponent, The End, to perish can be seen as a way to stall. This may be seen as what Galloway terms an *ambience act* (2006), in which the player is absent, and the machine is left alone, computing the game without inputs from the player, following the routines that give life to the game world. This may also be seen as similar to *idle games*, or *zero-player games*, designed for absent players (Björk & Juul, 2012). However, the difference between these types of games and one that stalls the player is that, in the former, the games progress while the player is away and they do not, therefore, require player inputs. However, while stalling, the game state is kept the same. In the case of The End, nothing changes in the game until the time limit is reached. The player can even turn off the game console—the game system does not even need to be running—and return in about a week to continue playing. In idle games, the game keeps on developing, and therefore the game system needs to be kept working.

Another example can be found in *Twelve Minutes* (2021), a temporal puzzle game that makes the player go into an endless loop of events until they find the right combination of actions to progress, which upon failure makes the loop restart. In this case, stalling manifests in taking the player back to the beginning over and over again, only to progress when the right combination of conditions is verifiable by the game system.

Other forms of stalling may include luring the player into a wild goose chase, a pursuit of something unattainable, or, in a more common strategy, offering side quests, challenges, or activities that do not contribute to advancing the game or changing its state. Endgame states in some games, such as *Diablo IV* (2023), can be an example here, as the game runs out of progression but still offers the player several activities to be enrolled in. Another example is by injecting bloat content into a game, something much common in open world games such as in the *Assassin's Creed* series, that acts as filler to try to keep the player engaged in the game for longer than needed.

We can also argue for some games being designed to progress by stalling, i.e. to progress without progressing. Such is the case of infinite runners, or *Candy Crush Saga* (2012) and similar puzzle games, where the goal is not progress itself but rather the continuation of the same actions that maintain the same state, endlessly or seemingly endlessly.[6]

4 Four Types of Stalling

Either as an act of the player or of the designer, stalling is commonly seen as being a *transitory* action, usually ruled by a particular condition that determines its duration, either time-based or other.

Typically, goals are defined by the game, being mandatory requisites or conditions players need to meet to progress (Zagal et al., 2005). A game's goals constitute the motivation for players' actions and "define the game states that the players should try to achieve by manipulating the game through their actions and those of the other players" (Björk & Holopainen, 2005, p. 18). When players ignore or reject the game's predetermined goals (p. 310)—the set of goals defined by the game designer—their play relies on a game of balance between these goals and a second set of player-defined goals (p. 317). The power relationship between these two forces determines if stalling for players is transitory (when players accept the game's predetermined goals) or becomes permanent (when players reject such goals to pursue their own).[7]

Even on the side of the machine and the designer, stalling as a permanent action is less common but still possible. Conventional thinking imagines designers having the goal to make players progress, as that progression is indispensable for engagement and closure. However, as we will see, that may not always be the case, and

[6] The scarce literature and state of the art on this subject determines these group of examples to be a small opportunistic sample rather than a selection of an extensive inventory of cases on the phenomenon. However, they are still a good depiction of diverse ways stalling is expressed in videogames.

[7] We can still argue for games without predefined goals, such as *The Sims 2* (2004), as "[t]he game has no imperative, no demands on what the player should do, yet Sims (the characters in the game) generally become miserable if the player does nothing." (Juul, 2007) On another example, we can also name games such as *Donkey Kong* (1981) or *Tetris* (1985), in which to beat them, or to find closure with a sense of winning, the player must play until the game system stalls permanently, achieving the famous and much sought after *kill screen*.

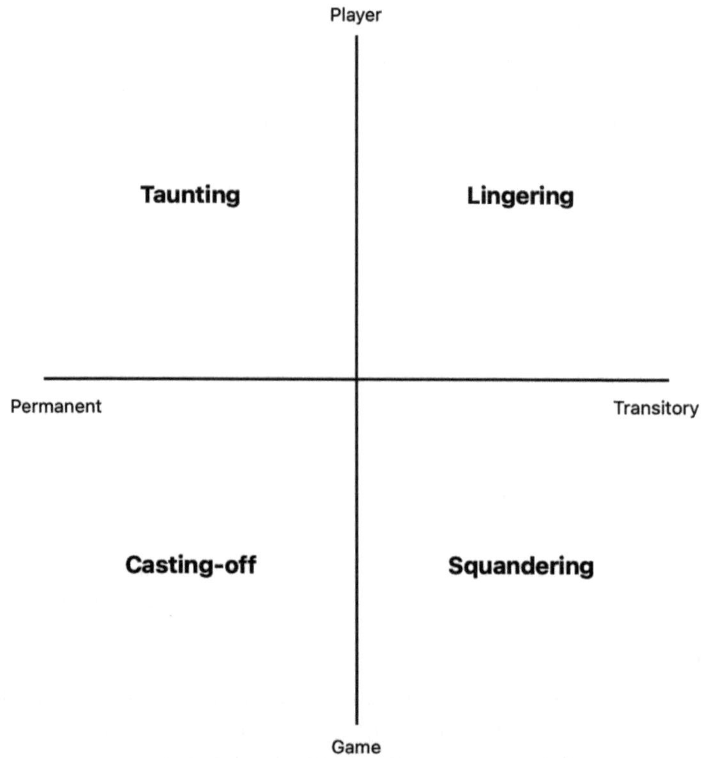

Fig. 1 A model of stalling in computer games

the ambivalent stance of the game, its adversarial and dialectical relationship with players, can be leveraged to other goals.

We can then consider two axes, the first dedicated to the two parties engaged in a game, the player and the game itself, and the second to the nature of the stalling developed, either permanent or transitory. By superimposing these axes, we obtain a model where we can find the four types of stalling in computer games: *Lingering* (Player/Transitory), *Taunting* (Player/Permanent), *Squandering* (Game/Transitory), and *Casting-off* (Game/Permanent) (Fig. 1).

4.1 Lingering (Player/Transitory)

A lingering player is a passive player, who waits for the game to present an opportunity to change its state, or that just waits for the game itself to change its own state. These are players that find themselves in a favourable state and want to hold on to it. In this sense, stalling may not be an adversarial behaviour, as it can also be motivated by reasons that we may describe as *aesthetic* (Hunicke et al., 2004), i.e. reasons related to the game's enjoyment and to the pleasure that is derived from it.

> Games are more than play, more than the free exploration of novel experience—games are also *anti-work*. In games we exert great effort, expending valuable resources and precious energy, in pursuit of arbitrary, nonsensical goals. We pretend to work; we act out a dark reflection of work in which we apply ourselves vigorously and passionately to a kind of intense problem solving in which no actual problems are solved. (Lantz, 2023, p. 49)

This type of stalling may happen whenever players, revelling in the familiarity and comfort of a certain state of the game, find themselves driven to maintain stasis and to preserve such a state and its cosiness. This can be achieved by repeating challenges or by taking side quests that the player knows will not contribute to their progress, even replaying the entire game from scratch with new characters (or with the same character), or engaging in non-competitive versions of games, such as *Assassin's Creed*'s Discovery Tour modes. Although these behaviours need to counter the game's stated goals and progression system (Juul, 2013), at their core, they are not anti-game behaviours, as their motivation is fundamentally to prolong the game's enjoyment, to preserve a given state of the game world and to enjoy the magic circle.[8]

4.2 Taunting (Player/Permanent)

While taunting, the player aims to mock other players, the game or even the game designer. Taunters stall the game to break it. They deliberately leave the magic circle to halt it, testing its limitations.

> The player who trespasses against the rules or ignores them is a "spoil-sport". (…) the spoil-sport shatters the play-world itself. By withdrawing from the game he reveals the relativity and fragility of the play-world in which he had temporarily shut himself with others. He robs play of its illusion—a pregnant word which means literally "in-play" (from inlusio, illudere or inludere). (Huizinga, 1950/2016)

Taunting players will stop when the game breaks or when they lose to the game system. Taunting players want to deconstruct the game. They are not interested in playing according to the established rules, but rather create their own ruleset and interact with the game to break it apart. In this sense, taunting can be seen as something of a meta-game, a game that is played against the game, against its rules, and against its mechanics. But taunting is also a game that the player may win—if they manage to prolong the taunting or even totally collapse the game system, should this lead to a crash—or that the player may lose if, regardless of the attempts at taunting, the game nevertheless persists in progressing and, ultimately, defeats the player thus punishing their inaction. Taunters delve into the game's inner workings, they try to

---

[8] Huizinga (1950/2016) defines "magic circle" as a defined space created by play, separate from the 'real' world, and governed by its own set of rules and conventions.

see if they can make it burst by its seams. In the same way as glitchers, which exploit the game, and speedrunners, which need to study mechanics and actually treat the game as a system too (and not as a magic circle) in order to succeed in the speedrun, taunters seek the artificiality of the system and reject the diegesis of the game world and of its lore, seeing the game system for what it is, a set of mechanics, rules, and potentials for action, and as a playground where all and any of these are up for grabs. The difference is that glitchers and speedrunners act like this to progress in the game while taunters do it for the opposite reason. For this kind of player, the game is a system to be tested, and stalling is the means to suspend its natural course of action, to put it in a suspended state, an endless loop of sameness, that reinforces the artificiality of its structure and behaviours.[9]

4.3 *Squandering (Game/Transitory)*

While squandering, the game delays players, making them pass or lose an opportunity to progress and change the game's state. Optional quests, challenges, or activities in a game can be seen as a strategy to squander. While these may provide players with items or score (or score-equivalents as, e.g., experience points) that may ease their traversal in later stages, they do not directly contribute to the development of the game itself, thus preserving the overarching game state.

Some games are designed with squandering in mind, generally with the purpose of making players spend more time in the game by delaying closure. It may be strange to think that players may feel motivated to keep playing when a game does not change. However, players often engage in activities that do not contribute to closure, and some games seem to actually be designed for this, offering many side tasks, sometimes in absurd amounts. In some cases, these tasks may even become part of the charm or the identity of the game, as in *The Elder Scrolls V: Skyrim* (2011) or the *Grand Theft Auto* series of games, for example. It is common for players of these games to spend more time exploring and engaging in these side activities than on pursuing the game's primary goals.[10]

An alternative route to squander may be the consequence of glitches or bugs in the game system that lead to emergent behaviours that also block progression of the game. Resetting quests that force players to restart or repeat tasks, items that do not work consistently or as expected, non-playing characters that refuse to do

[9] Taunters, glitchers, and speedrunners are types of players related to what we elsewhere called an exploiting traversal of the game (Cardoso & Carvalhais, 2013).

[10] This is related to what we called elsewhere a bending traversal (Cardoso, 2016).

their assigned jobs,[11] or time freezing in the game's diegesis.[12] All of these can temporarily affect, sometimes severely, the ability to progress in a game.

4.4 Casting-Off (Game/Permanent)

Casting-off is one of the most uncommon actions and unconventional game design practices. It is a permanent stall where the player is kept in a permanent state of sameness or resetting. For example, this can be seen in *Earthbound* (1994) which, when played with a pirated copy, deliberately crashes during the fight with the final boss. Because of this, players have no choice but to reset the game, only to find out that all their saved progress has been automatically deleted by the game system and that they need to start over their entire progress.

But not all casting-off actions are as nefarious as this. The endgame feature present in many games can also be seen as a casting-off technique, as the game will not progress further because it has been concluded. Therefore, stalling becomes the permanent state of the game. In opposition to other types of stalling that aim to prevent the game from developing to closure, in this one, the game has already been concluded, and the only way to retain players is to allow them to keep on playing all the side activities that were not undertaken yet. Open-world games like *The Legend of Zelda: Breath of the Wild* (2017) or the more recent *The Legend of Zelda: Tears of the Kingdom* (2023) are examples of this.

Some games may be designed with the goal of achieving permanent stasis. Some games are designed with short cycles that permanently restart, as in battle royales, racing games and other sports games, or even puzzle games, where each consecutive level brings the player back to the start of a problem. If, in some cases, this cycling results in progression (of difficulty, skills, buffs or nerfs), in other cases, the progression can be illusory. Even if the player keeps playing, surpassing puzzle after puzzle, level after level, there may be no actual increase in difficulty, no learning or skill development, but rather just the development of a state of stasis. Such is the case of non-games such as *Vanitas*[13] (2010), which purports to induce a meditative experience and presents itself as a *memento mori*. Here, this lack of progression, or a progression in a phase-space where one is whilst in the game, is intended as a feature and as a commentary on the ephemerality, fragility, and preciousness of life. Another

---

[11] A bug in *Dwarf* Fortress (2016), where the tavern keeper in a fully equipped tavern that the player builds, refuses to work and just states "I don't work here", not fulfilling any orders or renting rooms. See http://www.bay12games.com/dwarves/mantisbt/view.php?id=9327. Las accessed on 2024/04/07.

[12] A bug in Cyberpunk 2077 (2020) causes time to stand still and the in-game clock to get stuck, thus stalling several game possible game actions. See https://forums.cdprojektred.com/index.php?threads/bug-time-freeze.11121796/ or https://www.reddit.com/r/LowSodiumCyberpunk/comments/kc3a81/ingame_clock_stuck/. Last accessed 2024/04/07.

[13] More info at https://tale-of-tales.com/Vanitas/index.html. Last accessed on 2024/04/07.

good example can be found in *Mountain*[14] (2014), an idle simulator that, after a set of initial questions, offers little interactivity to players and not many events to witness besides the looping of day and night cycles or seasons. In *Mountain*, the game state may progress, but this is so infrequent and unpredictable that it is unexpected to players. Casting-off and the stasis it leads to are aesthetic resources that the game's designer, David OReilly, uses to great effect.

Other games may use these resources for different purposes. They may even construct an illusion of progression, displaying mounting scores, level numbers, incentives or praise for the player's performance while trying to, ultimately, maintain stasis. This is sometimes the case with endless runners or puzzle games, designed to retain players through incentivization and persuasion strategies whilst not really progressing because changes to mechanics, skills required, or any other familial element in the game may ultimately negatively affect player retention.

Finally, we may also regard permanent glitches, malfunctions or games that depend on online functions and are no longer supported but nevertheless still run, as particular and unintended cases of Casting-off. *Counter-Strike* (2000) or *Minecraft* (2011) abandoned servers can be examples here.

5 Conclusion: Stalling as a Strategy for the Design of Games

This chapter presented stalling as a potential action of the player or of the game that intends to preserve a given game state. Stalling is trying to maintain a stable equilibrium and achieve homeostasis. It is to explore play by maintaining a particular game state, temporarily or permanently.

In this context, we presented a model from which four types of stalling emerge: Lingering, when stalling is a transitory action of the player, when they wait for the game to present opportunities to change the game state, or for the game to change its own state; Taunting, when stalling is a permanent action of the player, to mock other players, the game or the game designer, trying to break or deconstruct the game and suspend the rules; Squandering, when stalling is a transitory action of the game, making players pass or miss opportunities to progress in the game; and Casting-off, when stalling is a permanent action of the game, making the player be kept in a permanent state of sameness or resetting.

The purposes of stalling diverge depending on type and are varied within each type. From getting advantage, to filtering and establishing minimum requirements for players, to aesthetic pleasure, to mocking, to extending or prolonging the game and delaying closure, to achieve dramatic or narrative tension, to punish players, and so on, stalling is a versatile strategy.

[14] More info at https://web.archive.org/web/20230305220322/mountain-game.com/. Last accessed on 2024/04/07.

Future work will look into further developing this model. Are there other types of stalling? Can this model be expanded somehow? Can we consider other axes? How can game designers promote each type of stalling in ways that are meaningful for the experience of the player? How can guidelines and patterns for the design of stalling be developed? How can practical prototyping be developed around a stalling framework, and how can these artefacts contribute to make the theory and the framework more robust? These are some of the questions that remain to be explored in further studies that try to find the place for stalling, a concept that defies conventional game design practices but that can be seen as a strategy for the design of playful and meaningful experiences with games.

References

Arjoranta, J. How are Games Interpreted? Hermeneutics for Game Studies. *Game Studies*, 22(3), (2022).

Bjork, S., & Holopainen, J. *Patterns in Game Design*. Charles River Media, (2005).

Björk, S., & Juul, J. *Zero-Player Games Or: What We Talk about When We Talk about Players*. Philosophy of Computer Games Conference, (2012). http://www.jesperjuul.net/text/zeroplayergames/

Cardoso, P. *Playing in 7D: An Action-Oriented Framework for Video Games*. Universidade do Porto, (2016). https://hdl.handle.net/10216/82685

Cardoso, P., & Carvalhais, M. *Breaking the game: the traversal of the emergent narrative in video games*. Journal of Science and Technology of the Arts, 5(1), 25–31, (2013). https://doi.org/10.7559/citarj.v5i1.87

Cardoso, P., Melo, R., & Carvalhais, M. *Breaking the Hedonistic Loop: Meaning Before fun in videogames*. ARTECH 2019: Proceedings of the 9th International Conference on Digital and Interactive Arts, (2019).

Carvalhais, M., Cardoso, P., Raimundo, J., & Melo, R. Designing games that prioritize meaning over fun. *Contemporânea - Revista do PPGART/UFSM*, 2(4), 1–8, (2019). https://doi.org/10.5902/2595523341302

Carvalhais, M. Designing (with) Computational Objects: From Metamedia to Metaenvironments. Joelho, *Journal of Architectural Culture* (14), 129–140, (2023).

Crawford, C. *The Art of Computer Game Design*. Osborne/McGraw-Hill, (1984).

Csíkszentmihályi, M. *Flow: The Psychology of Optimal Experience*. HarperCollins, (2008). (Original work published 1990).

Frasca, G. *Play the Message: Play, Game and Videogame Rhetoric*. IT University of Copenhagen. Copenhagen, (2007).

Galloway, A. R. *Gaming*. University of Minnesota Press, (2006).

Huizinga, J. (2016). *Homo Ludens: A Study of the Play-element in Culture*. Angelico Press (Original work published 1950).

Hunicke, R., LeBlanc, M., & Zubek, R. MDA: A formal approach to game design and game research. In M. LeBlanc (Ed.), Game Design and Tuning Workshop Materials, Game Developers Conference 2004, (2004). https://users.cs.northwestern.edu/~hunicke/MDA.pdf

Juul, J. *Without a goal*. In Tanya Krzywinska and Barry Atkins (eds): Videogame/Player/Text. Manchester: Manchester University Press, (2007). http://www.jesperjuul.net/text/withoutagoal/

Juul, J. *The Art of Failure: An Essay on the Pain of Playing Video Games*. The MIT Press, (2013).

Lantz, F. *The Beauty of Games*. MIT Press, (2023).

Monteiro, A., & Carvalhais, M. How we Construct Meaning in Interactive Digital Narratives: a structurally coupled relation. *Journal of Digital Media and Interaction*, 6(14), 21–32, (2023).

Neto, A., Cardoso, P., & Carvalhais, M. Asymmetric Gameplay: Types and Perspectives. In N. Martins & D. Brandão, *Advances in Design and Digital Communication III* Cham, (2023).

Sicart, M. *Playing Software*. The MIT Press, (2023).

Soderman, B. *Against Flow: Video Games and the Flowing Subject*. MIT Press, (2021).

Zagal, J. P., Mateas, M., Fernández-Vara, C., Hochhalter, B., & Lichti, N. *Towards an Ontological Language for Game Analysis*. DiGRA'05—Proceedings of the 2005 DiGRA International Conference: Changing Views: Worlds in Play, (2005). https://dl.digra.org/index.php/dl/article/view/136

Ludography

Assassin's Creed series. Ubisoft, (2007–2023, series).

Candy Crush Saga. King, (2012).

Cyberpunk 2077. CD Projekt Red, (2020).

Counter-Strike. Valve, (2000).

Diablo IV. Blizzard Entertainment, (2023).

Dwarf Fortress. Bay 12, (2016).

Earthbound. HAL Laboratory, Ape, Inc., (1994).

Grand Theft Auto. Rockstar Games, (1997–2021, series).

Minecraft. Mojang Studios, (2011).

Metal Gear Solid 3: Snake Eater. Konami, (2004).

Mountain. David OReilly, (2024).

Super Smash Bros. HAL Laboratory, (1999).

Tetris. Alexey Pajitnov, (1985).

The Elder Scrolls V: Skyrim. Bethesda Game Studios, (2011).

The Legend of Zelda: Breath of the Wild. Nintendo EPD, (2017).

The Legend of Zelda: Tears of the Kingdom. Nintendo EPD, (2023).

The Sims 2. Maxis Redwood Shores, (2004).

Vanitas. Tale of Tales, (2010).

Analyzing How Metaphorical Design Enhances the Construction of Meaning Across the Four Orders of Design

Xie Zeyuan and Jung Euitay

Abstract Metaphor design originated from the fields of linguistics and cognition. The existing metaphor classification method fails to consider the combination of design elements from a holistic perspective and cannot be effectively applied to the context of design. This paper combines metaphor design with the four orders of design to establish a new paradigm of metaphor design structure and redefine the scope of each level of metaphor design. According to the four orders of design and the triple design theory of emotional design, metaphor design is divided into four quadrants: symbolic metaphor design, event metaphor design, behavioral metaphor design, and conceptual metaphor design, and the components of each quadrant are briefly described. Finally, TikTok is selected as a case study to analyze how metaphor design accurately conveys brand concepts and completes the emotional cycle with the audience. The research results prove the importance of considering the weight and coherence between multiple metaphors in the design process. This study adopts a combination of literature review and empirical analysis to explore how metaphor design constructs a reflective level in emotional design, thereby improving user experience and design quality, and providing more targeted guidance and iterative methods for design theory and design classification.

Keywords Emotional design · Reflective level · Metaphorical design · Four order of design · Reflection

---

X. Zeyuan
Graduate School, College of Design, Hanyang University ERICA, 15588 Ansan, South Korea
e-mail: xiezeyuan1123@163.com

J. Euitay (✉)
Faculty of Graduate School, Communication Design, College of Design, Hanyang University ERICA, 15588 Ansan, South Korea
e-mail: junget@hanyang.ac.kr

© The Author(s), under exclusive license to Springer Nature Switzerland AG 2025

D. Brandão et al. (eds.), *Perspectives on Design and Digital Communication V*, Springer Series in Design and Innovation 50, https://doi.org/10.1007/978-3-031-76156-0_19

1 Introduction

1.1 Research Background and Current Research Status

Marco Diani once remarked that design has always existed between two poles dominating our culture: one being technological and industrial reality, and the other being production and social utopia scaled to human dimensions [1]. Presently, we find ourselves amidst the third wave of Human–Computer Interaction (HCI), which emphasizes human values, the creation of meaning, situational knowledge, and experience [2], following in the footsteps of Bannon (1986). It is evident that the current core objective of design ultimately focuses on realizing human values and creating meaning. Design, originally "technology-driven," should evolve towards being "meaning-driven." The construction of meaning is not only a necessity for emotional design but also a demand of the contemporary era. In some countries and fields, there is still an emphasis on efficiency, scalability, and standardization of production. Design, influenced by this broader context, tends towards industrialization, standardization, and practicality, gradually becoming alienated from its origins as a creative tool. To avoid the trend of excessive industrialization in design, a conceptual distinction between "manufacturing" and "design" is necessary, leading to the emergence of emotional design. It is through the incorporation of emotions that the concept of design expands from mere "creation" to meaningful "experience."

Donald Norman's proposition of "user-centered design" [3] in 1986 has gradually become a mainstream design ideology. Designers, in their process, need to consider not only the realization of basic functionalities but also pay particular attention to the completion of consumers' emotional experiences. Currently, research on emotional design mostly resides within the cognitive discipline, posing the challenge of how to construct comprehensively and holistically meaning in the process of design practice.

Metaphors pervade everyday expression, and designers consciously or unconsciously employ metaphorical design to shape products and create meaning. However, the systematic utilization of metaphorical design remains ambiguous. While surface-level linguistic metaphors, visual metaphors, and product metaphors are easily perceived in design practice, deeper layers such as action metaphors, gesture metaphors, systemic environment metaphors, and thought metaphors are challenging to discuss in detail. Yet, their significance, akin to reflective levels, serves as a criterion for distinguishing the excellence of a product. Presently, metaphorical design struggles to provide designers with a comprehensive theoretical framework. The four orders of design are a comprehensive and flexible theoretical framework within the discipline of design. They are currently applied to describe design activities, aiding in understanding the essence of design and its impact, used in design education [4], design strategy [5], and collaborative design [6] in virtual environments.

Currently, there is limited theoretical integration of metaphorical design into design structures and frameworks, and there is limited systematic research on the synergistic interaction between comprehensive metaphorical design structures and emotional design. This paper aims to establish a new metaphorical design framework by integrating metaphorical design with the four orders of design, deconstructing, and analyzing it. By combining this new framework, further exploration into the construction of meaning in the triple design theory of emotional design is pursued, delving into how to influence and promote the construction of reflective levels.

1.2 Research Objectives, Methodology, and Significance

Research Objectives: Based on the endeavor to construct the meaning layer in emotional design, this study aims to systematically explore emotional design, metaphorical design, and the four orders of design. Firstly, it aims to elucidate the basic concepts, developmental trends, and major application areas of these three design theories. Secondly, building upon a solid understanding of these theories, it seeks to identify their commonalities and corroborate their scientific and rational aspects through integration. Lastly, it proposes a new classification standard for metaphorical design by integrating metaphorical design with the Four orders of Design, thus enhancing the construction of design theories, and enriching their content.

Research Methodology: This study employs analytical methods from emotional design, metaphorical design, and the four orders of design, combined with literature review, case comparisons, and practical analysis to investigate how affective design connects with the Design Quartet. Furthermore, conclusions are drawn after logically examining the four criteria of the newly proposed metaphorical design:

Clear and effective classification hierarchy in design aids designers in reflecting on the use of metaphorical design at the reflective layer, providing users with profound insights when using products.

Conceptual metaphorical design serves as a criterion for distinguishing between ordinary and excellent products.

When dealing with multiple metaphorical designs, consideration must be given to the internal weighting, logical coherence, and consistency among them.

Research Significance: The subjectivity and individuality of emotions make affective design challenging to capture and evaluate, unlike traditional designs, which remain elusive. The infusion of new content into metaphorical design, Design Quartet, and other design theories is imperative in the contemporary era.

Design theories and concepts require certain standards for judgment and frameworks for reference. By integrating affective design with the Design Quartet, the study aims to enrich the initially weak structural framework, providing designers with practical guidance. Utilizing the framework and structure of the Design Quartet to provide structural support and phase division for affective design is anticipated.

Simultaneously, for the four orders of design, it presents an excellent opportunity to intersect and integrate with affective design, providing a solid background for exploring whether theoretical frameworks need emotional supplementation and coordination. It highlights the indispensable role of behavioral metaphorical design, systemic environmental metaphorical design, and conceptual metaphorical design in constructing meaning, ultimately facilitating iterative research, and providing robust theoretical and contextual support for user experience.

Additionally, the integration of design theories and concepts serves as a valuable insight for designers, urging them to broaden their design perspectives and not confine themselves to traditional design paradigms. Design should not only satisfy product functionality but also enhance user autonomy, focus on user participation, and consider the construction of user reflective levels to produce practical solutions that are warm, empathetic, and capable of evoking user emotions. The design will inject new vitality as per the demands of the times, expanding its vision and scope of application accordingly.

2 Theoretical Background

2.1 Theoretical Foundations and Practical Implications of Emotional Design

Following the emergence of emotional design, a substantial body of scholars has delved into researching this field. Emotional design, broadly conceptualized, refers to designs capable of evoking emotional resonance in consumers [7]. Donald Norman's seminal work in emotional design laid the groundwork, emphasizing that positive emotions can lead to more favorable evaluations and memories of products, thus facilitating consumption. Building upon principles rooted in cognitive psychology, Norman established the "Triple Design Principles [7]." of emotional design, dividing it into the visceral, behavioral, and reflective levels. Through the example of the Juicy Salif, it is illustrated that effective emotional design can sometimes sacrifice product functionality, indicating that the criteria for evaluating emotional design differ from those for evaluating products solely based on functionality. The absence of behavioral aspects does not impede the construction of reflective aspects, highlighting the reflective level as the ultimate evaluative layer for emotional design.

Pieter M. A. Desmet, another prominent scholar in emotional design, expanded upon Ortony et al.'s classification of three types of emotions: goals, standards, and attitudes [8]. Subsequently, Desmet and Hekkert (2002) experimentally validated these three emotional types and introduced four parameters—appraisal, concern, product, and emotion—forming the basic model of product emotion [9]. Through empirical studies using real product examples, they demonstrated the emotional processes involved in "instrument product emotion," "aesthetic product emotion," "social product emotion," "surprise product emotion," and "interest product emotion." [10]. They proposed a theoretical concept called "design for wow," [11] encapsulating the amalgamation of three emotions: fascination, pleasant surprise, and desire. Furthermore, they conducted research on the conditions inducing emotions by setting emotional experiences as the sole variable in experiments, aiming to monitor emotional changes during specific experiential activities. Paul Hekkert extensively discussed and elaborated on the product emotion model within product experiences, comprising aesthetic, emotional experiences, and meaning of experience [12].

In summary, current research on emotional design necessitates analyzing and elucidating the factors contributing to emotional arousal through products. This analysis requires considering the external structure of products, the sensory experiences of the audience, their intrinsic emotions, and the stimuli for reflection. Additionally, the materiality of products needs to facilitate emotional arousal, with reflection selecting products and spaces as metaphors and carriers of meaning. Designers encode and imbue products with meaning through symbols, while users, through product usage, undergo a decoding process, acquiring their understanding of symbolic representations on products and forming reflections, thereby eliciting emotions. Ultimately, scholars' discussions emphasize the importance of the reflective level in emotional design. Emotions and feelings are different, emotions are short-lived, while feelings typically arise after user reflection and endure. The visceral and behavioral levels represent stages of functional product realization but are not determinants of emotional design. Conversely, the construction of aesthetics, experiences, and meanings—the reflective level—is the key to shaping user emotions. Continuous exploration and stimulation of the visceral and behavioral levels are necessary to achieve the construction of the reflective level.

2.2 *The Role of Metaphorical Design in Constructing Reflective Levels and Its Structural Limitations Within Emotional Design*

Metaphors are ubiquitous linguistic and conceptual constructs encountered in daily life, with an inherent presence in human cognition [13]. Metaphors aid in problem reflection and meaning construction [14], facilitating the escape from constraints imposed by initial problem formulations [15]. Metaphor design can be viewed as a design tool consciously or unconsciously employed by designers, aiming to evoke emotional resonance among consumers through metaphorical associations. Metaphor design involves the use of design elements such as text, graphics, symbols, and colors to visualize the commonalities between two entities through techniques like analogy, symbolism, and implication. For users, metaphor represents a relatively unfamiliar concept (the target domain) elucidated through a concrete object (the source domain). The essence of metaphor lies in the use of one thing to understand and experience another [16]. Rational utilization of metaphorical design facilitates users in intuitively grasping the functionality, value, and usage of unfamiliar objects, thus reducing learning costs, accelerating information assimilation, and enhancing cognitive effects to achieve profound communication and even evoke emotional resonance. Metaphors influence individuals' reasoning, perceptions of the world, categorization of experiences, and integration of ideas [17]. This design approach leverages people's cognitive and emotional responses to specific symbols or representations, thereby enhancing the attractiveness, comprehensibility, and emotional connection of products metaphors [18], services, or experiences. Metaphorical design not only provides functional solutions but also creates emotionally meaningful and humanized experiences, allowing users to enjoy, understand, and accept designs more readily.

However, metaphorical design has certain flaws and shortcomings.

Lakoff and Johnson's book *Metaphors We Live By* is an important foundation for understanding metaphors. Metaphor is not only a linguistic phenomenon but also a cognitive mechanism of human beings. However, the starting point and background of their research mainly focused on the role of metaphor in language and cognition but did not explore the application of metaphor in design practice in depth. This led to early research focusing more on the conceptual level of metaphor rather than specific design applications [13]. A similar situation is also reflected in Gibbs's research. In *The poetics of mind: Figurative thought, language, and understanding.* Gibbs emphasized the importance of metaphor in daily language and thinking, which made the design field pay more attention to the theoretical background of metaphor but paid less attention to the practical application of metaphor in design [19].

Krippendorff and Butter emphasized the importance of semantics and metaphor in design, but mainly focused on the semantic level of product design and user interface design, without in-depth exploration of the application of metaphor in other design fields such as interaction design and service design [20]. In addition, Lakoff and Johnson pointed out that the understanding of metaphor is highly dependent on personal cognitive experience and background. Different users may have different interpretations of the same metaphor, affecting the consistency of design and user experience [13]. The same metaphor may have different meanings in different cultures and may even cause misunderstandings [20]. Marcus pointed out that the application of metaphor in international and cross-cultural design is often restricted by cultural background, which leads designers to prefer visual metaphors because visual elements are relatively easy to convey consistent meanings between different cultures [21]. The scope of metaphorical design is not clearly defined. Metaphorical design, as a tool for reflecting the reflective level in emotional design, needs to be more compatible with the design field. Currently, the corresponding classification of metaphorical design also needs further refinement. Metaphorical design still mainly remains at the surface level, where metaphorical design in the instinctive level of emotional design can easily be achieved through graphics, colors, images, symbols, sounds, smells, etc., but lacks exploration into higher levels [22]. Metaphorical design, intended to stimulate the reflective level in emotional design, is limited to the initial stage and only stays on the surface of visual metaphorical design.

2.3 *Designing the Fundamental Concepts and Research Status of Four Orders of Design*

Richard Buchanan is a renowned design thinker and philosopher, and one of the founding figures in interaction design, who has made significant contributions to the formation of modern design education and the discipline of design. In his paper "Wicked Problems in Design Thinking," he not only extensively explores the "wicked problems" often encountered in design, thereby broadening the scope of concerns in design, but also argues against the stereotypical impressions of the design field, thereby expanding the significance and connotations of design as a discipline. Furthermore, the preliminary formulation of the four orders of design proposed in this paper, delineates the dimensions and orders of design objects, later recognized as a primary prototype for the classification of design disciplines. This garnered substantial attention in both the design and education communities, providing a basis for the professional categorization of design disciplines. In his subsequent works, Buchanan explicitly delineates the content of the four orders of design, dividing the scope of design processes into four fundamental dimensions and orders, namely the communicative issues of the first order indicated by symbols and signs, the construction issues of the second order indicated by artifacts, object, and things, the action sequence represented by actions and events in the third order, and the integration issues represented by systems and environments in the fourth order [23].

(Table 1) It is easy to find contrasting relationships among the four orders of design within the current classification of design disciplines in higher education. Symbols correspond to graphic design, artifacts to product design, actions and events to interaction design, and systems and environments to environmental design [24]. However, Buchanan (1992) does not believe that each design object belongs exclusively to a particular discipline. He points out that each order is a site for rethinking and reconceptualizing the essence of design. The various fields are interconnected and interrelated. This framework summarizes some objectivities of human experience [23], symbols and images derive from fragments of worldly experience, distilled perceptions of material products. Products serve as engagement tools for the perception of actions and systems, while interfaces and concepts create emotional connections for experiences.

With the advent of the third wave of Human–Computer Interaction (HCI), design has begun to emphasize the construction of user experience, reflective levels, and meaning layers. A plethora of scholars have demonstrated the efficacy and significance of emotional design, elucidating the decisive role of reflective levels in user experience. The elicitation of emotions has become an indispensable criterion for designers in providing user experiences. Scholars from various disciplines have extensively discussed the construction of reflective levels as a crucial stage in completing the loop of emotional design.

In exploring the process of constructing reflective levels from a design perspective, the integration of the Design Four Orders Theory with design practice illustrates metaphorical design as a mode of expression utilized by designers. However, due to

Table 1 Four orders of design as per the overlay of tables illustrated by Richard Buchanan in 1998 and 2001

	1st order problem of communication symbol	2nd order problem of construction things	3rd order problem of action action	4th order problem of integration thought
Symbol	Word Symbol Images **Graphic design**			
Things		Physical Object **Industrial design**		
Action			Activities Services Processes **Interaction design**	
Thought				Environments as organizations and system **Environmental design**

the current limitations of concepts related to metaphorical design, there is a pressing need to enhance the standards and frameworks of metaphorical design from the disciplinary standpoint of design. This enhancement is essential for effectively enabling designers to deeply engage with symbols, actions, and environmental codes in the construction of products and experiences, thus inspiring reflection, as evident in the reflective level of emotional design. Further exploration is required to elucidate the assistance provided by deep-level metaphorical design in the context of reflective level, and urgent efforts are needed to refine the standards and frameworks of metaphorical design from the perspective of design discipline. This refinement aims to strengthen design theory for better guiding design practices.

3 Metaphorical Design and the Integration of Four Orders of Design

3.1 The Fusion of Metaphorical Design and the Four Orders of Design

The practice of exploring the world initially relies on the assessment of human cognitive recognition and the initial bodily exploration experiences. The body serves not only as a tool for our thinking and perception but also directly participates in and shapes our cognitive experiences and modes of understanding [25]. Due to the inherent limitations of the scope accessible to the self, humans face constraints in conceptualization and cognition in their daily lives. As new elements and technologies continuously integrate into later stages, individuals begin to utilize metaphors, allegories, and implications to simplify cognitive processes, reduce cognitive difficulty, and disseminate ideas. Metaphors are crucial for generating familiarity and affinity with unfamiliar objects, playing an important role in enhancing user experience and fostering reflection. Layoff and Johnson proposed the concept of conceptual metaphor theory in their book, which categorizes conceptual metaphors into structural metaphors, orientational metaphors, and ontological metaphors [13]. However, this classification method is not convenient for design applications.

The four orders serve as the foundation of design discipline classification and stipulate the main research and learning directions of each discipline of design (Table 2). Per Donald Norman's three-fold design principle for emotional design, and Richard Buchanan's definition and classification of design taxonomy, the theoretical category of metaphorical design is reclassified. Metaphorical design is subdivided into symbolical metaphorical design, object metaphorical design, behavioral metaphorical design, and thought metaphorical design.

Table 2 Reclassification of four-levels metaphor design

Classification	Keywords
Symbolical metaphorical design	Symbols, colors, smells, graphics, pictures, glyphs, sounds and other non-verbal symbols
Object metaphorical design	Physical attributes, shape, size, texture availability, etc.; product positioning, product differentiation
Behavioral metaphorical design	Through behaviors, users' emotions are elicited, accommodated, guided, and constrained. This includes non-verbal forms of expression
Thought metaphorical design	Ideologies, prevalent design concepts, align with the characteristics of the era or region, catering to underlying intellectual demands; they constitute the demarcation between ordinary and exceptional products; attention to integration embodies a systemic culmination

Firstly, symbolic metaphor design encompasses sensory "fragments" such as symbols, colors, shapes, graphics, patterns, typography, sounds, etc. It is important to note that at this level of symbolic metaphor design, it specifically refers to non-verbal symbols.

Secondly, material metaphor design involves considering the physical attributes of products and artifacts, including their appearance, shape, texture, and availability, emphasizing the material properties of products. When analyzing software applications, one can approach it from the perspective of product thinking, highlighting product positioning through aspects like layout and promotional language.

Thirdly, behavioral metaphor design refers to the metaphorical effects of behaviors, actions, gestures, etc., adhering to ergonomic principles. It involves non-verbal expressions that enhance the sense of experience and embodiment. By guiding, planning, or limiting user behavior, emotional interaction is facilitated during the process of user-product interaction. Planning and designing should align with user behavior expectations from the perspectives of service design and interaction design, ensuring consistency and predictability of user behavior, while also considering adaptability to context and situation. It's important to integrate the first three levels with product logic in a localized manner.

Fourthly, thought metaphor design involves combining abstract concepts with concrete images innovatively, guided by the collective cognitive influences of historical, cultural, and ideological factors, to meet the needs of the mass society background, thereby guiding or conforming to people's thinking, perception, and behavior to achieve the design of excellent products.

These four categories correspond to Donald Norman's Triple Design Principles [7] of the emotional design and include the elements in each category. Symbolic metaphor design and object metaphor design correspond to the instinctive/visceral level, behavioral metaphor design corresponds to the behavioral level, and thought metaphor design corresponds to the reflective level. This classification method aims to understand and apply metaphor design more systematically and improve the overall effect of design and user experience through different levels of emotional response and cognitive experience. There isn't a strict hierarchical relationship among these four levels; instead, integration and coherence are required. In the first order, symbolic metaphor design presents fragmented visual elements, necessitating integration, positioning, and reflection within the system and environment, using products as carriers. When the analyzed product does not align with the materiality of the second order, specific analysis should be conducted from the perspective of product positioning and differentiation based on actual circumstances (Fig. 1).

The Table 3 will illustrate, with one most representative case selected for each category of metaphor design, and note the differing emphases required within each of the four metaphor design categories.

By analyzing examples of four categories of metaphorical designs, it is evident how each type of metaphorical design plays a crucial role in emotional design between brands and consumers, particularly in the construction of reflective levels. As visual symbols and objects cease to be the focal point, designers, and design theorists' endeavor to comprehend products from within—not the physical interior, but the

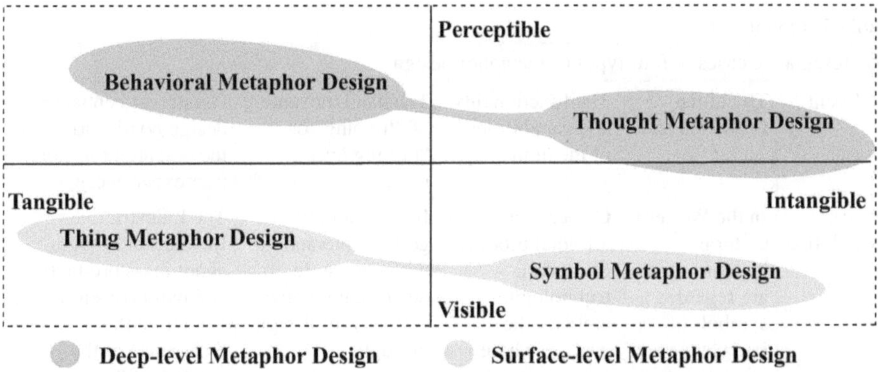

Fig. 1 Place four metaphorical designs onto a Cartesian coordinate system for weighted analysis and subsequent classification aggregation. Case illustration of the integration of metaphorical design with the design tetrad

Table 3 Analysis of representative cases represented by four types of metaphorical designs

Representative cases of four types of metaphor design				
	Symbolical metaphorical design	Object metaphorical design	Behavioral metaphorical design	Thought metaphor design
Case	The logo of Apple Inc.	Surveillance cameras	Interactive gestures and actions when reading e-books	Less is more
Image		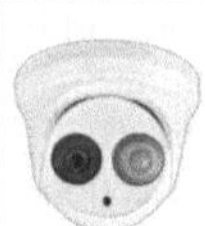		**LESS IS MORE**
Ontology	The bitten apple	Camera equipment	The action of swiping left with one's finger	The principle of minimalist and streamlined design

(continued)

Table 3 (continued)

Representative cases of four types of metaphor design				
Referent	The bitten forbidden fruit	The functionality and capabilities of the human eye	The hand movement of "flipping" or "turning over" pages	Greater and enhanced design possibilities and the potential for more user experiences
Case description	In the Western cultural lexicon, apples are regarded as symbols of knowledge and wisdom, often referred to as "fruits of knowledge." The concept of forbidden fruit is depicted in the Bible. Apple Inc., a globally renowned company in the realm of innovative technology, employs the image of a partially bitten apple to symbolize its fervent pursuit of innovation and knowledge	Cameras, as artificial products of modern technology, embody the process whereby human cognition of its own functions and daily life experiences are transformed into artifacts. Retaining a semblance to the human eye in both form and function, cameras highlight through metaphorical means their similarities to human vision, encompassing perceptual, comprehensive monitoring, and situational observation capabilities	In the realm of gesture interaction with electronic devices, it involves a process of design through metaphorical actions. For instance, when reading electronic books, the motion of flipping pages mimics the habitual action retained from reading physical books. Our memory and interpretation of such actions extend to other electronic products as well. For example, in social networking applications, swiping left signifies actions akin to "turning the page" or "disliking," while swiping right implies actions akin to "being interested" or "liking"	The Industrial Revolution brought about mass production and mass consumption, leading to the emergence of the concept of "less is more," which emphasizes functionality in pursuit of making industrialization more accessible to the masses. Regardless of right or wrong, it merely responds to demands. This notion, aligning with historical contexts and public consumption psychology, is widely regarded as fashionable. Consequently, it shapes aesthetic standards in the design realm, where streamlined design is equated with good design

experiential interior of the humans who manufacture and use them within societal and cultural contexts [24]. Metaphorical design entails a process of conforming to sensory logic and invoking reservoirs of knowledge to ultimately grasp the design intent. This form of design is not merely a conveyance on a visual surface but rather a key to establishing profound connections between brands and consumers on an emotional level. The selection and utilization of various metaphorical design types can guide consumers to resonate with brand narratives, fostering emotional resonance and deepening consumer identification and loyalty to the brand. Cultural symbols, product symbolism, and the association with the brand itself aid in establishing deeper emotional connections and resonance. The premium effects offered by the brand provide consumers with a sense of satisfaction and accomplishment symbolically.

4 Case Analysis

4.1 Take TikTok as a Design Case

Sensor Tower recently released its "Q1 2023: Store Intelligence Data Digest" report, revealing that TikTok once again ranked No. 1 by worldwide downloads for the eleventh consecutive quarter. Taking the TikTok mobile short video app as an example, the report analyzed its application of four newly proposed metaphor design standards. By exploring TikTok's status as one of the hottest applications from the perspective of users, the report delved into the utilization of metaphorical design in its product logic and how such design aligns with user behavior patterns, ultimately achieving a reflective effect in stimulating emotional design within the levels of emotional logic.

TikTok's Symbolic Metaphor Design (Table 4)

Sound: TikTok's short videos are usually accompanied by popular music or sound effects. Sound not only increases entertainment, but also evokes specific emotions and atmosphere. It promotes the spread and popularity of content like memes.

Color: The application interface and logo use bright, vivid and dynamic colors, and create a lively and pleasant atmosphere. Such color design can quickly capture the user's attention and stimulate their desire to explore.

Fragmented vision: Whether it is the selection of TikTok's logo or the presentation of short video content, it adopts eye-catching and instinctive symbolic metaphor design factors. TikTok's short videos are usually edited quickly, presenting a fragmented vision. This design conforms to the attention mode of modern users, can convey a lot of information and emotions in a short time, and keep users at a high level of engagement.

TikTok's Object Metaphor Design (Table 5)

Carrier: The video content itself is the main carrier, and the short video format is convenient for users to quickly consume and share. The length of the video is usually between 15 and 60 s, which can provide enough entertainment information.

Availability: TikTok's interface design is simple and intuitive, and users can easily record, edit and publish videos. The provision of various filters, special effects and stickers enables users to easily create interesting and attractive content, enhancing users' creativity and sense of participation.

TikTok's Behavioral Metaphor Design (Table 6)

Table 4 Using four-levels of metaphor design to analyze symbolic metaphor design elements in TikTok

TikTok APP				
Symbolical metaphorical design		Logo	Quaver (eighth note)	The notes represent rhythm, music, and entertainment. It explains the functional positioning of TikTok as a music short video platform
		Color	Main: black and white	Black and white are the colors of piano keys or staffs, highlighting the attributes of music;
			Minor: red and green	It symbolizes the jitter and vibration of the light ball and sound waves and symbolizes the gorgeous moment. and symbolize dynamics through visuals
		Icon	Like—heart Collection-stars	The heart symbolizes love, and the star symbolizes preciousness and scarcity, used as a metaphor for collection. It is a common symbolic metaphor design

Affirmative actions: TikTok's design mainly encourages users to engage in affirmative interactions, such as likes, comments, and sharing. And the arrangement and internal logic of the actions conform to the metaphor of behavior. These simple interactive actions not only enhance the social connection between users, but also promote the dissemination of content and the activity of the platform.

TikTok's Thought Metaphor Design (Table 7)

Historical Context: In the era of the fast-paced pursuit of energy efficiency, the development of products with social attributes necessitates attention to and utilization of users' fragmented time. The success of TikTok is closely intertwined with the product logic that aligns with the spirit of the times.

Modes of Dissemination: Traditional media such as radio, television, and news belong to the "one-to-many" top-down linear communication mode, emphasizing authoritative narratives. In contrast, TikTok's dissemination resembles a decentralized "many-to-many" "point-to-surface" communication, focusing on individual narratives and marginal narratives.

A significant reason for TikTok's success lies in its alignment with contemporary demands. In the present era, people are more inclined towards the presentation of content based on the product logic of short videos, which embodies profound

Table 5 Using four levels of metaphor design to analyze object metaphor design elements in TikTok

TikTok APP			
Object metaphorical design	Name	TikTok	Tik has a light pronunciation and expresses product attributes in a light and fast pace, while the "Tok" part may be related to "talk" (talk) to symbolize the product in the form of short videos and its social attributes "Tick-tock" symbolizes time, and combined with product features, it highlights that TikTok is a short video measured in seconds, highlighting the characteristics of editing and production
	Slogan	"Make your day"	Encourage users to make full use of every moment and every second to record the beauty of life, no matter how short or small the user's creation is. Users can create and share videos to showcase their thoughts, talents, and creativity. Recording the beauty and creativity in life
	Flow layout	News feed Single-column feed	Social apps can usually be divided into text feed, picture feed and Video Feed represented by Tik Tok. TikTok takes advantage of the design advantages of a single feed stream to improve the user's concentration, the clarity of the page, the immersion and the convenience of promotion and monitoring The layout rolls like a waterfall At the same time, the form of feed stream is also designed metaphorically, symbolizing that users are indoctrinated and fed information by the platform

metaphysical design. There is a shift away from grand narratives towards a focus on micro-narratives and marginal narratives. This transformation signifies attention to individual narratives and emphasizes decentralization. In this process, TikTok endeavors to confront the absurdity of postmodernity by highlighting individual and marginal stories, disrupting the meaninglessness brought about by grand narratives. Decentralization of power becomes a crucial principle in its design, intending to break the monopoly of traditional meanings through decentralized content creation and dissemination. Therefore, TikTok's product logic is not merely a functional design but also a powerful response to the nihilism of postmodernity, aiming to redefine the construction of meaning and dissemination pathways.

Table 6 Using four levels of metaphor design to analyze behavioral metaphor design elements in TikTok

TikTok APP			
Behavioral metaphorical design	Tap	Like, comment, share and follow	When users like, comment or follow, they interact with the user by clicking on these positive gestures, expressing positive emotions such as choice, love, affirmation, trust, and recognition through the affirmative action suggestion of "clicking"
	Push/slide up	Quickly scroll through the news stream and skip the content that doesn't interest you	The gesture symbolizes the sliding away exit interface, and the user expresses his lack of interest and insufficiency through the gesture of sliding away quickly At the same time, this sense of control increases the user's sense of control and autonomy over the content
	Pull-down	Quickly browse the full video and refresh the updated information	The design of the swipe or pull action can be seen as a behavioral incentive that encourages the user to actively engage and explore more content Through this suggestive action, users can assist the positive visual content, and at the same time, it is a metaphor for the continuity and infinity of the platform content

Table 7 Using four levels of metaphor design to analyze thought metaphor design elements in TikTok

TikTok APP	
Thought metaphor design	**Content provision**: The content on the TikTok platform covers a wide range of content, from entertainment, education to current events. Such content diversity meets the different needs of users and attracts users of all ages **Follow the trend of thought**: TikTok's algorithm can push personalized content based on the user's viewing history and preferences. This design that conforms to user interests and social trends allows users to always find content that interests them, thereby enhancing user stickiness and satisfaction

4.2 Analysis and Design Recommendations

Based on the analysis in the above table, two important points can be observed. Firstly, there is an accumulative effect of multiple metaphorical designs, and it is crucial to note the intermodal correspondence between metaphors. Secondly, there is coherence among multiple metaphorical designs themselves.

A single metaphorical design can target a design objective. Multiple metaphorical designs can collectively target the same design objective, or even multiple design objectives. The existence of such multiple metaphorical designs provides a richer and deeper expression of the product's concepts and values. When multiple metaphorical designs simultaneously target a design objective, they reinforce each other, emphasizing the clarity and consistency of product positioning. However, it is also essential to recognize the differentiation in weight and priority among multiple metaphorical designs. In practical applications, continual adjustment and balancing of the weights and priorities of these different design metaphors are necessary to ensure the overall effectiveness of product design and the achievement of objectives.

A product is often composed of multiple overlaid design metaphors, implying that each metaphor serves its own purpose and function, and they complement each other rather than being independent. Different metaphorical structures are typically combined, where the coherence between metaphors becomes more crucial than the structure itself [13]. Each metaphor has a singular purpose, and when purposes overlap, so do the metaphors. However, since one metaphor cannot fulfill all purposes simultaneously, multiple metaphors are needed to fully express a concept. Thus, the coherence of metaphors makes the overall design more organic and easily understandable. The assessment of the weights and priorities of these metaphors needs continual refinement through practice and reflection.

In metaphorical design, each metaphor focuses on one aspect of argumentation, and this shared implication of metaphors can establish inter-metaphor correspondences, creating coherence between different metaphors, thereby making the entire design more consistent and comprehensive.

Hence, coherence exists among them. Allowable mixed metaphors belong to this overlap, providing a more comprehensive perspective and understanding when expressing complex concepts. Therefore, maintaining coherence and consistency in metaphorical design is crucial, as it helps ensure effective communication of the design and deep understanding of the product by users.

5 Conclusion

In this paper, we explore the significance of constructing layers of meaning in affective design, with a particular emphasis on the metaphorical designs utilized by designers in their daily practices to bridge the four orders of design. Metaphorical design is categorized into symbolic metaphor design, object metaphor design, behavioral metaphor design, and conceptual/thought metaphor design. These design elements, through emotional triggers, can guide users towards emotional resonance, thereby enhancing user experience. Symbolic metaphor design can evoke user emotions through symbolic meanings, while object metaphor design evokes emotional engagement through the shaping of product forms, plot settings, and developments. Behavioral metaphor design shapes emotional connections through user behavioral patterns and feedback, while thought metaphor design guides user emotional experiences through the core ideologies and values of the product. Collectively, these designs foster emotional interactions in product narratives, not only establishing emotional connections between users and products but also serving as vital pathways to enhance user engagement and loyalty.

Through case analyses, it is found that when audiences can comprehend metaphorical designs well, there are significant advantages in constructing layers of meaning. Metaphorical design necessitates designers not only to focus on surface-level symbolic metaphor design but also to integrate and plan, from a comprehensive perspective, behavioral metaphors, product metaphors, and system metaphors tailored to users, ultimately aligning with contemporary conceptual metaphors to position products. In multi-layered metaphors, designers need to balance the weights of various metaphorical design elements to maintain consistency and fluidity among them.

However, it is crucial to acknowledge the limitations of this study. This paper selects products that are relatively outstanding in the market and does not discuss scenarios where metaphors fail to function, the imbalance of weights in multi-layered metaphor design, mismatches between metaphors and product positioning, ideological environments, etc. Therefore, we anticipate that future research will further explore situations where metaphorical design fails to function, aiming to enhance the effectiveness and applicability of metaphorical design in constructing meaning and reinforcing emotional design.

References

1. Diani, M.: Immateriality takes command. Design issues, 6–11 (1988).
2. Bødker, S.: Third wave HCI, 10 years later—participation and sharing. Interactions, 22(5), 24–31 (2015).
3. Norman, D.: User centered system design. New perspectives on human-computer interaction (1986).
4. Duman, S., & Timur, Ş.: Expanding Orders of Design and its Implications for Design Education. Online Journal of Art & Design, 8(3) (2020).
5. Liu, X., & Chen, Y.: Digital Media Design Strategy for Stage Based on Four Orders of Design. In E3S Web of Conferences (Vol. 179, p. 02034). E3S Web of Conferences (2020).
6. Meluso, J., Johnson, S., & Bagrow, J.: Flexible environments for hybrid collaboration: Redesigning virtual work through the four orders of design. Design Issues, 38(1), 55–69 (2022).
7. Norman, D.: Emotional design: Why we love (or hate) everyday things. Basic books (2007).
8. Ortony, A., Clore, G. L., & Collins, A.: The cognitive structure of emotions. Cambridge University Press (2022).
9. Desmet, P. M., & Hekkert, P.: The basis of product emotions. Pleasure with products, beyond usability, 60–68 (2002).
10. Desmet, P.: A multilayered model of product emotions. *The design journal*, *6*(2), 4–13 (2003).
11. Desmet, P. M., Porcelijn, R., & Van Dijk, M. B.: Emotional design; application of a research-based design approach. Knowledge, Technology & Policy, 20(3), 141–155 (2007).
12. Desmet, P., & Hekkert, P.: Framework of product experience. International journal of design, 1(1), 57–66 (2007).
13. Lakoff, G., & Johnson, M.: Metaphors we live by. University of Chicago Press (2008).
14. Madsen, K. H.: A guide to metaphorical design. Communications of the ACM, 37(12), 57–62 (1994).
15. Snodgrass, A., & Coyne, R.: Models, metaphors, and the hermeneutics of designing. Design issues, 9(1), 56–74 (1992).
16. Lakoff, G., & Johnson, M.: The metaphorical structure of the human conceptual system. Cognitive science, 4(2), 195–208 (1980).

17. Casakin, H. P.: Factors of metaphors in design problem-solving: Implications for design creativity. International journal of design, 1(2), 21–33 (2007).
18. Hekkert, P., & Cila, N.: Handle with care! Why and how designers make use of product metaphors. Design Studies, 40, 196–217 (2015).
19. Gibbs, R. W.: The poetics of mind: Figurative thought, language, and understanding. Cambridge University Press (1994).
20. Krippendorff, K.: The semantic turn: A new foundation for design. CRC Press (2005).
21. Marcus, A.: International and intercultural user interfaces. User interfaces for all: Concepts, methods, and tools, 47–63 (2001).
22. Cooper, A., Reimann, R., Cronin, D., & Noessel, C.: About face: the essentials of interaction design. Wiley (2014).
23. Buchanan, R.: Wicked problems in design thinking. Design issues, 8(2), 5–21 (1992).
24. Buchanan, R. Design research and the new learning. Design issues, 17(4), 3–23 (2001).
25. Dourish, P.: Where the Action Is: The Foundations of Embodied Interaction; MIT Press: Cambridge, MA, USA (2004).

Designing Cookbooks for a Phygital World: Recipes (from the Past and) for the Future

Suzana Parreira

Abstract Cookbooks involve personal, social, and cultural practices that created a large editorial mass market with food being recorded in several conventional publishing formats, alongside the channels and platforms used to circulate content. Together with handwritten cookbooks and print magazines, nowadays new branches powered by the internet also cover food tv channels, blogs, recipe platforms, podcasts and more recently food apps and subscription newsletters, not to mention the digital form of print cookbooks, the e-cookbook. This paper uses this overlapping territory (and the gap between print and digital) as motivation to analyse selected Portuguese cuisine cookbooks, taking the national food scene to discuss the cookbook phygital experience. Complementarity between physical and digital versions of products with different user experiences show an appetite for cookbooks with content made available on multiple media, in joint formats and on different platforms. The concept of phygital offers a specific approach to understand the cookbook market dynamics where the coexistence of different food-related mediascapes reveals a "pluriverse" that characterises the phygital cookbook experience in the present. The increase of interactive features and multimedia content which allow for extra personalization and customization provide a more engaging and immersive experience for the cookbook reader in the future.

Keywords Portuguese cookbooks · Visual narratives · Communication design · Food design · Phygital experience

1 Introduction

Food is a form of communication that connects people over geographies and languages, with recipes and stories that have been kept in handwritten journals or circulated as printed material while building a common platform for understanding

S. Parreira (✉)
Faculdade de Belas-Artes, Centro de Investigação e de Estudos em Belas-Artes (CIEBA), Largo da Academia Nacional de Belas-Artes, Universidade de Lisboa, 1249-058 Lisboa, Portugal
e-mail: s.parreira@belasartes.ulisboa.pt

© The Author(s), under exclusive license to Springer Nature Switzerland AG 2025

D. Brandão et al. (eds.), *Perspectives on Design and Digital Communication V*, Springer Series in Design and Innovation 50, https://doi.org/10.1007/978-3-031-76156-0_20

the world. In fact, it can be argued that the history of cookbooks is the history of humanity itself. As a literary genre, the cookbook plays an active role in shaping norms about gender, class, race or sexuality. But to fully understand the implied meanings and its impact in society, we must also consider the cookbook's publishing history [1]. Cookbooks involve personal, social, and cultural practices that created a large editorial mass market, anchored in needs, dreams and goals concerning food that every individual and every society builds across time. This book genre gained a new surge with printing, and through the last five centuries, became part of a diffusion circuit of culinary recipes, turning a minor business into a mass-market industry [2].

Regardless of all the recipes readily available in digital form, in the present, physical cookbooks remain the reader's first option because the experience in the kitchen with a print book provides memories and a purpose for experimenting that can't be replicated uniquely with digital devices. Thus, the cookbook of the future is phygital, reinstating a new paradigm that entails the combination of both physical and digital realities [3]. Although the concept originated in the field of marketing, it has been increasingly used in other fields to describe these two different dimensions together in symbiosis, rather than replacing each other.

Powered by technology, cookbooks evolved from a personal or familiar context to a broader (sometimes global) audience, reflecting habits and memories of smaller or larger groups of people [2]. The cookbook as a source of collective experience considers primarily culinary recipes collected across time and kept as handwritten instructions passed by oral tradition. Secondly, it relies on print cookbooks driven by a combination of personal and professional motivations, with chefs providing content to a new publishing market or female authors who create cookbooks for the domestic cook, usually other women. Nowadays, with the digital era, those recipe collections become part of a shared global world, with platforms like blogs or social media as part of the loop between printed paper and the screen that consolidates into a phygital approach [3].

A combination of words and images provide the perfect vehicle for the cookbook's technical-scientific and narrative nature [4], which incorporate both instructions and tales as well as visualising the dish or the environment the author wants the reader to connect with. In the last two decades, cookbooks have been produced with aesthetics as a priority, a strategy to captivate based on the use of photography, design and quality printing. The cookbook as an artefact translates into a collection of recipes and stories that set a unique voice for its author, designed to be used in and out of the kitchen as an instruction's book as well as a coffee table book to assert a certain lifestyle. The challenges for the e-book to match a print cookbook are not only the interface but also the connection with the reader and the (physical) memories it involves [5].

Cookbooks supplied a way for understanding human history across time while also prescribing behaviours and shaping (new) markets. Both the recipe itself and the stories that it unveils make cookbooks not just a reflection of cultural sensibilities but also capable of creating a certain food culture [6]. The cookbook as a medium acts as a channel or route in the communication process, with particular languages that translate into ways of living or create specific food tribes. As part of an experience that is simultaneously physical and digital, the print book may offer a connection with supplementary online content that presents an alternative reading through videos or interactive infographics.

2 Recipes from the Past

Traditionally, cookbooks are collections of recipes and cooking processes set for the domestic kitchen, either with a reference to a specific cuisine or as part of family heritage. Reading (and cooking from) a cookbook which reflects a kitchen practice, allows the user to enter a food culture and be part of the foodscape because food is not just nutrition but also preparation, presentation and consumption as a complex communicative practice that must include the meal's design and its whole field of experience [7]. The use of more than one media in a cookbook and the combined practice of image, sound or video is common in the digital environment where different formats converge to create a complete experience. However, food as a language has been used for centuries as part of a multidimensional encounter between people using diverse tools and channels to produce meaning (personal, social or global).

2.1 Community Cookbooks and the TV

Any recipe collection represents the individual person who wrote it but always also reflects some "collaborative knowledge passed down from mother to daughter; from neighbor to friend" (p. 5) [8]. Community cookbooks are an extraordinary record of collective memory while providing a snapshot of the lived experience of a particular group, where a recipe "reveals other stories too: of family sagas and community records, of historical and cultural moments or changes, and also personal histories and narratives of the self" (p. 2) [9]. Considering Maria de Lourdes Modesto seminal cookbook, *Cozinha Tradicional Portuguesa*, which originates from a quest set in motion on TV by the author, both the impact of a collective experience and the dissemination power of television created an everlasting effect.

In 1958, the first culinary show on the newly created Portuguese television launched Maria de Lourdes Modesto. Her experiences centred on French cuisine and the TV show was meant to raise awareness of that food culture among housewives. The first cooking show on Portuguese television aired for 12 years (between 1958 and 1970). In 1967, the book *Receitas da TV* (Recipes from TV) was first edited, and recently in May 2019 a facsimile version was re-edited and re-released. With television becoming popular, a new type of approach was created, with cooking TV shows frequently mimicking the mother-daughter teaching scenario, which made different recipes and techniques widely available and reproducible to the public [2]. Later, in 1982, Maria de Lourdes Modesto would play a fundamental role in promoting traditional Portuguese cooking with the most iconic cookbook in national cuisine, *Cozinha Tradicional Portuguesa*. A compilation of selected recipes sent by the TV viewers, the book has become the "bible" of Portuguese Traditional Cuisine, both for home cooks and for chefs (as part of their professional training). It's the best-selling cookbook of all time in Portugal, having already sold more than 400 thousand copies, which illustrates the potential of community cookbooks [1].

Now and then, TV presenters and chefs became public personalities with the influence to write cookbooks that created a new market. Food TV channels like *24 Kitchen* set a platform for different voices to have their shows from which, invariably, is released a new cookbook with the broadcasted recipes. Already in its 9th season in Portugal, chef Henrique Sá Pessoa keeps a well known culinary TV show *Comtradição* (a word play between "with tradition" and "contradiction") where he "reinterprets traditional Portuguese cuisine on a journey to the roots of national cuisine" always with a twist or a provocation. The recipes are available online (together with videos) at the channel's website, and also in its *YouTube* channel but have been compiled in a cookbook (2021). The hardcover, with a glossy printing work, is mostly intended for TV viewers to complement their multidimensional, and phygital, experience. So, phygital is nothing new in food contexts, as the physical part of the equation has been frequently connected with digital (or at least dematerialized) content ever since TV became part of everyday life. What the present complementarity between print and digital shows is new hybrid paper-and-screen reading habits, and "how our online and offline lives have become intertwined" [10].

2.2 From Handwritten to Print (and to Digital) Cookbooks

Handwritten cookbooks are a tradition dating back to the 19th century, with compilations of recipes that are casual and random, commonly not meant for other cooks but the author. Usually, these books have no special organisation rather than the timeline that marks the interval between the beginning and the end of its use, characterised by the recipe selection that follows the author's everyday life and personal experiences. The handwritten cookbook reinstates itself as "a material support for an immaterial tradition that combines culinary knowledge with commensality practices" (p. 107) [11].

Although technology may evolve, as it happened with the printing press and the proliferation of printed books, people's habits do not change rapidly. Many still keep manuscript books, despite the abundance of printed editions "which, however, did not replace the tradition of handwritten cooking notebooks probably because of their flexible structure which encapsulated a personal identity" (p. 108) [11]. As print cookbooks didn't completely replace manuscript books in the past, the same can be said about e-books concerning print books. Since the 2010s, publishers have been making a strong investment in the digital business model, transforming their processes to offer content in multiple formats (print and digital) and on all platforms.

Regardless of all the e-books' proclaimed advantages (storage, distribution, interaction), print cookbooks kept thriving [3]. For example, Edite Vieira's *The Taste of Portugal: A Voyage of Gastronomic Discovery Combined with Recipes, History and Folklore* represents a trajectory from print to digital (and phygital) after its first edition as a print book in 1988, and then 1995 (both by Hale Publishers and in hardcover format). The cookbook had a new edition in 2000 (with a new publisher, Grub Street) and was reprinted in 2003, and 2005. A version in 2013, revised and updated (with a new cover and photographs) marks the simultaneous release of an e-book Kindle version. Although there is no public info to discuss the success of the digital version, in 2018 a paperback version with new cover was launched but the same e-book Kindle (from the 2013s edition) was kept. It can be due to minor changes between both versions that didn't justify a new e-book or the assumption that the digital version was of lesser importance.

The cookbook's historical path is traced in adapting mode from pen to paper, and then to pixel, continuously following technology and social change. Although different periods see distinct trends in cookbook use, the replacement of the old by the new doesn't occur, instead diverse cookbook typologies coexist in time. The increase of phygital experiences is part of the digital era and consequently, in the present, the same content can be available in multimedia formats that are used simultaneously by the reader [5].

2.3 Cookbook is the Medium (and the Message)

The medium through which food-related content is conveyed plays a vital role in the way the message is received and interpreted, being at the same time the result of a certain culture and a cultural producer itself. The language of cooking is a cultural matter as it relies on conventions and contexts previously set in which cookbooks act as part of a social dynamic. The double-dimensional nature between the instructional function and the aspirational way of living creates a critical field for cookbooks, considering "how an 'object as discourse' meets 'reflection in use'" (p. 34) [12]. Historically, preserving knowledge is a function cookbooks have embraced by creating followers, whose numbers grew in order to pass the information and know-how from generation to generation. Nowadays, a cookbook can assume many forms and exist through different media without losing its nuclear format: a food-centred text (and images) that can take the shape of recipes, places and experiences that are shared with a more or less large number of people.

In 2017 Cristina Castro started to publish *A Doçaria Portuguesa*, a cookbook collection about the history, practice and traditions of sweets in Portugal, serving both as an itinerary and a guide to the South, Center, North and the Islands confectionary. Each book describes each sweet, its history, who makes it and where and "it is explained how the sweet should be eaten, because this is also part of the tradition. It talks about people who currently make those sweets". In parallel, she offers a *YouTube* channel called No Ponto (www.youtube.com/@NoPonto_pt) that collects videos concerning the stories and recipes of sweets and the people that make them. With only a handful of recipes, the cookbook collection is built around the traditions in each place and the people that cook, bake and eat the sweets for which the videos available offer a context, a story and a living culture. Although the print cookbooks can be used without the project's digital part, the combined exercise of reading the books and watching the videos add to a more complete sensorial experience, both tactile, visual and auditory. If, as a consequence, the reader tastes a sweet from the book and the video, it becomes a total adventure with gustatory and olfactory experiments included.

How the cookbook is used involves different practices and ideologies that forge personal, social, and cultural dynamics within the experience. The memories created are set to be part of a personal cultural legacy that also translates into a collective formation settled on tradition. Just by existing as a medium, the cookbook sets a chain of effects beyond the content it displays or the concrete food topic it shows. Because "our interactions with food-related media can help us understand the ways they both shape and reflect culture" [10], the cookbook establishes itself as a way to crystalise memories, as well as create new ones in an unique manner. This trend only increased with the digital era, and became part of an intricate net of connections that settles the cookbook in a multidimensional market with interconnected branches that come together to fulfil the reader-cook-internaut dreams and needs.

3 The Phygital Cookbook Experience

When Chris Weil, in 2007, invented the term phygital to explain the blended reality between physical and digital that characterised several industries, this point of view (and the word) was mostly adopted by marketing experts. Over time, phygital emerged as a promising subject defined as the use of technology to link the digital and physical worlds with the intention of supplying a special interactive experience for the user [13]. As the connection of distinct environments and formats amplified the integration of print and digital in the cookbook world, the market changed into a complex phygital field that can only be completely perceived from a holistic point of view.

To understand the cookbook market is crucial to realise food is a multifold experience [7], covering preparation, presentation and consumption at the same time as it considers the cultural side and the food-related mediatic dimension (TV shows, newspapers, magazines). From the publishing perspective, food has historically been recorded in several conventional formats, alongside the channels and platforms that it uses to circulate its content. With the internet surge, a broad set of new branches also cover food tv channels, blogs, recipe platforms, podcasts and more recently food apps and subscription newsletters, not to mention the digital form of print cookbooks, the e-cookbook. These different forms coexist and coincide as (food and book) consumers live phygital lifes that combine the physical world with the ever present digital environment [3].

Thus, the phygital cookbook experience is directly (and indirectly) the result of print and digital overlapping areas concerning formats, platforms, and media in which food is presented, shared, and discussed. What the phygital mindset brings is a simultaneity and ubiquity of the content, bridging together space and time for a complete multi sensorial experience. The complexity inherent to the cookbook ecosystem in the present is visible in the relational diagram (Fig. 1). Considering the physical, food handwritten journals and print food magazines intersect with print cookbooks, which today remains the most important format in food-related publishing ink-on-paper [2]. Even if print cookbooks face the same challenges as other book genres trending for digitalisation, this market keeps thriving as it acknowledges the importance for print media in the foodspace, reinforced by e-cookbooks as part of a phygital experience. Throughout history, print media "promoted not only new foods, kitchen technologies, and methods of food preparation, but also introduced novel culinary traditions and ideas, influenced social behaviors, and contributed to a rapidly evolving culinary landscape" (p. 75) [14].

Traditionally, handwritten journals cover daily eating with stories and recipes to illustrate a personal connection, and this format has been part of the food scene for centuries. Starting with royalty, personal manuscripts represented a legacy from high nobility ladies such as Infanta D. Maria de Portugal who, in the 16th century, was responsible for the oldest Portuguese recipe's manuscript which can be found in the National Library of Naples [15]. Although relevant to understanding the ingredients and techniques present in the kingdom's kitchens at the time, it was not before the

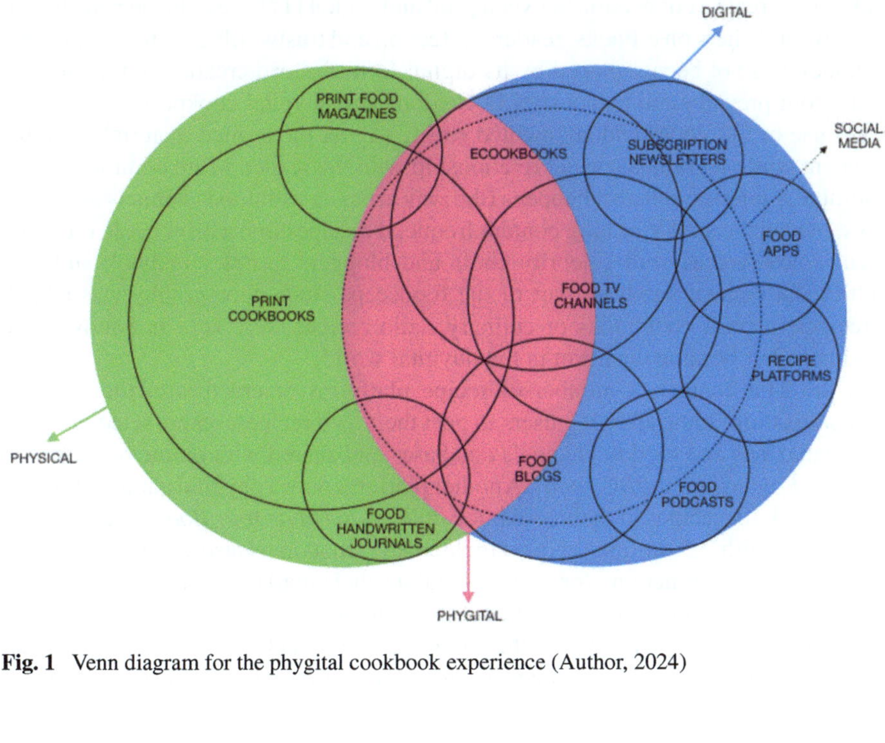

Fig. 1 Venn diagram for the phygital cookbook experience (Author, 2024)

1960s that the manuscript was printed and published in Portugal, still being available today, also as an e-book. The *Manual de Cozinha da Infanta D. Maria* started as a handwritten manuscript in the 16th century, was later printed in the second half of the 20th century and then transformed into a digital version in the 21st century.

Print food magazines also represent a 20th century trend when high-gloss mags on coffee tables and in the kitchen initiated a food revolution for the everyday cook. Directed by Maria Emília Cancela de Abreu, from March 1960 until 1974, the first Portuguese food magazine *Banquete* marks the moment chefs identity began to emerge in specialised print. Another iconic Portuguese culinary magazine *Tele-Culinária* was first published in October 1976, whose technical director for more than 30 years was Chef Silva (who became a celebrity with his TV show). The weekly magazine featured one main recipe, previously filmed and shown on TV, with tips about cooking techniques and utensils, and illustrated with photos. Today, the magazine is available in digital version, following the recent print mags shift but its history shows the phygital food media's nature. Since the second decade of the 21st century, as the world becomes more interconnected, the rise of online content threatened conventional food magazines sales, only to see an independent food magazine's rebirth as a market niche in the 2020s, one of several changes in the magazine industry in recent times [16].

Presently, e-cookbooks form part of the digital food territory, together with food tv channels and food blogs, demonstrating the potential in dematerialised publishing, as well as the role of self publishing, concerning recipes, food events and lifestyle. Many print cookbooks result in digital versions, either to address new readers looking for e-books or to create a connection between print and digital [17]. Despite the investment made by publishers on e-books, readers' affection and trustworthiness for the printed cookbook has not been replaced by its digital form, instead creating a new market where both prevail simultaneously [3]. Seldom, the phygital cookbook experience makes use of QR codes and augmented reality to link the printed material with the e-content while it crafts a special relationship with the reader. More commonly, the print/digital intersection also happens (the way around) with food channels and food blogs, in which case TV or blog content frequently shapes into a print book, creating singular new voices with celebrity chefs and bloggers turned cookbook authors. Multimodal content has been part of the foodscape since photography was added to recipes in print cookbooks or culinary radio recipes were kept in handwritten cookbooks but became the norm in the phygital world.

In the 21st century, a number of recipe platforms emerged with the internet democratisation, some allowing users to post their own recipes, others selected from food magazines and food tv channels databases and shared with online readers (for example, *Epicurious* or *BBC Food*). Another platform with a phygital nature allowing users to look for recipes in their cookbook collection is *Eat Your Books*, a cookbook mega-index with 2.5 million recipes. Incidentally, food apps also launched planner and manager new functions for cooks to curate their marked recipes and use as a customised digital cookbook. Food Podcasts are a fairly new addition to the culinary landscape, usually associated with the author profile as a chef, journalist or blogger and used to broadcast audio content (such as *As Receitas da Tia Cátia*, a culinary podcast in *Smooth FM*). More recently, food subscription newsletters (for example, through *Substack*) have allowed many cookbook authors and bloggers to share (and, more importantly, monetise) their recipes and food content. Also, kitchen robots connected to the internet display recipe collections that enable cooking by directing the user to place certain ingredients and follow directions through different steps. These robots added to a new experience where the device contains both the screen with the recipe and the machinery needed to prepare the food [18].

In spite of being fragmented and diverse, social media is omnipresent to every food-related activity: print cookbooks and e-cookbooks, magazines, handwritten journals and blogs, tv channels and apps, recipe platforms, kitchen robots, subscription newsletters and podcasts all appear and may have a social media profile as "social media encourage the rapid spreading of food-related information" [19]. From recipe sharing to food research, all publishing types end up, one way or another, as part of social media posts, either with the intention to promote and show the content or to produce and create new ones. For example, *Instagram* has become a food hub for photography, recipes and food-related topics, with specialised profiles that showcase authors and cookbooks. Users, as well as authors, create collaborative community-oriented spaces through food to share content while constructing identities using social media [20]. Cookbooks, print and digital, are enjoyed as a whole through a sensorial experience, and social media plays a relevant role in the way cooks and readers connect with recipes and books.

4 The Future (Phygital) Cookbook Reader

As Roger Chartier refers, a new definition of book arises in the transition from manuscripts to the printed page with the text, the object and the author all connected in a way that is impossible to disentangle or separate [21]. With significant technical revolutions the text may remain the same but the reading changes and takes different courses of action [22]. As a result, the phygital cookbook experience is marked historically by a connection between those who authored the book but also those who read and cooked from it. For a long time, the cookbook bore a personal connection through experience with the person who wrote it, in many cases being used and valued exclusively in the household where it was written. With the publishing market, editors became a piece of the process as they selected those who were printed, a position pulverised by the digital revolution as the "cookbook itself, as an object, is also under transformation as the opportunities offered by new media and such changes in the publishing landscape as quality self-publication have expanded the possibilities of their use and value. This has, both been caused by, and prompted, a rethinking of traditional models" [10]. From a phygital perspective, the cookbook has become a multimedia artefact and medium set for a multilayered experience where content travels between formats and platforms, frequently in self-publishing or DIY mode. This is reinforced by social media, which remains a catalyst for accelerating print and digital blending, and represents a convergence for every phygital cookbook experience that may still increase in the future.

Concerning the technology used, cookbooks are artefacts that rely on design to build messages around food, forging a specific format that connects cooks, readers and designers [23]. As technology develops and establishes new ways to share food-related content, cookbooks unfold into multiple media and different configurations. Regarding layout, interactivity and accessibility, print cookbooks and e-books may share part of content but bare distinct profiles as readers fail to transition straight from print to digital. The phygital cookbook experience is technology-based as habits become more interactive with features that can enhance e-readers (like Kindle) with their own unique advantages and disadvantages but indicates a continuous preference for traditional books [24]. Nevertheless, because of e-books portability and their ability to be altered and changed, it's important to consider the potential for creating new habits that will coexist with print cookbooks, similarly as handwritten journals did with printing material [17]. The content's mobility, from print to digital, changed its nature to become "polyphonic and palimpsestic, open and malleable, infinite and shifting" (p. 9) [25], disrupting the idea of originality, authorship and the reader's ability to intervene. Recipe platforms and food apps offer a convenient way to access recipes and cooking tips without time or space limits but still fall short of creating an intimate relation with the reader similar to print cookbooks. Interestingly, some platforms, devices (like kitchen robots) and apps connect with cookbooks either supplying interactive features such as videos and step-by-step instructions for printed recipes or offering indexing to print cookbooks or e-cookbooks from the reader's own collection. The increase of interactive features and multimedia content which allow for extra personalisation and customisation provide a more engaging and immersive experience for the cookbook reader as part of a phygital experience.

5 Conclusions

As a mass-market industry, the cookbook's spectrum is multidimensional, progressing from an individual to a collective endeavour, seen both as an object and an experience, and assumed as a medium used to convey a message. Frequently, for the cookbook of the present, content is made available on multiple media, in joint formats and on different platforms—several elements, not limited to text and image, may also include audio or video to complete a phygital experience. The concept of phygital offers a specific approach to understand and explain the cookbook market dynamics since the "scientific debate about phygital has allowed to identify thematic specialisation in managerial, technical and social fields" [13]. A multilayer experience combines both print and digital in different formats for a phygital reader who interacts with food publishing platforms in order to create mixed connections. The coexistence of multiple food-related platforms reveals a "pluriverse" that characterises the phygital cookbook experience, which sets new and innovative ways to engage with books and food content in the future.

References

1. Driver, E. (2009). Cookbooks as primary sources for writing history: a bibliographer's view. *Food, Culture & Society*, 12(3), 257–274. https://doi.org/10.2752/175174409X431987
2. Notaker, H. (2022). *A history of cookbooks: from kitchen to page over seven centuries* (Vol. 64). Univ of California Press.
3. Parreira, S. (2024). No More Cookbooks? No, More Cookbooks. Reflections on a Print Book in the Age of Digital Media. In: Martins, N., Brandão, D. (eds) Advances in Design and Digital Communication IV. DIGICOM 2023. Springer Series in Design and Innovation, vol 35. Springer, Cham. https://doi.org/10.1007/978-3-031-47281-7_26
4. Ferrara, C.: Cookbooks. Narrative spaces and user manuals. *Progetto Grafico* (35) (2019). https://hdl.handle.net/10447/393340
5. Leer, J., & Povlsen, K. K. (Eds.). (2016). *Food and media: Practices, distinctions and heterotopias.* Routledge.
6. LeBesco, K., & Naccarato, P. (2016). Politics and the future of food and media. *Food and Media: Practices, Distinctions and Heterotopias*, 197.
7. Bartz, C., Ruchatz, J., & Wattolik, E. (2023). Food-Media-Senses Preliminary Observations. *Food-Media-Senses: Interdisciplinary Approaches*, 100, 9.
8. Cirina, L. E. (2017). Rewriting the recipe: trauma, memory, and the modernist cookbook. https://scholarworks.calstate.edu/concern/theses/sf2686787
9. Forster, L., & Floyd, J. (2003). *The recipe reader: narratives, contexts, traditions.* Ashgate Publishing Limited.
10. Brien, D. L., & Wessell, A. (2013). Cookbook: A new scholarly view. *M/C Journal*, 16(3). https://doi.org/10.5204/mcj.688
11. Iliescu, L. J. (2022). The Handwritten Recipe Notebook as a Place of Memory. Martor. *Revue d'Anthropologie du Musée du Paysan Roumain*, (27), 107–112.
12. Mazé, R., & Redström, J. (2009). Difficult forms: Critical practices of design and research. *Research Design Journal*, 1, 28–39. https://www.diva-portal.org/smash/get/diva2:1042616/FULLTEXT01.pdf
13. Del Vecchio, P., Secundo, G., & Garzoni, A. (2023). Phygital technologies and environments for breakthrough innovation in customers' and citizens' journey. A critical literature review and future agenda. *Technological Forecasting and Social Change*, 189, 122342. https://doi.org/10.1016/j.techfore.2023.122342
14. Pipes, M. L., & Janowitz, M. F. (2013). Op-Ed: The Influence of New Technologies, Foods, and Print Media on Local Material Culture Remains in Nineteenth-Century America. *Northeast Historical Archaeology*, 42(1), 6. https://doi.org/10.22191/neha/vol42/iss1/6
15. Arnaut, S. D. (1967). A arte de comer em Portugal na Idade Média. In: Arnaut, S. D. & Manuppella, G. (Eds.) *O Livro de Cozinha da infanta D. Maria de Portugal.* Universidade de Coimbra, pp. XXIII–CXXX.
16. Holmes, T. (2020). Magazines, Megazines, and Metazines: What Is a Magazine in the Twenty-First Century? The handbook of magazine studies, 1–19. https://doi.org/10.1002/9781119168102.ch1
17. Albala, K., & Larson, C. (2016). The evolution of cookbooks in the Digital Age. In *Food & Communication: Proceedings of the Oxford Symposium on Food and Cookery.* London: Prospect Books.
18. Fonseca, E., Oliveira, I., Lobo, J., Mota, T., Martins, J. & Au-Yong-Oliveira, M. (2019). Kitchen robots: The importance and impact of technology on people's quality of life. In *New Knowledge in Information Systems and Technologies*: Volume 2, 186–197. Springer International Publishing. https://doi.org/10.1007/978-3-030-16184-2_19
19. Steils, N., & Obaidalahe, Z. (2020). "Social food": Food literacy co-construction and distortion on social media. *Food Policy*, 95, 101932. https://doi.org/10.1016/j.foodpol.2020.101932
20. Beardsley, A. (2022). Feminist Food Rhetoric: Women's Rhetorical Strategies Across Instagram, Food Podcasts, and Community Cookbooks. https://hdl.handle.net/11244/335404

21. Chartier, R. (1994). *The order of books: Readers, authors, and libraries in Europe between the 14th and 18th centuries*. Stanford University Press.
22. Feather, J. P. (1986). The Book in History and the History of the Book. *Journal of library history*, 12–26.
23. Parreira, S. (2013). Alimentação, comida e design. In *Design, crise e depois*. Editora: Faculdade de Belas-Artes da Universidade de Lisboa, 116–121.
24. Hancock, G. M., Schmidt-Daly, T. N., Fanfarelli, J., Wolfe, J. L., & Szalma, J. L. (2016). Is e-reader technology killing or kindling the reading experience. *Ergonomics in design*, 24(1), 25–30. https://doi.org/10.1177/1064804615611269
25. Rabot, C. & Chartier, R. (2020). From Print to Digital: A Revolution in the Order of Speeches. An Interview with Roger Chartier. *Biens Symboliques / Symbolic Goods* [Online], 7. https://doi.org/10.4000/bssg.479

Correction to: Chandra-Padma: Design and Developing a Non-linear Narrative Based Augmented Reality (NNAR) Experience

Sajini Lankadari and Buddhika Rodrigo

Correction to:
Chapter 14 in: D. Brandão et al. (eds.), *Perspectives on Design and Digital Communication V*, Springer Series in Design and Innovation 50,
https://doi.org/10.1007/978-3-031-76156-0_14

In the original version of Chapter 14, the typo in the chapter title has been corrected. The chapter has been updated with the change.

The updated version of this chapter can be found at
https://doi.org/10.1007/978-3-031-76156-0_14

© The Author(s), under exclusive license to Springer Nature Switzerland AG 2025

D. Brandão et al. (eds.), *Perspectives on Design and Digital Communication V*, Springer Series in Design and Innovation 50, https://doi.org/10.1007/978-3-031-76156-0_21

MIX
Papier aus verantwortungsvollen Quellen
Paper from responsible sources
FSC® C105338

If you have any concerns about our products,
you can contact us on
ProductSafety@springernature.com

In case Publisher is established outside the EU,
the EU authorized representative is:
Springer Nature Customer Service Center GmbH
Europaplatz 3, 69115 Heidelberg, Germany

Printed by Libri Plureos GmbH
in Hamburg, Germany